CADDO
INDIANS

 WHERE WE COME FROM

Caddo Indian Nation in Oklahoma, by Billie Ruth Huff (Silver Moon II).

CADDO
Where We Come From
INDIANS

by Cecile Elkins Carter

UNIVERSITY OF OKLAHOMA PRESS
Norman

This book is published with the generous assistance of Edith Gaylord Harper.

Library of Congress Cataloging-in-Publication Data

Carter, Cecile Elkins, 1928–
    Caddo Indians : where we come from / by Cecile Elkins Carter.
      p.   cm.
    Includes bibliographical references and index.
    ISBN 0-8061-2747-3 (cloth)
    ISBN 0-8061-3318-X (paper)
    1. Caddo Indians—History. I. Title
    E99.C12C37 1995
    973'.04979—dc20   95-3395
                                                       CIP

Text design by Cathy Carney Imboden. The text typeface is Kennerly.

2   3   4   5   6   7   8   9   10

To the archeologists who rediscover Caddo
culture, the historians who research Caddo
history, and the Caddos who preserve
traditions.

CONTENTS

Contents

ILLUSTRATIONS

Illustrations

x

ACKNOWLEDGMENTS

Many people have taught and encouraged me, some without realizing how much they contributed. I have found, for instance, that Caddoan archeologists, whether professional or avocational, are an exceptional group of enthusiastic teachers. I am grateful for the contributions of the late Clarence H. Webb of Shreveport and the late R. King Harris of Dallas, both of whom gave generously of their time to satisfy my curiosity at the beginning of my study; and Dr. Ann Early and Dr. Martha Rolingson, of the Arkansas Archeological Survey, who introduced me to the elements of archeology. I also appreciate the communica-tion of Dr. Timothy Perttula and Dr. Jim Bruseth, of the Texas Historical Commission; Dr. Jim Corbin, of Stephen F. Austin State University in Nacogdoches, Texas; and Dr. Frank F. Schambach, Southern Arkansas University and the Arkansas Archeological Survey.

The Arkansas Archeological Society, Oklahoma Anthropologi-cal Society, and Texas Archeological Society are especially com-mended. Their publications and the field schools they sponsor have been vast sources of information.

I am indebted for access to the archives of the University of Oklahoma Library, Western History Collections; the Oklahoma Historical Society; the University of Texas Libraries at Austin; and the Detroit Public Library, Burton Historical Collection. These collections are invaluable.

In particular I wish to thank Dr. Hiram F. Gregory, professor of anthropology, Northwestern State University of Louisiana, in Natchitoches, for the help and encouragement he has given from the midpoint of my work through a reading of the manuscript. The comments offered by Dr. Elizabeth John and Dr. Helen Tanner were important to the final preparation.

I am very pleased with the decision to issue a paperback edition of this book (2001) and wish to thank John Drayton, Jo Ann Reece, and the entire University of Oklahoma Press production team. I especially appreciate the opportunity to make minor corrections and add new material about the Caddo language. For forty years, Caddo individuals fluent in our tribal language have welcomed visits to their homes from "that nice man who talks good Caddo." That nice man is Wallace Chafe, a distinguished linguist at the University of California Santa Barbara. I am grateful for his willingness to share his skill and knowledge with readers who are curious about Caddo words found on the pages of this book and thank him for his "Note on the Caddo Language."

My deepest gratitude is reserved for my Caddo family and friends, who treated my ignorance with kindness and taught with patience. I am thankful for personal memories and knowledge shared by Julia Edge, Lillie Whitehorn, Leon Carter, the late Grace Akins, and Patricia Carter. And I am indebted to Doyle Edge and Gayle Satpauhoodle for contributing their experiences. I also appreciate the indirect contributions of many others, among them Reathia Cussens, Barbara Constein, the late Nellie Decker, Randlet Edmonds, the late Fallis Elkins, Billie Ruth Huff, Madeline Frank, and Helen Tate. Finally, I thank my husband, Jack, who gave me praise when I needed it and criticism when it was deserved and would not let me quit when I became discouraged.

A NOTE ON THE CADDO LANGUAGE
Wallace Chafe

★ Some of the sounds of the Caddo language are very different from the sounds of English, and the structure of its words can be unusually complex. The following list provides a standardized spelling and other information for some of the Caddo words mentioned in this book, with numbers in parentheses showing the page number of the first mention of the word. The symbol ʔ stands for the glottal stop (a catch in the throat, as in the middle of the English expression "uh oh"). The k' and t' are so-called ejective stops, which are made by closing the mouth for a ǩ or t, closing and then raising the larynx, and then releasing both. Double vowels and consonants are longer than single ones. Accented vowels are spoken on a higher pitch.

aʔah	father (368)
hááyuh	above (368)
habashkuʔ	sour, also a meat preparation (357)
hadikuʔ	black (122)
hakuhduʔ	cold, also winter (125)
hak'uushuʔ	bitter, also medicine (367)
Hak'uushuʔ Kaʔayʔtsiʔ	Medicine Screech Owl (367)
Hasfínay	Caddo, Hasinai (72)
hawaʔin	disease (127)
háyú kahdíí haʔimay	God, big leader above (80)
haʔimay	big (55)
haʔímáychiʔ	old people (173)

kahdii	leader, chief (23)
kakkáhnin	thunder (368)
kat	knife (55)
kaʔayʔtsiʔ	screech owl (367)
kiyuh	horn (73)
kunah	healer, doctor (83)
kuná kahdii	Chief Healer (123)
kunáʔitsiʔ	little doctor (80)
kúsinah	that's enough (32)
k'ántuh	head (122)
nihih	horned owl (371)
nish	moon (73)
Sa	Ms. (364)
Sa Kaduh	Ms. Caddo (?) (182)
Sa K'ándikuh	Ms. Black Head (122)
sak'uh	sun (73)
shiwah	squirrel (369)
sukatih	buzzard (369)
tááshah	wolf, coyote (74)
Táyshaʔ	friend, ally (61)
Tsa	Mr. (73)
Tsa Kiyuh	the devil, literally Mr. Horn (73)
Tsakápbiʔ	February (133)
t'ámmaʔ	spokesman, master of ceremonies (44)
wááhih	shoe, war party (43)

Since the nineteenth century the name Cadohadacho has been erro-
neously interpreted by anthropologists and others as meaning
"true chiefs" (179). The Caddo word is ḳaduhdááchuʔ. The last
two syllables mean "sharp" (the adjective alone is hadááchuʔ). The
beginning of the name is no longer interpretable, but it is not
unusual for the origin of proper names to be lost over time.

PROLOGUE:
WHERE WE ARE NOW

Red dust rises with the passing of cars along un-paved farm roads near the west-central Oklahoma town of Ana-darko. The dust settles like powdered pigment, painting the leaves of brown-eyed susans and long-bladed grasses. Every mile or so the post-and-wire fences that frame the fields on either side of the roads are interrupted by side drives leading to solitary houses. Many are owned and lived in by Caddos—descendants of once-strong con-federacies of tribes whose presence provoked missionaries to zeal, governments to exploitation, and frontier settlers to murder.

Approximately thirty-five hundred Caddo men, women, and children were listed on the tribal roll in the early 1990s. Most gave their postal address as Binger, Gracemont, Fort Cobb, or An-adarko, Oklahoma; a few lived outside the state; but all traced their ancestry to Louisiana. Considering that when the United States purchased the Louisiana Territory from France in 1803, the territory's boundaries were vaguely defined as west from the Mississippi River to the Rocky Mountains and north from the Gulf of Mexico to British America, a Caddo speaks truthfully when he or she says, "Our people come from Louisiana." By today's boundaries, however, it is more accurate to say the Caddos came from Louisiana, Arkansas, Texas, and Oklahoma.

On a modern map the southern border of Oklahoma, dividing that state from Texas, is marked like a line drawn by a shaky hand. The line represents the Red River. It flows past Oklahoma's eastern limits into Arkansas, where, near the city of Texarkana, it makes an almost ninety-degree turn to the south toward Shreveport, Louisiana. From there it runs diagonally for 150 air miles to a juncture with the Mississippi River.

When the first white men reached the banks of the Red River in the sixteenth century, ancient Indian villages with Caddo names were spread along wide fertile prairies bordering the great bend in the Red River. In time all the people from the great bend region were called Caddo, a shortened form of the tribal name, Cadohadacho. Kinship and culture linked the Cadohadacho to two other tribal groups. One, lower down the Red River, was called Natchitoches. The other group, with settlements dotting the streams along the banks of the upper Neches and Angelina Rivers in east Texas, called themselves Hasinai. Each tribe within these three regional groupings had an individual identity and was independently governed, but all had a common language, followed the same social and religious customs, and shared traditions. Their direct descendants are listed on the tribal roll of the Caddo Indian Tribe of Oklahoma in the twentieth century. My name is on the Caddo tribal roll, but before 1960 I knew almost nothing about Caddo history, not even the sketchy bits I have just written.

Perhaps if I had grown up among my father's Caddo people, I would have learned some of the information included in this book at an early age, but I grew up in southeast Oklahoma, where I lived with my mother and her family. My father, Fait Elkins, met my mother, Thelma Perkinson, when he came to play football at the college in her hometown, Durant, Oklahoma. When they were married, a few days after he set a championship record in the 1927 national decathlon, they went to live in Lincoln, Nebraska, where he was attending the University of Nebraska. I was born while he was in Holland for the 1928 Olympics. Unable to compete because of an injury, he was an observer-reporter. Afterward he played professional football in Philadelphia, Pennsylvania, and when the marriage ended, he remained in Philadelphia, while my mother and I returned to Oklahoma.

During my school days I learned that before Oklahoma became a state, it was the Indian Territory and that the U.S. government had moved tribes there from other states. Later, when my geographical boundaries broadened, I met people who saw in me my father's features and coloring, and I had repeated exchanges.

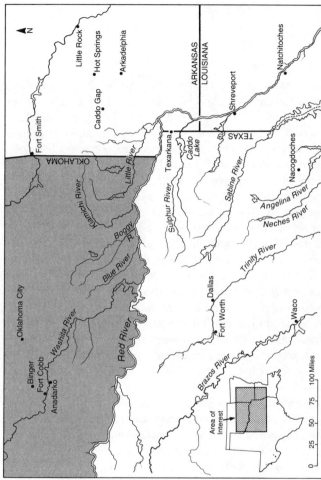

Red River, marked on maps like a line drawn by a shaky hand. The Caddo Tribe of Oklahoma, descendants of the Caddo, Natchitoches, and Hasinai tribes, whose ancestral homeland was southwest Arkansas, northwest Louisiana, northeast Texas, and southeast Oklahoma, now maintain a tribal complex located near Binger, Oklahoma, as the center for government and cultural activities.

"You're Indian, aren't you?"

"Yes."

"What tribe?"

"Caddo."

"Never heard of 'em."

Most of these people thought they knew about Cherokees, Choctaws, Comanches, Apaches, Sioux, and some other tribes. They had seen movies and read about American Indians in western novels. A few history students were familiar with more tribal identities. But so far as I know, no one has ever made a movie or written fiction in which Caddo Indians played a major role. If Caddo tribes are mentioned at all in standard American history books, it is in a sentence or two, at most a brief paragraph.

Through a friend of mine, Dr. Victor Oliver, head of a science department at Ouachita University in Arkadelphia, Arkansas, I learned that a Caddo conference hosted by Henderson University, also in Arkadelphia, would be held in the spring of 1975. I did not know what group was meeting or what its purpose was, but I went and met archeologists, anthropologists, ethnologists, and histo- rians who gathered for annual conferences because of their special interest in Caddo Indians. That summer I enrolled in the Arkan- sas Archeological Survey's two-week training program for ama- teur archeologists. It was conducted in conjunction with the University of Arkansas Field School at a Caddo site in southwest Arkansas.

Archeologists say that prehistoric people lived in the eastern half of Oklahoma's Red River basin and the adjoining areas of Arkansas, Louisiana, and Texas at least eleven thousand years ago. Those who stayed there became farmers, kept close and constant contact, and by A.D. 800 developed a distinctive culture defined as Caddo. They were builders who constructed great earthen mounds as ceremonial centers for worship and elaborate burial rites. They were artisans who designed pottery of astonishing beauty and wove fine rugs and mats from strips of cane. The mute evidence uncovered by archeologists has been linked to historical records written by explorers, traders, missionaries, and government officials.

Clarence H. Webb, M.D., a pediatrician whose long and dedicated avocational interest in Caddoan archeology made him a recognized authority, was the first to direct me to John R. Swanton's *Source Material on the History and Ethnology of the Caddo Indians,* a Bulletin of the Bureau of American Ethnology published by the Smithsonian Institution in 1942. Swanton compiled the principal materials relating to the Caddos from French and Spanish sources and drew his historical and ethnological content from both early and late informants. His work is a standard source but not exactly a common listing in ordinary library catalogs. Gregory Perino, archeologist and, before his retirement, director of the Museum of the Red River in Idabel, Oklahoma, gave me one of the rare copies of William J. Griffith's *The Hasinai Indians of East Texas as Seen by Europeans, 1687–1722,* volume two of the Philological and Documentary Studies of the Middle American Research Institute and printed in 1954.

Swanton and Griffith wrote that the Caddo tribes had a superior culture before the arrival of the Europeans and were historically significant afterward. The brief excerpts from five centuries of letters, diaries, journals, and official reports which documented their work stirred, rather than satisfied, my curiosity. What more had those people written about their early contacts with Caddo, Natchitoches, or Hasinai tribes? How much influence did background, sense of duty, and social mores have on the observations of those early writers? How did the Caddos lose their place in history? If their presence was historically significant, why was that position little known now, especially among the Caddos? The last question was the only one I thought I could answer—no one had ever written about the Caddos for the Caddos or for anyone else without a specialized academic interest. The Caddos' past was a scholarly secret stored on reference shelves. By then I had experience as a researcher, a writer, and a teacher. I began digging for more answers in university libraries, people's memories, and the earth.

The bibliographies provided by Swanton and Griffith gave me guidance. Most of the printed material was published before 1930, when a small number of people did a large amount of work translating Spanish and French documents. Their articles and translations appeared in numerous periodicals, mostly those of state historical societies. The outstanding scholar was Herbert E. Bolton. His archival research brought to light Spanish documents that had been unattended. Swanton drew on his expertise; Griffith, a former student of Bolton's, used his data. In 1977 I took a semester's leave of absence from teaching in Michigan and spent the time searching the archives of state and university libraries in Arkansas, Louisiana, Texas, and Oklahoma. I would have been saved a lot of time and energy if Bolton's comprehensive study *The Hasinais: Southern Caddoans as Seen by the Earliest Europeans,* edited with an introduction by Russell M. Magnaghi, had been published before 1987. I also haunted new and used bookstores, hunting for Bolton's *Athanase de Mézières and the Louisiana-Texas Frontier, 1768–1780,* first published in 1914 and reprinted by Kraus Reprint Company in 1970. Before I finally located a copy, I had added quite a number of books to my personal library. More had been written about the Caddos than I had first thought, but no book for general readership had a full account of the Caddo tribes as its single subject.

Before 1975 my visits to the Anadarko area had been brief, infrequent, and basically purposeless. I started going back more often and staying longer, talking with relatives, finding new friends, and recording some of the present-day thought and traditions that are unique to the Caddos. I discovered that contemporary Caddos have little real knowledge of the distant past. They have heard their parents and grandparents talk about the times when the Caddos were forced to leave Louisiana or make their exodus from Texas, but the events they recall are sometimes confused with stories of later troubles during the Civil War, when many Caddos temporarily fled their new homes in the Indian Territory. I also discovered that parents and grandparents had taught dances still performed, rites still practiced, and beliefs still held.

More than one Caddo elder has explained to me, "God gave special ways to the white man and special ways to the Indian—they are different. We don't know why, but they are. The white man writes things down for others to read and learn; the Indian tells what has happened and expects his children to listen and remember."

There is weakness in both ways. Written documents reflect the bias of the writer. People's memories are filtered through emotional shadows that flutter on the edge of consciousness and can neither be captured nor pinned down for examination. The Indian way of preserving history was weakening, and I feared that for the Caddos it would soon be lost.

That is why I began work on this book. I wanted to make it easier for readers to learn a significant part of Caddo history in a single, accurate, readable account. The information I had gathered was fragmented, like the broken parts of an exquisite pottery bowl found in an ancient burial mound. By piecing them together, I could rediscover the beauty of the form and the talent of the potter. Cracks are visible in the vessel I have pieced together, but those who look at it will, I hope, be able to see the shape of Caddo history as it was molded by many hands. Nothing new has been added to old materials except my perspective and glimpses of contemporary Caddo people.

Reading descriptions written by the missionaries, explorers, and officials who first came in contact with the Caddo, Natchitoches, and Hasinai tribes, I was struck by how the voice of the Caddo, which once spoke strongly for a nation of power and prestige, has diminished to a whisper. The tribe's population, political structure, and leadership are, of course, quite different now. Nevertheless, I seemed to recognize dances, traditions, stories, and religious observances that are almost the same today. Given the historical circumstances, I believe it is testimony to the strength of an unusual culture that any traces have survived. To invite comparison of where we come from and where we are now, I have at times interrupted an otherwise chronological account with the insertion of a later observation.

By bringing together from many sources what I have learned about the Caddo people from their prehistory to their removal to the Indian Territory, and interspersing it with impressions of their present lives, I offer a blending of the two ways of preserving history. My narrative is best described by the words of my Caddo friend Lillie Whitehorn: "I don't say that I know this; I'm just going to tell you the way I heard it" — and the way I read it and the way I saw it.

CHAPTER 1

THE ARCHEOLOGISTS

Caddo Gap, Arkansas, is in the Ouachita Mountains, a series of ridges beginning near Little Rock and extending west into Oklahoma. Clear, swift streams with rocky bottoms and gravel bars flow through the Ouachitas. Most of them follow the narrow east-west valleys, but a few, like the Caddo River, flow south through a break in the ridge. Caddo Gap can be reached by following Interstate 30 southwest from Little Rock. There is a junction with Arkansas Highway 70 a few miles south of that city. The state highway runs west through Hot Springs to Glenwood, where it intersects the blacktop on Number 8 leading through the valley like a loosely wound grosgrain ribbon.

At 6:30 A.M. in mid-June 1975, mist fogs the Caddo River valley. Turning off Highway 8, a group of archeologists—all members of the Arkansas Archeological Society—bump along a dirt road, cross the Caddo River on a low concrete bridge, and stop to open, pass through, and close the gate to Dick Standridge's pasture. They bounce across the ruts of a cow path past Otis, the patriarch of the herd, to an area assigned for parking. They each pocket a steel measuring tape and a hand trowel and walk the rest of the way to the dig site.[1]

Sunlight begins to seep into the gap, and the mist rises lazily like a late-sleeping cloud. Morning rays slip between the thick trunks of pine and oak along the footpath leading to a low, grassy knoll on the flat of the Caddo River bank. Here the archeologists mark an area with stakes and string to define the dig site for society members and to keep Otis and curious members of his family out. U.S. Geological Survey maps and instruments are used in marking the boundaries so that the exact location of whatever is found can be recorded.

Inside the excavation area, a grid of two-by-two-meter squares is laid out with stakes and string. Each square is assigned to one or two workers, who spade away the grass cover to its root level and then begin to remove layers of earth. Using hand trowels, they begin to scrape dirt from the top of the square. At a depth of five centimeters, they scrape the bottom smooth and level; they do this again at another five centimeters, and another. They keep the sides of the deepening pit carefully parallel. As they remove dirt, they sift it by hand through a fine mesh wire screen. When a load of screen dirt accumulates, they trundle it by wheelbarrow to a place outside the excavation area.

The sun that had appeared so shyly in the morning is blazing boldly before noon. An odd assortment of people work the dig, sweaty from the heat, grimy from the soil, sore from hours spent in bent positions. A flutist from New York who rode her Harley-Davidson across the country to join the dig, a graduate student from Finland, a petite, white-haired woman and her husband, who looks like Santa Claus—all work alongside other amateurs, college students, and professional archeologists. The professionals belong to the Arkansas Archeological Survey, a state agency responsible for salvaging and preserving the archeological riches of Arkansas. Each summer during an Arkansas Archeological Society–sponsored dig like the one at Caddo Gap, the survey archeologists direct a field training program for society members who are, or want to become, lay archeologists. The director of excavations for the Caddo Gap dig is Dr. Ann Early, a survey archeologist stationed at Henderson University in nearby Arkadelphia.

During the day Ann Early moves from one excavation pit to another, giving instruction, offering encouragement. She wears a battered, short-brimmed, soft hat jammed over two ponytails and typically walks with her hands stuffed in the pockets of her jeans, a bounce to her step like that of a nine-year-old wearing a new pair of sneakers. As the day's dig continues into the heat of the afternoon, some of the first-timers need Early's encouragement.

The work is tedious and unrewarding. Even experienced members of the crew begin to slow down, but they do not give up because of what they might find—proof that people lived here hundreds of years ago.

They are looking for evidence—minute fragments of bone, charred bits of wood or seeds, broken pottery pieces, which are called sherds. They watch for changes in soil color that might show the stains of decayed posts or of middens—places where prehistoric housekeepers piled their trash. They keep meticulous records for each five centimeters examined because archeologists can put records together with the artifacts (human-made objects) and other bits of evidence that are found and draw a profile of the people who inhabited a place before their written history began. Small cloth sacks tagged with numbers identifying each two-meter square are kept handy so that the diggers can bag pieces of evidence. The contents of the bags will be analyzed in a laboratory.

The next few days are much the same. The pits get deeper, and some new ones are opened. Then aching backs and sunburned necks, cramped fingers and scraped knuckles, are forgotten when the charred remains of a thatched roof are uncovered. Trowels are discarded for fine picks and soft brushes as the first evidence of a burned, collapsed, Caddoan structure is exposed.[2]

The Field Training School at Caddo Gap was a three-week activity. Survey archeologists continued work at the Standridge site through August 1975, and a second session was held there the following summer. As excavation continued, the pattern of post molds showed that the first structure uncovered near the surface of the knoll in 1975 had a rectangular shape about twenty-one by thirteen feet. A line of posts marked the walls of an extended doorway, with an entrance to the house facing southeast. In the center of its baked clay floor was a shallow, circular fireplace protected by a raised rim. Very little debris was under the collapsed, charred roof. The users of the building seemed to have cleaned the inside before it burned; only a piece of a jar in one corner and a group of cobblestones in another corner were left.

Beneath the first structure was a second, similar building, which had been cleaned, burned, and blanketed with earth before the topmost building was erected. Below the second structure was a third building, circular in shape, a little more than twenty-six feet in diameter. It, too, had a cap of soil spread over its baked clay floor, but, unlike the two rectangular buildings that had covered it, the circular building did not appear to have been destroyed by fire.[3]

Just to the west two more rectangular structures were found, one on top of the other. Both had the same architecture as the other rectangular buildings, and both had been burned. But excavation of the one on top revealed an unexpected feature: a large grave in the center. Three persons were buried there. Twenty-two pottery vessels, a drinking cup or dipper made from a conch shell, some tools made of stone and bone, two rattles made of tortoise shell, projectile points, and some tiny turquoise beads had been placed in their grave. Some of these items were rare among Caddo people and could mean that someone of high status was buried there.[4]

The circular building was the only one containing evidence that people cooked, ate, slept, and worked on tools inside its shelter. The rectangular structures all seem to have been used for a special purpose, probably religious. Analysis of the way the structures were built—one on top of another, with a separating cover of soil—together with the identification of artifacts and the use of sophisticated laboratory techniques for measuring the age of charred wood samples showed that the activities of a small group of Caddo people centered on this special place at Caddo Gap for at least one hundred uninterrupted years during the fourteenth and fifteenth centuries.

Ann Early had hoped to locate a simple Caddo farmstead. What she and the others found was far more complex. "What seems to have happened at Standridge," she concluded, "is that in its initial Caddoan occupation the site served dual purposes as both a residence and a location for small scale rituals. From this beginning it evolved into a location used exclusively for special purpose activities, but on a seemingly small scale."[5]

The burning of a structure, followed by a layer of leveling dirt cover and successive rebuilding, burning, and covering, created a low earthen mound on the flat terrace by the river at Caddo Gap. Elsewhere in Arkansas, Louisiana, Oklahoma, and Texas, near major rivers and streams, the people who were ancestors of today's Caddos built other earthen mounds. They built single mounds on the natural surface of the earth and constructed multiple mounds around a broad plaza. They built flat-topped mounds, cone-shaped mounds, and pyramidal mounds with level tops. The mounds were monuments to the dead buried in them and religious or political centers for the living.

The flat-topped mounds served as a platform for a succession of houses dedicated to special uses. The platform grew higher when the house, or "temple," was destroyed and the charred remains were covered over by earth before a new one was built. New stages were added at varying intervals, perhaps whenever the principal leader died. The other mounds rose as they were built to cover or contain the graves of certain honored persons. The mystique of the mounds and the people who built them has challenged the skill and imagination of archeologists. Gradually, painstakingly, they have sifted a part of the past from the earth.

The Caddos' past, like that of all people, is divided into two parts—the prehistoric, for which there are no written records, and the historic, which has been recorded in writing. Archeologists are prehistorians. In general they agree that prehistory for the Caddos began about A.D. 800. For a long period of time before then, from around 9500 B.C. to 500 B.C., wandering bands of hunters and gatherers had small temporary camps in Arkansas, Louisiana, Texas, and Oklahoma. They left little evidence of their lives—a few large, broad dart points and some stone tools and ornaments. Then people started to settle more permanently. Some of their settlements became larger, growing into villages that covered from two to ten acres. They began to plant seeds and harvest vegetables, make pottery, smoke tobacco in long-stemmed pipes, construct burial mounds, and develop ceremonial traditions that were ancestral to the culture of the Caddos.[6]

Ceremonial practices may have begun with simple rituals for planting and harvesting or efforts to seek protection from drought and flood. The use of burial mounds could have started because a grave without a marker was soon lost; a mound of earth, if large enough, marked a place for generations yet unborn. No matter how simply it all began, the introduction of new ideas brought about complex rites intended to nourish the living and sustain the dead.

Professional archeologists give credit to Clarence H. Webb, a pediatrician from Shreveport, Louisiana, for providing the basic

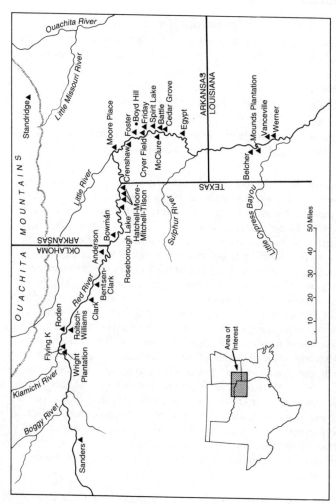

Important Caddo archeological sites along the Red River, redrawn from Schambach and Rackerby, *Contributions to the Archeology of the Great Bend Region* (Fayetteville: Arkansas Archeological Survey, 1982), fig. 6–1; and Perttula, *The Caddo Nation*, fig. 14

framework of Caddoan archeology of northwest Louisiana.[7] Webb's interest in archeology began when he helped his young son collect arrowheads for a Boy Scout merit badge. Before long the doctor was using his leisure time for more systematic explorations, and his knowledge expanded with experience. Beginning in the 1930s and continuing until his death in 1990, archeology was, for Webb, "a pure intellectual joy."[8]

Discussing the multiple burials revealed during mound excavations, Webb said:

> Some of them [the mounds] have evidence that there were successive burials; others have evidence of placement all at one time. And in these instances, we are strongly suspicious that there was retainer sacrifice. Generally these are huge pits . . . fifteen to twenty feet in length and twelve, fifteen feet in width with fifteen, twenty, twenty-five individuals laid in a long row, and very often, a single paramount or important individual with a different placement and surrounded by very rich offerings. In other instances . . . the [paramount] individuals themselves may have had only a few offerings placed around them but the pit itself contained massive placements and this looks like the burial of an extremely important person who was not only furnished with food, for which we find evidence with containers, with all kinds of burial furniture—weapons and so forth, but also furnished with people to go along with him for the afterlife. . . . We have never found any dismemberment of bodies or any direct evidence of how these people were killed. . . . We found one burial at the Mounds Plantation, about ten miles north of here [Shreveport, Louisiana], in which there were two intrauterine fetuses in females. So, they were all the way from fetuses, babies, children, youths, adults and old people. Could possibly be a clan, a family.[9]

In the graves of such high-status leaders there were beautiful ceremonial objects, many made with materials not available in the area occupied by the Caddos. The work by ancient artisans was represented by long slender celts—a kind of chisel or spatula-shaped tool—made of glowing, polished greenstone; conch shells engraved with intricate designs; plates of beaten copper and carved cedar wood objects overlaid with thin sheets of copper; finger covers and hand symbols cut out of copper and big earspools made of wood or stone and covered with copper. Webb believed that the source for all this copper was the Upper Peninsula of

Michigan and Isle Royal in Lake Superior. He pointed out that the sort of far-reaching trade routes that brought copper all the way from Lake Superior to the Gulf Coast were well established by 1000 B.C. Other archeologists argue that the most likely source of the copper was the southern Appalachians.[10]

Whatever the source, Caddo artisans used copper in crafting some of their most intriguing objects. During 1938 while excavating the Gahagan site (about forty miles down the Red River from Shreveport), Webb found a shield-shaped wooden mask made like a stylized face and covered with a thin layer of copper—the mysterious "long-nosed god." The nose was a very long triangle. The eyes were large and round; the mouth, a slit. There was a narrow band across the forehead, and above the band a headdress was represented. The top edge of the headdress was cut straight across, except for a notch in the center and a step-down on each side. A resemblance to ancient Mexican and South American carvings is easy to see. Only six pairs of the long-nosed god—it has always appeared in pairs—have been found in the United States. The only other long-nosed copper masks in the Caddoan area were uncovered in two mounds at Spiro, an immense ceremonial center in east Oklahoma. Short-nosed masks made of shell and dating from a later time have turned up in Arkansas.[11]

It took powerful and intelligent leadership to maintain the kind of trade network that brought rare materials to the mound centers. Skillful organization and strong leadership were also required to direct the building of huge earthern mounds or the digging of deep shafts by people whose only moving equipment was their own bodies, baskets woven with strips of cane, and tools made of wood, bone, or shell. Tons of dirt were dug and carried, a basketload at a time, to shroud a burned temple or cap a tomb. Many were built up five to ten feet or more; one to a height of thirty-four feet. There were large mound centers that covered as much as twenty acres of land and included multiple mounds, plaza areas, a large village, and cemeteries.[12]

Most of the ceramic vessels placed with burials were molded from the clay of the river valleys in the Caddos' homeland. Caddo potters made exquisite bottles with long spouts and bowls shaped like the carina (keel) of a ship. They decorated their bottles and bowls with circle and scroll designs. The vessels were often fired a gleaming dark chocolate–black color. Archeologists recognize the

Distinctive shapes and designs help define Caddo pottery (*Clarence H. Webb Collection, Louisiana State Exhibit Museum, Shreveport; photo 1994.1.1*)

bottle form, the carinated bowl, and engraved decorations of curvilinear lines as distinctively Caddoan ceramic features. Their shapes and designs help define the Caddo culture area and limit it to the Red River basin of southeast Oklahoma, northeast Texas, southwest Arkansas, and northwest Louisiana; the Arkansas River basin of east Oklahoma; the Ouachita River basin of south-central Arkansas and north Louisiana; and the basins of the Sabine and Neches-Angelina Rivers of west Louisiana and east Texas. The Caddo-language-speaking people lived in those same river valleys when they met and were written about by Europeans in the sixteenth and seventeenth centuries.

The ceremonialism that caused the Caddos to furnish graves so lavishly reached its height between A.D. 1000 and 1200. Villages with large populations that were once part of some of the mound centers had been vacated by the eleventh century, and only religious or political caretakers lived at the ceremonial sites. The mounds were still the focus of ceremonial activities, but the ordinary people had become farmers living in small, separate clusters of homes and tending their individual fields of corn. Family compounds dotted the countryside out from the great mounds—satellites spread over many miles. Whatever belief inspired several hundred years of mound building seems to have lasted longer around the great bend of the Red River than elsewhere, and for that reason the region is called the heartland of the Caddoan area.

In the small homesites below the present ground surface and in the mounds that rise above, archeologists find the clues that identify Caddo people. Most homesites, hidden as they are now, will never be discovered, but archeologists are persistent, and more sites are recorded each year. Mounds disappear only when they fall into flooding rivers or are leveled by modern machinery, and they continue to give up secrets from the past.

Sadly, the visibility of mounds and the knowledge that cemeteries often lay nearby make them vulnerable to "pothunters"—diggers who desecrate and destroy sites while searching for Caddo pottery and ceremonial objects that bring high prices in the collectors' market. State and federal legislation makes such looting illegal and punishable by fine or imprisonment, but it is easy to escape detection when digging up ancient burials in rural fields and woodlands. Pothunters who plunder graves do not share information. They do not record their sites, document their collecting methods, or catalog the objects they take. They disturb the evidence of past lives, desecrate graves, and leave empty holes.

Archeologists dig to learn about prehistoric and early historic Caddo people, asking questions such as, What happened here? Why did it happen? To answer those questions, archeologists look at more than pottery and tools, the way houses and mounds were built, and the way the dead were buried. They study the area's geography and geology, soil and mineral resources, changes in climate, and courses of rivers. They analyze plant and animal remains and evidence of human diet, disease, and injury. Reviewing known facts and collecting new ones, they extend Caddo history beyond the memory of living Caddos.

CHAPTER 2

THE EXPLORERS

The intensive period of mound building was over by the time the first Europeans invaded Caddo land in 1541. In that year the Spanish explorer Hernando de Soto entered Arkansas and the prehistory of Caddo tribes began to merge with history. The chronicles of his expedition gave the first written descriptions of people and places with Caddo names.

De Soto landed at Tampa Bay, Florida, with an army of 600 men; 100 or so camp followers, servants, and slaves; more than two hundred horses; a herd of hogs; some mules; and bloodhounds for tracking down Indians. He crossed Florida, Georgia, North and South Carolina, Tennessee, Alabama, and Mississippi, winding his way deeper and deeper inland, lured by the prospect of finding gold. Depending on native granaries for provisions, he chose the more thickly settled country for his march, plundering Indian villages, compelling tribal leaders to act as guides, and placing captives in chains to serve as servants and burden bearers. By the time the expedition crossed the Mississippi River into Arkansas in June 1541, many soldiers, a great number of horses and arms, and almost all of the expeditioners' clothing had been lost. Not much of European manufacture was left for twentieth-century archeologists to find.

In the late 1930s a group of scholars reconstructed the route of the De Soto expedition by comparing its members' descriptions of the country that was crossed, the native people met, and events that took place with geography, known Indian tribes, and the small amount of available archeological information. The trail west of the Mississippi was the most difficult to trace. There was much discussion of where exactly De Soto crossed the river and considerable doubt about the identity of the first tribes he encountered in modern-day Arkansas. Rivers, mountains, and places where salt was extracted were major clues. De Soto reached the mountainous region of western Arkansas in the fall of 1541, and in October he clashed with the Tula who were, wrote De Soto's private secretary, Rodrigo Ranjel, "the best fighting people that the Christians met with." The conclusion of the De Soto scholars was, "We know now that they [the Tula Indians] were one of the Caddo tribes and feel safe in locating them about the present Caddogap and on Caddo River."[1]

To commemorate the Tula tribe and the westernmost point reached by De Soto and his men, a full-figure statue of an Indian was placed atop a pedestal in the center of the village of Caddo Gap. The Indian's bronze eyes stare toward the gap in the Ouachita Mountains where his home was supposed to be, but he stands and looks in the wrong place. By 1990 De Soto scholars could be far more precise in matching actual locations with those described in the Spanish narratives. The Tula were a Caddo tribe with links to the Indians who lived at Caddo Gap, but they lived and fought the Spaniards at a place farther north in Arkansas, some thirty-five to forty miles southwest of the Arkansas River.[2]

Even though Tula does not sound like a Caddo name, the tribe was probably the first Caddo band to come in contact with Europeans. Its language was different from any the Spaniards had heard before, and De Soto had trouble finding an interpreter among his Indian captives. Possibly Tula was the name the tribe was given by non-Caddoan speakers. Other Caddos with tribal names and locations that became familiar in historic times were met by De Soto's men in the months that followed their battle with the Tula.[3]

After suffering the bitterly cold winter of 1541–1542 encamped south of present-day Little Rock, Arkansas, De Soto took his men back to the west bank of the Mississippi River. In need of reinforcements, he intended to build boats to send down the river and across the sea to Cuba or New Spain (Mexico), but before he could carry out his plan, he became ill and died.

Luis Moscoso de Alvarado was elected to lead the army. Nearly half the original force and 100 horses had been lost. The remaining expeditioners wanted out of the country the fastest way possible. They knew that there were two ways to get to New Spain: down the river in their boats, which could not weather a storm, and across the sea, for which they had no charts; or over land where provisions could be taken from Indian towns along the way and riches might still be found. They marched west.

Beyond going west, Moscoso had only a vague sense of the direction the expedition should travel to reach Mexico. He needed the Indians of the country to direct his course and to supply enough corn to keep alive more than three hundred men, as many as five hundred captive Indians, about forty horses, a herd of hogs, and a pack of hounds. Among the Indian captives were several boys and girls who had learned to speak Spanish and had been able to act as interpreters of native languages, but none knew the language spoken by the Caddo tribes. Lack of an interpreter, wrote one of the expedition's chroniclers, "was so great a hindrance to our going, whether on discovery or out of the country, that to learn of the Indians what would have been rendered in four words, it became necessary now to have the whole day: and oftener than otherwise the very opposite was understood of what was asked; so that many times it happened the road that we travelled one day, or sometimes two or three days, would have to be returned over, wandering up and down, lost in thickets."[4]

Moscoso spent the next six months crossing southwest Arkansas, passing through the Red River heartland of Caddo country, and circling through northeast Texas. Archeologist Frank F. Schambach, with more than twenty years of field experience in southwest Arkansas, remarked, "There are at least 20 ceremonial centers, each with from one to eleven mounds, distributed in a 40 mile wide band along the general route that the Spaniards must have taken from Arkadelphia, Arkansas, towards Texarkana and the Red River Valley. Many of them were in use during the sixteenth century, so the Spanish were probably always within 20 miles of an active temple mound, whether they knew it or not, and they must have seen farmsteads and other types of compounds everywhere."[5]

An attempt was made to stop Moscoso and his army before they reached the Red River. Two bands of Caddo warriors attacked from different directions. They fell back quickly, dividing the Spaniards by getting those on horseback to give chase. Then two other Caddo bands, hidden until the mounted Spaniards went in pursuit, attacked. Spanish accounts admitted that many of the men and horses were wounded but claimed a great number of Indians were killed.

One Indian was captured. They learned from him that the leaders of three Caddo tribes had brought many warriors together. The Spaniards recorded the tribal names as Maye or Amaye, Hacanac, and Naguatex. The Naguatex leader was in command. The Maye are archeologically linked to a Caddo tribe known later as Nasoni. The identity of Hacanac is still uncertain, but historical documents and archeological evidence make clear that the Naguatex leader, a man powerful enough to unite three bands of warriors in a single force, was a Cadohadacho.[6] The Cadohadacho dominated both sides of the Red River valley from the vicinity of Fulton, Arkansas, to Shreveport, Louisiana. A sign of their dominance is that the largest known Caddo mound and six other mound sites are within the area called Naguatex by the De Soto chroniclers and Cadohadacho in later documents.[7]

The Indian leader that English speakers generally call "chief" and Spaniards called *cacique* is called *caddi* (cah' dee) by people who speak the Caddo language. The title is recognizable in the name Cadohadacho, which loosely translated means "true chief" or "real chief." The name strictly applied to only one group, but all the closely associated kindred bands that lived along the big bend of the Red River eventually became known as Cadohadacho.[8]

Moscoso ordered the right arm and nose of the captured Indian cut off. Then he sent the Indian back to his leader with a message: Moscoso would march into Naguatex the next day and destroy it. The Spaniards marched directly toward the place where the Naguatex caddi lived on the west side of Red River, but stopped on the opposite bank.

There were good reasons for Moscoso to call a temporary halt. Many of his men and horses were wounded, he did not know where the river fords were, and a force of Indians was posted in defensive positions on the west bank. He sent another message to the Naguatex caddi, saying that, "should he come to serve and obey him, he would pardon the past; and if he did not, he would go to look after him, and would inflict the chastisement he deserved for what he had done."9 The caddi kept Moscoso waiting a few more days, then sent word that he would come.

Naguatex protocol for such a meeting was as formal as a meeting between twentieth-century heads of state. A large group of representatives, principal men among them, came to announce the approach of the Naguatex leader. He arrived about two hours after the announcement and came forward flanked on each side by a file of attendants who walked one behind the other. The Spanish narrative recorded:

> They arrived in the Governor's presence weeping. . . . The chief, making his proper obeisance, thus spoke: VERY HIGH AND POWERFUL LORD, WHOM ALL THE EARTH SHOULD SERVE AND OBEY: I venture to appear before you, after having been guilty of so great and bad an act, that, for only having thought of it, I merit punishment. Trusting in your greatness, although I do not deserve pardon, yet for your own dignity you will show me mercy, having regard to my inferiority in comparison with you, forgetting my weakness, which to my sorrow, and for my greater good, I have come to know.
>
> I believe that you and yours must be immortal; that you are master of the things of nature; since you subject them all, and they obey you, even the very hearts of men. Witnessing the slaughter and destruction of my men in battle, which came of my ignorance, and the counsel of a brother of mine, who fell in the action, from my heart did I repent the error that I committed, and directly I desire to serve and obey you: wherefore have I come, that you may chastise and command me as your own.10

Since the Spaniards were without interpreters who understood the Caddo language, it is remarkable that they could have recorded such a speech. What the caddi actually said will never be known, but whatever it was, when Moscoso and his troops finally crossed to the west bank of the Red River, they found houses but no people. Moscoso again sent word to the caddi, demanding a guide. When days passed without any response, Moscoso ordered his captains to set fire to the houses and crops and capture any people they could find. The caddi then made his single concession—he sent three guides to Moscoso.

The Spanish narrative recounted, "Two days' journey on the way, the Indians who guided the Governor, in place of taking him to the west, would lead him to the east, and at times they went through heavy thickets, out of the road: in consequence, he ordered that they should be hanged upon a tree."[11] They were by then near the territory of the Hasinai, a strong branch of the Caddo nation occupying the northeast section of the present state of Texas. Like the Cadohadacho in the Red River heartland, the Hasinai were direct descendants of people whose ceremonial activities focused on mound centers beginning about A.D. 800.[12]

Marching through Hasinai settlements, the Spaniards stripped villages and farmsteads of corn, slaughtered inhabitants who resisted, tortured captives, and forced them to become unwilling guides. When the Spanish believed again that they were being deliberately led in the wrong direction, they threw one Hasinai guide into their pack of bloodhounds. Finally, reaching the Trinity River in Texas and discovering that the people on the other side lived in poor huts and spoke another unknown language, the expeditioners decided to return to the Mississippi.[13]

Passing again through villages they had devastated the first time through, Moscoso and his men had a hard time finding food until they reentered Naguatex, where the Cadohadacho homes had been rebuilt and storehouses were full of corn. Going on to the Mississippi, they spent several months building bargelike boats to launch on the river. On September 10, 1543, the boats carried the men, by then an exhausted, ragtag group clothed in deerskins, into a Mexican port.

On paper the latest reconstruction of the Spaniards' route through northeast Texas looks like the loop of a limp lariat. They followed a south-southwesterly direction for more than half the distance, then meandered toward the east before looping south-west to northeast and rejoining the trail they had made coming in.[14] Except for these brief encounters with De Soto's troops, the Cadohadacho and Hasinai were undisturbed by outsiders until late in the seventeenth century.

One hundred forty-four years after De Soto's horde moved through Hasinai country, green prairie grasses bent beneath the feet of a small party of men and then sprang back, leaving little trace of their passage. Their journals and memoirs, however, offered the first detailed descriptions of the Hasinai. The leader of the group was the French explorer La Salle.[15]

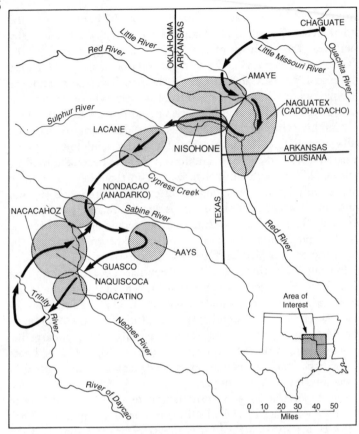

De Soto's route through southwest Arkansas and northeast Texas, redrawn from Schambach's reconstruction based on archeological research, "The End of the Trail," fig. 2. Schambach identifies Naguatex as Cadohadacho and Nondacao (Nadako, Anadarko) as probably the first Hasinais encountered by the Spanish.

Historians have documented the adventures that brought René Robert Cavelier, Sieur de La Salle, to lead a trek across the plains of Texas. They began in 1666 when he joined his older brother, Abbé Jean Cavelier, who was a priest of St. Sulpice in Montreal, Canada. La Salle spent sixteen years learning the region and languages of Indian tribes in Canada and the Great Lakes district before he came down the Illinois River to the Mississippi and followed its twisting course to the Gulf of Mexico.

As the first European to explore the river all the way to the sea, La Salle claimed the Mississippi basin for the king of France. The claim included the length of the river and a vast expanse on either side. He named the country Louisiana and envisioned control of the domain, with a French and Indian colony on the banks of the Illinois River and a fort and another colony at the mouth of the Mississippi. The Illinois River colony would be a defense against the unfriendly Iroquois Indians and would serve as a storage place for furs and hides brought there by western tribes. The colony at the mouth of the Mississippi would be a defense against English or Spanish interference and serve as an outlet for the furs collected from the Illinois and Mississippi valley trade. La Salle went back up the Mississippi to the Illinois River and built Fort St. Louis. Then, leaving Henri de Tonti (or Tonty) in command there, he went to France to win approval from Louis XIV for a gulf port colony.[16]

King Louis favored the plan, and La Salle sailed from France in 1684 with nearly four hundred people aboard four ships. There were soldiers, mechanics, and laborers; gentlemen and well-to-do merchants; families; single women; and missionaries. One of the ships was seized by Spanish buccaneers near the West Indies. The other three sailed past the mouth of the Mississippi and coursed on westward in the Gulf of Mexico. La Salle's bold plan began to founder when the ship carrying stores was wrecked while trying to enter Matagorda Bay in the Gulf of Mexico and his royal navy escort vessel returned to France. The plan was doomed when the last remaining ship, a ketch named *Belle,* was wrecked in an exploration of the east end of the bay.

The colonists were stranded, ill, without supplies, and endangered by marauding Gulf Coast Indians. La Salle oversaw the construction of a fort on the Garcitas River about five miles above its entry into Matagorda Bay and gave it the same name as the one he had built on the Illinois River, Fort St. Louis.[17] La Salle then chose twenty men to accompany him and set out on a march overland to find the Mississippi. His plan was to save his foundering colony by going up the Mississippi and Illinois Rivers to Canada and bringing back help. In his party were his nephew Crevel de Moranget, his brother Abbé Jean Cavelier, Father Anastase Douay, and a Shawnee Indian called Nica who had been with La Salle since he first left Canada.

The men reached Hasinai country by walking across continuous plains, the horizon unbroken except for immense herds of buffalo. They crossed many rivers and streams flooded by spring rains and passed through meadowlike fields dotted with groves or skirted by fruit trees and vines. Finally, said Father Douay, "we entered countries still finer than those they had passed, and found tribes that had nothing barbarous but the name."[18]

A Hasinai man and his family, returning from a successful hunt, saw the strangers trudging in the direction of his village. Their clothing—the long, loose robes of a religious order and patched European garments—was alien. They had packs and weapons slung on their backs. Some carried kettles and axes. The Hasinai hunter came closer to inspect the bedraggled group. He gave one of his horses and some meat to La Salle, invited them all to his home, and leaving his wife, family, and game as a pledge, went swiftly ahead to his village. Nica and La Salle's servant went with him.

Two days later a Hasinai delegation met the French a few miles outside the village. Several chiefs and a company of warriors, all dressed in fine skins decorated with feathers, brought two horses loaded with provisions. They approached ceremoniously carrying an ornamented long-stemmed tobacco pipe used in rituals to cement friendships—a peace pipe, called a *calumet* by the French, who had seen them among other North American tribes.

The Hasinai community was large and populous. It covered at least fifty miles, the people living in individually named clusters of ten to twelve cabins.[19] La Salle was lodged in "the great chief's cabin." A crowd gathered and loaded the visitors with presents and all kinds of food. Young warriors stood watch, relieving one another night and day. La Salle, afraid that some of his men might molest the women, ordered them to camp a distance away from the village.

The French stayed three or four days, bartering for horses and supplies. The Hasinai were more than willing to trade a horse for an ax. One of the Indian traders took a fancy to the hood of Douay's robe and offered a horse in exchange for it. The Hasinai had many horses and could easily get more through friendly trade with other tribes, which acquired them from Spanish settlements in New Mexico. Pieces of money, silver spoons, lace, and clothes came to the Hasinai in the same way.

So much evidence of Spanish goods made La Salle uneasy. France and Spain were bitter rivals in the possession of American colonies, and he really did not know where he was in relation to Spanish strongholds. During his years in Canada he had gained much experience in dealing with Indian nations, and even with-out knowing the Hasinai language, he was able to communicate with signs. He had the Hasinai draw a map on a piece of bark, showing where their country was in relation to that of their neighbors and the Mississippi River. Distance was reckoned by the number of days traveled, and the Hasinai counted six days to the place where the Spaniards lived. They said the Spaniards had not yet been in their country — the clothes, horses, and other things came to them by trade with the Jumano Indians or by Hasinai warriors joining the Jumano "to go war on New Mexico."[20] To counteract any favorable impression made by Spanish riches, La Salle told the Hasinais that "the chief of the French was the greatest chief in the world, as high as the sun, and as far above the Spaniards as the sun is above the earth."[21] His stories about the great French chief's victories caused his listeners to burst into exclamations and show astonishment by placing their hands to their mouths.

Having gained horses and food, La Salle and his party left to continue their search for the Mississippi. They crossed a river that divided the village where they had traded from another on the east bank and made camp for the night about ten miles beyond. Before morning four men decided that life among the Hasinai was preferable to following La Salle and crept away to return to the villages. Then came an experience worse than the loss of four men: La Salle and his nephew, Moranget, woke with violent fevers. Their illness kept the group from moving for more than two months. Weakened and almost out of gunpowder by that time, La Salle decided to go back to Fort St. Louis near the Gulf of Mexico.

The French deserters settled comfortably among the Hasinai as the season advanced through autumn and the tall field grass rustled dryly when winds whipped across the prairie. The Hasi-nai set fires to burn off the dry blades so that tender new shoots would be free to raise enticing tips in game-grazing areas. Chill air chased most village activities indoors, where families gathered around the central fireplace and busied themselves with shaping clay utensils, weaving cane mats, and designing and repairing footwear, clothing, tools, and weapons. Men concentrated on plans for the winter hunt. A successful hunt required prudent preparation, with careful attention given to weapons and maximum organization. Buffalo were usually mild mannered and sluggish, but they were capable of great speed and rage. Then, too, there was always the danger of a clash with a hostile tribe, which added to the natural perils of hunting on the plains.

At Fort St. Louis on the Gulf, La Salle planned a return trip to the Hasinai villages. From there he expected to reach the Mississippi and travel its course upstream to the Illinois River fort, where he had left Tonti in charge. La Salle started out after the first of the year in 1687. His brother, his nephew, Father Anastase, Nica, and several of the men who had been with him on his first trip to the Hasinai villages were with him again. A younger nephew, seventeen years old, who had been left behind on the first trip because of his youth, was included this time. Pierre Talon, a few weeks away from his eleventh birthday, was also a member of the company. The most reliable man in the group was Henri Joutel, who had been left in charge of the colonists during the last trip. The plan was for Joutel and Jean Cavelier to go from the Illinois River fort to Canada and then on to France to get help for the Gulf Coast colony. La Salle would bring more immediate aid back from the Illinois fort. The Talon boy was to be left with the Hasinai to learn their language and act as an interpreter when La Salle returned. Altogether the party totaled eighteen. Left behind in the settlement were twenty men, women, and children, the only remaining colonists.

La Salle led the way toward the Hasinai villages, following much the same route as before. The horses obtained from the Hasinai made this journey less burdensome, but heavy winter rains made travel slow and difficult. Rivers that the French had forded before were swollen. In some places the prairie had become a sodden mire. There were times when a downpour forced them to halt for days.

Hunting parties populated the country they passed through. They met Indians from various tribes almost every day. Near the end of February Nica was scouting ahead when he saw from a long way off a single Indian following a herd of buffalo. The sun spilled winter-weakened warmth over the nearly silent scene. The shaggy beasts were almost motionless, the hunter concentrating on getting close enough to make an accurate shot without giving warning.

Nica managed to close the distance between them without being seen until he stepped directly into the path of the hunter. Startled, perhaps angry with himself for failing to notice the approach of a possible enemy, the Indian stood his ground. Nica came closer, concealing his gun by holding it flat against his side and thus appearing unarmed. Their showdown changed to friendly recognition. The buffalo hunter was from the village where La Salle had bartered for horses.

Glad to find a friend instead of facing a stranger, Nica and the Hasinai hunter drove the buffalo herd together. The Hasinai shot several arrows, but they fell short. Nica raised his gun and dropped a cow with one shot. For a long moment the Hasinai stood still and speechless, the sound of the gun's blast roaring in his ears. Then, jogging to the side of the dead beast, he examined the hole made by the shot, amazed by the size of the wound and admiring the effect of the French weapon.[22]

Nica easily persuaded the Hasinai hunter to come with him to La Salle's camp. La Salle immediately remembered the hunter as one who had traded him a horse, and he asked about the four men who had deserted on the last journey. The Hasinai answered that one was in his own village, that two others lived in the neighboring village of Nasoni, but that he knew of no other.

The Hasinai man went back to his own camp when night came. There were four or five camps, fifteen hunters in all, near the range of the buffalo. The French came to one the next day. Women and children were hard at work there. Men did the hunting, but dressing and packing the kill were women's jobs. La Salle tried to trade for the group's two horses, but the women explained that they needed the horses to carry meat and hides. They did, however, offer the French both fresh and thinly cut, smoke-dried strips of meat, and La Salle gave knives in return.

La Salle learned that the hunters would soon be breaking camp; they wanted to join some Hasinai men who had already gone to fight an enemy tribe. They would show La Salle the way to their village if he wanted to wait for the hunt to be finished. La Salle chose not to wait, but he traveled only a little distance before he came to a marsh area that he was hesitant to cross unguided. He sent word back to the Hasinai camp, asking some of the hunters to go along with him. A few came to guide his way, sometimes going ahead, sometimes trailing behind, and sometimes walking along with the French.

Two and a one-half weeks later, in the middle of March, the Indian guides were spectators at the murder of La Salle. Five of the French explorer's own men, full of anger and resentment toward their leader's nephew, Moranget, killed him. Since Nica witnessed the murder, they also killed him. La Salle's assassination inevitably followed.

The assassins seized control of the party's supplies and declared themselves in command. Father Anastase, Abbé Jean Cavelier, the young Cavelier boy, and Joutel were told that their lives would be safe so long as they offered no opposition. Joutel, whose journal gave the best account, said that because they hoped to survive and carry out La Salle's plan to reach Canada, they did not resist.

The fragmented party followed their Hasinai guides over a faint footpath to the bank of a river about twenty miles from the Hasinai village. The river was too rain-swollen to wade across. Most of the French, including Joutel, Abbé Cavelier, and Douay, could not swim. They stopped to build a buffalo hide canoe, while the Hasinai guides swam across and went on to the village.

There was little to eat in the French camp, and Joutel was appointed to go trade with the villagers for some corn and, if possible, another horse. Three of the men now in control of the group went with him. They had gone some distance when they saw three horsemen coming toward them from the village. Two were Indians. The third looked like a Spaniard. He was dressed in Spanish fashion, wearing a blue doublet with embroidered white sleeves, very straight breeches, white stockings held by woolen garters, and a broad-brimmed, flat-crowned hat.

Joutel held his gun ready and called out a few words of Spanish. No answer. He tried Italian. Dark eyes peered intently from beneath the Spanish hat. "Coussica," responded the wearer. The word relieved the French. Joutel said that they realized the speaker was Hasinai and that they thought the word meant, "I do not understand you."[23] It seems just as likely that the Hasinai Indian stopped Joutel from speaking any more words that he could not understand by saying, *"Koo' see nah,"* "That's enough."

The Hasinai village had sent the three men to welcome the visitors. The one who spoke had donned prized clothing in their honor. Two large gift baskets filled with parched cornmeal were tied over the back of a fine gray mare ridden by another. Joutel asked a number of questions, but the only information communi-cated by the Hasinai spokesman was that the French were ex-pected by the chief man in the village.

Following the messenger, Joutel had his first view of Hasinai dwellings. The impressive structures were forty or fifty feet high. To build the form, trees as thick as a man's thigh were stripped of their branches and placed in a circle that was sometimes sixty feet in diameter. After the trunks were securely erect in the holes dug to hold them, the tops of the trees were lashed together, and the resulting dome shape was thatched with meadow grass. The round-top houses reminded Joutel of a giant beehive or rick of hay. Fifteen or twenty people could, and did, live comfortably in so large a house. Individual homes were built wherever there was a natural clearing and ground suitable for planting fields and gar-dens to feed the household. In other places there were unoccupied buildings used as assembly houses for council meetings and special community events.

The French were led past many houses before nearing the village center, where twelve spectacularly dressed elders came to meet them. The deerskin bands they wore flung over their shoul-ders were painted with patterns of different colors. Several of the old men had pieces of white linen draped from shoulder to shoulder. Their heads were crowned with colorful feather plumes. Six or seven of them carried square, Spanish-style sword blades, with great bunches of feathers and several hawk bells fastened on the hilts. Some held clubs, called head-breakers; others, bows. All their faces were daubed with black or red paint.

The elders approached formally, walking in the center between files of young men and warriors. Joutel had almost no experience with this sort of Indian custom. His unfamiliarity kept him from recognizing the honor given by the formal welcome. He wrote in his journal, "All the old men lifted up their right hands above their heads, crying out in a most ridiculous manner; but it behoved us to have a care of laughing. That done, they came and embraced us, using all sorts of endearments. Then they made us smoke, and brought to us a Frenchman of Provence, who was one of those that had forsaken the late M. de la Salle at his first journey."[24]

The warmth of the Hasinai welcome may have been caused by

the need for a strong ally. The French had arrived at a time when the tribes were preparing for a major battle; a victory would be assured if the French, with their guns and powder, could be persuaded to join the warriors. The elders escorted Joutel and the men with him to the home of the caddi and, after a short time there, to an assembly house. Mats had been spread on the floor for the visitors to sit on, and a meal was brought to them. The elders sat with their guests and began a discussion of war plans. After the meal they lit a pipe and passed it around.

Neither Joutel nor the men with him showed any interest in the plans for war. They gave their hosts some knives and some strings of beads for their wives and told them that they wanted to trade for corn. The elders readily promised the corn, but the man from Provence who had been living in another Hasinai village told his compatriots that there was a greater store of corn where his cottage was. They decided to go to that place. Still intent on making these men into allies, the elders agreeably prepared to go with them. A large number of young men joined them, and the entire group left together.

It was night when the men arrived and were greeted in the same way as in the first village, except there was less ceremony. Joutel and his traveling companions stayed in the house where the French deserter lived. It was the largest in the village, the home of a caddi who had recently died. Although it was occupied by more than one family and there were no interior walls, each person had the privacy of a nook for sleeping and an individual place for storing pottery, baskets, food, and other belongings. The beds, made of sturdy cane poles and mats of woven cane strips, were raised two or three feet off the ground. Buffalo robes and soft deerskins served as mattresses, quilts, or blankets. Closely woven mats, decorative as well as utilitarian, were hung to separate one bed from another. Joutel noticed that the pottery used for cooking was skillfully made, as were the cane baskets that held fruit and other provisions. The only thing families in the household shared in common was a central fire. It was never allowed to die out, and all took responsibility for keeping it burning.

In the morning the French were again taken to an assembly house, where the day was spent in active trade—corn, meal, and beans for needles, knives, rings, and other trinkets. Joutel's prize of the day was a fine horse; for the Hasinai trader, it was the ax he got in exchange. The three men who had come to the village with Joutel led the horse, packed with the new provisions, back to the riverside camp where the rest of the French party waited. Joutel was told to stay in the village and continue collecting supplies.

Joutel felt insecure among people whose speech he could not understand, but he did not protest being left because he hoped to talk privately with the men who had deserted La Salle the previous year. He was still determined to part from La Salle's murderers and needed to know if the deserters living with the Indians had heard any talk about the Mississippi River. He gave a knife to a boy as a gift and asked him to return the favor by telling the French who lived among the Hasinai that he wanted to see them.

Joutel spent his days engaged in trade, his nights in fretful sleep, needlessly suspicious that someone might steal his merchandise. The elders came frequently to sit with him. Using sign language, they told him again and again about their war against enemies they called the Cannokantimo, who boiled captives alive.[25] Joutel sometimes nodded his head in agreement with their signs, but most of the time he did not know what they meant.

Activity in the village was divided between preparations for the coming battle and ordinary daily tasks. The warriors rallied for war in the assembly house and would not go back to their homes until they returned from battle. When the time came for the war party to set out, it would set fire to the assembly hut and burn it to the ground. Women brought food, which young men served to the warriors before eating their own share.[26]

After the warriors ate and smoked, they trained the young men. Joutel, a man who had made a career of soldiering, especially enjoyed watching the daily exercises. Two posts were set in the ground some distance apart. The youths were lined up in a row and at a starting signal began a foot race to see which one could circle the markers the most times with the greatest speed. After the races came practice in shooting with bow and arrows.

There was a special ceremony for boys who had just become old enough to be warriors. A specific stool in the assembly house was used in the ritual. The young man's garments, usually no more than a breechclout, his bow, and a quiver of arrows were placed on the stool. One of the old men stretched his hands out over them while he spoke, or, according to Joutel, muttered a few words.

When the old man finished blessing the garment, bow, quiver, and arrows, they were presented to the owner, who was then a new warrior prepared to serve his people.

Watching other ceremonies, Joutel began to realize that these people believed, not in the god that he knew, but certainly in a superior being. The same stool used for the dedication of young warriors was also used when the first corn ripened. A basket full of corn was placed on the stool, and one of the elders held his hands over it and talked for a long time. The corn was then distributed among the women, but no one was allowed to eat any of the newly ripened crop until eight days after the ceremony. Joutel saw the same sort of ritual before a meal that was served when the people were called together for an assembly. The main dish was sagamite, a kind of cornmeal mush or porridge that was boiled in a great pot for the occasion. The pot was placed on the stool, and one of the elders went through the same blessing.

Joutel began to understand, too, that his hosts were not normally inclined toward violence. He saw one hundred men and as many women work together day after day to prepare fields for new crops at a succession of households. Joutel's father had been a gardener for La Salle's uncle, and memories from boyhood made Joutel appreciate the Hasinais' labor and the way it was shared. They broke the surface of the ground with a wooden tool, rather like a small pickax, made by splitting one end of a thick stick and fitting it with a shorter, sharply pointed piece of wood. With so many workers, it took only part of a day to prepare a family's field for sowing. The family to whom the field belonged then furnished food for everyone, and the rest of the day was spent in eating, lighthearted talk, and dancing. Seeing the way the Hasinais shared work and the goodnatured way they enjoyed leisure made Joutel conclude that the people about him became fierce and revengeful only when they were wronged or attacked.

Two men who had deserted La Salle got Joutel's message and came to see him. Joutel said they had turned half savage. Like Hasinai men, they saw no need to wear outer garments when the climate was warm. When cold winds did blow in from the north, they covered themselves with buffalo or deerskin cloaks. The deserters who came to see Joutel wore only a kind of coat and some turkey feathers on their shoulders. Neither wore anything on his head or feet. One had cut his hair like the Hasinai men—short, with a small lock on the crown left long—and he was tattooed in Hasinai fashion, with marks on his face from the top of his forehead, down his nose, to the tip of his chin. The Hasinai made tattoos by pricking the skin until it bled, then rubbing in a fine charcoal powder. They used this method to draw animal, leaf, and flower designs on their shoulders, thighs, and other body parts. Joutel thought that Hasinai men were generally handsome— except for the tattoos.

The French deserters had gained a reputation by taking part in their adopted tribe's war parties, killing enemies with their fire-arms. After they ran out of powder and balls, their weapons became useless, and they had learned to shoot with bows and arrows. Both men had Hasinai wives.

Hasinai women, said Joutel, were shapely and quite attractive, but in his opinion they, too, marred their appearance with tattoos. Some not only streaked their faces with the forehead and chin pattern but also added marks at the corners of their eyes and figures on other parts of the body, particularly circling their breasts with cosmetic design. They wore their hair neatly plaited and knotted at the back of the head and covered themselves from the waist to halfway down their legs with a sort of petticoat. Some owned small coats made from pieces of coarse blue cloth brought back from visits to Spanish territory.

Joutel learned from the deserters that the Indians said there was a great river, forty leagues northeast of the Hasinai villages, where many nations lived and where white men also lived. Joutel felt sure that the river they described was the Mississippi and that the whites were French. If somehow he and trustworthy companions could go there, they would be able to reach Canada and eventually return to France. First, however, they had to reclaim some supplies and separate from the assassins.

The men who conspired in the murder of La Salle could no longer consider going home, where they would hang for their crimes. As they saw it, they had two choices: return to the dying settlement near the Gulf Coast, or live the rest of their lives among the Indians. Discord grew. Tempers flared and two of the assassins shot and killed two others. When the day the Hasinai set for going to war came, six Frenchmen—the two deserters and the remain-ing conspirators—took the six horses that belonged to the French party and rode out with the warriors. Joutel, Abbé Cavelier, the young Cavelier nephew, Father Anastase, the Talon boy, and another youth were left in the village with the Hasinai women, children, and men too old to fight. Without horses, guides, or supplies, all they could do was wait for the return of the warriors.

The old men tried to use signs to relay news from the warriors as it came in. Indian tribes with different languages communicated freely that way, but Joutel and the men with him did not know the signs. Neither did they understand why, from time to time and seemingly without cause, the women began to weep. They were alarmed because La Salle had often told them that Indian women began to wail when someone was about to be killed, and the French were afraid that the tears were for them. It did not occur to them that Caddo women also cried for their own lost people.

The Hasinai women and old men found it just as strange that the French repeated a set of mysterious words and actions each morning and evening. For all the Hasinai knew, the daily devotions of the Catholic faith were meant to cast some sort of evil spell on the village. They came and watched intently while the two priests led the observance of religious duties. The absence of the warriors and the inability to communicate kept everyone uneasy.

The war party had been away for several days when Joutel was surprised by a large number of women coming at daybreak to the house where he stayed. "Their faces all besmeared with earth, and they set up their throats, singing several songs as loud as they were able, whereof we understood not one word. That done, they fell a-dancing in a ring, and we could not tell what to think of that rejoicing, which lasted full three hours, after which we were informed they had received advice of the victory obtained by their warriors over their enemies. The dance concluded, those in the cottage gave some bits of tobacco to those without."[27] Joutel did not say so, but to understand the information given to him, he must have begun to understand some sign language.

After the dance the women began to work pounding corn, boiling meal to make a porridge, and baking bread to carry to the returning warriors. Joutel recorded in his journal:

The same day the victorious army returned, and we were informed that their enemies, whom they call Cannohatinno, had expected them boldly, but that having heard the noise and felt the effects of our men's firearms, they all fled, so that the Cenis [Hasinai] had either killed or taken forty-eight men and women. They had slain several of the latter, who fled to the tops of trees, for want of time to make their escape otherwise; so that many more women had perished than men.

They brought home two of those women alive, one of whom had her head flayed for the sake of her hair and skin. They gave that wretched creature a charge of powder and a ball and sent her home, bidding her carry that present to her nation, and to assure them they should be again treated after the same manner—that is, killed with firearms.

The other woman was kept to fall a sacrifice to the rage and vengeance of the women and maids, who having armed themselves with thick stakes, sharp-pointed at the end, conducted that wretch to a by-place, where each of these furies began to torment her, sometimes with the point of their staff and sometimes laying on her with all their might. One tore off her hair, another cut off her finger, and every one of those outrageous women endeavored to put her to some exquisite torture, to revenge the death of their husbands and kinsmen who had been killed in the former wars; so that the unfortunate creature expected her death stroke as mercy.

At last one of them gave her a stroke with a heavy club on the head, and another ran her stake several times into her body, with which she fell down dead on the spot. Then they cut that miserable victim into morsels and obliged some slaves of that nation they had been long possessed of to eat them.

Thus our warriors returned triumphant from that expedition. They spared none of the prisoners they had taken, except two little boys, and brought home all the skins of their heads, with the hair, to be kept as trophies and glorious memorials of their victory.[28]

Compared to the way some tribes dealt with prisoners, the Hasinai treated their victims mercifully. Today's Caddos, far removed from that time, are ready to deny that Joutel's revolting account is true, but further on in his description of the victory celebration, faint traces of traditions followed today can be recognized. Joutel wrote:

The next day twenty savages assembled and went to the cabin of the chief whither all the scalps were brought as trophies, as well as the heads. They then began to rejoice greatly, and it lasted all that day at the aforementioned cabin; but the ceremony lasted three days, since they went then to the cabins of the most noted among them, whom they call cadis, which signifies chiefs or captains. They invited the six Frenchmen who had gone with them to take part in their rejoicings since they had taken part in their victory: so that, as we were in a cabin belonging to one of the most distinguished men, they came there after having finished at the cabin of the head chief.

I wondered at the way in which they behaved.

After all had arrived, the old men and the most esteemed took their places on the mats, on which they seated themselves. Then one of the aforesaid ancients, who had not been with these, and who appeared to be the orator, and acted as chief of the ceremonies, made for them a kind of eulogium or discourse. . . . A short time afterward the warriors who had slain enemies in battle and had taken scalps, marched, preceded by a woman carrying a great reed and a deer skin; then followed the wife of the said warrior bearing the scalp; and the said warrior followed with his bow and two arrows, and, when they reached the place where was the orator or chief of ceremonies, the said warrior took the scalp and put it in the hands of the said orator, who, having received it, presented it toward the four quarters of the earth saying many things which I did not under-stand; after which he laid the scalp on the ground, or rather on a mat spread out for this purpose. Another then approached until each one had brought his scalp as a trophy. When all that was completed, the orator delivered a kind of discourse, and food was served, the women of the aforesaid cabin having taken care to cook hominy in many big pots, knowing that the crowd was going to come. After they had eaten and smoked they began a dance, in the nature of a round dance, but which they did not close up. They kept a kind of cadence which they marked with their feet and with fans made of turkey feathers. . . . Their ceremony ended with some presents of tobacco, which the occupants of the aforementioned cabin made to the old men and warriors.[29]

Joutel and his companions watched the women's victory dance and the Hasinais' three-day celebration in May 1687. Three centuries later whenever Caddo people hold a traditional tribal dance, it is usually a three-day event and always begins with the women's Turkey Dance. Modern Caddo dances usually start Friday afternoon. In past years when families came to the dance ground in wagons and on horseback, they set up camps and stayed until after they had rested on Sunday. Now, arriving in cars, some go home to sleep the first night, but hardly anyone leaves during the second night, when the drum is stilled for only brief intervals between the beginning Turkey Dance and the Morning Dance that greets the next day.

To start the dancing, the singer-drummers take their places around a big drum in the center of the otherwise vacant dance arena. They each take hold of a drumstick and hit the drum in unison with a steady beat. They sing out together, calling the women, who begin to enter the ring from wherever they have been sitting or standing talking with friends and relatives.[30]

The songs and steps for the Turkey Dance come from so long ago that no one today knows their origin. Several versions are told, but all say that the songs recount history—the closeness of the people and their strength, the battles they have fought, and their victories. The dance of the women may have been given its name because the steps and body motions are patterned on the movements of turkeys, but the songs that set the rhythm carry messages from the past that are far more important than associations with turkeys.

In July 1967 a researcher from the University of Oklahoma came to visit with Caddos near Binger, Oklahoma. He attended a dance and taped several interviews with a Caddo woman named Sadie Weller. Throughout her young years Sadie was cared for by her grandmother, whose name was Sabedoka (Sah Bedoka).[31] At the age of two Sadie contracted polio and so spent many childhood hours sitting on her grandmother's lap, listening to stories about times past. Visitors often arrived on horseback or in wagons and stayed overnight. After supper they would sit until almost midnight, talking idly and reminiscing. The grown-ups conversed in Caddo, which was Sadie's first language. She was sixty-six years old at the time of the interviews and spoke in English.

The interviewer, Kenneth Beals, placed a microphone to pick up both their voices, started the recorder, and began asking questions:[32] "Today I'd like to talk about the Turkey Dance, and one of the things I'd like to ask you is whether or not there is a story about how the Caddo got the Turkey Dance and where it came from. Could you tell me about that?"

She answered, "Well, the[y] said once upon a time there was a special man that composed these songs and whenever the runner came in, why then he related the story of the battle or whatever the outcome had been and then this old man would compose the songs within the hour before the warriors came in.

Winona Williams, wife of former Caddo Tribal Chairman Melford Williams, dressed for a Turkey Dance in the summer of 1978. The age of the leader's cane she is holding is unknown, but it is believed to predate the Caddos' move to Indian Territory.

"There are different versions of the story of how this dance came to be but it's always been considered as a victory or either a scalp dance and this dance is never danced after late hours. It's always been the late afternoon because the Caddos never went on the warpath at night. They always went by day. . . . See, prior to the time that the warriors went, they always had that Big Osage [dance]. It's where they went from camp to camp like I told you. They had that drum, you know in the middle, and everybody followed the warriors, and then in the camp whoever had anything that they could give, such as food, . . . this deal was in the first part of the turkey dance."

Sadie explained that Big Osage had another name that meant, "They're on the war path. . . . That's the interpretation for that Wahu, where they came to camp and collected materials."

Beals asked, "Do you know how the name Turkey Dance became associated with it? Why they call it the Turkey Dance today?"

Sadie's answer was prompt. Her grandparents "said once upon a time there was a man who got out to hunt, and they said that he saw a bunch of turkeys and they were all, I guess they must be in the mating season or something, I don't know what it is they were all going around and around out in the timber somewhere wherever he saw them and then when he told of this story, that's how come the Turkey Dance. . . . That's the version that I had from my grandparents."

Beals was confused, "Did you say that the Turkey Dance and the Wahu are the same dance?"

"Well," answered Sadie, "the Wahu dance is supposed to be prior to this. Of course, since we don't have no war parties we don't have that part of it, but it's called the Big Osage dance."

"Who was this Big Osage that you're talking about? Was he a certain person?"

Sadie was a patient teacher, repeating her information. "No, that's the name of the dance. Wahu and Big Osage, both are the same name. . . . Now, they dance it at the last."

Still puzzled about Big Osage, Beals asked, "Do you know what this name, Big Osage, means or how it got associated with the dance—Was there any reason for that?"

Sadie gave the obvious answer, "After the Osages at the time. . . . That's the Little Osage that they dance now."

"What's the difference between the Big Osage and the Little Osage?"

"There's a difference in the song."

"Is there any difference in the way they do the dance?"

Sadie replied, "Yes, uhuh. Big Osage is from camp to camp, where they gather material and supplies for the trip."

"Oh, you mean that when they went from camp to camp they did the Big Osage, but when they came back from the warpath they did the Little Osage?"

Sadie almost sighed. At last, he understood.

Beals took up another topic. "You were telling me about these runners, too. Could you tell me some more about how they decided who would be the runner and how he would get back?"

"Well, see they relayed like, the villages were so far apart. I don't know just how many miles apart, see there was Hinai [Hainai], and the Caddodacho. . . . They were up in the thousands and each community and each village had their own spokesman and their own what we call tamma."

Tamma is an ancient Caddo title given to certain tribal officials and recorded by Spanish observers in the seventeenth century as either tamma or tanma. These officials informed the people about decisions made by their leaders and saw to it that those decisions were carried out.

Sadie continued, "Nowadays it would be what we could call an MC. Now this [tamma] . . . got up in the morning and he would announce for the day what activities would be within the camp and they used to do that a long time ago . . . these boys that were the runners, they were of the athletic type and could defend themselves in case of enemies or something."

Beals was still trying to get the dance sequence right. He asked, "Would they have this dance, or would they start the dance as soon as the runner got back?"

"No. See, the runner comes in and he tells the story to the man that composed the songs. There was one certain man that did that, and then when the runner came and he told the story, they'd be ahead of the warriors. He'd tell them what they were bringing and how many were lost or whatever they had to do. So then they'd go ahead and this man when he sees them coming, he'd hit the drum and the women are ready because the tamma would announce that certain parties were coming and to be ready. Regardless of what they were doing they'd all come in. The pole was there where they hung the scalps. Most generally, Osages would be their enemies."

The interviewer was curious. "What kind of pole would this be that they'd hang the scalps on?"

Sadie wasn't quite sure. Her answer, less pat than it had been to other questions, was, "Well . . . maybe a good cedar pole. . . . They said that they had certain poles that they used and I don't know because I never did—I should have inquired and I would have been told."

"When would they put the scalps on the pole? Would the runner bring the scalps with him?"

Her answer was again confident. "No. The warriors themselves. The leader. Whoever they had as a leader they would give him the scalps and he'd put them up and they didn't wait regardless of what anyone was doing. You were supposed to drop your work and get out there and honor the warriors."

"Would they tie them onto this pole?"

"Yeah, they tied them way up at the top, just like you do a flag now. That's the way they had them and they'd hang there, fresh you know. They'd hang them up and then each of the warriors would tell the story of what happened and how they acquired those scalps."

During the dance he attended, Beals heard the Caddo tribal chairman talk about the time when the Turkey Dance was revived. Beals asked Sadie Weller to tell him how it been lost and how it got started up again.

She replied, "Well, it wasn't really lost, but after our oldsters died, why then there were very few that could sing those songs because it wasn't just anybody that could sing them. Like my grandpa, he was one of the singers. His name was Wildhorse. He stayed with us and he taught my brother the various songs and various traditions. I used to say, 'I wish grandpa would quit talking,' but he was always telling. Now I realize that if I had been able to write at that time and took interest as I should have, perhaps I would know more about it."

Beals again changed the subject, saying, "There was something in this dance the other day that I really didn't understand . . . something about a woman putting tobacco on the drum. Could you tell me about that? What it means?"

It was difficult to explain old customs to someone who had so little acquaintance with the way things were done. The incident was intertwined with how Caddos show appreciation to someone who has helped them. It was also the old way of showing that a period of mourning was over, that a man whose wife had died was free to remarry. Sadie tried to explain, saying, "Well, that's way back in tradition. . . . As she [the woman who had placed tobacco on the drum] said, this wasn't a war story. It was a story of appreciation. . . . See, she put that tobacco there for tobacco leads in all our deals. . . . She put that tobacco there for the drummers. And I don't know, she may have put money there. If you have money, it goes along with that to pay the drummers for the singing. That's the way it's supposed to be."

The interviewer returned to the idea that the Turkey Dance had been revived. He asked, "Was there a certain length of time that the Caddos didn't do this dance?"

"Oh, they've always danced it, but the ceremonial part we didn't carry on."

"When did that happen? When did the people decide to do that?"

"Well, it was after the war."

"After the Second World War?"

"Uhuh. After the Second World War."

One afternoon seven years after Sadie Weller's interview, one of the Caddo drummers, Leon Carter, sat at his desk in the Indian Agency office building talking about Caddo dances. He was one of the first Indians to be employed — as a civil service accountant — when the federal government decided that it was appropriate for Native Americans to work at office jobs in the federal Indian agency. Now, in 1972, he was looking forward to retirement the following year.

Leon had been a singer and drummer since he was a boy. Both his parents were Caddos, and he was proud of helping to preserve this part of his culture. It was important to him that the tradition be understood. He leaned forward and spoke earnestly, describing the form and meaning of the dances.[33]

"Just about all of them are social, purely social. No costumes or anything, you just get out there and dance. The only traditional dance we have in costume is the women's Turkey Dance. That is

Leon Carter (1978)

danced only in the daytime—the sun goes down, that's it. There's some significance to that, I don't know what it is, but . . . as I understand it . . . the women danced this because their men were gone off to war or off hunting or in a skirmish.

"In the last stages of the dance there's a certain song in which the women go out and catch the men, partners. What they used to do—I've heard two versions—they would get as a partner the brother of the one that was away or his cousin or some near relative to take his place in the dance. Never their father-in-law, but always his brother or his cousin.

"The other version is that they might go after any of the men, and whoever they catch has to dance with them, or he's considered a coward. Nowadays it's all in fun, but even so, if any of the men refuse to dance, they are supposed to give the lady something—a token, you know, maybe a scarf or a silk handkerchief or maybe even a dollar or something like that.

"The dance goes through several stages. It's a kind of a shuffle to

start with. After those songs are finished, there's another sequence. They call it the grazing series. Well, I don't know whether
they call it that or not, but that's what I call it. See, they all mostly
go in single file or double file, but when this grazing series of songs
starts, they scatter—you know, you've seen chickens or turkeys
feeding here, and there—they just break up just any old way. It's a
different kind of step, and they dance all over the place. Some even
come close to the drum, probably tip somebody's hat or hit them on
the back or something like that—all in fun.

"Then there's another series where they go sideways, and that is
graceful. Traditionally this was danced around a fire. For the next
sequence they have a beat, it's just a quick shuffle [he rapidly
slides the palms of first one hand, then the other, across the
desktop] like that. That's when everybody goes in toward the fire.
Then they start that song over again, and they move back, just
walk backwards. They hit the drum again, and they move toward
the fire—it's colorful!

"After a few songs of that, they go like they did when they
started off. After that is the song where they go out and catch men,
and they dance face to face. As the drum beat changes, the man
and woman turn around and face each other. They dance with a
[he beats lightly on the desktop, PAT-pat-pat-pat-PAT-pat-pat-pat-
PAT-pat-PAT] or maybe just like walking along [PAT-PAT-PAT-
PAT] facing each other. After that's over with, they go into what
we call the Osage Dance. . . . It's another type of song entirely.

"That's in the afternoon. At night we have other dances."

For one of the most important dances, the Drum Dance, the
drummers carry the drum and the people fall in behind them.

"That's what we start with in the evening," remarked Leon.
"They just go around the fire." The Drum Dance was also a kind of
victory dance long ago, but the form changed over the years. So
did the pattern of the procession. "Originally they'd start from the
west end here," he said, beginning to draw on a pad of paper, "and
sing their song till they'd get over to here, then sing another song
and get over to here, another song over to here, and back to here,
making a square. But now they don't have many people that know
these songs, and we have to make them last, so we just go clear
around to here and over here." He placed the pencil point on the
northeast and southwest corners of the square.

"Those are the only ones that I know that aren't purely social dances except for the War Dance, and our War Dance was never a show type of dance like it is now. But now we don't have many war dancers, just the young fellas, boys, and they're growing up learning these fancy steps." Fancy steps had been incorporated into the "war dances" that young men and boys performed for exhibitions and judged competitions. The shows and contests were often intertribal.

"So we have what as sacred dances? The Turkey Dance and the War Dance and then this Drum Dance or Victory Dance."

In the last decade of the twentieth century those dances, like the Caddos who perform them, descend from those watched by Joutel during the days of victory celebration in the seventeenth century.

Joutel, Abbé Cavelier, and Father Anastase reached an agreement with the murderers of La Salle when things settled down after the victory celebration. It was decided that those who wanted to could continue their search for the Mississippi. The seven men in Joutel's party were given six horses, a scant supply of gunpowder and balls, and thirty-odd axes and knives for use in trade with Indians. The Hasinai furnished three guides.

The ten men crossed the Neches River, which divided the village where the French had stayed from one on the east bank, and traveled on for two or three days, passing a few houses each day along the way before coming to another village, which the people called Nahouidiche (Nawidish). Joutel said that the name meant "place of salt." A handful or two of the sand from a nearby sand bed, when soaked in water, produced saltwater, which was poured into beans and other foods for flavoring. The French traded for supplies and accepted the caddi's offer to go with them as far as Nasoni, the next village.[34]

The way to Nasoni led a short distance north and east through fertile Hasinai country. Flat plains gave way to rolling hills and prairie valleys. Grass grew thick and tall from rich, black earth. Black land changed to sandy red soil, and the landscape gradually became more tree-covered until it was blanketed by pine forests. Woodland growths of fruit-bearing bushes and vines fed and sheltered abundant wildlife. Dwellings were located in natural clearings near creeks and streams. It was the planting season, late

May into June, and Hasinai women were busy sowing their gardens with corn, beans, watermelon, pumpkin, sunflowers, and other crops. Both men and women worked to till the soil, but only the women planted.

It rained almost continually for two weeks, and the French stayed at Nasoni until the weather cleared. Then two men from the Nasoni village led the French toward the Cadohadacho. Progress was hampered by river crossings and marshy country, and one of the guides became ill. The other went to hunt fresh meat for his sick kinsman.

The Nasoni guide soon brought back a deer, and his sick friend recovered after only a day's illness. They led the French into a district that was easier to travel. Joutel tried to learn the names of Indian nations in the neighborhood and of those they were going toward. Whenever the Nasoni guides understood the questions, they answered as best they could with words and signs—in the direction they were going, they would reach the Cadohadachos, which sounded like "Cadodaquios" to Joutel.

On June 23, ten days after leaving Nasoni, the group was a little more than one mile from the first Cadohadacho village near the Red River. Fine tree groves bordered prairies where the grass grew so high and lush the travelers sometimes had to clear the way for the horses. A caddi mounted on a large gray mare rode toward them. He was attended by others from the village. "As soon as that chief came up to us," said Joutel, "he expressed very much kindness and affection; and we gave him to understand that we did nobody any harm, unless we were first attacked."[35] They smoked together, and then the caddi signaled for the French to follow him. He led them to the bank of a river and asked them to wait there while he returned to the village to tell the elders to prepare for their arrival.

A large group of people came back to the river with the caddi. Joutel and his companions were a little startled when seven of the young men approached them directly and knelt with their backs turned toward them. The Nasoni guides made the French understand that they should each mount the back or shoulders of one of the kneeling men so that they could be carried into the village with honor. It was a custom the French had not met with before, and Joutel was especially uncomfortable with it. He was a large man, loaded down with clothes, guns, ammunition, a kettle, and other implements, and he was also taller than his carrier. His feet scraped the ground until two more Cadohadacho men hurried to hold them up.

More than two hundred people were at the caddi's cottage, where the elders received their visitors with a ceremony that gave the French another new experience. It was customary for the Cadohadachos to bathe strangers when they first arrived, but since these guests were fully clothed, freshwater was brought in an earthenware vessel, and one of the elders washed only their foreheads. Next the caddi motioned for Joutel and his companions to be seated on a wood-and-cane bench, about four feet high, while he and three other caddis, from the same number of villages, spoke one after the other. It was midday and the travelers were tired by the heat of the sun as well as by the length of the speeches, but the words sounded like a welcome, so they sat patiently. When the speeches finally ended, the French tried their own form of communication. They made presents of axes, knives, strings of beads, needles, and pins and did their best to make their hosts understand that they were going to their own country but would soon return, bringing many things that the Cadohadacho needed.

After breakfast the next morning, one of the Frenchmen, De Marle, decided to bathe in the river they had been carried across. Young Cavelier followed and came to the riverbank in time to see that De Marle was drowning. He had gone too far into the water, stepped into a hole, and did not know how to swim. Neither did Cavelier, who ran back for help. A number of Indians answered his call, reaching the river before Joutel and the other Frenchmen but too late to save De Marle. Some of the Cadohadacho men dived to the bottom and brought up the body.

De Marle's friends tearfully carried him back to the cottage and gave him the last rites of their faith. With prayers and the reading of scripture, they buried him in a small field behind the cottage. The Cadohadacho showed great sensitivity and made the French understand through sympathetic actions that they shared their sorrow. They understood sorrow, they understood prayer, but they could not understand the meaning of a man turning the leaves of a book while speaking. The French were equally mystified by the actions of the caddi's wife. Each morning during the rest of their short stay in the village, she carried a small basket filled with parched ears of corn to De Marle's grave and left it there.

During the last days of the visit Joutel learned that he was in one of four allied villages; that together they formed one people, the Cadohadacho, but that only one place was called by that name. The place where the explorers stayed had the name Assony (Nasoni), the same as the Hasinai village they had left ten days before arriving in Cadohadacho territory. The other villages were called Nathosos (Nanatsoho), Nachitos (Natchitoches), and Cadodauio (Cadohadacho).[36] None of these associated villages was far apart, and people came from each to greet the French.

Joutel and his companions gave parting presents, particularly to the caddi and his wife, who had taken such good care of them, and left the last day in June. The caddi went along, personally delivering them to his friend, the Cadohadacho caddi. Other visitors were already being entertained there. They had come from the east-northeast, where they lived on the stream now known as the Ouachita River in Arkansas. They were called Cahinnio and were close to the Cadohadacho in every way but distance.[37]

The Cahinnio had come to get wood for making bows. The large Cadohadacho bows, superior to any others, were made from the wood of a tree that was abundant in the region. The French gave the bow wood tree the name "bois d'arc." It is also called Osage orange.

The Cahinnio visitors told Joutel and the others about white men who had guns and lived in a house near the Cappas (Kappas, Quapaws). Their own village, they said, was not far from the Cappas, and they were perfectly willing to take the French home with them. They were unwilling, however, to leave immediately, as the eager French wished. Finally, one young man reluctantly volunteered to serve as a guide.

They first followed close to the Red River, then made their way across lush country watered by many brooks, streams, and rivers. Five days after leaving the Cadohadacho village, Joutel and his party were eating a meal on a riverbank when they were startled by the sound of tinkling bells. Looking around, they saw an Indian standing on the opposite bank of the river. He held a sword—its naked blade was decorated with feathers of various colors and two large hawk bells. The bells rang again as he made signs for them to come to him. With more ringing gestures he made them understand that the elders of his village had sent him to meet them.

The Cahinnio village was different from all the others Joutel had seen. It was compact, one hundred or so cottages placed together. Near the end of the French travelers' first day with the Cahinnio, some elders led a company of young men and women into the cottage that had been assigned to the French. The young people were singing, and the elder at the head of the procession was carrying a very-long-stemmed tobacco pipe decorated with varicolored feathers. They stopped outside the cabin to sing a while, then entered and continued the songs for nearly fifteen minutes.

Cavelier, the priest, was taken as the leader of the white men, perhaps because he was the oldest. Supporting him firmly under the arms, the singers solemnly propelled him out of the cottage and seated him at a place that had been prepared for ceremony. One attendant laid a great handful of grass on Cavelier's feet. Two more brought a pottery dish filled with freshwater and gently washed his face. Next he was coaxed to sit on a skin that had been spread for that purpose.

When he was properly seated, the elders took their places, sitting around him. A leader placed two small, forked sticks in the ground and laid a straight stick across them. All three sticks were painted red. He covered the red sticks with a buffalo hide, overlaid that with a deerskin, and placed the pipe on top. When he finished the arrangement, the singing began again. Women's voices joined the men's, and the rhythm of the mixed chorus was accented by the rattle of hollow gourds filled with pebbles. A man who stood behind Cavelier again lifted the old priest and tried to coax him into joining the festivities by shaking and dangling his body in time to the beat of the music.

At the end of the song, the leader presented two young women. One carried a sort of collar, which she hung on the wooden fork by the end of the pipe. The second girl placed an otter skin on the fork at the other end. The singing resumed, and the master of the ceremonies directed the girls to sit on either side of Cavelier facing each other and extending their legs so that they interlaced. He then moved Cavelier's legs so that they lay on top and across those of the girls. While this arrangement was made, one of the elders tied a dyed feather to the hair at the back of Cavelier's head. The singing was tedious to the French priest, and he did not know the purpose of the embarrassing position in which he found himself. To escape his predicament, he signaled that he was not well, and two Indians immediately came again to support him under his arms while they took him back to his cottage. There they made signs to show that he should rest. It was by then several hours into summer darkness. The singing continued throughout the night, but Cavelier was left undisturbed.

With daylight, Cavelier was conducted from his cabin in the same manner as the night before and seated in the same place. The singing continued. The leader of the ceremonies took the pipe from its place atop the deerskin and lit it. He held it out and withdrew it six times, then put it in Cavelier's hands. Cavelier pretended to smoke and returned the pipe. It was passed around to the elders, Joutel, Father Anastase, and the other travelers, each whiffing in turn while the singers sang on.

By about 9:00 A.M. Cavelier's discomfort had been increased by the summer sun radiating on his bare head, and he signaled that it did him harm. The singing stopped. One of the elders put the pipe and the three red sticks in a deerskin case and offered it to Cavelier, assuring him that with it as a token of peace, he could pass through all the nations of all the tribe's allies and be well received.

Although the French had smoked as a sign of friendship before this, Joutel said, "This was the first place where we saw the calumet, or pipe of peace, having no knowledge of it before, as some have written. This nation is called Cahainihoua."[38] Twentieth-century authorities generally think that the Cahainihoua (Cahinnio) were the Caddoan group that De Soto's chroniclers called Tula. Only a few years after they feted Cavelier (sometime around 1700), the Cahinnio left the region of the upper Ouachita River in the present state of Arkansas, some moving southwest to settle with or near the Cadohadacho on the Red River, others going northwest to settle in the Arkansas River valley.[39]

Cavelier's ordeal seemed worthwhile to him when one of the Cahinnio men drew in the sand with a stick to show that they were not far from a great river. He showed that the river had two branches and pronounced the word Cappa while pointing to one of them. Cavelier remembered that La Salle had mentioned Cappa as the name of a nation of Indians near the Mississippi.

The French had a saber that they knew the caddi would like to have. Joutel said that the caddi's name, Hinmahy Apemche, meant Great Knife and that his eyes, like those of the other Cahinnio men, had often been drawn to gaze on the gleaming, metal blade. Joutel's translation of the caddi's name may have been fanciful. As used today, the Caddo word *haimay* means "big," but the word for "knife" is *ḳut*.

Cavelier took advantage of Hinmahy Apemche's attraction to the saber, telling the caddi that he could have the weapon if he would take the French to the Cappas. The caddi consulted his elders, then used hand signs to show that his own heart and the heart of a man he pointed to were like one and that he, Hinmahy Apemche, would lead the French to the Cappas through that man. Hinmahy Apemche was given the saber, and his proxy guided the French to the Arkansas River a few miles above the point where it joins the Mississippi.[40]

Looking across the river, they saw a great wooden cross and a short distance from it a house built in the French fashion. They had traveled, according to Father Anastase, 250 leagues, more than 660 miles, across country: 100 leagues from La Salle's settlement on the bay to the first Hasinai village, 25 leagues from the Hasinai to the Nasoni, 40 leagues from the Nasoni to the Cadohadacho, 25 leagues from the Cadohadacho to the Cahinnio, and 60 leagues from the Cahinnio to the French outpost.

CHAPTER 3

THE SEARCHERS

The French outpost on the Arkansas River was built by French Canadians who were led down the Mississippi from Fort St. Louis (on the Illinois River) by Henri de Tonti. They arrived at the mouth of the Mississippi, where Tonti expected to meet La Salle, in April 1686, the same month that La Salle first started overland toward the Hasinai villages. Unable to locate La Salle, Tonti started back up the river. Because some of his men wanted to settle on the Arkansas near the place where it joined the Mississippi, Tonti left them there to establish the Arkansas Post that Joutel and those with him were so happy to find. Tonti returned to his post at Fort St. Louis on the Illinois River.[1]

From Arkansas Post, Joutel, the Caveliers, and Father Anastase traveled up the Mississippi and Illinois Rivers to Fort St. Louis. They stayed there, living on Tonti's hospitality for several months, but did not tell him that La Salle had been murdered. When they left for Canada in March 1688, Tonti still believed that La Salle was alive and in good health at the settlement on the Gulf of Mexico. He did not learn the truth until the next year, when one of the men from Arkansas Post visited him.[2]

About the same time he heard La Salle was dead, Tonti learned that France and Spain were at war. He was a soldier who had been in the French service, both land and sea, for eight years, and he had lost one of his hands in combat before he joined La Salle. Cavelier had told Tonti that the Cadohadacho had offered to accompany the French if they fought the Spaniards. Believing he could marshal a force of Indian warriors and rescue La Salle's colonists from their vulnerable position on the seacoast, Tonti once more canoed down the Mississippi. He left the Illinois River fort in December 1689, taking five French, one Shawnee Indian hunter, and two Indian slaves with him.[3]

On his two previous trips down the Mississippi, Tonti had made friends with Taensa Indians whose village was located in northeast Louisiana. His plan was to get Taensa guides to lead him across land to the Naodiché (Nawidish) Indian village where he thought some of La Salle's men had stayed.

On his way downstream, Tonti made a brief detour by Arkansas Post. There he met Indians who "lived on a branch of the river coming from the west." These Indians, said Tonti, "did their best, giving me two women of the Cadadoquis nation, to whom I was going." Tonti expected the Cadohadacho to be grateful to him for returning the women.[4]

Tonti continued his journey down the Mississippi to the Taensa village. From there thirty Taensas guided him cross-country to the Natchitoches on the Red River. The Natchitoches and their relatives, the Ouachita and the Doustioni, lived separately.[5] Three village chiefs assembled at Natchitoches to meet with the one-handed man and thirty Taensas who had arrived unexpectedly in their midst. There was a sacred house—Tonti called it a "temple"—at the Natchitoches meeting place. Before any words were exchanged, the Taensas put down their arms and "went to the temple, to show how sincerely they wished to make a solid peace. After having taken their God to witness, they asked for friendship."[6]

The Taensas stayed a few days to trade for some of the salt that the Natchitoches produced from a lake in their neighborhood. After the Taensas left, Natchitoches guides directed Tonti to the Yatasi, who lived farther up the Red River about halfway to the Cadohadacho. The Yatasi anticipated and welcomed Tonti and his men with refreshments at a distance from their village. In the village the chief was cordial and gave feasts for his guests, but when Tonti asked for guides to the Cadohadacho, the Yatasi refused. Tonti claimed they were "very unwilling to give us any, as they had murdered three ambassadors [from the Cadohadacho] about four days before who came to their nation to make peace."[7]

He said he was finally able to persuade the Yatasi that no harm would come to them, and five men agreed to take him to the Cadohadacho.

Twelve days later Tonti was in Cadohadacho country. His group camped on March 28 beside a trail made by people and horses. The next day a mounted Cadohadacho reconnoitering party appeared. The scouts recognized one of the women brought from the Arkansas River as the wife of a chief, talked with her, and then left. On the following day a woman, who Tonti said governed the Cadohadacho nation, came to his camp with the principal persons of the village. Only dire circumstance could place a woman in this position. A caddi's wife could wield influence, but governance was traditionally the role of her husband or his male heir. Tonti's recollection of meeting the Cadohadacho leaders makes it clear that he arrived at a time when the tribe not only needed but also fully expected that Joutel and Cavelier's promises to aid in fighting its enemies would be kept. The two Frenchmen had smoked the pipe of peace and had said they would return with guns and ammunition to join the Cadohadachos in war.

Cavelier and Joutel had made false promises, but the woman said to be governing the Cadohadachos had no way of knowing that. She confronted Tonti with tears and demands that he revenge the deaths of her husband and the husband of the woman he had brought back home. Both chiefs had been killed by the Osage. Tonti's scruples were no greater than Cavelier's and Joutel's. In his memoir Tonti wrote, "To take advantage of everything, I promised that their death should be avenged."[8]

The Cadohadacho also had a sacred house where all things important to the well-being of the people were communicated to God. They took Tonti to that special place, and the "priests" spoke to God. Afterward, they took Tonti to the caddi's cabin. Before entering, they washed his face with water in the same ceremonial way described by Joutel.

Tonti stayed with the Cadohadacho only long enough to get the information and guides he needed—about one week. He, in effect, just passed through and learned little about the tribe that was not obvious. He noted that the men and women were tattooed on their faces and bodies, but failed to see any of them engage in any activity that he called work—except for making bows that he admired for their quality. The bois d'arc bows made by the

Cadohadachos were famous as trade items, even among distant Indian nations. Trade had brought about thirty horses to the Cadohadacho who called them *cavali*, a word adopted from the Spanish word for a horse, *caballo*.

The Cadohadacho called the river they lived on the Red because the water, colored by deposits of sand, was "as red as blood." Tonti learned that "Cadadoquis" and two other "villages" on the Red River, called "Natchitoches and Nasoui," all spoke the same language and were united. He observed that they did not occupy villages in the European sense, with houses tightly clus-tered, but built their cabins distant from one another. Although they had the prosperity of beautiful fields, plenty of game to hunt, and fish to catch, it seemed to Tonti that the villages were thinly populated because of "the cruel war" they waged.

Tonti was told that eighty leagues from Cadohadacho, in the Nawidish village of the Hasinai nation, there were seven French. He was eager to go there, but the Canadians who accompanied him were disgusted with the roundabout and difficult search for La Salle's colony and refused to go farther. Tonti therefore traveled south toward the Nawidish with a single Frenchman, "his little Shawnee Indian slave," and five Cadohadacho guides.[9] Before taking the trail, he made a gesture toward keeping his promise to the chief's wife. He put some ammunition in a small box and left it in her hands.

On his way south, Tonti and his guides met some Nawidish hunters, who assured him that Frenchmen were staying with them, but when he finally came close to the Nawidish village and was met by the chiefs, he was disappointed and angered by their response to his questions. They told him that the French were no longer there. The French, they said, had gone with the chiefs to fight against the Spaniards, seven days' distance away, and the Spaniards had surrounded them with armed men on horses. The Nawidish said that their chief had spoken in favor of the French and that the Spaniards, as an act of friendship, had given them horses and arms. From others Tonti heard that three of those he sought had been killed by an enemy tribe and that the four still living were gone in search of "iron arrowheads." Tonti believed the Nawidish had killed all seven of the French, and he told them so. The women present began to cry, and for Tonti their wails were proof that his accusation was true.

When the chief offered a peace pipe, Tonti would not accept it. Instead, he gave the chief seven hatchets and a string of large glass beads and announced he wanted four horses for his return trip. Horses were common among the Nawidish. Tonti counted four or five at every cabin. Four horses were brought to him the next day.

It was not just the Nawidish who angered Tonti; his own men proved unmanageable. The only one who stayed with him was an incompetent who lost most of their ammunition when he fell into a river. Irritated by this lack of ammunition and frustrated by an inability to locate any of La Salle's men among the Nawidish, Tonti left the Hasinai village at the end of April 1690. He turned back from his search without knowing that he was already too late to save La Salle's colonists.

Spanish records indicate that Tonti was mistaken in his belief that the Nawidish had killed the French who lived among them. Spaniards had started to search for the French as soon as the news of La Salle's colony reached Mexico. While La Salle was traveling the Texas plains looking for the Mississippi River, Spanish brigs were coasting the Gulf of Mexico. The wrecks of the French vessels were sighted, and Spanish officials thought that La Salle's expedition was lost, but rumors of French among the Indians north of the Rio Grande caused them to begin a series of land searches led by Alonso de León.[10]

De León first crossed the Rio Grande near Eagle Pass in 1688 and found an old Frenchman living like a petty king among the Indians there. The identity of this Frenchman has remained a mystery, but it has been speculated that he was one of the early deserters of La Salle's colony.[11] The Frenchman was captured, taken to Mexico, and used as a guide for De León's second expedition north of the Rio Grande in 1689. During the second search De León located La Salle's ravaged colony and tracked down two of the Frenchmen who were living with Hasinai tribes.[12]

De León's 1689 expedition began in late March, traveled for three weeks, and crossed the Guadalupe River before finding any trace of the French. Father Damian Massanet, eager to expand his mission field, was in De León's company. In mid-April, a year before Tonti left the Nawidish, they had come across an Indian who said that four Frenchmen were in his nearby village. At the village, however, De León was told that the French were not there; they had gone on to the Tejas four days before.

Tejas (*taysha*) is the Caddo word for "friend" that Hasinai tribes used to greet allies. Missionaries and soldiers learned that a number of tribes were called Tejas, but they first used the term to identify the dominant Hasinai tribes that lived east of the Trinity River between the Neches and Angelina Rivers. Reports about these people, from whom the state of Texas got its name, began as early as 1650. Their name is spelled differently in various documents, usually Texas or Tejas. Gradually the name was applied to a broader geographical area, and Spaniards called their entire northernmost province Tejas.[13]

Having been told that the four French they pursued had gone to the Tejas, De León took sixty of his men and followed, but the French continued to elude him. The country was unknown, and the main body of the Spaniards fell farther and farther behind. De León and Massanet decided to quit their chase, compose a letter to the French, and send an Indian to deliver it. The letter, written in French, said the Spaniards would wait for the French in the village they had recently left. It urged the French to come there within three or four days. Massanet added a Latin postscript in case one of the four was of a religious order. He and De León also had the forethought to send a sheet of paper for response.

De León's native informants told him that most of the other strangers who had built houses on "the little sea" (the Gulf of Mexico) had died of smallpox three moons before the rest were massacred by a coastal tribe. De León found La Salle's vacant, vandalized settlement five days after the Indian carrier had left to deliver the letter to the French with the Tejas. A few days later De León received a response to the letter. Written in red ocher, it said that the French were tired of living among the Indians and would come to De León's camp in two days. The letter was signed by Jean L'Archevêque, one of the conspirators in La Salle's murder.

When the French did not arrive within that time, De Léon took thirty men to look for them. He returned to camp bringing L'Archevêque and one of the men who had deserted La Salle on his first trip to the Hasinai. A Hasinai chief and eight of his men accompanied the two French.

The chief impressed De León, who described him in a letter to the viceroy as "an Indian of great faculty" who "asked me to furnish him an Indian guide, saying that he would come with his brother and six other Tejas Indians to this province [Coahuila in

Mexico], because they wished to communicate with Christians, and that they greatly desired to know the evangelical law."[14] The chief's motives for wishing to communicate with Christians may have been less pious than those De León attributed to him, but the missionary Massanet had the opportunity he sought. His own description of the event was as follows:

> Two Frenchmen came, naked except for an antelope's skin, and with their faces, breasts, and arms painted like the Indians, and with them came the governor of the Tejas and eight of his Indians. Through that day and night I tried my utmost to show all possible consideration to the said governor, giving him two horses, and the blanket in which I slept, for I had nothing else which I could give him. Speaking Spanish, and using as an interpreter one of the Frenchmen whom we had with us, I said to the governor that his people should become Christians, and bring into their lands priests who should baptize them, since otherwise they could not save their souls, adding that if he wished, I would go to his lands. Soon the afore-mentioned governor said he would very willingly take me there, and I promised him to go, and to take with me other priests like myself, repeating to him that I would be there in the following year, at the time of sowing corn. The governor seemed well pleased, and I was still more so, seeing the harvest to be reaped among the many souls in those lands who know not God.[15]

The man Massanet described as the "governor of the Tejas" was from Nabedache, the westernmost Hasinai village that lay along San Pedro Creek, a few miles west of the Neches River in the northern part of what is now Houston County, Texas.[16]

The Spanish advance northeast from Mexico had been slow. They had barely begun frontier missionary activity in the district of Coahuila bordering on the south bank of the Rio Grande by 1670. Natives of south Texas who regularly traded with the Hasinai carried many tales back to the missionaries who served in the Coahuila province. The missionaries were encouraged to think there was a fertile field for their efforts, but it was another six years before the bishop gave his support. He wrote his superiors, saying:

> Coahuila has as a neighbor on the north, inclining somewhat to the east, a populous nation of people, and so extensive that those who give detailed reports of them do not know where it ends. These [who give the reports] are many, through having communicated with the

people of that nation, which they call Texas, and who, they maintain, live under an organized government (en policía), congregated
in their pueblos, and governed by a casique who is named by the
Great Lord, as they call the one who rules them all, and who, they
say, resides in the interior. They have houses made of wood, cultivate
the soil, plant maize and other crops, wear clothes and punish
misdemeanors, especially theft. The Coahuiles do not give more
detailed reports of the Texas because, they say, they are allowed to go
only to the first pueblos of the border, since the Great Lord of the
Texas does not permit foreign nations to enter the interior of his
country.[17]

These and other reports about the "Great Kingdom of the
Texas" stirred interest, but it took the presence of a rival European
power to spur Spanish officials into action and place De León and
Massanet on the trail to Hasinai country. Their expedition signaled the beginning of extended stays by the Spaniards in the land
of the Hasinai and by the French in the territory of the Cadohadacho and Natchitoches. Beginning with the missionaries, the
letters, diaries, and official reports written by representatives of
Spain and France reveal most of what is known about the three
branches of the Caddo nation during the years that the two rival
European nations competed to influence and control the Tejas
tribes.

CHAPTER 4

THE MISSIONARIES

Massanet and the three priests with him appeared to bring the blessings of God to the Hasinai when they entered the outskirts of the Nabedache settlements on May 22, 1690. It had rained very little during the year, and the corn was suffering from drought, but on the day the priests arrived, rain started to fall and continued with a heavy downpour for eleven days.[1]

The day following their arrival, the priests, De León, and a command of 110 soldiers formed a procession from their camp to the house of the caddi, about a half-league's distance. Singing a litany and carrying staffs bearing a crucifix, the four priests sloshed along the rain-drenched path through knee-deep puddles. Before them waded a lay brother holding high his lance, to which a piece of linen with a picture of the Virgin Mary painted on it was attached like a banner. Most of the soldiers marched behind the priests; De León, with twenty or so men, formed a mounted guard.

The procession ended in front of the caddi's house, where a number of the village men, women, and children had gathered. While the missionaries knelt to bless the house before entering, some of the onlookers, including the caddi, stepped forward to touch Massanet's robe, lifting the cloth to their lips. They may have heard this ritual described when they visited with Indians who lived near the Spanish missions and therefore went through the motions as a courtesy, or they may simply have been curious about the feel of the cloth. Massanet accepted their act as true reverence.

The caddi had already invited the four priests to live with him, saying that there was room for all. Now he invited them to come inside his towering thatched house (Massanet estimated it at twenty varas, more than forty feet tall) and ushered them through the extended entryway. Stepping into the spacious interior, Massanet viewed the windowless room by the light of the ever-burning fire in its center. On one side were ten bedsteads, each made by attaching a ruglike reed mat to four forked sticks. They stood about three feet off the floor and were made comfortable with buffalo-skin coverings. Another rug, lined with a vibrantly colored piece of woven reed matting, formed an arch over the bed, giving a sleeper the privacy of a decorative alcove. On the other side of the house, shelves ranged the walls about five feet above the floor. The shelves held large, round reed baskets and a row of oversized earthen pots. The baskets stored staples such as corn, nuts, and beans; the pots were used to make *atole* (cornmeal porridge or mush) on ceremonial occasions when there was a crowd to be fed. Six wooden mortars, used for pounding corn indoors in rainy weather, lay on the shelves with the baskets and pots. On fair days corn was ground outside in an area like a courtyard or patio.

On this day the courtyard was bright and cool. The guests were seated there on small wooden benches, which Massanet noted were skillfully fashioned, and food was brought. The missionary described the pleasant mealtime, saying:

> They brought us a lunch consisting of the tamales they make, with nuts, pinole of corn [a flour made of parched corn], very well prepared, a large crock full of corn cooked with frijoles, and ground nuts. Soon I noticed outside the patio, opposite the door of the governor's house, another long building, and no one lived in it. I asked who dwelt therein or what purpose it served, and was told that the captains were lodged in that house when the governor called them to a meeting. On the other side I saw yet another and smaller vacant house, and upon my inquiring about this one they answered that in the smallest house the pages of the captains were lodged, for the law provides that each captain shall bring his page when the governor assembles the captains, according to the custom which they observe. As soon as they arrive they are lodged in that

house, and for each one is laid a large brightly colored reed mat, on which they sleep, with a bolster made of painted reeds at the head; and when they return home each one carries with him his mat and pillow. While they attend the meeting the governor provides them with food, until he sends them home.[2]

Massanet's interpreters were a young man named Pierre Meunier, about twenty years old, and fourteen-year-old Pierre Talon. During the time since Joutel and Cavelier had left them in the Hasinai village, both had learned to speak the native language fluently. One of De León's officers spoke French, and through roundabout translations—Spanish to French to Caddo and back again—Massanet and De León could ask questions and receive answers. The information they gathered in this way was often ordinary, sometimes mysterious.

Domestic arrangements in the house of the caddi, Massanet learned, were fairly commonplace. They included the services of ten women, who came each day at sunrise. The women arrived loaded with firewood; swept out the house and the patio; ground corn for the atole, tamales, and pinole; and carried water from a brook some distance away. The river was closer, but its water was not as good as that of the brook. After a day of housekeeping, the women returned to their homes for the night. What Massanet found most extraordinary was that he was not allowed to use a little wooden bench that stood in front of the central fireplace in the caddi's house. He was admonished "not to sit upon it," he said, "lest I should die. I was curious to learn what mystery there was connected with it, and they told me that no one but their lord, the governor, might sit upon that stool."[3]

On the second day with the Nabedache, a makeshift chapel was prepared for the priests to use in observance of the Feast of Corpus Christi. De León distributed clothing and small gifts and notified the caddi that he should summon all his people to come the next day to witness the first high mass celebrated in their village. The large number of Hasinai who assembled could hardly have helped being impressed by the spectacle of painted banners and thunderous gunfire. "The soldiers had been given leave to fire as many salutes as they could during the procession, at the elevation, and at the close of mass. . . . In the name of His Majesty the royal standard bearing on one side the picture of Christ crucified and on the other that of the Virgin of Guadalupe" was hoisted. For Massanet, it was "a memorable feast, which was rendered a source of great consolation by our being able to carry the blessed sacra-ment exposed and to walk in procession as Christian Catholics are wont to do."[4]

The missionaries having completed their duties, De León ful-filled his. The Nabedache became subjects of the king of Spain when De León

> accepted the obedience which they rendered to his Majesty, and in his royal name promised to befriend and aid them. I delivered to the governor a staff with a cross, giving him the title of governor of all his people, in order that he might rule and govern them, giving him to understand by means of an interpreter that which he should observe and do, and the respect and obedience which he and all his people ought to have for the priests, and that he should make all his families attend Christian teaching, in order that they might be instructed in the affairs of our holy Catholic faith so that later they might be baptized and become Christians. He accepted the staff with much pleasure, promising to do all that was desired of him, and the company fired three salutes.[5]

For the caddi, whose nation's policy was to buffer its borders by making friendship pacts with peripheral tribes, this ceremony was an elaborate new way to seal a familiar agreement that promised, in effect, "We will be your friends and you will be ours; your enemies will be our enemies and ours, yours; we will help protect you as you will protect us."

Massanet delicately declined the caddi's offer to share his home. The priest praised the house, saying that it was very fine and that he appreciated the invitation to become part of the household, but that the missionaries had to build a church and needed to live near it. The caddi had no trouble understanding—the Hasinai had a house dedicated to the Great Leader Above, and their spiritual leader on earth lived next to it. He said that he would show the missionaries suitable places and that Massanet could choose the one he thought best.

The caddi first showed the Spaniards the place La Salle's men had chosen for their camp. Massanet thought the location on the bank of the Neches River too far away from the Indians he wanted to convert. The site he selected was in the middle of the principal string of settlements and close to a brook and fine woods that delighted Massanet—the plum trees there reminded him of those in Spain. Massanet proudly envisioned "the harvest to be reaped among the many souls in those lands who know not God," but the Hasinai's ancient belief in a supreme being was already firmly imbedded in their tradition.[6]

The caddi prudently decided that it was time for the Hasinai spiritual leader to meet these new men who served God. Special messengers went to pay him honor and invite him to come for a visit. Massanet had already learned:

> These Tejas Indians have always had among them an old Indian who was their minister, and presented their offering to God. They observed the custom never to taste any eatable without first taking a portion of it to their minister for sacrifice; they did this with the products of their lands—as corn, beans, watermelons, and squash- es—as well as with the buffalo meat they obtained by hunting. This minister had a house reserved for the sacrifices, and they entered therein very reverentially, particularly during a sacrifice. They never sacrificed to idols, but only to Him of whom they said that He has all power and that from Him come all things, who is recognized as first cause.[7]

After a customary three days and three nights of songs and dances, the Nabedache returned home, bringing their most re- vered leader with them. Massanet said:

> He came, advancing slowly, and bearing himself with much dignity, and with him was a crowd of Indians, men, women, and children. He appeared extremely serious and reserved, and as soon as he reached the place where we were the governor bade him kiss our robe. This he did, and when we sat down to dinner I asked the governor to let our visitor sit by his side.
>
> When the Indian priest took his first mouthful, instead of asking a blessing, he made with the food, as he took it out of the dish, a sign like that of the cross, pointing, as it were, to the four winds, or cardinal points. After dinner we gave him clothing for himself and his wife, and he was well pleased.
>
> Later we were told by an Indian who was then with the Tejas but came from the country beyond—from Coahuila—and who spoke Mexican, that the above-mentioned priest of the Tejas had told all the captains and other Tejas, "Now you will no longer heed me, for these priests who have come to you are the true priests of Ayimat

Caddi" —which name signifies, in their language, "The Great Captain." This was the name he gave to God, for since the only rank or
title they know is that of captain, they call "Great Captain" him
whom they consider as great above all things.[8]

Massanet recognized the influence of the Hasinai's spiritual
caretaker, but he was confident in his belief that Catholicism
could supersede their ancient beliefs. One night the caddi asked if
he could have a piece of blue fabric to make burial clothes for his
mother when she died. He did not care what kind of cloth, so long
as it was blue. The missionary, struck by this insistence on the
color, asked why he was so attached to blue. The caddi explained
that his people were fond of the color, especially for burial clothes,
because in past times they had often been visited by a very
beautiful woman who came down from the heights. She wore blue,
and they wished to be like her. The caddi said he had not seen the
woman —she had come long before his time —but his mother and
others who were very old had seen her.

The caddi's explanation excited Massanet. He was sure the
beautiful woman who came down from the heights was Mother
María de Jesús de Agreda, a Spanish nun who sixty years earlier
had told her confessor that she had miraculously flown from her
convent in Spain to minister to the natives in the New World. The
revelations of the young abbess and his own call to the ministry
had inspired Massanet to come to New Spain and push his way
into the interior of Tejas country.[9]

With Indian help, the missionaries had two houses —one to live
in, one to worship in —less than a week after Massanet had
selected the building site. A tall cross of carved wood was set in
the ground in front of the church, and on the morning of June 1,
1690, the church and the village around it were dedicated to Saint
Francis. After dinner De León sent the main company on the trail
back to Mexico. He and Father Massanet followed the next day.

Three priests and three soldiers were left in charge of the newly
founded mission of San Francisco de los Tejas. De León would
have left a military contingent of forty or fifty men, but Massanet
objected. The priest did not trust the soldiers' behavior. Fights
broke out among them almost every day, and there had been
complaints about the way they entered homes uninvited. Worse
still, there had been an attempt to rape the wife of the caddi's
brother. Massanet argued that the missionaries did not need the

With one exception, the Spanish missions and European communities established in Hasinai territory beginning in 1690 were short-lived. Among the missions were El Santísimo de Nombre María (1690–92), Nuestra Señora del Pilar de Bucareli (1773–79), Guadalupe de los Nacogdoches (1716–19, 1721–72), Nuestra Padre San Francisco de los Tejas (1716–19), Presidio Nuestra Señora de los Dolores de los Tejas (1716–19, 1721–30), Purísima Concepción (1716–19, 1721–29), San José de los Nazones (Nasonis) (1716–19, 1721–30), and San Francisco de los Tejas (1690–92). Missions on the fringe of Hasinai territory were no more successful: Nuestra Señora de los Dolores de Ais (1716–19) and San Miguel de los Linares de los Adaes (1716–19, 1721–73). Presidio Nuestra Señora del Pilar de los Adaes, established in 1721, developed a sizable Spanish community, but was abandoned in 1779. The only European community destined to survive was Natchitoches (1714–present). This map is based on Perttula, *The Caddo Nation*, fig. 22.

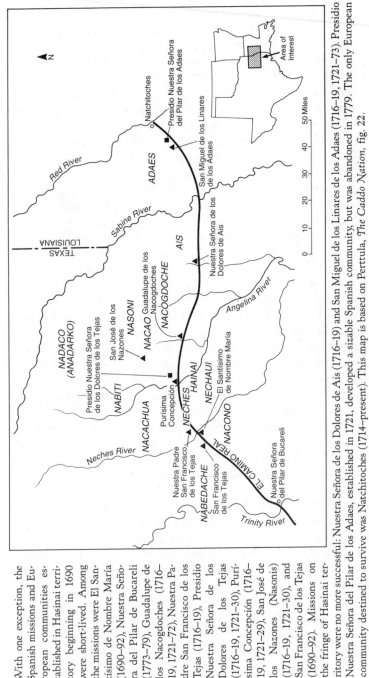

protection of soldiers since the Hasinai had welcomed them with nothing but affection and goodwill. The caddi himself had promised to take care of the fathers and had pledged his friendship by promising that his brother, two other relatives, and a nephew would be sent to visit Mexico, going with Massanet when he returned to Mexico. The caddi's only demand was, "Do not permit anyone to demand service from these men whom you take with you, nor to make them work," which was evidence for Massanet that the Tejas had "among them the idea of rank, and that they distinguished their nobles from the mass of the people."[10] It might also have meant that the caddi knew more than was suspected about the way Spaniards misused Indian labor in New Mexico.[11]

Communication among the three divisions of the Caddo nation was steady and largely responsible for the peace and prosperity of the Hasinai, Cadohadacho, and Natchitoches. Reports of events that might affect the security and well-being of one were efficiently transmitted to the others by messenger. This network plus the promotion of friendly relations with neighbors logically reinforced the belief that "the Great Lord of the Texas does not permit foreign nations to enter the interior of his country."[12] Either there had been a change in Tejas policy toward foreign nations as described to the missionaries in 1676, or the Great Lord of the Tejas had decided to make an exception for non-Indians.

De León was as impressed with the affability of the Nabedache as was Massanet. The commander of the soldiers had also found that the land occupied by the Tejas tribes was pleasing and productive. He believed that the only way Spain could protect the potential that the country offered was to provide garrisons (presidios) and establish settlements. His judgment was influenced by information about French activity that he gleaned during conversations with the caddi.

The questions asked and the attitudes expressed by the white-skinned strangers who penetrated Hasinai, Cadohadacho, and Natchitoches territory made clear that they represented rival nations. The Nabedache caddi may not have known the reason for Tonti's singular journey to the Hasinai, and he may not have understood De León's declaration of possession by Spain, but he may very well have played on a knowledge of rivalry when he chose to tell De León about the French party. Responding to De León's probes for information about French intruders, the

Nabedache caddi told his visitor that on the same day he had learned that the Spaniards were coming, he had received a message that French, seeking friendship, had stopped at a Hasinai settlement that was a three-day journey in the opposite direction. One of them had had only one hand. The Nabedache caddi said he had sent word to those strangers that they could not come to see him because he was expecting a visit from his friends the Spaniards. After the French were told this, he said, they had gone back toward the east, crossing one large river before going on to a second where they had a settlement. De León returned to Mexico convinced that unless Spain moved vigorously to protect its rightful possessions, the land and the four thousand souls who lived on it would be lost to France.[13]

One of the priests who remained at the mission of San Francisco de los Tejas was Fray Francisco Casañas de Jesús María. He was thirty-five years old, born in Barcelona, Spain. His mother was of royal French blood, and his father was a Spanish gentleman who commanded royal troops. As a child Casañas had built chapels of cypress boughs in the garden of his home. He had decorated the boughs with flowers and surrounded his chapel with a miniature garden fence made of reeds. His biographer said this favorite childhood pastime was prophetic of the thatched missions in unexplored Texas.[14]

Casañas gave vigorous attention to his missionary duty. He followed dim paths beneath tall pines through the thickly wooded east Texas country to learn the extent of Hasinai territory and visit the people in their scattered settlements. Two rivers, the Neches and the Angelina, flowed through the country, and homes were built in natural clearings in the river valleys. The distance from one end of the district to the other was thirty-five leagues, about seventy miles. Casañas was hampered by the distance and by his scanty knowledge of the language. De León had taken the French captives, Pierre Meunier and Pierre Talon, with him to Mexico, and the missionaries had only the meager vocabulary that they had managed to record before being left alone.

It was Casañas who discovered that the correct name for the province was Hasinai ["our people"], not Tejas, as the Spaniards thought. "Teja" [taysha] simply meant friend. All the tribes allied by long-standing friendships, even those with a different language, were called Tejas. Casañas explained to his superiors in

New Spain that the term Teja should only be used to identify a tribe. Casañas also dispelled the Spanish idea that the Tejas, or Hasinai, formed a kingdom in the European sense of a region ruled by one person. The Nabedache together with eight other tribes, formed the Hasinai nation, but the closest they came to being governed by a king was that they were all subject to a leader called the "grand *chenesi.*"[15]

A variant spelling of Chenesi was Xinesi. Because the term is not recognized by Caddo people today, it is only possible to speculate on its meaning. There are Caddo words (*Tsa-kee-yooh,* "devil," for example) that begin with a *ts* sound similar to the *ts* sound at the end of plural English words such as "habits." Either *ch* or *x* could have been a Spanish attempt to transcribe this sound. If so, Chenesi or Xinesi sounded like *Tsa nesi. Tsa* in Caddo roughly translates as "Mr." The word for "moon," is most often written *neesh, nishe,* or *nici.* Was the grand chenesi "Mr. Moon"?

The old Caddo grandfathers told stories about Moon. They said that in the beginning there was only darkness. No sun, or moon, or stars, or earth, like we see now. Only darkness. After a while there was a man, the first human being. And pretty soon after that a village sprang into being—thousands of people living together in the darkness. The people did not know who the man was, but they noticed that he seemed to be everywhere.[16]

The man disappeared for a time, and when he came back he had all kinds of seeds. He called all the people together, told them that the seeds were for eating, and gave them to everyone. He told them that soon Darkness would go and that the people would see because Darkness had promised that they would have a man by the name of Sah-cooh (Sun) and that he would be given power by the Great Father Above. The man said that the direction the Sun came from should be called east and that the way of its going should be called west. The unknown man told the people that whenever that time came, he would be called or taken away from his mother, from Great Mother Earth Below. He announced, "I was the first being created, and I have been given power by the same Great Father Above, and I must carry out my work."

Then this man told the people that it was very necessary that they have one man abler and wiser than any other among them to be their headman, that they should call him caddi, that the people should do whatever the caddi commanded, and that they should look on him as a great father. The man said, "Go back to your homes, hold a council among yourselves, and select a chief."

When the people returned to their homes and got together in the council, a man called Ta'sha (Wolf or Coyote) told the people that the powerful unknown man should be called Neesh (Moon) because he was the first man created on earth. When the unknown man called them together to ask if they had selected their headman, Wolf told him they had decided that he should be their caddi and that they had named him Moon.[17]

After Moon came to be caddi, he selected a *tamma (tum'mah)*, an "errand man," to go around among the people to call them together whenever Moon wanted them. One time the errand man told the people that the caddi had very important news and that they should come quickly. When they came together, Moon told them they would all have to move away from the world they were living in to another and better world, that he knew the way and he was going to lead them through.

Before the people were ready to leave, Moon sent the errand man around to tell them to divide into groups because there were so many people. Each group, he said, had to have a leader, known as *canaha* (cah-nah-ha). After the groups formed and each selected a leader, the caddi called all the leaders together and gave each a drum. He told them to sing and beat their drums as they were moving along. He cautioned them never to look back the way they had come and warned that, if people stopped, they would have to stay where they were—in darkness.

First, an old man climbed up carrying fire and a pipe in one hand, a drum in the other. Next came his wife, bringing corn and pumpkin seeds. All the people and animals began moving westward, coming out of the Old Home in the Darkness to another world. Wolf began to look around. He told the caddi that the world was too small for all the people, and then he turned to see how many were behind him. Some say that Wolf saw a figure with horns and a tail and stopped to warn those who had still not come out. Anyway, the people still coming stopped, and half of them went back. Those who had come up into the new world of light sat down and cried for the ones left in darkness, and where they sat became known as Cha-cah-nee-nah, the "Place of Crying."

The Caddo creation legend as illustrated by noted Creek-Pawnee artist Acee Blue Eagle (courtesy of Caroline Dorman Collection, Cammie G. Henry Research Center, Watson Memorial Library, Northwestern State University of Louisiana)

The people traveled westward until finally the chief picked up some dirt and threw it in front of him and formed very high mountains. The people stopped and began to make their first homes and villages. Moon went to the top of the mountains and looked about and saw that not all the people had followed his trail.

Some had scattered and gone in different directions. When the people had all been together, they had spoken only one language, Caddo; but now that they were scattered, each group spoke a different language. That is why the many tribes of the present time speak different languages.

Casañas moved among the nine southern Caddo tribes—the Hasinai—introducing himself into homes, listening to words he barely understood, and watching all that went on. He learned that hospitality and courtesy ruled the households in the Hasinai nation. No guest ever asked for anything to eat; as soon as visitors arrived, hosts offered whatever they had to share. Meat, boiled or roasted without broth, was served on small, pretty platters that the women made from reeds. Other food was placed on earthen plates. Eating took a long time because there were singing and talking, even whistling from time to time. Men were supposed to eat everything served them, but anyone who was gluttonous earned no respect. Anyone who ate only a little was teased and taunted. After a feast the guests were supplied with pipes and tobacco. Smoking was a way of giving thanks, the first four whiffs being directed into the air, toward the ground, and to either side.

To celebrate special events, if the host was a person of rank, he invited the whole village to come to his house. The caddi came with all the rest and, before the feast began, took a bit of everything and threw one portion into the fire, another on the ground, and one to each side. When that was done, the caddi stepped away from the fire, and the villagers joined together, ready to celebrate with a dance. The caddi spoke some final words of thanksgiving, saying that the corn should allow itself to be eaten, the snakes not to bite, the deer not to be bitten. Then, having consecrated the whole harvest, he declared that the Father Who Lives Above had said that they might now eat and that if they did not, they ought to die of hunger.

If a host could not afford an elaborate feast, the man of the house took food to the caddi to be blessed before anyone started to eat. On returning, he threw the bits of the food blessed by the caddi into the fire and to the four winds. He then said that everyone was free to begin eating.

Ordinarily there was plenty to eat. There was not much open space for planting in such a thickly wooded area, and human-made clearings were nearly impossible with only wooden, bone, and flint tools, but the rich soil in natural clearings nurtured vegetable gardens and cornfields. Hunters were able to supple-ment the produce with deer, rabbit, and birds found in the woods as well as waterfowl and fish from creeks and the river. When the nearby woods and streams did not supply enough, a group of hunters was sent to find buffalo. They traveled in organized groups because the nearest place to find buffalo was four days away, and there was always a danger of meeting enemies on the plains.

While attending feasts, Casañas was able to unravel the mys-tery about the seat that Massanet was forbidden to sit on. The high seats resembled small tables and were reserved for use at special ceremonies. Only a caddi and the chenesi had the privilege of sitting so high above everyone else that their feet were placed on a bench. Casañas observed that when a caddi or chenesi sat on one of these seats, "whatever this official says or does is carefully heeded, just as the Catholics obey the Holy Gospels. If he issues a command it is more strictly obeyed by these Indians than the ten commandments are observed by the Christians."[18]

There were times when, without a command, the people acted in a charitable way. For instance, when a house caught fire and burned to the ground, destroying everything the owner had, everybody came together to build a new house and to furnish it comfortably with food and other essentials. The same sort of helpful kindness was shown when someone became ill. Visits were made, consolation was offered, and trinkets that might cheer were given or lent. Among Hasinai misfortune for one was the concern of all.

Both men and women were adept at dressing skins and hides. Deerskins and buffalo hides were skillfully tanned for clothing. Men were apt to go about the house naked in the middle of the summer, but the women and even the little girls always wore skirts. For special wear plain leather was transformed into fancy garments by attaching tiny, white, beadlike shells, or snake rattles, deer hooves, and other things that clicked and jingled with the movement of the wearer. Both men and women also added collars, pendants, and other ornaments to their festive dress. Glass beads and bells, received in trade with other nations, were particularly prized. Women liked to paint colored patterns on their skin from the waist up to the shoulders, particularly on their breasts. Men especially liked feathers for ornamentation.

If the men had a particular vanity, it was their hair. Those with the right kind wore it long and carefully combed so that it spread over their shoulders. Others shaved all but the top and left the hair in the center to grow all the way to the waist. They plucked their eyebrows and beards with shells utilized for tweezers. Before setting out on a war expedition, they used paints of various colors to disguise or camouflage themselves.

As Casañas became familiar with Hasinai traditions, he began to appreciate the way they contributed to a well-ordered society. He saw, for example, a young man approaching the parents of a maiden, offering presents for their daughter. The best possible gifts were knives or anything made of iron, such as axes and mattocks — valuable tools for building houses and planting food crops. Even before Spaniards came to the village, Hasinai men traded with distant tribes for such useful things as well as for treasures such as bells, glass beads, hats, and sky-blue woolen garments. Something that special could be among the gifts the man brought to the young woman.

Standing by the door to her home, the daughter focused first on what the man laid before her parents, then on his face, then on the faces of her mother and father, and then back on the gifts. Her father seemed to take forever before saying, "Our daughter may have these things." By accepting the presents, the parents gave consent for their daughter's marriage to the young man. The caddi would be notified, and if he also approved, the young man and woman would become husband and wife.

If the marriage did not work out, the two would first talk the matter over, each airing personal sentiments, and then arrange a parting. The woman might find a new man who offered her more, and the first man would be expected to either match the offer or leave quietly to look for another wife. If the man wanted to take a new wife, the first wife would be expected to leave him at once to search for another husband. Neither felt disgrace at leaving the other, and no stigma clouded their future lives.

Seen through the eyes of a gentleman cleric with royal Euro-pean blood in his veins, this sort of marriage, though admirable because a man never had more than one wife or a woman more than one husband, was a disgrace, and the lack of punishment for such loose conduct was deplorable. "Only the noblest families," observed Casañas, "consider this kind of a contract binding. Therefore, in *their* circles, no one dares to trouble another's wife."[19]

Casañas said that when a woman was called *aquidau,* everyone knew she was the wife of either the grand chenesi or a caddi. The title was given only to the wives of these officials and reflected the respect paid to the leaders. Each Hasinai tribe was governed by a caddi whose office, like the chenesi's, was hereditary.

If the section of the country occupied by a tribe was large, seven or eight *canahas,* "headmen," assisted the caddi; if small, there were only three or four canahas. Casañas reported it was their duty "to relieve the *caddi* and to publish his orders by reporting that the *caddi* commands this or that." Casañas also reported, "They frighten the people by declaring that, if they do not obey orders, they will be whipped and otherwise punished."[20]

When the caddi had an important decision to make, it was the job of the canahas to call the old men to the caddi's home for discussion. Deference was given to age. The eldest was the first to be seated and the first to speak. The others gave their views in order according to age. As soon as one stopped, another began. No speaker was ever interrupted—it was not polite to do so. By small signs, maybe a nod of the head or a hand gesture, the others showed they were listening with grave attention. To keep other distrac-tions to a minimum, no one else was allowed to enter the room after the council began. If something required attention outside of the assembly, a person appeared at the door and made the need known by signs. The caddi was the most intent listener of all, weighing the words of each elder. Then, deciding to do what he thought best, the caddi would explain, urging agreement from those whose ideas differed. Finally, there was unanimity, and the old men went away satisfied with the outcome of the council.

When the caddi went out with the hunters or warriors, the canahas directed the fitting up of a place for the caddi to rest, eat, and sleep. And when the occasion arose, a canaha brought the tobacco pouch and filled the pipe of peace before placing it in the caddi's mouth. Authority filtered on down to subordinates, called *chayas,* who did everything the canahas told them to do. The officials called tammas, messengers and overseers, saw to it that the caddi's orders were promptly executed, whipping idlers on the legs and over the stomach with sticks if necessary. After fifteen months of observing the community created by this civil govern-ment, Casañas observed, "The peace and harmony among the officials described is so great that . . . we have not seen any quarrels—either great or small. But the insolent and lazy are punished."[21]

Casañas was slow to learn the language, but he was quick to build another chapel. Within a few weeks he had founded a second mission, east of the first, on the banks of the Neches River. Its location was nearer the power center of the Hasinai—the place where the chenesi lived.

The power and position of the chenesi became clear to Casañas almost immediately. No one wanted to be the cause of this leader's displeasure. Like the monarchs of Europe, the chenesi's nearest male blood kin would succeed him when he died. The grand chenesi never left the house except to take a walk or to make certain visits. He was the keeper of a fire that burned day and night in the center of the main worship house, a fire so vital to the nation that he had special assistants to help attend it. He made sure that the flame was never allowed to die. The sacred fire temple was only a few steps from the chenesi's home within the territory of the leading Hasinai tribe—the Hainai.[22]

Casañas heard that the chenesi took care of two children who came from the other side of heaven to live in the sacred house. The little ones were called *cononici,* and through them the Chenesi talked with God, Ayo-Caddi-Aymay. No one Casañas tried to talk with had ever seen these children, but all believed that the chenesi spoke with them whenever he wanted. Throughout the year the people presented the chenesi with a portion of whatever they had—when the corn was gathered, the first ears were given to him; when a deer was slain, a part was cut out for him before anyone else took a share. The chenesi then tended to the children, giving them food and drink. He placed some of all he received in two small, woven reed boxes that were kept on the sides of a tall, wide table in the house of worship.[23]

In a time of great need—war, drought, or crop failure such as the Hasinai nation suffered for the first two summers the missionaries lived there—the chenesi called together all nine tribes. The caddis and old men entered the worship house and sat around the fire. Light from flickering flames chased shadows across their bare skins—no one came into the sacred house clothed. Stripped of any disbelief, they waited to learn what Ayo-Caddi-Aymay would have them do.

The chenesi lifted live coals from the fire with a pair of wooden tongs and dropped them into a mixture of tobacco and fat from the heart of a buffalo. He offered the burning incense to the cononici, then told the assembled caddis and elders that the little ones' boxes were empty. He moved to cover the fire and shut out the light coming through the doorway. Outside the men and women sang and danced. Inside the men sat silently in darkness.

The chenesi began to speak to the cononici. He asked them to tell God that the Hasinai were going to reform. He prayed for plentiful corn in the future, good health, fleetness in chasing deer and buffalo, good women in the tribes' homes, and strength when fighting enemies.

Next he took a small gourd, the kind used as a rattle, and threw it on the ground. It fell without making a sound. Its silence frightened the men—God was angry. He did not wish to speak to them. They cried out loudly, promising that they would bring offerings of every kind of food they had to the chenesi and the two little ones.

The chenesi picked up the rattle and began to make a noise. The voice of a child came from him. The child's voice said that Ayo-Caddi-Aymay was now speaking and that the chenesi should tell the others that if the tribe fulfilled the promises made, he Ayo-Caddi-Aymay would give them everything they asked for through their chenesi.

In his own voice, the chenesi then repeated what the children had said to him. He instructed the leaders to go out and search for meat and everything else they could find so that neither Ayo-Caddi-Aymay nor the cononici would be angered again. He threw open the door covering, and the men all rushed out, pushing their way through in disorder and crying aloud their alarm. Alone inside the house of worship, the chenesi stirred the fire, then took up a special mortar to grind meal for the children.

From the chapel not far away, Casañas set out to teach the Hasinai right from wrong as he perceived it.

[I] went to see what these two children really were and arrived at the door with two beautiful little images of saints I possess, the first thing he said to me was that I must undress before entering. He took off his own deerskin and laid it near the door. I told him that it made no difference if I went in with my clothes on. However, he warned me that I would surely die. I told him plainly that I would not die and that I would be afraid of some misfortune if I should go in naked. He laughed as if making a joke of my answer; but did not want me to go in. Nevertheless, I darted in and he followed behind me. When I asked him about the two children and where they were, he was at once frightened and put in my hands a round piece of wood like the cover of a sweetmeat box. This was covered with skin like parchment. Around the little box he had placed some crumbs from the bread which the Indians brought him as an offering. In the middle of the box was a hole into which tobacco is put. He told me that it was for tobacco for the two children to smoke. I saw that there was no trace of the children, and having heard the nonsense he had spoken, I reprimanded him in such a way that he would not be angered. I told him tactfully what the Lord inspired me to say. He listened to me without an outbreak. I told him it would be a good thing if I would throw the thing into the fire; that the two children I had brought in my hands should stay there with me, and stand guard over them; and that, in the future, whatever might be offered to what he called the two children should be consecrated to the two that I should place there; and that he would see that all this was nonsense; and that it was all a lie for no other purpose than to deceive his people in order that they might bring him quantities of supplies. He agreed for me to leave my two children there and for me to remain also; but he would not agree for me to burn his children because he and all the *Asinai* loved them very much. He declared that the reason I did not see them was because it had not been possible to see them since just after the time they had first come from Heaven. Then they were visible; but, now, the house that had been built for them when they came burned down and they had perished in the flames. Only what I saw was left. I knew that all this was a lie of his, and I wanted to throw them in the fire. But when I was on the point of pitching them in, he became very furious. I, therefore, desisted in order not to stir up trouble. I appeased him as best I could, telling him that it would be at least very well if I and my two children should remain. He said yes, composed himself, and we went out of the house in quite a good humor. I, with the determination to found a mission there.[24]

There were two elderly women in the chenesi's household. He went immediately to tell them that the Spanish priest wanted to move in. One seemed to agree to the arrangement, but the other argued vigorously against it. Casañas said he would find six or seven men to help him move his baggage, but the woman had influence and her argument had prevailed. The chenesi said no, he did not want Casañas to move. When he was talking before, the chenesi explained, he had not known what he was saying.

It was easier to construct chapels than to change the faith of the Hasinai. Casañas thought he had made a few conversions, but he could not supplant the chenesi. There were other men, too, who thwarted his missionary efforts. These men were *conas,* "healers." Because of their special powers and training, they could explain things that were mysteries to others. They could cure sick or injured bodies and spirits, and they could ward off evil and cause it to seek enemies of the Hasinai. But Casañas said, "The physicians do nothing without mixing it up with some kind of superstition. . . . If they throw ice on the fire they say the cold does not have to go and must be angry. If someone dies or a house burns up they say that death is angry. Therefore, they make an offering of something by hanging it on a pole in front of the house. When a house burns, they also say that the ground on which they lived, or the hill near the house, had been angered and burned the house; so they do not rebuild the home there but in another spot."[25] Casañas called the conas liars. He said they were all guilty of a thousand deceptions and that some of them were enchanters.

The conas certainly understood the power of ritual words and actions, and they were suspicious of Casañas and his fellow priests. Most particularly, they mistrusted the use of baptismal water. The sprinkled water, warned the conas, would cause sickness, even death.

Once as Casañas tried to baptize a woman, a cona interrupted by stepping in to perform an ancient formula to ward off evil. Casañas exploded with an exorcism, hurling oaths to drive demons from the medicine man. The cona was no match for such religious wrath. He turned and ran away. Another took his place, attempting to throw buffalo fat and tobacco into the fire. Casañas again invoked an exorcism, and the fearful sound of his incantation shook the man so that he dropped the bow and arrows he carried and fled.

A group of more than thirty people watched this spiritual struggle. The next morning when the cona was needed to cure a sick person, some of the witnesses went looking for him. They found him lying dead in a valley. After that, Casañas was satisfied to see, all the conas were afraid of him. Better yet, of the seventy-six people he was able to baptize while ministering to the Hasinai, five were medicine men.

CHAPTER 5

"GOD MUST BE ANGRY"

Fray Francisco Casañas de Jesús María wrote, "They are not ignorant of God. Indeed, all of them know there is only one God whom they call in their language *Ayo-Caddi-Aymay*. They try, in all their affairs, to keep him in a good humor in every way possible. They never in any manner venture to speak of him in jest, because they say that, when he punishes them for anything, he does it well and that whatever he does is best. They also believe that he punishes those who are angry with him."[1]

There was more sickness than usual in the Hasinai villages during the first months of 1691. Throughout the tribes healthy people became mysteriously ill and died. One of the missionaries became ill in February and died following a fever that lasted eight days. The conas treated patients as they always had, using heat and herbs, chanting, and rhythmic movement to drive the disease out of the house or into the fire. The missionaries ministered by seeking confessions and initiating the sick into the Christian order through baptism.

The number of mourners multiplied. Death often followed soon after a priest sprinkled water on the head of a sick person, and more and more people came to believe the conas who said the missionaries were the cause of this misfortune. Despair released stored doubts. Everyone knew the priest had killed a cona with a curse, had mocked the grand chenesi, had hidden inside robes when he entered the fire temple, and had threatened to throw the cononici into the fire. Ayo-Caddi-Aymay must be angry with the Hasinai for allowing such a man to live among them.

Casañas was unfaltering in his faith that with proper instruction, even the most perverse of the poor, misguided Hasinai would become proper Christians and vassals of the king of Spain. By the grace of God, he said, "as soon as the ministers are able to speak the language perfectly and when we have the protection and watchful care of the Spaniards," all the discord that the devil had planted in the country would be uprooted.[2] Casañas envisioned large mission settlements and believed that it would be easy to get the Hasinai to live there if they were provided with axes, knives, and mattocks. "What they will dislike most," he conceded, "will be to build new houses and to open new ground for planting." But, he countered, "if they have these tools, I have no doubt but that with the aid of the Spaniards and the helpful instruction of the ministers, they will locate in pueblos."[3] Pueblos, Indian towns set up according to Spanish law on specially assigned lands and governed by native officials who were supervised by the missionary fathers, had been the core of success in extending, holding, and Christianizing frontiers in Mexico.

Casañas was immensely pleased with one successful conversion. He officially reported, "Once when the xinesi [chenesi] was sick unto death, he called upon me to hear his confession. I made him confess the mysteries of our holy Faith and baptized him in bed in the presence of many Indians; and particularly in the presence of the person who was expected to become the xinesi. . . . The Lord justified his cause by restoring the xinesi to perfect health, thereby proving the efficacy of the Holy sacrament of baptism."[4] Every day afterward, said Casañas, this important person praised the holy sacrament, saying he felt better as soon as he received it and that he was stronger now than he had been before he became ill. Casañas said the chenesi gave his word that he would not do anything except what the missionary told him to do.

As was often the case, Casañas's good intentions overwhelmed his good judgment; he attempted to elevate the position of this man whose recovery had surprised everyone, especially the medicine men. He wrote his superiors:

I have honored him already by making him governor and have presented him with the staff of command. He is now no more than a *caddi,* and as such, he together with the other eight *caddices* is subject to a grand *xinesi*. But because of the things given him, it is impossible for him not to be recognized as the *xinesi* rather than as a *caddi*. This done, all the other caddices will feel obliged to recognize him as their grand *xinesi* since they have never known a higher authority than that of a *xinesi*.[5]

The true grand chenesi became ill and did not recover. His burial two days after his death required the presence of all the nine tribes. Casañas did not witness all of the observances, but he did see "a coffin which was as big as an ox cart" and symbols "such as placing the world in front of his door. This is done by setting up a very high pole with a large globe of grass on top. They indicate the moons by putting up some large sticks in the shape of the moon. Before these they dance ten days and nights and then they each go home."[6]

The Hasinai believed that when a person died, his or her soul went to another house where a man guarded everyone who came until all were gathered together. Once all the souls were together, they would enter another world, where life would begin anew. To let the master of the house know that someone was coming, they shot arrows into the air and cried, "Here he comes! Make him work until we are all united."[7] Because a person needed strength to reach this house and was weak from hunger at death, they buried all the person's arms and utensils with the body and for several days carried something to eat to the grave.

The ones who conducted the funerals of tribal leaders first ordered a coffin made. Then, Casañas said,

> two Indians put into it some tobacco and some of the herb which they call *acoxio,* and also a bow and arrow. All these things they move about over the coffin from one place to another while they walk to and fro around the coffin. They keep talking in a low voice as if they were praying. Their mode of speaking is so strenuous that they perspire even though it be cold. During this ceremony, the two wear skins. The ceremonies around the coffin being finished, the Indians go to the place of interment which is always near the house. There they talk again to themselves; but the grave is not opened until, with an axe, they have made a stroke at the place where the head of the dead man is to rest and another where the feet are to lie. While the grave is being dug, the two return to the house and give directions for placing the dead man in the coffin. Thereupon, they

talk to the dead man again as if they were speaking to a living person. After finishing the talk they retire a little, saying that they are going to talk to God. After a while they bring back what God has said to them. Then another man comes out who has the same office, but, as he is old, he does not serve like the others but stands in the midst of all those who are present; i.e., the old men and the most distinguished men. He comes out with a weapon in his hand—one of the best they have.

The person I saw on two occasions had a sword without a scabbard. He spoke for nearly an hour, talking very loud and earnestly, telling them how much they had all lost by the death of Mr. So-and-So who has always been fortunate both in war and in killing a great number of buffaloes and that he had been strong for work. He tells them that they must weep a great deal for him. He tells them all these things as well as many others of a similar nature. When he has finished the sermon, he goes to the dead person and sits close beside him, repeating to him, as if he were alive, all the things that he has said in his sermon, ending by saying to him that everybody loves him dearly; that everybody is weeping for him; that he must go in peace; that he must work in that other house with the others who have gone before, until those who have begun to work shall have assembled; that he must take up his hatchet and all the rest of the things that are wrapped with him.[8]

Casañas recorded that ceremonies for ordinary individuals were about the same as those for an important person, but without so much "pomp."

The missionary once attended the burial of a person he had baptized. Three times while the Hasinai elder was speaking, Casañas placed his hand over the speaker's mouth and told him to hush for a little while, that he wanted to speak to God, that what the Hasinai was saying was of no use, and that only what he, Casañas, was going to say to God would be useful to the dead man. The third time he was allowed to do what he wanted.

There is no way of knowing what the mourners thought, but Casañas thought their reaction favorable. He reported:

While I was singing the response everybody kept absolutely quiet. In some of them it aroused so much interest that they did not speak for some time after I had finished. . . . Twice they called upon me to keep singing as before. All these ceremonies being ended, they carried the dead body outside as fast as they could, shooting a great many arrows into the air. Then they put whatever clothes he had into the grave, placed the body on top of them, and closed the grave. The two men who served as priests talked earnestly and in low voice, while the others stood round weeping. When all was finished they went home; and the first thing they did was to carry him something of the very best things they had, placing it on top of the grave. Then they put some tobacco and some fire there and left a pot full of water. Then they all went away to eat.[9]

The deaths and desolation that darkened the winter months of 1690–1691 in Hasinai country did not disappear with spring. By March a smallpox epidemic was raging. The Hasinai had no immunity to diseases introduced by Europeans. Three hundred died in the mission area that month, and nearly three thousand deaths occurred within the bounds of the friendly tribes. Terror, cold and icy as the snow and sleet that swept down from the north in winter, froze what was left of the warm feeling the Hasinai had for the missionaries. Some plotted to kill the men they believed to be a source of evil.

Casañas discovered the danger and went directly to the caddi's house. The elders were in council, and as soon as the priest entered, they accused him of killing their people. Casañas considered the charge ridiculous—superstitious nonsense instigated by the conas. He confronted the members of the council, asking if they had killed the priest who had died or the soldier who had died soon after arriving in their country.

The elders all said, "No."

Casañas told them that they had spoken well, that they were quite right, that "it was God who killed him," and that "whenever He wishes He will kill us." He spoke passionately, telling the Hasinai leaders, "as sure as the sun sets my hour would come—while to some of those present it might come at dawn. . . . All who love God," preached Casañas, "must submit to His holy will. . . . When He wishes to do so, He will kill the Spaniards as He was now killing them [the Hasinais]."[10]

No one disputed Casañas. He believed the force of his arguments had made a great impression, and he was probably right. The Hasinai elders lost no time in repeating his words throughout the settlement, and the headman hastened to tell the other tribes that it was not the missionaries who were killing them—it was the missionaries' God!

The danger of plots against their lives was intensified by stories the missionaries heard about a one-armed Frenchman. They were told by leading men, Cadohadacho as well as Hasinai, that the French had been feasted in their villages and that the Cadohada-chos said a one-armed Frenchman had promised to come again, bringing many people with him. Fearing an invasion by the French and the disaffection of the Hasinais, the missionaries prayed for aid and protection.

The season of sickness passed. Some of the pain it left had eased by summertime when Father Massanet returned with fourteen priests and seven lay brothers to carry out a plan to establish six more missions, two in Tejas country and four among the Cad-ohadacho. Domingo Terán, newly appointed governor of Coahui-la and Spanish Texas, led the military escort.

The missionaries preceded the soldiers, who made a formal entry on August 4. Terán officially gave the title of governor to the caddi and distributed gifts for all the Nabedache. The soldiers marched to the church, bugles blowing and drums beating. At the end of the parade, six volleys were fired before the company followed the missionaries inside for mass.

The Nabedaches at first showed no open hostility toward the newcomers, but the soldiers' undisciplined behavior revived old resentments. In addition, horses and cattle brought by the Span-iards were not corralled, and they trampled through ripening cornfields. After staying twenty days, Terán left a small guard with the missionaries and took the main body of his men to the Gulf Coast to pick up provisions that had been shipped there from New Spain. There were a few raids on the Spanish livestock while the full force camped by the Nabedache village; after the main troop left, the herds were attacked more openly and often.

Meanwhile, the Nabedache were preparing to chastise a hostile tribe. Casañas described their preparations:

Before going to war, they dance and sing for seven or eight days, offering to God meat, corn, bows, arrows, tobacco, acoxo [acoxio], and fat from buffalo hearts, praying for the death of their enemies. They pray also for strength to fight, for fleetness to run, and for valor to resist. There is plenty to eat. In front of those who are dancing there is a pole and on it hangs a portion of everything they are offering to God. In front of the pole a fire is burning. Near by is a person who looks like a demon. He is the person who offers the incense to God, throwing tobacco and buffalo fat into the fire. The men collect themselves around the blaze; each one takes a handful of smoke and rubs his whole body with it. Each believes that, because of this ceremony, God will grant whatever he may ask—whether it be the death of his enemy or swiftness to run. On other occasions the incense is not offered by burning in this way. In this case a kind of a burned pole is taken and set up by the fire. This pole and the fat for the incense—which has already been burned—they offer to God. Every time a dance begins, a man steps forward as a preacher does and tells the people what they are to ask God for in the next dance. In these gatherings there are many abuses, they pray also to the fire, to the air, to the water, to the corn, to the buffalo, to the deer, and to many other similar things, asking some of them to permit themselves to be killed for eating. To others they pray for vengeance. They ask the water to drown their enemies, the fire to burn them, the arrows to kill them, and the winds to blow them away. . . . I trust in the Lord that when their language is learned, we can garner in a great harvest because many tribes are gathered together in these meetings.[11]

Casañas was still far from fluent in speaking the language, but after living among the Hasinai tribes for more than a year, he understood most of what he heard. He may, however, have given too literal a meaning to some of the words. Certainly the mission-ary priest's mind-set caused him to misinterpret the Hasinai use of tobacco, fire, smoke, and the tall pole—signs of faith retained far longer than he could have imagined.

Sitting alone in the back seat of the car, Grace Akins hardly occupied any space at all. A small, frail woman, she sat next to the window with a blanket tucked across her lap and legs. Sunshine streamed through the window and poured into her cupped hands, which lay relaxed on her lap. For seventy-seven years she had viewed her world with humor and pride. She had earned the love and respect of family members, and although forced by the cancer inside her to become increasingly dependent on them, she could still assert a wiry will.

Gazing now at the passing countryside, Grace's expression was both content and impatient, like that of a child holding a happy secret she was eager to share. Almost inaudibly she began to sing.

Chee-tah ay hey-o wanna a-ka-a-a-
Chee-tah ay hey-o wanna a-ka-a-a-a

Na-nah high-nigh a' hey-e-e-e
Hey-ya inay hey-e-e-e
High-nay itcha kaa-nah
High-nay itcha kaa-nah

Itcha kaa-nah meant "that kind of pole," said Grace. The song was one she had learned by hearing it often as she was growing up.[12]

Grandpa and Grandma White Bread made the pole from the heart of a tall, straight, cedar tree before Grace was born. At least twenty feet tall, the tree was black on one side, green on the other. When there was a Ghost Dance or some other special reason to use the pole, it was erected with the black side facing north and the green side facing south. The leader stood on the invisible dividing line at the west side of the pole. He faced east and began the first song, which told that the feather signifying the right to lead the Ghost Dance was given to seven men.

The Ghost Dance was first given to the Paiute prophet Wovoka in a vision. On January 1, 1889, a day of total sun eclipse, Wovoka was said to have died, but like the sun, he came to life again. He returned with a message for his people, who lived in Mason Valley, Nevada. God had told him that there would be an end to the poverty and disease brought to Indians by the white people.[13]

God, said Wovoka, was coming to live on the earth as an Indian because the whites had betrayed Him. When He came, all of the white people would be rolled back across the ocean to the lands from which they had originally come. Grass would cover the earth again. The streams would run clear and full. The buffalo would return. All of the tribes' dead would rejoin them on a regenerated earth, and life would be as it had been in the old days. Wovoka preached that until God appeared, coming to them from the west in the flesh of an Indian, there had to be no violence, killing, or thievery, and the dance-in-a-circle in his vision had to be performed.

Wovoka never left his valley home, but word of the Paiute's prophecy swept across western prairies like the hot winds of summer. In September 1890 a great dance was held by the Southern Arapaho and Cheyenne who had been assigned a reservation in Indian Territory. (Indian Territory became the state of Oklahoma.) The leader was an Arapaho named Sitting Bull, who had lived for a while with the Northern Arapaho in Wyoming. A convert to the doctrine of the Ghost Dance, he had returned to his Indian Territory home to spread the word. Thousands of Indians attended the dance, which was held on the bank of the South Canadian River across from land where the Caddos were settled. Some Caddo men took part in the dance, among them one named Moonhead.

Sitting Bull introduced the rituals that so often led dancers into a trance. Round and around the Indians danced. After a while one fell to the ground in a trance. Then another fell and another. Moonhead, known by his English name as John Wilson, was the first Caddo to go into a trance. When he regained consciousness, he told of seeing many wonderful visions, and he composed a new song—a Caddo song.

After the big dance on the bank of the South Canadian, Caddos started Ghost Dancing on their own grounds. In December Sitting Bull came to give further instruction. He presented a leadership feather to seven men: Moonhead, White Bread, Mr. Blue (Thomas Wister), Tsa owisha (John Shemamy), T'amo', K'aaka'i (Crow or Billy Wilson), and Mr. Squirrel, who was also called Tsa Biti (Mr. Cedar).[14] From that time on Caddos wove their own sacred lore into the Ghost Dance rituals. They had their own songs, and they had the pole.

Grace was born in 1900, and from earliest childhood she knew of the power of the pole. Strength came from the pole and "what-ever else they had on the pole. They had tobacco and some had feathers on there. These feathers were crow feathers." From her family's camp on the dance grounds or from the edge of the dance circle, she saw men fall to the ground and lie there as though asleep. When they awoke, they "knew things"—such as how to cure tuberculosis or what was going to happen at some future time.

Once, she remembered, "there was one real sick man while we were all in camp. We camp there for about five days. You know they dance for five nights. And he was real, real sick, and they call on these seven men. And they went over there, and after while here they come with him. Nobody knew what was going on—I know I didn't. They're just carrying him on a blanket . . . three men on each side and carrying him. They took him around this pole. And then after they took him around four times, they took him back over there to his camp." Her thin voice rose, and the

Grace, aged three.

Chief White Bread in a photograph made during a trip to Washington, D.C. (1888?).

words rushed out. "After while here he come!" Speaking quietly once more, she explained her wonderment at seeing the man walking back from his camp—well again. "I thought maybe he died and they took him back to his camp."

According to Grace, the government took away the Ghost Dance in 1914, but the pole continued to be used whenever there was a need. There were times when only one man used the pole, and Grace watched from in front of her home at Grandpa White Bread's. The house was at the top of a hill overlooking dance grounds below.

Chief White Bread died in 1915. Before his death he gave the pole to Mr. Squirrel. He was a "doctor" who could predict things. He was the one who prepared the dance grounds at the bottom of the hill in 1920.[15] A year or so later there was a summer drought that threatened the crops in all the district. Mr. Squirrel went alone to the dance grounds and set up his tent. He took the pole from its resting place in the crook of a tree and set it up in the center of a cleared circle. He prayed and danced around the pole for three days while the corn continued to burn in the unrelenting sun. His time was almost up, said Grace, and people were afraid he would not be successful in bringing rain. On the fourth day, however, the rain came, and the corn—just the Caddos' corn— was saved that season. Another time too much rain threatened to wash away the fields, and Tompmo (T'amo') used the pole to make the rain stop.

Squirrel died in 1922. One by one all the seven men died, and after Mr. Squirrel's death, a Caddo man named Joe Weller took care of the pole. When he became ill in 1945, he knew he would not get well, but he wanted to have the pole put up for one more dance before he died. That was the last dance with the pole.

As her illness progressed, Grace began to think more and more about the pole. No one seemed to know what had happened to it. She talked about it with her daughter, Madeline, and they remembered some men who had come to the house one day to ask about the dance grounds at the foot of the hill. The men were from a museum, and they were driving a truck.

Madeline went to the State Historical Society Museum. With the help of the people there, she located the pole. It was in the Stovall Museum at the University of Oklahoma in Norman.

Hey ya inay ke·y.
Hi nay itcha kaa nah.

Grace's singing floated high and clear from the back seat of the
car. "Just think," she said, "of all the hands that have touched that
pole. Seems like it's the whole Caddo tribe." Madeline found a
parking space directly in front of the museum, convenient for the
use of Grace's wheelchair. A granddaughter and a great-grand-
daughter were waiting in front of the building—four generations
of the family were going to see the pole. Grace was helped into the
wheelchair and rolled toward the door. Her anticipation, under
control for the length of the car trip, could scarcely be contained
any longer. Her back was arrow straight. She leaned slightly
forward as though hurrying the path to the pole.

The young curator was cordial and courteous. The pole, she
explained, was in the storage building next door. Because of its
height, the pole probably could never be displayed, but its preser-
vation was ensured, and the museum was glad to give people the
opportunity to see it. She had taken the pole out of storage and
placed it in the hallway for viewing.

Inside the utilitarian storage building, doors along the entrance
hall were closed, and some bore signs cautioning that they should
not be left open. The family was led through a doorway into
another long hall, which angled to the right. The side walls were
lined with glassed-front cabinets filled with reed baskets. Bare
bulbs, spaced at intervals along the ceiling, spread harsh, uneven
light along the corridor. Beyond the stacks of shelves, the pole lay
on the floor. Grace saw it first. Her quick intake of breath
resembled a sound of anguish. For a moment there was no other
sound.

Then she whispered, "It's so faded." She leaned over the arm of
her chair, stretching toward the pole. Her hand trembled. Quickly,
the pole was lifted so that it lay across her right shoulder, its tip
resting on the back of her chair.

Reverently, she stroked the smooth heart of cedar. Tears slid
into the fine-lined wrinkles on her cheeks. She prayed, the Caddo
words struggling through choking sobs. The prayer was short. In
the hush that followed, the spirit of the small, frail woman became
calm. Grace died nine months later.

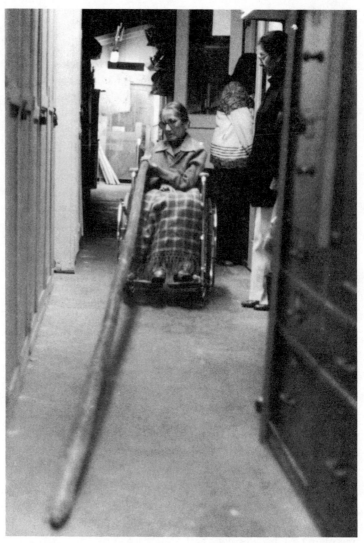

Grace with "that kind of pole" in a hallway storage area of the Oklahoma Museum of Natural History, Norman.

Preparing for battle in the fall of 1691, Hasinai tribes gathered to dance in front of the pole, make offerings to God, and pray for His protection. Because of the great number gathered, Casañas said he trusted that the missionaries could "garner a great harvest." But that trust was shaken when, before riding out with the war party, the caddi told Casañas he did not want to find missionaries among his people when he returned.[16]

Casañas blamed the loss of the caddi's friendship on the bad behavior of Terán's troops. A relative of the caddi, who had gone with De León to Mexico City and returned to Nabedache with Massanet and Terán, was probably another influence. In Mexico that relative had been baptized and given the name Bernardino. Several years later Spanish missionaries were told that Bernardino was very much against all matters of Christian faith, although he had lived for many years among the Spaniards as a young man and had been counted as a convert until he escaped from a Río Grande mission with some Indian women who had been left there.[17]

By the time Terán got back at the end of October from his trip to the coast, the missionaries were willing to leave. Terán, however, had other orders. The ship that brought supplies to the Texas Gulf Coast had also brought instructions for him to explore Cadohada-cho country.

Massanet and several missionaries went with Terán to the Cadohadacho villages on the Red River. The weather turned cold. The horses fought for footing on ice-glazed ground. Wind-driven snow burned the faces of the soldiers and missionaries and sent icy needles through their clothing. The Cadohadachos received them in a friendly fashion, but the difficult trip had depleted their provisions, and the plan to establish missions could not be carried out. Terán briefly surveyed the area, drew a map, and took soundings of the Red River. Massanet told Cadohadacho leaders that he would come back at a later date.

By the end of December Terán and Massanet were back at the Hasinai missions. On January 9, 1692, Terán started back to Mexico. Casañas and most of the other missionaries left with him. Massanet, two companions, and nine soldiers stayed at the Mission of San Francisco de los Tejas, and the Nabedaches tolerated their presence. Before the first missionaries came, the Hasinai had

had a strong belief in one all-powerful deity. Now, they told Massanet, "there were two, one who gave the Spaniards clothing, knives, hatchets, and all the other things they had, another who gave the Indians corn, beans, nuts, acorns, and rain for their crops."[18]

Floods swept away the mission Casañas had built on the bank of the Neches River. The soldiers and missionaries there retired to the mission of San Francisco. Two successive crops failed, one because of floods, the other because of drought. Disease wiped out most of the mission livestock. Disease again plagued people, too, and the Hasinai became more convinced than ever that baptismal water caused sickness.

Massanet decided that the Hasinai were not yet ready for conversion. He made up his mind to abandon the mission in July, but did not because relief arrived from Mexico in June. With ninety-seven packloads of provisions and gifts for the Indians, the mission could continue a while longer.

The Hasinai forced Massanet's final decision to leave. When Spaniards came offering useful things, the priests were permitted to stay. But the gifts were not worth the misery missionaries and soldiers brought with them. The same goods could be gotten by trading with the French, who also traded guns. Spanish policy forbade Indians to own firearms.

Bernardino, dubbed "the governor of the Tejas" by the Spaniards, began wearing a new cloth suit that was obviously woven and tailored by the French. Massanet confiscated from Indians at the mission four guns given as gifts by French traders. The corporal of the mission guard reported that Bernardino said his people were angry and did not want the Spaniards in their country any longer. When Massanet asked Bernardino if the corporal's story was true, the Indian made it clear—the Spaniards ought to leave if they did not want to die.

Massanet put on a bold front. He said he and his men were well armed and could defend themselves, but since the Indians did not want them any more, they would leave. Valuable ornaments from the mission church were secretly packed. Heavier things—cannon, bells, and such—were buried. On October 25, 1693, the mission was set on fire. Massanet, his companions, and the soldiers turned from the bright, sparking flames and slipped away like fugitives.

CHAPTER 6

THE FRENCH

A legend tells about an old Indian chief who lived on the banks of the Sabine River and had two sons. One day he said to his sons that the time had come for them to find a place of their own. The chief told one to face east, the other west, and then walk in the directions they faced from sunup of one day until sundown of the next. Where each found himself at that time was the place for his tribe. The one walking east found the fruit of the pawpaw tree, and his people were called Natchitoches, "pawpaw eaters." The one walking west found persimmon trees, and members of his family were called Nacogdoches, "persimmon eaters."[1]

Today the cities with these tribal names, Natchitoches, Louisiana, and Nacogdoches, Texas, are almost straight across from each other, and the one hundred or so miles between are nearly equally divided by the Sabine River. The Texas town rests on a foundation of sun-baked Spanish adobe, and the Louisiana city sits on plots laid out by Frenchmen.

France gained a shaky foothold on the sandy Gulf Coast east of the Mississippi when Pierre Le Moyne, Sieur d'Iberville put ashore the first members of his Louisiana colony in 1699. Early in January 1700 Iberville renewed the act of taking possession of the Mississippi River that La Salle had performed twenty years before. Iberville built a small fort a few miles above the mouth of the Mississippi and began exploration upstream.[2] The territory and the languages of its inhabitants were unknown to him, but he had some experienced help. La Salle's veteran lieutenant, Henri de Tonti, and a seasoned group of Canadian traders came down from the Illinois River country and entered Iberville's service. Two survivors of La Salle's colony, Pierre and Jean Talon, were already in his service.[3]

Pierre Talon and his younger brother Jean, who was found living with the Karankawa tribe near the Gulf Coast during Terán's exploration in 1691, were on board a Spanish vessel that was captured by a French warship in 1697. They were held in France for a year before the French minister of marine, Count Louis de Pontchartrain, heard about them. Pontchartrain was completing plans for Iberville's voyage. He had studied Joutel's journal and was keenly interested in what more could be learned from interrogating the Talons.[4]

In answering the minister's questions, Pierre Talon told about the Hasinai chief he had lived with and the chief's old father, who shared the same house. Talon said both had the title of chief, but the old man had given up the honor of command to his son; they were very close and lived together on good terms. According to Casañas, a caddi's authority extended to all sorts of civil matters as well as war, but Talon said this chief had authority only in matters of war. Even that authority was limited: a man could quit a war party and go home whenever he wanted.

Talon said the Hasinais' way of making war did not expose them to much danger because they used the element of surprise, attacking at night or in the dim light before sunrise. Warriors took scalps as trophies, and when they returned victorious from battle, there were celebrations with victory songs and dancing, and they showed off the scalps by holding them high. Each warrior kept the scalp he took, dried it, stuffed it with hay, and hung it on a stick at the top of his cabin. The one who had the most scalps had the most glory.

Talon reported that from time to time the elders gathered at the chief's house for conversation and entertainment. The chief treated them to drinks from a large jug of clear gruel made from corn and sometimes gave them presents of bows and arrows that came from Cadohadacho country. Shooting a bow was one of the first skills taught to children. As soon as they had enough strength, they were given small bows, and they continually practiced shooting little birds. By the time they were adults, they rarely missed a chosen target.

Talon said the "Cenis" (Hasinai) were a nation of strong and robust people, partly because a deformed child was buried as soon as it was born, partly because of a regimen aimed at physical fitness. Every morning at daybreak the Hasinai ran as fast as they were able to the nearest river and dove in. Even when the water was frozen, they made a hole in the ice and plunged in. Then, again running hard, they returned to stand before a large fire until they were dry. Afterward, wrapped in buffalo robes that had been rubbed soft as chamois leather, they walked around for some time. The men seldom missed a day of this exercise, which they claimed made them strong and supple and gave them fleetness of foot; women were only a little less faithful. Both men and women were excellent swimmers. The tribes that adopted the Talons tattooed their faces, arms, and bodies the same way they marked their own babies soon after birth, then taught them to run as fast as a "galloping horse" and shoot an arrow so accurately that they could "choose the exact place of the joints in the shoulders of a buffalo" and rarely miss a shot.[5]

The Talon brothers were placed in a company of Canadians held ready to ship from France with Iberville when he returned to prepare his second voyage. The company commander was Louis Juchereau de St. Denis, whose personal and family history entwined with that of the Natchitoches, Cadohadacho, and Hasinai tribes.[6]

Shortly after arrival in Louisiana, St. Denis was sent with Iberville's twenty-year-old brother, Jean Baptiste Le Moyne, Sieur de Bienville, and twenty-two Canadians to reconnoiter the Red River. They started upstream from the small fort built near the mouth of the Mississippi River and, as Tonti had done before, went to the Taensas Indian village and crossed over land to Natchitoches.[7] The year was 1700, and the month was late March, a season when it rained almost every day and night.

The reconnaissance party found an old Ouachita village on the Ouachita River in north Louisiana. Some of the Ouachitas had already moved to Natchitoches villages when Tonti passed through ten years earlier. Now only five cabins remained. St. Denis, Bienville, and the Canadians slogged on and met six Natchitoches who were carrying salt to trade to a tribe living near the Mississippi. Another week of wading through mud and water brought the party to a large lake, where they found two Natchitoches houses.

Natchitoches communities were built on natural levies in the floodplain of the Red River or on high ground above the mud and sand deposited by the river. Their houses and fields formed a series of hamlets fairly isolated by the river, especially when it was swollen with spring rains. The day after they first passed homes by the lake, St. Denis and Bienville were welcomed by a group of Doustioni men, who lifted them onto their shoulders and carried them to an arbor where the chief of the Natchitoches and others of the tribe were waiting. A song, which the French called a calumet song, was chanted, and the French gave presents to all the Indians, presenting the chief with a peace pipe as well as other presents.

St. Denis and Bienville led their group on up the Red River to the Yatasis. Several Cadohadachos and two Hasinais—a Nabedache and a Nadaco—were visiting there, and Bienville tried to learn from them how near the Spaniards were. His interpretation of what the Cadohadacho men told him was that thirty or forty Spaniards often came to their village on horseback, asked if the Cadohadacho had seen any more whites like them, and then left. Perhaps the Cadohadachos were disseminating misinformation or were misunderstood by Bienville. The only record of a Spanish party of that size to visit the Cadohadacho was the one led by Terán and Massanet nearly eight and one-half years before.

The Nabedache told Bienville that from where he lived, there was a Spanish settlement five and one-half days by horse. The settlement was probably near the Rio Grande; Fray Francisco Hidalgo, who had left the Tejas mission in 1693 when the Nabedache forced its abandonment, now worked there. The Cadohadachos visiting in the Yatasi village told the French it would take ten nights to reach their villages by boat at that time of year when the river was swollen and swift, but only two days during the summer months. St. Denis and Bienville decided to return to their base fort.

After a few weeks St. Denis came back to the Natchitoches settlement, bringing all sorts of attractive goods with him—shirts, hatchets, needles, knives, chisels, awls, vermilion, glass beads, and mirrors. The chief of the Natchitoches, called White Chief, and ten of his men guided St. Denis up the Red River to the Cadohadacho. It was the beginning of forty years of trade and trust between the Natchitoches and the man they named Big Leg.

Big Leg was then twenty-four. He was more than six feet tall, his body well proportioned and athletic. The Juchereaus were one of the prominent French families who had gone to Canada in the 1630s, served the colony in positions of leadership, and were granted letters of nobility. St. Denis was born in Canada but sent to Paris in his early youth for further academic and social education. He came to Louisiana from France as a "captain of the Canadians," but he was a volunteer officer unbound to any command.

Big Leg was in charge of the Mississippi fort in 1702 when the swirling, rust-colored water from the Red River rose to flood the fields and homes of the Natchitoches. They came to him for help, and he arranged for them to live beside the Acolapissa tribe, which had recently moved to the north shore of Lake Pontchartrain. St. Denis sent André Penicaut, a ship's carpenter who had come to Louisiana as an indentured servant, to conduct the Natchitoches to their new location.[8]

The relocation was advantageous for both the French and the Indians. The French colonists, headquartered at Mobile, were artisans, soldiers, traders, and novice adventurers — not farmers. Most of their staple foods came by ship from France. They already traded with the Natchitoches for salt, and with the tribe settled nearer the forts and French settlements, the colonists could also trade for produce grown by the Natchitoches and Acolapissa, who, barring natural disaster, were successful farmers. In return, French guns offered the Indians protection from their enemies.[9]

When the colony's food stores neared depletion and no supply vessel was on its way, it was the practice of the commander of the garrison to reduce the number of hungry stomachs by sending men out to live among the friendly tribes. Penicaut was one of those sent to live with the Natchitoches and Acolapissa during 1706. He later wrote a romantic account of his experiences.

Penicaut described the Natchitoches chief "as one of the most honorable men among the savages of that region," and the carpenter was pleased to be lodged in the chief's home, which had the added attraction of two daughters "that were the most beautiful of all the savage girls in this district." The older daughter was twenty. She was called Oulchogonime, which Penicaut said meant "good daughter." Her sister, two years younger, was the taller of the two. Her was named Ouilchil, "pretty spinner."[10]

In general Penicaut thought the Natchitoches were handsomer and had better figures than the Acolapissa, mainly because the

Acolapissa, both men and women, tattooed their bodies and the Natchitoches did not. The men shaved all but the hair on their head with shell ash and hot water. Besides, Penicaut said, the Natchitoches were naturally whiter.

Penicaut told about getting up late in the morning and being surprised by his host with a breakfast platter of fish fricasseed in bear fat and a bread made of cornmeal mixed with flour from small beans. The Natchitoches fished by a trotline method that fishermen still find successful. Penicaut said they tied a number of lines to a single long line, spacing them about a foot apart. From each line dangled a hook baited with a bit of dough or meat. The end of the long line was tied to a boat, and when the hooks were pulled up out of the water two or three times a day, there was always a good catch, many fish weighing fifteen or twenty pounds.[11]

The chief and Penicaut ate alone, but after a while Oulchogonime, Ouilchil, and their mother came back to the house with a big platter of strawberries freshly picked in the woods. That morning the girls wore their finest white aprons, which were made from a linenlike fabric woven with threads from nettle plants. Penicaut said they were made like the little taffeta ones worn by young women in France. Knowing he would please Oulchogonime and Ouilchil, he took from his supplies two pieces of white brocade woven with little pink and green flowers and gave one to each girl to make into an apron. His gift was almost spoiled when their father strongly objected, saying that Penicaut should keep the material for the daughter of the grand chief of the Acolapissa because that chief outranked all others in their settlement. The father was determined that his younger daughter should give her cloth back until Penicaut solved the protocol dilemma by producing another piece of brocade, which he said he was saving for the Acolapissa chief's daughter. Then everyone was happy, and Penicaut was thanked profusely and politely.

Penicaut spent ten months with the Natchitoches and Acolapissa. His idyllic description of life on the shore of Lake Pontchartrain is filled with tales of days spent hunting and nights spent dancing, of eating fresh fish suppers beneath the shade of peach trees in front of the house door, of teaching charming girls to speak French and dance the minuet. The idyll ended when a supply ship brought relief to Mobile in February 1707 and the men were notified to return.

The Natchitoches lived alongside the Acolapissa for eleven years. Then, because a letter written by a Spanish missionary found its way to the French governor of Louisiana, they were asked to return to their homelands on the Red River. The letter, written by Fray Francisco Hidalgo, asked the French to cooperate in founding a new mission among the Hasinai.

For seventeen years Hidalgo had tried to persuade Spanish authorities to resume missionary efforts among the Hasinai. He was even reported to have returned alone to live and work there for several years and may have been living there in January 1711, when he wrote the letter received by the Louisiana governor. Hidalgo hoped his letter would bring an answer he could show to his viceroy as proof that the French were closing in on Spanish territory, and thereby force reestablishment of the Tejas missions. Two years after the letter was written, it came to Governor Antoine de LaMothe Cadillac, who had recently arrived in Louisiana. He viewed it as pretext to enter Spanish territory and selected St. Denis to go to Hidalgo's mission and trade for horses and cattle there. The hidden goal was to gain access to the wealthy mining districts of Mexico by arranging a trade treaty with the Spanish government.[12]

St. Denis had become familiar with the Hasinai language, customs, and habits while he was in charge of the fort on the Mississippi. He had quit that post to make his home at St. John's Bayou, between Lake Pontchartrain and the Mississippi River, and engage in private trade. He maintained commerce with the Natchitoches, trading for skins, corn, fruit, and melons.

The old village site of the Natchitoches—inside French territory, within easy reach of the Cadohadacho, and just across the Red River from the Hasinai—was a strategic location for a supply base. St. Denis accepted the governor's offer of ten thousand livres of merchandise and twenty-two men to take into Tejas territory and sent Penicaut to ask the Natchitoches to return to their old home place.

The Natchitoches were willing to go, but for some unexplained reason, when Penicaut and the Natchitoches families started to leave, the Acolapissa attacked them with guns, arrows, and hatchets. Penicaut shielded the Natchitoches chief but could not prevent the deaths of seventeen Natchitoches who were close by. Fifty or more women and girls were seized by the Acolapissa; the rest of the tribe scattered and fled into the woods. Those who could crept from their hiding place at nightfall and joined Penicaut on the lakeshore. He took them to St. Denis's house at St. John's Bayou, where they stayed for several days, waiting for others to join them. Thirty or so found their way there.

St. Denis's supplies were moved to the bank of the Mississippi and loaded on boats for transport to the former Red River home of the Natchitoches. Nearing the island where they had traditionally lived, the Natchitoches saw others of their tribe who had escaped the Acolapissa and headed for home. With them were about two hundred Doustioni men, their old allied neighbors. The Doustioni had been unwilling to go to the Acolapissa village and had remained near their old homesites, wandering from place to place and surviving on game, fruits, and wild potatoes.

When St. Denis got to the island, he assembled the Natchitoches and Doustioni chiefs and told them that he had brought seed grains with him that would be distributed among their families. He said they had to sow seed and tend their fields because from now on there would always be French living among them, and it would be the tribes' responsibility to feed their French friends. If the tribes stood closely united, he told them, they would have nothing to fear from enemies.

Two or three days later when everyone was rested, St. Denis gave hatchets and picks to the Natchitoches and Doustionis and asked them to cut trees for building houses. As soon as Natchitoches Post—a warehouse for merchandise and a house for men— was built, St. Denis was ready to search for Hidalgo's Spanish mission.

Leaving ten men at Natchitoches Post with instructions to stay until he got back, St. Denis started overland with twelve men, including the Talon brothers. After twenty-two days, they reached a Hasinai settlement. The Talons' identifying tatoos were a passport, and the Hasinai welcomed St. Denis with a three-day calumet ceremony and an eager reception of his merchandise.

Hidalgo was not among the Hasinai. It had been at least five years since any Spaniard had been there. However, the Hasinai had plenty of horses and buffalo hides to exchange for guns, knives, beads, and cloth. Trade was so active that St. Denis had to make a trip back to Louisiana to pick up more trade goods and report to the governor before looking further for Hidalgo.

St. Denis stayed with the Hasinai for about six months before leaving for the frontier of Mexico. He left four of his French companions behind and took his valet (Jalot Medar) and the Talon brothers with him. Bernardino, principal chief of the Hasinai, and twenty-five Hasinai men accompanied St. Denis. They rode south and west until they reached the banks of the Colorado River, where they met two hundred Karankawas who greeted them with a shower of arrows. The rifles of the French won a victory for their smaller party. A truce was negotiated by the Indians, and except for Bernardino and three of his men, the Hasinai returned home.[13]

Captain Diego Ramón commanded the garrison at the Spanish frontier mission settlement of San Juan Bautista del Río Grande. He was General Alonso de León's old lieutenant and therefore must have seen the Talon children when they were found in Tejas country and taken to Mexico. On July 22, 1714, Ramón wrote Father Hidalgo at the missionary college in Querétaro, Mexico, where he had retired two years earlier, to tell him that St. Denis, Medar, and the two Talons had arrived at the garrison.[14]

CHAPTER 7

NEW MISSIONS

Almost two years passed before St. Denis brought Fray Hidalgo back to the Hasinai villages. St. Denis was first detained at San Juan Bautista (on the Rio Grande near present-day Eagle Pass), where he fell in love with Diego Ramón's granddaughter. From San Juan Bautista he was taken under arrest to Mexico City, where officials reacted much as Hidalgo had wished, decreeing that French intrusion on Spanish territory was prohibited and that missions had to be reestablished in Tejas country to help protect that frontier. St. Denis was offered a salary to guide the missionary expedition to the Hasinai. He returned to San Juan Bautista, married Diego Ramón's granddaughter, and waited for the arrival of the company he had agreed to assist.

Captain Domingo Ramón, an uncle of St. Denis's bride, was leader of the expedition, which included nine missionaries and three lay brothers. Fray Isidor Felís de Espinosa and Fray Margil de Jesús jointly headed the religious party. There were twenty-two soldiers in the military escort. Spanish authorities had learned one lesson from their previous abortive attempt to establish permanent mission settlements in northeast Texas: unmarried soldiers were prone to bad behavior, which the Hasinai would not tolerate. The new plan was for four missions, each guarded by two men. Five soldiers in Ramón's company were married, and another was married en route to Hasinai country. Civilians included two families equipped as settlers with plows, hoes, and oxen; drovers;

and muleteers. The total number of the company was sixty-five. Large herds of oxen, horses, mules, sheep, and goats raised dust along the trail.[1]

St. Denis rode in advance to the first Hasinai village to tell the caddi of the Spaniards' approach and help prepare for their arrival. The caddi sent messengers to call the people together, while a delegation of five chiefs and twenty-nine men rode out with St. Denis to meet the missionary expedition. They went armed with bows and arrows, as they always did when they left home, and those who had French guns carried them.

They came to the Spanish camp about eight in the morning of July 27, 1716. Ramón and the missionaries, centered between two files of soldiers, walked forward to greet the Hasinai who rode single file behind St. Denis. The headmen dismounted, gave their horses and arms to the care of others, and, keeping their file order, walked between the lines of soldiers to exchange embraces with the missionaries.

A green-bough arbor had been built for the occasion. Blankets carpeted the ground, and pack saddles served as low chairs. Under the shade of the arbor, Spanish and Hasinai leaders were seated in order of rank. The caddi lit a long-stemmed pipe decorated with white feathers, puffed smoke, and passed the pipe to Ramón. The pipe was solemnly handed from one person to the next until each leader had blown smoke. The missionaries served chocolate and afterward a caddi stood and delivered what Espinosa described as a "very serious discourse."[2] St. Denis interpreted, saying the Hasinai welcomed the missionaries into their midst with pleasure.

The next day the Hasinai delegation led the Spaniards to a large plain surrounded by trees. There were two lakes in the center of the open space and a brook flowing nearby. The Spaniards set up camp beside the stream.

Evening came. Ninety-six people from Hasinai tribes gathered near the camp and arranged their number in three files. Principal men, led by St. Denis, were in the middle; the rest lined up on either side. A short distance away the Hasinai who had first greeted the missionary expedition advanced and fired a salute.

Ramón lifted a banner painted with the images of Christ Crucified and Our Lady of Guadalupe. The priests and lay brothers took places on either side of him, and together they moved to meet the Hasinai ranks. Ramón delivered the religious standard to Father Espinosa, knelt before him, kissed the holy images, and embraced him. St. Denis did the same, and the Hasinai followed his example.

Singing a hymn, to which the soldiers fired salutes in response, the missionaries led a procession back to their encampment, where Hasinai and Spaniards seated themselves in the same order as the day before. The Hasinai talked briefly among themselves, then spread a beautifully painted deerskin. Each caddi took a handful of powdered tobacco and placed it on the deerskin. They stirred the tobacco together, showing their unity, and handed the skin and tobacco to Captain Ramón.

An exchange of gifts followed: young corn, muskmelons, nuts, tamales, and beans cooked with corn for the Spaniards; small blankets, hats, tobacco, and flannel cloth (which the missionaries intended for underwear) for the Hasinai. That night the Hasinai celebrated with a dance.

Around noon the next day eight more tribal leaders and their followers came to the Spanish camp, bringing a feather-adorned pipe made of brass. The smoking ritual was observed, the Spaniards made gifts of clothing, and there was more dancing.

Ramón spoke to the assembled tribes. St. Denis interpreted, telling the Hasinai the Spanish captain said that the gifts he distributed were tokens of love and that the Spaniards had come to look after the welfare of the Hasinais' souls, to bring them a knowledge of the holy law, and to impress on them a recognition of the authority of King Felipe V. Ramón asked the Hasinai to select one of their own to serve as a captain general so that they could have good government. The Hasinai withdrew for a short conference and put forward the youngest of their chiefs, the son of Bernardino. To signify his Spanish appointment as chief of the Tejas and governor of the Indians, Ramón gave the young chief his own jacket and a staff used by the Spaniards to symbolize authority.

Once all these courtesies and formalities were finished, the large body of Indians and Spaniards moved northeast to the spot where Father Massanet had established the mission of San Francisco de los Tejas in 1690. Ramón approved the natural clearing, not far from a medium-sized river and edged by a large lake, for the location of a presidio. Location of the four prospective missions was largely determined by the Hasinai who decided among themselves how the missions should be apportioned to the tribes. With St. Denis to interpret, leaders set out with the missionaries and Ramón to select the first site. Other members of the welcoming tribes stayed to build a house for the Spanish officer.

Four missions were established in rapid order: San Francisco de los Tejas near the Nabedache and Neche villages; Purísima Concepción at the main Hainai village; Guadalupe de los Nacogdoches at the main village of the Nacogdoches; and San José de los Nazones near the Nasoni and the Nadaco (Anadarko). The missions were placed so that all the Hasinai, four to five thousand men, women, and children, were within easy reach. Houses and churches were built with diligent and skillful assistance by the Indians.

Father Margil was in charge of Guadalupe de Nacogdoches. Father Espinosa was director of the other three. Espinosa appointed Hidalgo as minister of the first dedicated mission, San Francisco, located just east of the Neches River. He made his own headquarters among the Hainai at Purísima Concepción. Because the Hainai were the head tribe of the Hasinai nation, they were sometimes called Hasinai or Tejas even when their particular identity was indicated. Hainai homes stood on both sides of the Angelina River.

The Angelina River was probably named for Angelique, a Hasinai woman who had been reared and baptized in the mission of San Juan Bautista in Coahuila, Mexico. She was helpful when the missionaries tried to communicate the object of their coming to the people gathered to welcome their arrival, translating from Spanish to her own language. Frontier mission work was meant to extend beyond spreading the faith. Church and king expected missionaries to educate Indians to follow the daily routine that disciplined the lives of Christian citizens living in Spain and Mexico—building and living in towns near the church, wearing European clothes, planting and harvesting crops, caring for stock. When this job was accomplished, Indians resisted any other foreign influence and thereby helped protect the Spanish frontier. The first step was to persuade the Hasinais to come together for instruction. Angelique assisted in gaining her people's goodwill toward the missionaries, but when asked to come live by the mission, the Hasinai said they could not until they had gathered their crops.[3]

After the formal founding of the four missions was completed, St. Denis was permitted to go to Louisiana to gather his property. Ramón went to Natchitoches to see for himself what sort of establishment the French had there. Brother Margil and three other missionaries accompanied Ramón. They found a well-built house with a stockade on a small island in the center of the river and learned from two French there that a reinforcement of ten men was expected shortly. Ramón ordered the French to erect a large cross, and the missionaries celebrated mass in view of a large group of Natchitoches onlookers.

On the way back, certain that the French had considerable influence over the Indians in the neighborhood, Ramón and the missionaries stopped to establish two more missions: the mission of San Miguel de los Linares de los Adaes among the Adai, who lived near present-day Robeline, Louisiana, about twelve miles from Natchitoches; and the mission of Nuestra Señora de los Dolores de los Ais where the Ais (Eyeish) lived, less than one hundred miles west of Natchitoches, between the Adai and Nacogdoches.[4] With a total of six missions, the missionaries eagerly anticipated the conversion of many souls.

Although Hidalgo was the only one of the missionaries familiar with the Hasinai language and customs, Espinosa must have had some idea of what to expect. He had taken the Franciscan habit at the Colegio de Santa Cruz de Querétaro in 1696, when he was sixteen years old. Hidalgo and Casañas had come from the same institution, and it is reasonable that their reports, written and oral, formal and informal, were shared within its halls. The Hasinai, as Espinosa came to know them, showed little change from the time when Casañas had served in their country. The people still came together to communally build their houses, plant their crops, and hold celebrations. Peace was still preserved within their boundaries, civil leadership remained hereditary, the cona elicited respect, the dominance of the chenesi was undiminished, and the sacred fire still burned.

The peaceful relations that the Hasinai maintained with other tribes living near their borders were the result of caddis' skillful diplomacy. Espinosa, after stating that "the Province of the Assinais [Hasinais]" was commonly called "Texas," observed that "the Texas Indians maintain an inviolable peace with the surrounding nations and they all preserve their own customs without any occasion being furnished for trouble." He also said, "They never form a truce or make friends with an enemy."[5]

Hereditary succession to the position of caddi secured the promotion of able men because the boy in line benefited from years of tutoring. Even if the caddi died while his male heir was quite young, the child was recognized without controversy as the head of his tribe. He was given the counsel of able, high-ranking men, who acted in place of the caddi and carried him to all the council meetings, where he was assigned the highest seat. He sometimes slept or ran around like a bright, obstreperous kindergartner while elders held conferences, but by the time he was a man, he had been schooled to be a caddi.[6]

A caddi's duties were many. He kept order in his own village and contributed to the peace of the nation. He set the day for building a new house, approved marriages, called assemblies of elders when major decisions were to be made, hosted feasts, organized official welcomes for visitors, helped sponsor and offici-ate at planting and harvest ceremonies, conducted peacemaking ceremonies, supervised the division of gifts from foreign emis-saries, conducted councils for raising a war party and selecting its leader, and hosted victory celebrations. Since each caddi assumed these responsibilities in his community, there was little distur-bance within Hasinai borders.

Cases of dispute or accusations of theft were taken to the caddi. He and the council of elders made the guilty party give satisfaction in a manner that would cause no future trouble. If someone did damage to another tribe, for example, by stealing a horse, the injured tribe sent a principal man with notice that the caddi should call the council, bring the delinquent before it, and make him return the stolen property. The offender was sharply repri-manded and threatened with expulsion if he should repeat the offense.

Hasinai, Cadohadacho, and Natchitoches caddis followed an equally stringent protocol for taking action against enemies. Ac-cording to Espinosa:

> The way in which they most clearly show their civilization is in the embassies which they send to various settlements, especially when they wish to call them together for war. The captains receive the person who goes as an ambassador with great honor. They assign him a principal seat and, following their custom, give him a great

many presents while preparing the reply they are to give him. They are so strict in the observance of their pledges that they do not fail, even a day, in gathering together to go in search of the enemy.[7]

The Cadohadachos were especially honored when they traveled down from their homes on the Red River. An advance messenger announced their coming, and the caddi alerted every household to prepare. All the leading men dressed in their finest and formed a welcoming committee to ride out and greet the visitors before they reached the village. After they arrived at the settlement, there were dances and feasts and an exchange of gifts.

Natchitoches were grandly treated. Espinosa, whose Spanish allegiance made him sensitive to French influence, reported:

> They preserve close friendship with all the Indians who are subject to the French and when one party visits the other, the exchange of courtesies is very marked. The preparations for receptions are very great. These Indians have been so carefully trained in politeness by the French and our Indians try not to be outdone by them in politeness and courtesies. They do not yield a point in proving themselves equally as warlike and valiant. For this reason, they make a show of handling their guns with dexterity and of running on their horses at great speed, for, although the Natchitoches have a greater number of guns than the Texas Indians, the number of horses they have is limited. The latter thus travel on foot while the Texas Indians ride on horseback with great skill, their feet hanging loose and, traveling at a great rate, they guide their horses with only a slender cord which they use in place of a bridle.[8]

The most active time for visiting and feasting came after the crops had been gathered. The gatherings were often political as well as social. Each season the Hasinai entertained tribes that lived south of them. The annual event was a sort of trade fair with many families—men, women, and children—bringing items to trade for things they lacked in their own settlements. Old friendships were strengthened and new ones built. In the process, the Hasinai ensured that tribes outside their borders were "tayshas," allies who would assist in repressing enemies.

The Hasinais' harvest culminated in the most celebrated feast of the year, a gathering of the entire nation. Preparations began when a tamma went about the settlements collecting the first fruits of tobacco plants and delivering them to the house of the principal caddi nearest the fire temple. The caddi's duty was to pray for the right amount of rain to make good crops and to bless the first fruits of harvest. When the day for harvest festival was set, tammas announced it at each homestead so that families could prepare offerings for the feast. Six days before feast day, caddis, conas, and other leading men assembled at the house where the chenesi tended the fire. The old men prayed and drank large quantities of a warm, foamy brew of laurel tea. The chenesi gave young men orders to go out in all directions to hunt for deer. He cautioned them to return quickly and said that while they were away, he and the elders would pray, asking Ayo-Caddi-Aymay to favor them.

Camouflaged with white dirt smeared on their naked bodies and covering their heads with a dried deer head complete with neck skin and antlers, the hunters went into the woods to stalk their prey. They brought their kill back and went out for more deer the next morning. All but the head and the intestines of the deer was cooked for the feast.

Only those who were too old or ill, and those needed to care for them, stayed home during the celebration of the harvest festival. Families set up camp on the outer edge of a previously cleaned arena, and when darkness came, their campfires glowed like footlights on a stage. They brought their best clothing and orna-ments to wear on the feast day. Woolen apparel, received as a gift or acquired through trade, was kept for special-occasion wear, as were the finest deerskin garments. Women wore two-piece dresses of lustrous black deerskins made by a process that Espinosa said only the Hasinai knew. The women's dresses looked as though they had been made of very fine cloth and made graceful by a border of the small white seeds sewn on all edges. The tops, covering from shoulders to waist, were made from a large skin with a center opening cut large enough to slip over the head. Edges were fringed.

The women wore their neatly combed hair pulled back and plaited in a braid that was folded and fashioned into an unusual shape with the help of a strip of red-dyed rabbit skin. Men wove colored feathers in the thin lock of hair that they grew long from the tops of their heads. Brilliantly colored feathers from the Spanish chickens raised by the missionaries were a new source of plumage. Their finery included ear ornaments and strings of beads worn around their necks, ankles, or knees. On the night of the celebration they made their faces slick and red by painting them with a mixture of bear grease and vermilion.

On the night of the new moon in September, logs for a bonfire were laid in the center of a cleared space fenced by green cane sticks stuck in the ground. The conas, caddis, headmen, and servants remained inside the assembly house. Two old men sat praying in an undertone, then rose and stood before the central fire. For more than a hour they threw bits of meat and tobacco into the fire, then reseated themselves on the wooden benches reserved for them. Meat was served to the other elders and caddis, who drank a brew made from wild olives with the meal. The earthenware vases holding the liquid were refilled three or four times. Pipes of tobacco were passed all around, each leader drawing smoke and blowing it toward the sky, toward the ground, toward the north, south, east, and west.

Midnight approached. Outside, people started to come closer together. A crier began to call out for the families in order. They came by threes, a woman representing each house with an offering she had prepared—small pots filled with finely ground meal or rolls made of a thick paste of roasted corn and sunflower seeds. The food offerings were placed in large earthen containers and taken to be divided among the old men, conas, caddis, and other officials.

Some young conas slept. Others made a great effort to stay awake, playing instruments and singing to drive away sleep. Three or four youths, assigned to keep the bonfire burning high, continually fed its blaze.

From midnight on a sentinel was stationed to watch the stars for the moment the Pleiades were perpendicular over the house where the leaders stayed. The moment he sighted the six stars of the constellation, he alerted the chief cona, who together with one other came out to the circle of green cane surrounding the bonfire. The two men, leaders of the ceremony, seated themselves on a high bench. On their left all the women were formed in rows—the oldest sitting in front, married women and girls behind them, younger girls at the end with little girls. To the right of the masters of ceremony an arbor covered a second bonfire.

The women and children would begin to sing. Three old men cloaked in curious buffalo robes stepped rhythmically in a line, one following another, to the fire beneath the arbor. They paused, then danced back to the circle. The singing stopped, and the three men addressed the gathering in high-pitched voices. Their rapidly delivered speech made use of a special language unintelligible to the uninitiated. They proceeded around the circle, and as they arrived in front of each woman, she presented a little pot of meal and rolls. The women offered their gifts without rising, lifting them up for young men, novices in the ritual, to take. The songs of those in the circle continued uninterruptedly for another hour or so, until the old men's rattling of gourd instruments signaled the coming of dawn.

Day broke, the singing stopped, the three old men and the two leaders divided the women's offerings, and everyone anticipated sunrise. Appointed young men and boys were sent into the nearby woods to call as if speaking to the sun, telling it to hurry its arrival. When it appeared, they ran about joyously, lighthearted and thankful for the year's harvest. Men and boys of the same size and age lined up to race up to a tree a good distance from their starting point. They rounded the tree and returned to the starting point as many times as they could before giving out. Then both girls and boys ran the same race. Relatives watched the runners intently to see who would gain the advantage and be acclaimed as the strongest. Any man who was left behind or became too tired to finish was wept over by wives and female relatives—his lack of speed would cause him to be left behind, either captive or dead, when he went to war.

The last race was followed by a dance. Eight women took places around drums made of hollow logs with the bottom ends buried in the ground and green branches covering the tops. With sticks in each hand, they began to beat an accompaniment to the shaking gourd rattles held by the old men and the songs of a group of men and women. Everyone else danced. Women, girls, men, boys, and little children joined in a circle, men facing the women. They danced moving only their feet in time to the music until midday, when tired, sleepy, and content, everyone went home.

If, from observation of large gatherings, the missionaries expected the tribes to come together and form mission settlements after the crops had been gathered, they were disappointed. The rainy season commenced in September. Cold months followed. Women went into the woods to gather nuts and acorns, but most of their time was spent inside their homes, where dampness and chills were warded off by the warmth of central fireplaces. The season was right for domestic tasks: cooking, making pottery and clothing, teaching the young ones. Little children were instructed by their elders from the time they were old enough to learn and recite the rituals and traditions of the tribe. Espinosa's opinion was, "If some of the old women who are steeped in superstition could be removed, all the young women would gladly listen to all that is offered them by the evangelical minister, both because they are naturally good and because they would not hear these fables with which the leaders have fed them."[9]

A quarter of a century earlier, Casañas had reported a

> gross superstition . . . which all of them believe implicitly, is that the old men made Heaven and that a woman, who sprang from an acorn, first gave them its outlines; and that it was done by placing timbers in the form of a circle and that Heaven was formed in this way. They further declare that the woman is in Heaven and that she is the one who daily gives birth to the sun, the moon, the water when it rains, the frost, the snow, the corn, the thunder, and the lightning; and many other similar absurdities.[10]

At the same time, the early missionary noted that the whole Hasinai nation held the belief that Caddi Ayo (the leader above) created everything and that He rewarded good deeds and punished evil ones. It was Espinosa's view that the Hasinai were naturally civilized and had good minds but that they were disfigured by false beliefs handed down from parent to child.

The main religious center for the Hasinai was less than ten miles from Mission Purísima Concepción, where Espinosa made his headquarters.[11] The sacred house was rebuilt in December 1716, a few months after the founding of the mission. Espinosa said it was like a parish house or cathedral for the Hasinai. It was in this house that men gathered to consult and hold war dances and to pray for rain when there was drought. Nearby were two small houses, which the people said were the houses of the two cononici. Espinosa was told that the boys whom Caddi Ayo had sent from above had been in the houses until a little more than two years before. He understood through an interpreter that the cononici were there until the Hasinais' enemies the Yojaunes (a Tonkawa band) had burned the houses. That was when the children were seen rising skyward with the smoke, and they never came down again.

Inside one of the houses were two small chests, in which Espinosa and another missionary priest found four or five shield-shaped vessels of black wood. They were carved with four feet, a head, and a tail in the form of a duck, an alligator, or a lizard. Feathers of various colors and shapes nestled with the carvings in the chests—handfuls of wild bird feathers, a white breast knot, rolls, crowns, and a bonnet of ornamental feathers. There were musical instruments in the chests—flutes or fifes made of little carved crane bones or reeds and other small instruments used in dances.

The Neches had a small fire temple of their own, and the Nacogdoches had one shared with the Nasonis—but the fires that burned in those places were brought from the main Hainai fire house. Family fires throughout the nation also came from the principal center, supplied from there when the homes were built. If ever the fire went out, the people considered it a sign that all the family would die. With great ceremony, they brought new fire from the source fire.

Espinosa said, "They are very much afraid of angering the fire and they offer up to it the first tobacco and the first fruits of their crops." He had no understanding of Hasinai reverence for fire. When the missionaries fanned flames to brighten the blaze of their own fires, alarmed Indians would move to take the fan from them, saying, "You are a fool or crazy to do such a thing. Such a snow or cold spell will soon come that everything will be killed. You are not afraid because you are covered with clothes."[12]

Lillie Whitehorn was a religiously minded person. She attended mass and altar-society meetings regularly. As a girl she had attended St. Patrick's Mission School in Anadarko, Oklahoma. "But," she said, "I didn't learn too much. . . . I was a dumb-head."[13] She was not. Her memory was a data bank of tribal history, native lore, and information gleaned from reading the somewhat limited number of books available to her. Sorting through a seventy-six-year collection of fact and lore, weighted with teachings Christian and Caddo, she struggled to cross-index and make sense of what she knew.

Lillie Whitehorn (1978)

"I'm just going to tell you according to what I heard and what I was told. I don't say I know it; I don't say that it's truth or I know this. I'm just telling what my—" She interrupted her statement that her father had told her many things and explained, "Of course, Indians, they don't put it down. They tell you like this. . . . They expect you to know it and keep that in mind. That's the way they teach, you know."

There was a cadence to her speech, a dropping of final conso-nants that hinted that her first language was not English. As a child she was called Sah K'un-dee-ku, Miss Black Hair. Her father was the Caddo chief Enoch Hoag. Her mother was a Delaware woman, Nellie Thomas, who "took the Caddo ways."

Lillie lived alone, having "buried two husbands." She was lonely living by herself in the house on Kentucky Street in Ana-darko, which her husband had bought two years before his death.

The comfortably furnished living room was kept excessively warm during the cold winter days. Heat radiated from a small, freestanding gas parlor stove of the type found in many older homes in Oklahoma. Cold weather caused the arthritis in her knees and ankles to be even more painful than usual. She drew her chair closer to the heater.

Waving a hand toward the windowpane brushed with large, light snowflakes, she related, "Father used to say, 'He's a king, this snow out here. I don't care how much crack it is, he's gonna get in there. No matter little bit of space, he's gonna get in there. He'll make you cold!' And he say there's a story that Christ, one time when he was a little boy, he went and visit the Snow King. This is the story now.

"Christ, one time when he was a little boy, he went and visit the Snow Man.

"He goes over there. He takes his bow and arrows. Nobody dare go over there. They're afraid of that king cause if you go to him he'll kill you—he'll get you!

"He wouldn't kill you like this." She stabbed the air with her finger. "He'll freeze you to death.

"Well, this little boy, he come to that king, and that king told him, 'Come on in little boy. Where did you come from?' He already knows where he come from, but he says, 'Where did you come from? You come up here to see me? Nobody comes up here, but you brave enough to come over here!'

"The little boy comes with his bow and arrows, and he's not going back that day cause it's a long ways. The king told him, 'All right, I give you a place to sleep.'

"It's cold, you know, and he gives him cover and cover him up. Then he put that snow on him."

Lillie pantomimed patting a mound of snow; then her eyes laughed and she triumphantly said, "In the morning that lil' boy was still alive! That Snow King done with all his might to get rid of him, and he did not get rid of him! That little boy was just sweatin', and he throw his covers to one side, and then the king told him, 'Yes, I know who you are—I know you. I know who you are because nobody comes up here—you're the first one. You're the person that they call Kuna Cah-dee. That's who you are.'

"Now Kuna Cah-dee means Christ, Christ the healer. That's what it means in Caddo, Kuna Cah-dee. Snow King couldn't get rid of him. That's the story of the snow. That's one story my father used to tell us."

Espinosa and his fellow missionaries reproached the Hasinai who warned them of the folly of disturbing fire. The Hasinai defended their belief by saying that the missionaries' fire was different because it was made by striking iron against a rock. When Espinosa asked why the Hainai and Neche did not all leave their houses during buffalo time, when all the Nasoni and Nacogdoches left theirs, he was told it was so that the fire would not go out if wood failed. The Nasoni and the Nacogdoches could leave their fire hanging up in their houses because they had a different kind of fire, which they made by rubbing two little sticks together. The fire of the Hainai and Neche could not be allowed to die since it came from their forefathers, kept alive from that time to this.[14]

CHAPTER 8

HA-COO-DOOH
(WINTER)

There was severe weather in Hasinai country during the winter of 1716–1717 and much suffering from the effects of cold, floods, sickness, and death. To carry on their ministry, Espinosa and his brother missionaries crisscrossed miles of woodland covered by barren branches and paved with frozen pine needles. They had to go to the people—the Hasinais did not come to the missions.

Father Margil's mission for the Nacogdoches was built near the center of twenty-two small settlements spread over a north-south distance of twenty miles. The religious leaders and Ramón had expected the Nacogdoches to form a settlement at the mission after harvesting their crops. The Spaniards anticipated more than four hundred prospective converts. Instead the Nacogdoches claimed that their southern neighbors, the Bidai, who they said had wicked and powerful witches, had caused damage to Nacogdoches crops, and they all moved to the northern section of their territory. The mission, left isolated on the southern edge of the new location, was nearly eight miles from the nearest household and more than one hundred miles from the most distant.[1]

Homes visited by the missionaries were often filled with sickness, and the conversions they sought were frustrated by the people's faith in the curative powers of a cona. Conas were the nemeses of Espinosa, as they had been of Casañas in his time. "The number of these medicine men," fumed Espinosa, "is so great that even when one of the heads of this hydra is cut off by death, additional heads in the persons of new ministers of lies raise up at every step."[2]

Young men took great pride in learning to become healers of the body and spirit. Those who excelled were initiated as conas at about twenty years of age. Espinosa maintained that the devil was "the instigator of all this foolishness" and scorned their initiation, saying:

> A great number of the old fakirs or saints, with a bunch of medicine men, gather together, dressed for a feast in all the finery they have. They offer drinks to the prospective medicine men. The latter consume great quantities of tobacco. This, with their drinks, causes them to lose their senses, to make faces, and to fall upon the ground like drunken men. Here they remain either really senseless or pretending to be, for twenty-four hours, as if dead, until they decide to come to and begin to breathe. They then relate what they have dreamed or whatever their imagination suggests to them. They say that their souls were far from them. The candidate then begins his song and this discordant music continues for eight days, the novices relieving each other and the assembled women adding their discordant cries.[3]

To cure a sick person, the conas painted themselves heavily and wore their own particular insignia of feather headdresses and snakeskin necklaces. They built a bonfire and used a collection of fifes and an abundance of feathers in their rituals. After drinking a foam-covered herbal brew, they began playing instruments — small polished sticks with slits like snake's rattles that they rubbed against a hollow skin. Singing a chant accompanied by these instruments, they danced in place.

The patient lay sweating from the heat of coals heaped under his or her bed. From time to time the cona stopped singing and dancing and bent over the sick one. He placed his mouth on the sufferer's flesh to suck out the pain or sickness, spat it out, and resumed his singing and dancing. The treatment went on from the middle of the afternoon until near dawn — intervals of chanting interrupted by sucking and spitting.

Espinosa believed the conas used sleight of hand, putting a worm or blood into their mouths and saying they took it from the body of a patient. He admitted, however, that in treating snake-bite, they really sucked and spit out the poison. With other patients, the conas covered the liver with stones and sucked the blood. If a prominent person was in need of treatment, there was a gathering of the medicine men, and each one tried his own prescription. Espinosa conceded that some of their remedies called for the application of medicinal herbs growing abundantly in the country and that many cures followed.

The conas said, and the people believed, that sickness came from neighboring nations—"Bidais, Ays, and Yacdoas" were named by Espinosa—whose many witch doctors came in secret or sent *aquian* ("disease") to the Hasinai. Aquian, explained Espinosa, is "a pointed thing that has a sharp point like an arrow, that it is shot from a bow which they call *texino* and we called the devil, and that it strikes the patient."[4] The conas said aquian was like a big white needle, and before commencing treatments to remove it, they prayed for the powerful Bidai medicine men to come help. The Bidais came, they said, in the shape of owls. Whenever the hoot of an owl was heard, the Hasinai gave a shout of joy. The conas also called on *ynici*—a being who they said came to help because he was moved by their songs and prayers.[5]

The conas applied their treatments and herbs, prayed, threw tobacco and bits of meat on the fire, and lifted handfuls of smoke toward each of the main directions and up to Caddi Ayo. If a patient died, or if a healer's reputation was harmed by too few cures, bereaved relatives sometimes put him to death. The missionaries prayed, offered incense at their church altars, and baptized with holy water. If the few Hasinai who accepted baptism became sick, the conas would have nothing to do with them, saying that the waters of baptism had caused a disease that all their skill could not cure. Some abandoned patients sought help from the missionaries, and sometimes they recovered, but if they died, belief that life was destroyed by baptismal water was reinforced.

Espinosa saw many burial ceremonies for unbaptized souls that winter. The body was kept at home for several hours while mourners succumbed to their grief. Those who prepared the body for burial first bathed it, then clothed it in fresh deerskins or the best clothes owned by the person who had died.

Large quantities of meal, corn, and other eatables were provided for burial with the deceased. A man's bows, arrows, knife, and other things needed in life were buried with him. A woman's domestic utensils, canisters, mortars, and pottery vessels were placed in her grave. Espinosa said this practice occurred "because they say the dead will have need of them where they are going. When asked where the souls of those who die go, they answered, that, as soon as the souls leave the body they travel towards the west and from there they rise once more into the air and go close to the presence of the great captain whom they call *caddi ayo*. From thence they go to wait in a house located towards the south, called the House of Death."[6]

For the Hasinai, death was the last stage of life; the human being left the body to reside in a better place. Those who were left behind grieved only for themselves. When Espinosa asked "what death was and if it was not eternal, [they said] that they believe or persuade the old people to believe that every body is very happy there and that there is no hunger, nor sickness, nor suffering, and that every body remains in the condition they were when death overtook them, so that if a woman dies when she is pregnant she will continue to be in this condition, while if she dies with a child at her breast, she will continue to nurse it — and other errors of a similar nature."[7] Espinosa could not accept such a concept, but the funeral honors he observed forced him to admit, "These Indians understand well and confess a belief in the immortality of the soul."[8]

Early in the twentieth century, many Caddos buried family members on their own land, near their homes. The head of the grave was always at the west, facing the sunrise. The gravediggers stood at the east end, and one fired a shot into the empty grave. The blanket-wrapped body was then lowered into the earth, and the things that should be taken along were placed there, too. A woman needed cooking utensils, plates, and a knife for protection; a man, blankets, a bow, and arrows. Someone in the family kept a fire burning at the east end of the grave for the six days a spirit stayed before starting on its way. All personal possessions, such as clothes owned by the one who had died, were hung on a pole set beside the fire to be bathed in its smoke. At the close of the six days, items unfit for further use were burned. Everything else was given to friends or relatives. Family members came to the grave-side fire for a ritual cleansing of the spirit, bathing their faces, hearts, and bodies in the smoke of the fire and then in the water of a clear-running creek. All others at the graveside washed their faces and hands with water from a pot placed there; then each in turn threw a handful of dirt into the grave. At noon a meal was served beside the grave—a feast to celebrate the soul's release from earth. Food pots were set in a circle. The man in charge of the honors spooned food from each pot into his hand and put it on the middle of the grave. At this same time of year for the next two, three, or four years, a memorial feast would be held for the one who had passed on.[9]

Most old ways have disappeared from use, erased by civil laws governing death and burial. Now, with rare exceptions, interment takes place in Christian cemeteries. Within the privacy of homes and the closeness of community, however, Caddos still find solace in traditional observances.

Like thousands of other American women in the 1990s, Pat Carter goes to work in an office five days a week. She is attractive and intelligent, the working mother of two children. What makes her different is her heritage.

Pat's father is Caddo; her mother, Kiowa. Her father's mother was the center of the family and past eighty when she died. Tradition was one of her legacies.

Pat recalled, "You know, it wasn't so hard when Grandmother died. My sister and I dressed her. Grandmother used to say it was a heavy job dressing the dead, and I never knew what she meant until we finished her dress. I just felt like some sort of a heavy burden came off my shoulders—not that it was a sad task; we did love her so much—but we were so busy trying to remember and do everything the right way. It was a good feeling, knowing we were doing everything the way she had told us.

"She never sat us down and told us how to do things. She just taught us over the years. We'd be talking along about things, and she'd mention something—we never realized we were being taught.

"We painted the red circles on her cheeks. I don't know what that's for, she never told us, but it has to be done. And we put ashes on her earrings. That's to give light—to light the way through the dark. We put her best moccasins on her feet and slit the soles. Grandma always told us, 'Never put anything heavy on a dead person—that would weigh them down.'[10]

Patricia Carter and daughter Hallie in traditional dress (1972).

"We had dinner on the sixth day at noon. If a person dies after noon, you count the next day as the first. Grandmother didn't say 'noon'—she'd point to the west and say, 'When the sun is on that side.' If a person dies in the morning, the day of death is counted as one.

"The old people often say, 'There's a reason for what we do,' and sometimes I don't understand the reason. Like the family stays together for ten days—they don't go out at all. If they need groceries or anything, someone outside the immediate family brings them to the house. It never made sense to me to stay shut up that way, but now I understand. There's comfort in the closeness. And after ten days your mourning is over—you're ready to go out and about your business without carrying that deep grief around with you.

"There are a lot of Caddo ways that are different, like prayer. Sometimes Grandmother would be talking, as if to herself, softly. I'd ask what she was doing, and she'd say, 'Praying.' She always said the Caddos are not like the others—'We are not proud and boastful when we pray. We know we are very small to God. For so many years we have been so poor, had so many hardships. We try to be very small when we pray.' "[11]

Although the winter of 1716–1717 was burdensome, many troubled spirits were placated by the return of St. Denis in early December. He had sold his property in Louisiana and collected the three years' salary owed him for his service as commandant of the fort on the Mississippi. The value of the sum was given him in merchandise—bundles of thread and dozens of pairs of fine-quality woolen hose, both red and blue. There were bolts of lace and lengths of cloth—linen, blue and green twill, satin, scarlet flannel, and blue wool. He transported the merchandise to Natchitoches and purchased horses to carry his boxes and bundles to Mexico. He was ready to begin a business to support his wife and children and was on his way to rejoin them, but finding the conditions at the missions grim, he delayed the reunion.

All six missions were in distress. No supply train had come to relieve the need for food and clothing that became acute within a year after the missionaries had arrived in Hasinai county. They were infrequently visited by members of the tribes and had received no further assistance from them after the churches and houses had been built. St. Denis made three trips back to Natchitoches and, paying out of his own pocket, bought corn for the missions.[12]

CHAPTER 9

SPRING

The winter-weak sun began to regain strength, spreading more warmth over the fields and houses of the Hasinais in the month of February, Tsa-cup-bee.[1] A cardinal posed on a branch of a low bush, gave a tentative call, and with a flicker of red moved to a higher perch. Each day as spring became more certain, he moved a little higher and sang a little stronger, until he was flying from the tops of the trees and calling clearly the notes of the new season. A child watching quietly from a spot bathed in sunshine joined his own song with that of the red bird, *yodoos*.

Ah ho wah hey yea ah
ho wah hey yea
Yodoos nah ba ka no cah
doos ah day a cha wah nah
Ah ha wah hey yah ah
A ha wah hey yea

The child's song said, "Listen to the red bird. He's singing around. It's getting toward morning."[2]

Everyone's spirits lightened with signs of spring. Tsa-cup-bee was the time for an annual gathering of all Hasinais. Fresh game— rabbits, wild cats, birds, badgers—and dried meat were prepared for a feast. Women measured a portion of cornmeal, or whatever else their households had to eat, to take to the mass meeting.

The celebration began early in the day. All the healers and wise old men entered the assembly house for private ceremonies. They spent the morning drinking a tea that two or three of them had brewed from laurel leaves. Later in the day they turned their faces toward the wall and began prayers to Caddi Ayo. A pipe of tobacco continuously passed from hand to hand. Ground tobacco was thrown on the fire. An eagle's wing was given the motion of flight to show that their request for consultation on the weather for the coming year rose high up to Caddi Ayo. After hours of exertion, they knew the forecast and emerged from the assembly house to announce the almanac for the year 1718. They said the year wound be "abundant in nuts and acorns but not in corn because the water would fail at the best season."[3]

The Hasinai planted early corn when the rainy season stopped, usually late April. Before planting occurred, certain traditional tasks had to be performed. Women, girls, and children wove special small mats with little strips of cane brought to them by an old woman who supervised their work. Finished mats were presented to the caddi, who took them to the fire temple as an offering. Men and women met at the caddi's house near the fire temple and worked together collecting black-walnut wood to make hoes, clearing a good-sized area, and stacking a quantity of wood in piles.

Except for the use of a few iron hoes acquired from the French and Spanish, the age-old Hasinai way of tilling the soil was unchanged. The chenesi's field was prepared first. Tillers went next to the caddi's houses, then to those of other leading men. Fields for the rest of the homesteads were tilled in an order fixed by headmen. Men and women worked communally to dig the earth, first with seasoned walnut hoes, then with iron hoes. Hoeing a field took two or three hours. After preparing a plot, the workers enjoyed a large meal served by the householder and moved on to the next in line.

Sowing was done by the individual families. Usually an old woman placed the seeds into the earth; a pregnant woman was never allowed to do the planting. It was believed she might spoil the harvest. Early corn grew less than one foot high, but the mature stalks were covered from top to bottom with small, full ears. This first corn crop ripened in May. It was harvested, the field again cleared, and a different variety of corn planted for gathering in July.

Beans, sunflowers, squash, melons, and tobacco were planted at proper times. Forked cane sticks were stuck in small bean plant hills so that the vines grew up the canes and were protected from mildew and small animals. When it was time to gather the crop, the women simply pulled up the canes wound with pod-heavy vines and carried them home to pick and shell the beans. Sunflowers grew huge, producing edible seeds. Tobacco never failed to produce in season.

When the first corn planting ripened, family and friends gathered, and a cona was called. A cona's blessing was required before a single ear could be eaten or one stalk cut. Anyone who did not wait for the proper prayers would surely be bitten by a snake. Everyone knew someone who had suffered snakebite because he or she had dared to eat too soon. Even dogs, known to be very fond of new corn, were tied with a leg or paw fastened to the neck so that they could not get to the corn before the right time.

The crop was cut while a cona prayed. Some of the corn was toasted, some ground to be made into atole. At the end of his prayers, the cona was given a portion. He threw a bit into the fire and ate the rest. The crowd of family and friends watched, the smell of the roasting corn tingling their taste buds. After the cona had finished eating, everyone was free to eat as much as she or he wanted.

Each season a selection was made of the best ears of corn, as many as needed for two years' planting. In that way, if the coming year was a dry one, there would still be seed for a second year. The ears of corn were strung with the shucks left on and hung high on a forked stick in a place reached by smoke from the home fire pit. Shelled corn was stored in large reed baskets and covered by a thick layer of ashes to keep out rats.

Even if corn stored for cooking had been eaten, the seed corn was left untouched. Instead the family traded for corn at a household where the crop had been better. During lean years when drought or floods caused crop failure throughout the district, the Hasinai gathered and cooked dry seeds produced by wild-growing grasses.

Hasinai celebrations at the beginning of May when the first corn sprouted green in the fields reminded Espinosa of May Day festivals held in Europe. There an elm tree was stripped of all but its top branches and set up as a centerpiece for games and contests.

The Hasinai cut a very tall, straight, slender pine tree and removed the branches, except for those at the top, before setting it up in a level space. They cleaned a circle around the pole to make a wide, smooth path for runners.

Runners took to the path at sunrise. They raced to test endurance more than speed. As runners tired out, the women gave them refreshments. The one who circled the pole the greatest number of times without pause was given enthusiastic approval. Strength and stamina won victories in fights with enemies.

The nation as a whole elected a warrior to serve as a general during wars. Contrary to Pierre Talon's 1697 description of Hasinai war parties — which made them sound like every-man-for-himself sorties — Espinosa said:

> When they set out on a campaign they obey him [the elected leader] implicitly, without disregarding an order in the slightest degree. Even though they may have traveled all day without taking food, they do not even moisten their tongues from the water holes they pass until the leader makes camp — after exploration has been made to see that no enemy is near. After they have gained a victory over their adversaries, the leader sends out a number of the Indians he has with him, others remaining to guard the camp and the rear.[4]

Talon may have misled his French interrogators, or perhaps during the time between his stay with the Hasinai and Espinosa's, Hasinai warriors had learned the value of discipline.

Other conditions had indeed changed since Pierre Talon lived among the Hasinai. Then their weapons were bows and arrows. "But at this time," said Espinosa, "they have secured so many guns, due to their proximity to the French, that they know how to manage them skillfully and use them for war, for hunting when at home, and always carry them when traveling."[5]

The skulls of defeated adversaries were trophies brought back from battle and hung in a tree. On an appointed night there was a gathering at the place where the skulls hung. A number of bonfires were built, and musicians and singers wearing black paint and covered from head to foot with buffalo robes sat with bowed heads while they sang and played mournful-sounding instruments. The people danced to the music without moving from the spot where they commenced; women in one line, men to one side. The dance lasted the greater part of the night. Espinosa described what followed:

> A decrepit old Indian with certain young men surround the tree where the skulls are, each with an arrow pointed in the same direction. They all give a shout or cry. They then turn in another direction and do the same thing. From time to time they shoot a gun towards the skulls and raise a confused cry in unison. When the morning comes they cover their faces and arms with white dirt and carry the skulls and inter them in the cemetery which is near the fire temple where they spend the rest of the day in celebration. The whole thing seems to be the work of hell, the songs as well as the ceremonies connected with it. They offer to these skulls ground *pinole* and other foods which the living instead of the dead con-sume, after they have said their prayers and gone through with their superstitious ceremonies.[6]

If Hasinais died in war or otherwise while away from home, certain honors or funeral ceremonies were held for them. Espinosa related:

> All the people are invited for the appointed day and sufficient quantities of the foods available at the season are provided. Almost a gun's shot from the house, they build a pile of small wood. All gather together, the mourners, men and women stretched upon their beds. A leader among their holy men appears and speaks a few words to them. They set up a weeping, or it might better be called a howling in which the mourning women join. About seven men leave the house, turn their faces toward the east and say their prayers. In front of them they have a very small vase in which there is moist corn meal. After the leader of the old men finishes a prayer they take part of the ground corn from the little vessel and scatter it to the four winds. Three of them, who serve as patrons of the funeral, eat the rest of it. They then re-enter the house and the mourners renew their clamor. All the captains sit down in their order. The patrons seat themselves near the mourners and tobacco and meal is then offered to the old saint. He takes it and walks around the fire which is in the center of the house. He repeats the formula, throws some of the meal and tobacco into the fire, and then turns and presents it to the patrons. This done, two or three Indians come forward and present bows and arrows to the wife or mother of the deceased. Then, one after another, the captains step forward and offer one, six, or eight arrows to the bereaved, according to the condition of each. The women then express their condolence and present their gifts of

beads, a knife, or clothing. This is all collected and all the ornaments of the deceased are added to it. The Indians roll this up, add some fine deer skins, and cover it with a mat woven of reeds. In the meantime an old man and a young man unite in singing a very mournful song. One of the patrons takes the roll on his shoulders and carries it to the fire. Another carries a handful of dry grass and another fire. When they reach the pile of wood, they set fire to it on all sides, throw the mat and all the arrows and clothing on top of it, and burn them to ashes. The confusion is increased by the mournful cries of the mourners and friends. In the meanwhile some of those in the circle laugh and joke. The whole ceremony is crowned by a feast which is divided among all those present. This ended, the company disbands. All this, so they say, is in order that the soul of the deceased may go to the house of rest and when it returns to view its body it will find what has been done with it.[7]

Snow lay six inches on the ground across most of western Oklahoma in mid-February 1978, but except for some icy patches, the highways were cleared. Drivers steered cautiously over the pavement where a rutted turnoff led to the Caddo Community Center. At 11:30 that morning a dozen or so people were already inside the one-room frame building preparing for a memorial dinner. Among them were the daughters and sons of a woman who had died one year ago.

In the kitchen, separated from the rest of the long rectangular room by a counter, a woman stood by the range watching over a kettle of cooking oil that was almost hot enough for her to start dropping in pats of cornmeal dough for fry bread. Other women spread red-and-white-checked cloths over tables set end to end from the counter to the entrance door. At the end of this long dining table nearest the door, they placed a separate, small table.

Cold gusts of air swept into the warming room as people entered in an almost steady procession. They arrived carrying boxes, bowls, pans, and ladles, which were placed on the table. The bad weather had kept many of the oldest homebound, but within the next hour more than fifty friends and members of the deceased's family came. The table was crowded with food brought for sharing.

Cakes, cookies, pies, and a large cardboard box filled with apples, oranges, and bananas were grouped at the head of the table;

vegetable dishes and salads were placed in the center. Two men brought in one, then another, huge canister of water and lifted each onto a smaller, separate table. The sweet, heavy smell of yams baking in the oven began to fill the now-crowded hall.

The daughters, women in their twenties and thirties, finished slicing thin strips of beef and filled three large iron pots with the meat. They put on warm jackets and carried the brimming kettles outside to a wood fire burning a few feet from the building. Snow had been shoveled from the area around the fire pit earlier in the morning, and now small wood logs were burning red hot under the grill on which the pots were set.

When the meat began to simmer, the three women stirred it with oar-shaped wooden paddles. They laughed, talked, and traded teases with a small group of young men and women clustered near the fire's warmth. One of the brothers fed additional sticks to the blaze at intervals until the heat was intense enough to sizzle the grease in an iron skillet placed on the grill for cooking more fry bread.

When the meat was tender and rich in its own gravy, the pots were carried back inside and placed on a space left clear on the long table. Social talk chattering throughout the room fell to a hush as two solemn women started walking slowly around the food-laden table. One held a small cup into which the other spooned a minute portion from each of the dishes. While the cup was being ritually filled, the sisters and brothers stood silently facing the leader chosen for their mother's memorial. A man in his sixties with graying hair, nothing visibly marked him as exceptional, yet he appeared touched by a special dignity. He was holding a handful of cedar sprigs.

Having completed the circuit of the table, the two women carried the filled cup to the semicircle facing the leader. He began to speak so quietly that even in the silence, only those directly in front of him heard his words. A movement of his hand indicated that the eldest daughter should take the cup. After a few more words, he led the way out the door to the still-burning fire. Everyone followed with hardly a sound.

Using sticks as tongs, the leader lifted a few bright coals from the fire bed and arranged them in a mound a few feet distant. He placed a few green cedar twigs on top, and aromatic smoke began to wisp skyward. With hushed intensity, he prayed in the Caddo language: "Everyone that lives must someday die. Yet every person who dies lives. The evergreen reminds us. The cedar smoke rises to carry a message. . . . 'Look here. See, we do not forget the one who has left us.' Bless the one who has passed on. Bless those still living here. We share our blessing and are blessed in return. We remember our loved one who walked with us and spoke with us, and we want her to know we remember."

The eldest daughter emptied the bits of food from the cup onto the smoldering coals. Setting the cup aside, she made a cup of her hands and bent toward the smoke to scoop its gray-white wisps. She drew back erect, face uplifted, and passed her hands over her face, her shoulders, and down the length of her body as though bathing with the smoke. With hands then relaxed at her sides, she lifted one foot, then the other, so that the sole of each was bathed in the rising smoke. Leaving her position, she circled the fire clockwise in a stately walk and stopped on the far side. Each of the sisters, followed by the brothers, other family members, and friends, stepped forward individually and followed the same pattern of "smoking" their bodies before circling the fire.

The surrounding banks of snow and cold air formed a crystalline capsule around the spiritual observance. Its reverent quiet was shattered by the sound of shrill voices and penetrating laughter from a few children playing away from the ceremony. Two or three adults quickly separated from the observers and brought the chastened children back into the circle. The youngest were assisted by a mother or father; hands were guided in the motions of bathing with smoke; tiny feet were extended over the wafting warm air. The last solemn act completed, the leader returned the dying embers to the fire pit, and everyone went back inside to take seats at the table.

No one started to eat. Even the youngest remained quiet, attentive. The leader spoke: "You all know why we are here. Everything we do when we come here has a special meaning. Today we are blessing," he faltered, emotion choking him momentarily, "the one who—the relative who has passed on. Many times I have listened to her words, and that is why I. . . ."

Again his voice broke, and tears slid down his cheeks. "I will try to say a few words now. The children, the grandchildren, I see them. It is for us to let them know the meaning of these things. I am sad that some do not get along so good for when we do these things, the spirit is blessed, the food is blessed. For some of us now, maybe we don't feel so good; we eat the food and we feel good—it does that. We drink this water, and it will make us feel good. It is that way because there is meaning in what we do.

"Now I will try to say a few words." He spoke in the Caddo language, repeating in English what he had said, but conveying less because many times there were no English words to carry the full meaning of the Caddo.

The talk finished, every person silently rose. Forming a moving line, each person paused by the small table holding the containers of water, received a dipperful in a cup, drank it, and returned to his or her place at the dining table.

After the last in line returned to a seat, the room erupted in social sounds as plates were filled and the meal was eaten. Sometime later cold air rushed in as the door was opened and closed by departing friends and family.[8]

As foretold during Tsa-cup-bee, the weather in 1718 produced drought. The previous growing season had also been a dry one. Both the mission and native households suffered deprivation, but they managed to gather their resources for a gala reception in October when the Spanish governor of the province, Martín de Alarcón, arrived with supplies for the missionaries and gifts for the Indians.

The greeting was according to custom. A welcoming party rode out a short distance from the mission to meet the Spaniards. One Hasinai took Alarcón's spurs; another, his sword; and a third, his baton.[9] The Spanish governor was lifted onto the shoulders of the principal Hasinai leader. Another supported his feet. He was carried in this fashion to the mission, where his face was washed and he was presented with a pipe full of tobacco before being lowered onto a "throne" padded with buffalo robes. "This," said Espinosa, "is the ceremony by which they declare anyone a captain-general among them."[10]

After waiting three days for people from throughout the nation to arrive, Alarcón was honored further. The night was lit by bonfires and the Spanish official comfortably seated. Espinosa said, "They put on his head a very curious feather" and began a ceremony that lasted nearly half the night. There was singing, accompanied by fifes and drums; speeches were made one after another in the name of the various settlements; and gifts were offered of beautifully dressed skins or jars of food. The festivities continued until Espinosa asked that the visitors be allowed to rest. Using Hasinai language, he made a speech in the name of the governor, thanking the Hasinais for their politeness and promising them that the Spaniards would always favor them.

Alarcón concluded his visit near the end of November. Before leaving, however, he briefly visited Natchitoches to see what fortifications the French had there.[11]

CHAPTER 10

THE TRADERS, 1719

The first small Natchitoches post, built by St. Denis before he left to set up trade with the Hasinai, was bolstered with the posting of a sergeant and a half-dozen soldiers soon after his departure. Fortifications, however, remained minimal. A wooden wall enclosed the quarters, storehouses, and magazine. There were no cannons or mortar guns. The compound was built on a small island in the Red River, close to a larger one where the Natchitoches had lived since returning to their ancestral home with St. Denis and settling into a mutually beneficial relationship with French traders. The number of soldiers posted at Natchitoches increased after the Spanish missions were established among the Hasinai in 1716. An estimated 150 Natchitoches, Doustioni, and Yatasi households were only "a pistol shot" distant from the fort, which stood the same distance away from Spanish territory.[1]

The nebulous, undefined border between the territory the Spanish considered theirs and that claimed by the French was frequently crossed. The Hasinai found Natchitoches a friendly place to trade, well supplied with French trade goods brought by a river route from the port of New Orleans. The missionaries — close to Natchitoches and distant from a Spanish supply source — sought and received aid from the officer in charge at Natchitoches during the two years of drought that left them in dire need. While the Spanish government struggled to secure its hold on Hasinai territory and thus protect its border from real or imagined French encroachments, the French sought to consolidate their influence with the Natchitoches and Cadohadacho tribes.

In the spring of 1719 the Nasoni chief, a man about seventy years of age, sat waiting for guests at his house near the Red River, a few miles west of the present city of Texarkana. Chiefs of the Nanatsoho, Cadohadacho and Natchitoches waited with him. A messenger had come the day before to announce the approach of a group of French. The Nasoni war chief and six leading men had gone to take horses to them. Bread, a variety of corn dishes, fish, deer and buffalo meat were laid out for a welcoming dinner beneath a brush arbor beside the Nasoni chief's house.[2]

The leader of the French was Bénard de La Harpe, who had received a concession from the Company of the Indies, the trading company governing Louisiana at that time. The Crown had given the company a monopoly on trade in Louisiana along with the business of colonizing; the company then gave large grants of land, called concessions, to individuals who were responsible for bring-ing in settlers and developing enterprises profitable to themselves, the company, and France.

La Harpe's concession gave him command of a post among the "Nassonites [Nasoni], Cadodaquious [Cadohadacho], Nadsoos [Nanatsoho] and Nagodoches [Nacogdoches], savage nations above the Natchitoches," and instructed him to do his "utmost in order to succeed at entering into trade with the Spaniards of the province of Texas, the Kingdom of Leon, and New Mexico and to spare nothing in order to make discoveries in the western part of Louisiana."[3] The more La Harpe expanded French trade, the greater his personal profits would be. Carrying a letter written by Louisiana governor Bienville and addressed to Alarcón, the gover-nor of the Spanish province of Texas, La Harpe brought twenty-five people and large boatloads of European merchandise up the Mississippi and Red Rivers from New Orleans to Natchitoches. A detachment of six soldiers and a sergeant from Natchitoches Post were assigned to go with him.[4]

Father Manuel, head of the Adaes mission, came to say mass at Natchitoches while La Harpe was there. From him La Harpe learned that Governor Alarcón had proposed a Spanish settle-ment among the Upper Nasonis, whose village was about two leagues above the Cadohadachos on the Red River. This news caused La Harpe to waste no time in getting to his post. Guided by the Natchitoches war chief and twelve warriors, La Harpe and his men traveled up the Red River with the boats full of merchandise until they reached the place where the Bear River (Sulphur River on modern maps) entered from the west. At that point the group split, with La Harpe and some of the guides taking a shortcut up the Bear River in a dugout canoe and a portage to the Nasonis, while the others continued on the longer route up the Red River.[5]

The early April sun had moved three hours past noon when La Harpe and his escort arrived at the Nasoni chief's house and were served a silent feast. La Harpe said nothing, and, according to the way of the Cadohadacho, it was impolite to ask questions of a guest before he was refreshed. The hosts' curiosity waited.

After dinner La Harpe spoke to his hosts through an interpreter, saying that he bore a message from the great French Chief, who had learned of the cruel wars made on them by the Chickasaws, the Osages, bands of the Tunicas, Quapaws, and other tribes living along the Arkansas River. La Harpe said the great French Chief had sent him with several soldiers to help defend and protect them against their enemies. He told them he had already sent an order to their enemies warning them to cease their hostilities or he would declare against them.

The chief of the Cadohadacho was older than the Nasoni chief, nearly eighty. He was the most esteemed leader and an eloquent spokesman. After listening to La Harpe, this chief addressed the other chiefs, telling them the time had come to change their tears into joy. It was true, he reasoned, that the greater part of their brothers had been killed or made slaves by their attackers and that they were now no more than a small number. But, he declared, the arrival of the French would prevent the tribes' entire destruction. Their enemies would make no more war on them because they were allies of the French. He counseled them to give thanks to the Great Spirit, whose anger was satisfied, and at the same time assist the French with all the tribes' power to keep their friendship. "They knew by experience," he reminded the other chiefs, "that since the arrival of one of these soldiers in their village, the Naouydiches [Nabedaches] and other wild nations had made peace with them; that it was said that their compatriots who had been killed could not take part in the common joy and add this pleasure to the glory of the life that they had sacrificed for the liberty of their country."[6] It is not clear which soldiers or what enemies the old chief was recalling from his long years of experience, but the emotions roused by his words were obvious. By the time he concluded his talk, the faces of the other chiefs glistened with tears.

After the chief's speech, La Harpe questioned the tribal elders—where were the nearest Spaniards, and what Indians were in the country to the west? He was told about the Spanish mission at the village of their allies, the Nadakos (Anadarkos), twelve days south, and the mission at the Nabedache village fourteen days distant by a road leading south-southwest. The elders told La Harpe that there were several nomadic nations on the north bank of the Red River sixteen days west and that these nations warred against the Apaches of New Mexico. They said that powerful tribes lived on the borders of a great river twenty days northwest of their homes but that they did not know that country very well.

La Harpe observed that his informants' measure of an ordinary day's journey equaled five leagues (thirteen and one-quarter miles), and he was impressed by the accuracy of the information he was given.[7] "It is remarkable," he wrote, "that the savages do not make any mistake when they show the part of the world where the nation dwells of which they have knowledge, and that, taking the bearing of the places with the compass, one is certain of their situation."[8]

La Harpe had been welcomed by the four chiefs at the Upper Nasoni chief's house on the south side of Red River but he found that the Upper Nasoni, Upper Natchitoches, Nanatsoho, and Cadohadacho villages were all on the north side of the river. The Natchitoches lived about eight miles upstream (west) of the Nasoni; the Nanatsoho lived between the Nasoni and the Cadohadacho, whose village was a little more than five miles downstream, east of the Nasoni village. The communities were not villages according to the usual definition. Homes or small family compounds were isolated—spread a distance apart so that enemies would be unable to destroy them all at once. The theory made little sense to La Harpe, who thought the consequence of failing to form a compact village was a weakness that caused destruction. He said the total population had shrunk drastically during the ten years before his arrival, from more than twenty-five hundred to about four hundred. The population had slightly increased with the addition of some Yatasi families about 1717. The Yatasi had been nearly destroyed by attacking Chickasaws. Those who survived took refuge in different directions, some with the Cadohadacho, others with the Natchitoches lower downstream.

One of the men La Harpe brought with him was a geometrician able to check the distance and direction of their travels. Together they took a dugout canoe and made their way upstream in search of a suitable place for La Harpe to locate his establishment. About twenty-seven miles up the Red River, they found a former village of the Nanatsohos. It was a fine location with a small hill jutting out into the river—suitable for the placement of a fort. The soil below looked fertile, and they could see vast prairies, sources of good water, and many fruit trees. La Harpe would have chosen this place if it had been closer to the Cadohadacho, but since he had to depend on them to provide food during his first year, he decided to build his post a short distance from the Nasoni chief's house on the south side of the river, across from the main Nasoni settlement on the opposite bank.

La Harpe's boats, taking the longer route up the Red River, arrived sixteen days after their commander. The next day the four branches of the Cadohadacho began an uninterrupted, twenty-four-hour celebration of their new alliance. They sang, played instruments, removed the clothing they wore, and gave it to each other. La Harpe remarked, "This generosity takes place only among these people; for, in regard to the French, they content themselves only with presenting them some deer hides and these even in small number."[9] For his part, La Harpe made liberal gifts from his stock of European merchandise, "knowing the necessity of drawing them into the interests of the Company, as much on account of the proximity of the Spaniards of the province of Texas as for their alliance with the Nadacos [Anadarkos] and Amedichez [Nabedaches]."[10]

The festivities also gave La Harpe the opportunity to offer the Nasoni chief an additional gift and to ask if he would cede his ground with its cabin and arbor. The Nasoni chief consented, and the other chiefs pledged thirty men to bring cypress wood for the construction of the log house that La Harpe wanted to build.

The Cadohadacho nation celebrated the French alliance again the next day, this time honoring the Natchitoches war chief who had guided La Harpe to the Nasonis and was now preparing to return home. During the previous day's festivities this chief had stripped himself and presented all he had to the Nasoni chief. Recognizing that fact, La Harpe gave some merchandise to the ceremony in honor of his guide.

La Harpe employed his own men to help those the chiefs assigned to bring timber. They soon completed a building 110 feet by 20. The French post, known from then on as the Nassonite Post, was built on a natural levee that rose slightly above the river's floodplain. Great flocks of ducks and geese covered a five-mile-long lake near La Harpe's chosen spot, and though the soil was sandy, it was fertile. La Harpe was gratified by the way corn, beans, all sorts of garden vegetables, and tobacco produced. He was particularly impressed with the number of bolls and the quality of the cotton he harvested from his first planting.

About a half-mile from the river, sandy soil turned to rich black earth and prairies full of indigo plants, strawberries, mushrooms, and morels. Trees common to the area provided a habitat where game thrived. La Harpe listed "red and white cypress, cedar, pine, sweet gum, white woods, willows, ashes, oaks, walnuts, pecans, whose nuts are very good, mulberries, persimmons, which pro-duce a fruit similar to the medlar, but much better, plums whose fruits are very good and an infinite abundance of grape vines, whose grapes are very delicate; my men made six casks of good strong wine there."[11] Bear, deer, rabbit, turkey, and other wild fowl were not far away. Buffalo ranged only twenty leagues from the new post. La Harpe discovered in a short time what the Cadohadacho had known from the time of their ancestors: that their Red River country was generous in providing all basic needs.[12]

The day after work started on the building of his post, La Harpe sent a corporal to Hasinai territory with letters for the Spanish governor and the head of the missions. La Harpe wrote a bold, complimentary letter to accompany the one given him by the governor of Louisiana for delivery to the governor of the province of Texas, and he penned an even bolder one to the head of the missions. His letter to the governor announced that he would joyfully execute his orders from the Louisiana governor "to render all the services that rest with me to the Spanish nation established in the province of Texas."[13] He outlined these services more specifically in his letter addressed "To the Reverend Father

Marsillo, of the Order of the Recollects, Superior of the Missions of the province of Texas, for the Assinais." He wrote:

> Your fervor is great; but you have need of assistance. Touched by these reflections, I have the honor of offering to you a singular and certain means for succeeding there; write to your friends in New Mexico, in Paral and the Kingdom of New Leon that they will find at the Nassonites or at Natchitoches all the merchandise of Europe, of which they could have need, at a reasonable price, upon which they will make undoubtedly considerable profits. I am setting the prices for them, with the proviso that you shall receive from me five per cent of the total sales.[14]

The letter was delivered along with ten pieces of cloth made in Brittany and one piece of damask.

After such a smooth start, trouble seemed unlikely, but La Harpe's own men disrupted the initial ease of his assignment. Four of them evidently decided that life was more pleasant in Hasinai villages than within the confines of a post settlement. They deserted on May 1. La Harpe called on Cadohadachos to pursue them, and they were returned. He intended to punish the defectors but changed his mind when more of his men threatened mutiny unless he issued pardons.

A few days later a soldier told La Harpe that he had learned from an Indian woman that the Nasoni war chief was inciting several other chiefs to scalp all the French. Although La Harpe doubted the information, he took precautions: digging trenches around his post, positioning defensive weapons, and setting six big iron pikes up at the places subject to attack. He next sent his sergeant and six soldiers to escort the war chief to the post. The war chief was brought in and put in irons, and La Harpe sent out a call for the head chiefs of the four Cadohadacho tribes.

The four chiefs were confronted with grim possibilities as La Harpe reproached them for ingratitude and said he wished to leave their place. He warned that if he did leave, they should expect to be destroyed by the Indian nations that were French allies. He stated his resolve to punish the injustice of their war chief by putting him to death in their presence so that it would be clear to them that, although he and his men were few in number, they were not at all afraid of the Cadohadacho, Nasoni, Nanatsoho, and Natchitoches.

The effect of these harsh words, according to La Harpe, was that "the chiefs of these nations testified to me, with tears in their eyes, that it was undeservedly that I accuse them of so dark a perfidy, that they had not forgotten that I was their Calumet chief, that, very far from wishing to destroy us, they were ready to sacrifice their lives for our service."[15] They said it was true that the war chief had the imprudence to hold bad talks, that he had had some discussion with a soldier of La Harpe's nation, but that he was a young man who had talked without reflection. Whatever he had said was of no consequence because he had no authority — the title of war chief had been conferred on him because at age sixteen he had killed two warriors of the Chicacha (Chickasaw) nation who had taken the scalp of his father. The chiefs asked that he be pardoned. La Harpe did pardon the offending war chief, but in the presence of the chiefs of the four tribes, he had the French soldier put in irons.

The corporal La Harpe had sent to the Hasinai with letters for the Spanish governor of Texas and the head of the Hasinai missions brought back responses in early June. The governor's letter asserted that La Harpe was occupying Spanish territory and that all land west of the Nasonis belonged to Spain. The missionary's letter said that he would write his friends about La Harpe's proposal, but since it was unbecoming for a friar to participate in commerce, his correspondence with La Harpe should be kept secret. He also said that the missionaries were not strong friends of Governor Alarcón and that he was not expected to remain in the province for long.

When La Harpe's letter carrier returned to the French post, the Anadarko chiefs came with him. They celebrated four calumets with La Harpe and promised to maintain a good union with the French. La Harpe gave presents to the Anadarko chiefs and entrusted them with a letter to Alarcón. His letter refuted any Spanish claim to the land he occupied and stated that Bienville, who was perfectly instructed on the limits of his government, knew that all the rivers that flowed into the Mississippi and the lands between them belonged to the king of France; that even the province of Texas was French, since La Salle had taken possession of it in 1684 and possession had been renewed by St. Denis.

Eight days later several Anadarkos arrived at La Harpe's post with a confusing story that the Spaniards were angry with the

French because they had been chased away from the Adai [Adaes] mission by French soldiers from Natchitoches. The Anadarkos said the Spanish governor and his soldiers were withdrawing from Hasinai territory. La Harpe rightly judged from this news that France was again at war with Spain. To be sure, he sent his corporal back with the Anadarkos to find out what was going on.

In another four days a Doustioni man who lived at Natchitoches came to tell the Cadohadacho that the French were at war with the Spaniards. His chief sent him to ask the Cadohadacho to take sides with the French. The Cadohadacho chiefs did not want to take part in trouble between the French and Spanish and said so. They did agree that if the Spaniards attacked their place, they would go to war against them.

France declared war against Spain on January 9, 1719. The declaration made in Europe did not reach Natchitoches until June, and the Spaniards at Los Adaes knew nothing about it until the lieutenant in command at Natchitoches led six men to rout them from their Texas post. The seven mounted French soldiers charged into the mission yard, where a flock of chickens peacefully pecked, and took the only two Spaniards there, a lay brother and a soldier, by surprise. Amid a flurry of flapping wings and noisy cackling, a horse spooked, its rider was knocked to the ground, and the lay brother escaped. He made his way as fast as he could to the next closest mission, Nuestra Señora de los Dolores de Ais.

The thoroughly frightened lay brother arrived at the mission and informed Brother Margil that war had been declared and that the French intended to drive the Spaniards out of Texas. He said that 100 soldiers were on their way from Mobile and that the only hope was retreat to the Rio Grande. Brother Margil was startled but not inclined to believe it all. However, since he had only two soldiers and a few faithful Indians to defend the mission, he decided it would be best to abandon the Ais mission and take refuge at Purísima Concepción, where Espinosa had his headquarters and there was a larger military force.

Word of the French attack preceded him, and panic reigned among the soldiers and Spanish families stationed at Purísima Concepción. Fathers Margil and Espinosa argued in vain that some two hundred miles separated the mission's inhabitants from the French. The Hainai, who had grown quite fond of the brown-robed Franciscans, begged them not to leave and offered to send out scouts who would warn the Spaniards of the first approach of their enemy. The Hainai said they would help in case of a fight, but the soldiers, their families, the captain, and even the missionaries and lay brothers chose retreat. They abandoned their station and went to San Antonio, where a mission and supporting presidio had been established.[16]

The corporal sent by La Harpe to check on the situation between the French and Spanish returned to the Nassonite Post accompanied by Hasinai chiefs, who came to assure La Harpe of their friendship. French-Spanish rivalry over borders had benefited, rather than bothered, the Hasinai, Cadohadacho, and Natchitoches tribes. They accepted the gifts and trade items intended to buy allegiance to one king or the other and remained neutral. Long before either the French or the Spanish took up residence in these tribes' territory, the caddis had practiced the art of trading for things they could not manufacture or produce, and they had protected their borders by making allies of their nearest neighbors. The soldiers, traders, and missionaries who crossed their boundaries were too few in number to be considered dangerous, and the European goods they offered were too desirable to refuse the Europeans entry. The French had proved most acceptable because they willingly provided the things most helpful, including firearms and ammunition, and they asked for no more than skins, hides, salt, bear fat, corn, and other garden produce in return. The Spaniards claimed they wanted nothing in exchange for their presents of clothing and tools, but it was evident that they expected the tribes to alter their way of life.

CHAPTER 11

THE RETURN

★ The missionaries waited more than a year for supporting forces to escort them back to their Hasinai stations. The Marqués de San Miguel de Aguayo took office as the governor and captain general of the provinces of Coahuila and Texas in December 1719 and immediately started preparations to enter and recover the Texas province for the dominion of the king of Spain. But months passed and the war between France and Spain was over before all the men, equipment, and supplies could be brought together. The battalion he organized finally left from Monclova, Coahuila, south of the Rio Grande, on November 15, 1720.[1]

A picket of veteran soldiers, familiar with the terrain, headed the column. Five hundred mounted infantry followed in order of seniority. They were divided into eight companies, each company with its own complement of horses and equipment. Next came 500 mules loaded with food and supplies and an additional 400 with no packs. Herds of cattle and flocks of sheep followed the mules.

The battalion reached the Rio Grande in a little more than a month. Because the river was deep and wide, it took another three months to deposit everything on the north bank. During the time it took to cross, Father Espinosa, who had been in Mexico City, joined the expedition. Father Margil and two other missionaries, who had retreated after the French capture of Los Adaes, waited for the caravan at San Antonio along with another apostolic preacher and two friars who were going to the frontier for the first time.

On July 9, 1721, Aguayo's expedition made camp on the west side of the Trinity River. It took very little time for the Hainai caddi to learn they were there. When the Spaniards failed to reach his village as soon as he had expected, the caddi set out to meet them. He was accompanied by eight principal men and four women. One was Angelique, the woman who had helped the missionaries when St. Denis escorted them to Hasinai country.

The Hainai caddi rode into a camp of more Spaniards, more cargo, and more livestock than he had ever seen massed. At first he was speechless. When he did blurt out a welcome for Angelique to interpret, tears choked his words. He said he had been informed of the Spaniards' arrival at the Trinity River fifteen days before, and becoming impatient of so much delay, he had set out to meet them. "He [also] said he really felt the absence of the Spaniards when the Padres and Captain Ramón left [the land of the] Texas," and if the Spaniards had delayed longer, he would have gone to San Antonio looking for them.[2]

Aguayo assured the caddi that the king of Spain had a love for the Texas Indians, "which is verified by having sent the Spaniards to bring them peace and protect them from their enemies" and "the missionary Fathers to instruct them in our Holy Catholic Faith."[3] He gave the caddi a set of clothes—overcoat, jacket, and woolen breeches—and confirmed his title as captain and governor of all the Texas Indians by presenting him with the Spanish symbol of office, a silver-headed baton. The men and women who accompanied the caddi were given clothing.

The caddi and Espinosa rode ahead to the site of the mission where Casañas had begun his service in 1690, near a stream called San Pedro about six miles west of the Neches River. By the time Aguayo arrived at this old Nabedache mission site, the people there had prepared a greeting for him. Women and children from nearby homesteads welcomed the new Spanish governor with gifts of flowers, corn, watermelons, pinole, and beans. He received them affectionately, and to make sure that they went back to their homes feeling content and grateful, he distributed enough clothing to completely dress them all.

Before the day was over, a group of sixty Neche men and women had ridden in firing a salvo with their muskets. As a sign of peace, Neche and Spanish tobacco was mixed and smoked from a single pipe. The Neche caddi spoke of his pleasure in seeing the return of the Spaniards. He offered the service of his people and said they were grateful for the kindness of the Spaniards and hoped it would continue. Aguayo assured him that it would. He gave the Neches meat and corn to eat that night and the following day, but saved the act of clothing them for his arrival at the mission of San Francisco near their home place.

The next visitor to arrive that evening was received with far less pleasure. He was a Frenchman sent by St. Denis from the main Hainai village with a message for Aguayo: if Aguayo guaranteed St. Denis's safe conduct, he would come to relay the orders he had received as commander of the French forces on this frontier. Aguayo offered his guarantee.

Spain's protective trade policies made officials leery of St. Denis's movements. Even though he was married to a daughter of the distinguished Ramón family and had assisted with the establishment of missions among the Hasinai, he was arrested when he made a second foray into Mexico in the spring of 1717. He was accused of carrying contraband and was jailed in Mexico City, but managed to escape and return to Louisiana.

Aguayo continued on toward the old mission sites, reaching the edge of the Neches River. It was overflowing its banks, as were other rivers in the region, and for the next six days the soldiers sawed, butted, and nailed to build an eighty-eight-foot-long, twelve-foot-wide span across the river.[4] On the second day of bridge building, about one hundred Indians, including women and children, came to greet the Spaniards. These Indians lived at Nacono, a Hasinai settlement about five leagues away.

The Nacono had a blind leader. Juan Antonio de la Peña, the diarist for the expedition, wrote:

> Their [Indian] captain, who also happens to be their pagan high priest, is blind. It is presumed that after having been a chief for many years, he took out his eyes in order to become their high priest as is the custom among them. . . . With the greatest of power and natural eloquence, and with signs, he made a long address to His Lordship expressing great happiness for the coming of the Spaniards. To prove his love further, he said that what he esteemed most were God, the sun, moon, stars and the Spaniards. [He added] that the water, airs and fire did not merit such a comparison.[5]

A custom of self-inflicted blindness is not mentioned by any other known firsthand observer. If the Nacono leader was indeed a "pagan high priest"—a true chenesi—and if his words were accurately translated, a major change in Hasinai beliefs had occurred since missionaries first confronted the authority of a keeper of the fire.

Aguayo's interpreter was a soldier who had come in Ramón's 1716 expedition to the Hasinai and had learned their language and signs while stationed at one of the missions. The Nacono leader was told that the Spaniards were sent to bring peace to this large province, to leave it protected with many Spaniards who would remain there, and to bring the preaching missionaries to establish the Catholic religion for the benefit of the Indians. Perhaps with St. Denis in mind, or with the knowledge that Apaches had begun to rampage throughout nearby country, Aguayo explained with extra care that many more Spaniards would be sent to help defend the people from all their enemies as long as necessary.

The blind man spoke long and earnestly to his followers, telling them they should all live as good friends of the Spaniards and join them in whatever wars might occur. He told the Naconos to hunt turkey, deer, and bear and bring food from their homes as gifts. They brought their gifts the next day—tamales, watermelons, corn, pinole, and beans. In return, Aguayo presented each person with a blanket-wrapped bundle. The blankets alone were fine gifts, but Aguayo was more generous. As the blankets were unrolled, an assortment of prized items was uncovered—sets of clothing and a selection of head coverings (like those worn by Indian women in Mexico), ribbons, glass beads, hand knives, large knives, hoes, rings, mirrors, combs, awls, scissors, and chain links. The blind leader was given a silver-headed baton and full Spanish dress, while his wife received twice as much as any other person.

St. Denis rode into camp before the end of the day. Scarcely three years had passed since the king of Spain's decree that St. Denis not be allowed to return to Texas and that both he and his wife be deported to Guatemala.[6] In escaping from Mexico, St. Denis had had to leave his wife behind. Now, representing the French Louisiana government, here he stood, in Hasinai territory, face to face with a Spanish governor. After exchanging formal courtesies with Aguayo, St. Denis asked to be excused, saying he was tired from the sun and his trip and would like to rest, spending the night with his friends the missionaries. Aguayo agreed to postpone their conference until morning.

After morning mass Aguayo summoned his officers and called St. Denis to an official meeting. When asked to give the reason for this visit, St. Denis answered that he was now commander of the French forces on this frontier and wanted to know if Aguayo would observe the truce that the rulers of their two countries had signed in Europe. If so, St. Denis said, he intended to do the same.

Aguayo replied that his orders were to uphold the truce, provided St. Denis evacuated the entire province of the Texas Indians, took all the French back to Natchitoches, and neither directly nor indirectly interfered with the reinstatement of Spanish forces in all of Texas, including Los Adaes. Considering the Spanish force in sight, St. Denis could do no more than comply, but he argued against the Spanish reoccupation of Los Adaes, saying the site was unhealthy and unsuitable for farming. His argument was discounted by Aguayo, who firmly believed that the French wanted Los Adaes to use as a communication link with their post among the Cadohadacho where the opening of a route to New Mexico could begin.

Probably St. Denis had already accomplished the purpose of his overnight stay. Soon afterward, Espinosa and Margil wrote the viceroy asking that St. Denis's wife be allowed to join him in Natchitoches. Telling Aguayo that he would take his men back to Natchitoches without delay, St. Denis left the Spanish camp that same day, but traveled only a little more than twenty miles before stopping for a three-day conference with some Cadohadachos and Indians from other tribes.

On August 2, 1721, with only the Neches River to cross before reaching their former missions, Espinosa and another of the returning missionaries plunged their horses into the river and swam them across to reach the nearest mission, San Francisco de los Tejas. Two other friars left for Purísima Concepción near the main Hainai settlement. Aguayo sent a detachment to help with the work at each of the sites.

The churches and living quarters abandoned two years earlier had decayed or disappeared. At the Neches mission both the church and the living quarters had to be rebuilt. At Concepción only the church was not entirely in ruins. The mission of San José de los Nasones lay in ruins, and no trace of buildings was left at the Nacogdoches mission.

The bridge over the Neches River was completed the day after the missionaries swam their horses across, and Aguayo led his contingent over to reoccupy Texas east of the Neches. They went through the heart of Hasinai country and across the Sabine River to the presidio at Los Adaes only fifteen miles from Natchitoches.[7] The sheer size of his forces, his lavish distribution of gifts, and his intelligent attention to proprieties impressed the Hasinai.

The founding of the four Hasinai missions was marked by celebrations of solemn high mass. Large groups of Hasinais who came to watch and listen had their senses saturated by the sights and sounds. Salutes fired in unison by all the companies roared toward the sky, the ringing of bells vibrated in the air, the clear notes of horns called across clearings, and the roll of drums echoed through the woods.

Clothing gifts were distributed to 185 Hasinais at the refounding of San Francisco de los Neches, more commonly called San Francisco de los Tejas; to 400 at Concepción, near the Hainai settlements; to 300 at San José de los Nazones; and to 390 at Guadalupe, close to the Nacogdoches. Chosen leaders were presented with silver-headed batons, outfitted in elegant Spanish suits, and given the title of captain. Special favor was shown to Cheocas, the Hainai caddi recognized as the leader of all the Texas tribes. Aguayo outfitted him from his personal wardrobe. Cheocas became the proud owner of a blue suit heavily embroidered with gold lace, a matching vest embroidered with gold and silver, and all the accessories that completed the dress of a marquis.

About eighty Cadohadachos attended the ceremony near the Hainai village on the east bank of the Angelina River. Their two leaders were given bundles of clothing for themselves and gifts, like those given the Hasinai, to take home for their people. Peña's diary reported, "The Governor saw fit to do so in order to make them friendly to the Spaniards and also because they are confederates of the Texas [Indians]."[8]

Aguayo was shrewd enough not to accept any gift, even a deerskin, that could be seen as a sign of recompense for those he gave. His message to the Hasinai was:

> The main reason for this trip had been the zeal and desire of His Majesty to save their souls and bring them under his Royal and benign protection and to defend them from all their enemies. . . .

The [French] were only interested in their chamois, buffalo, and horses and especially in their women and children for slavery. . . . Our Lord the King [may God protect him] did not ask for anything. Instead, [the king] would gift them in abundance as they had just witnessed. . . . All [the king] wanted was for [the Indians] to enter the fold of the church. For this reason it was necessary for them to congregate and unite at the said Mission and form a pueblo like the Spaniards. . . . It should not be like before when they did not congregate. This time they were to carry it out without fail.[9]

Espinosa fluently repeated Aguayo's words in the native language, and the Hasinais present unanimously declared their willingness to do as Aguayo said—as soon as they harvested the corn crop in their fields.

The last act in establishing a Spanish mission was to give possession to the Indians it was to serve. In the name of the king of Spain, Aguayo formally gave the Hasinai permanent possession of the land and water rights of missions they were supposed to settle. If they understood Aguayo, it made little difference to them. They knew that the land they stood on was theirs and had been since the time of their forefathers. Aguayo installed a company of twenty-five soldiers at the old Presidio de los Tejas. Then, having provided four missions and a presidio for the Hasinai, he moved on to reclaim the eastern frontier of the Spanish Province of Texas.

Father Margil was sent ahead with a detachment to reconstruct the mission of Dolores de Ais. The mission buildings there had disappeared without a trace. Margil selected a new site about a half-mile south of the present city of San Augustine, Texas. Aguayo arrived and a church for the new mission was built in a single day.[10] There were the usual formalities, and clothing was distributed to 180 Indians.

Unlike Aguayo's arrival at other mission sites, where crowds gathered to greet the Spaniards, not a single Indian was in sight when the expedition reached Los Adaes, about two miles from the present town of Robeline, Louisiana.[11] Soldiers found the Adai living ten or fifteen leagues away, and their chief brought a large, cheerful group to see Aguayo. The chief said they were glad to see the return of the Spaniards because all the Indians of that country wanted to live under their protection. He said they had been forced to move to a more distant and harsh land because the French and the Natchitoches Indians were hostile to them, taking some of their men, women, and children captive. The reason for their hostility, he claimed, was that the Adai had shown regret for the retreat of the Spaniards when the French invaded San Miguel de los Adaes.

More than four hundred men, women, and children were in the group of Adai. Aguayo increased their professed pleasure by handing out clothing and gifts for all of them. He told the Adai that a presidio with 100 soldiers was being established less than one mile away and that San Miguel would be rebuilt for them. They agreed to congregate at the mission when it was reestablished.

Aguayo outlined the construction of the presidio, a hexagonal fortress that he named Presidio de Nuestra Señora del Pilar. Six pieces of cannon brought from Mexico fortified the new installation, which was on the road leading to Natchitoches. One hundred soldiers were assigned to the frontier fortress. Thirty-one men with families formed the nucleus of a Spanish settlement. Fiestas for the dedication of the Los Adaes presidio and its church were held on October 12, 1721, but plans to rebuild San Miguel were deferred—too few Indians appeared for the establishment of this mission to be celebrated.

Aguayo had completed his objectives. The goodwill of the Indians had been won, missions had been restored, and two presidios had been reoccupied. He left the province of Texas confident that it was securely in the dominion of the king of Spain.

Shielded from French intrusion, with permanently established missions and a sufficient military guard to command respect from the Indians, the missionaries were confident that their endeavors would be successful. But the Hasinai were as resistant as ever to submitting their bodies to mission discipline or their souls to Christianity. They grew genuinely fond of the selfless brown-robed Franciscans who visited their homes and helped tend their sick, but seven years passed and not one household came to live at the missions. Only Guadalupe de Nacogdoches could claim some friendly, industrious Indians, but the friars were unable to convert them. A small group of Indians, none of them converts, lived at Los Ais, and not a single Indian came to stay at Los Adaes. The leaders who had promised that people would come either did not have the authority to speak for the tribe or thought a flat refusal was impolite.

The presidio soldiers became accustomed to a comfortably relaxed routine. Because they had no hostilities to deal with, they mostly helped tend the mission crops and cattle. One or two sometimes escorted the missionaries on their visits to Hasinai settlements. When General Pedro de Rivera made a tour of inspection in the spring of 1729, he was disgusted by the unmili' tary appearance and practices of the garrisons. He condemned Presidio de los Tejas as an unnecessary expense to the Crown and ordered it abolished. The general was only slightly more approving of conditions at Los Adaes. On his recommendation, the force there was reduced from 100 to 60 men.[12]

The missionaries to the Neches, Nasoni, and Hainai vigorously protested the removal of the garrison at Presidio de los Tejas. Although they had suffered no attacks, they were convinced the soldiers had shielded them from disrespect and possible thievery by the Indians. Their missions were 60 leagues from the Los Adaes presidio and 150 from San Antonio. If Indian or French attack ever did come, help could not arrive in time.

Seven years of labor had proved fruitless for the missionaries. With the loss of the Presidio de los Tejas, they were discouraged enough to ask for transfer to a more fertile field. The request was granted. Missions Concepción, San José, and San Francisco were moved to San Antonio in 1730, leaving Guadalupe at Nacog' doches, Dolores de los Ais, and Los Adaes presidio as lonely outposts for Spain's claim to the territory of the friendly "Tejas" tribes.

CHAPTER 12

BIG LEG

✴ St. Denis was appointed commandant of Natchitoches in 1722. His family had been allowed to join him by then,
and he built a fine hilltop home on the west side of the Red River
overlooking the small island where the fort and warehouse stood
and the nearby larger one where about two hundred dwellings
formed the main Natchitoches village. There were other French
families settled in the community. Several had farm homes spreading west from the bank of the Red River. In time, the blood of some
of these neighbors would blend to produce respected new families
of French-Natchitoches parentage.

The Natchitoches, Cadohadacho, and Hasinai tribes knew St.
Denis as a man who could be trusted. He kept his promises and
traded fairly. He never required that they accept alien ways, and he
respected theirs. He never tried to overwhelm them with many
words of little meaning; he used their language and spoke as they
did, simply and directly. But he also appreciated, as they did, the
use of symbolic acts when the importance of an event or idea
called for dramatic communication.

Leading men among the Natchitoches, Cadohadacho, and Hasinai displayed outward signs of authority in their dress and bearing. In keeping with their rank, they wore brilliantly feathered
capes, the finest skins, and silver and shell ornaments. They also
possessed an air of dignity. St. Denis more than measured up to

these marks of a leader. He was admired for his handsome ward-robe and his confident carriage. He dressed in continental fashion, his clothing cut from velvet, taffeta, damask, or other rich fabrics and trimmed with lace and silver braid. The colors of his surcoats were bright scarlet, blue, green, or glossy black. Buttons of gold and silver glittered on his coats, and his vests were embroidered with scarlet and gold thread. Snug-fitting knee breeches, usually bright red, covered his long legs to the tops of silk or cotton hose, which followed the shape of his calves. The Indians named him "Big Leg" or "Beautiful Leg," and when they received a paper on which he had drawn the symbols for war and the outline of a well-shaped leg, they answered the call immediately.[1]

As commandant at Natchitoches, St. Denis cemented the tribal friendships he had already formed and paved a path for new ones. The Natchitoches had enjoyed the longest allegiance. The Cado-hadacho, with French traders in their midst since La Harpe had founded the Nassonite Post in 1719, benefited from a regularly traveled trail connecting them to Natchitoches. Skillful French traders had no trouble entrenching themselves in Hasinai villages. The Hasinai were ostensibly governed by Spain, whose commer-cial policy strictly regulated trade with Indians and totally prohibited supplying them with guns and ammunition, but the French were secure among people accustomed to welcoming St. Denis and paid little attention to the slight chance of being caught and punished. In fact, there was not much animosity between the Spanish at Los Adaes and the French at Natchitoches. In 1726 France sided with Spain in a war between Spain and England, and relationships on the Louisiana-Texas border actually became friendly.[2]

While French traders under the direction of St. Denis were peacefully increasing trade with the Cadohadacho and Hasinai tribes, friction between whites and Indians along the banks of the Mississippi was mounting. France was no less wary of the influ-ence of traders from the English colonies than Spain was of the Louisiana French. English traders and slave raiders, vying for control, kept the southeastern tribes stirred up, brief wars broke out, and in 1729 inept handling by a commandant named Chépart turned a conspiracy within the powerful Natchez Indians into a full-fledged uprising. Driven from their homes on the Mississippi by a force of French troops with Choctaw allies, the Natchez regrouped and sought revenge by launching an attack on the post at Natchitoches.[3]

The cane brakes and marshes, the willows that shrouded the shallow water in the bayous and lagoons that wound through the lowlands along the Red River, quivered with invasion in the fall of 1731. A Natchez war party made up of 150 or more warriors trained and experienced in warfare against Europeans moved toward Natchitoches. There were 20 settlers, 40 soldiers, and only enough weapons to arm 42 men at the Natchitoches fort when St. Denis got word of the Natchez advance. He alerted the Natchitoches chief, rushed a request for reinforcements to New Orleans, dispatched a message asking the Spanish at Los Adaes for aid, and sent runners to carry his Big Leg call for help to the Cadohadachos and Hasinais.

The attack came on October 5. The Natchitoches stood as the first line of defense, but they had only 40 warriors and were forced to abandon their village and fall back to the fort. Stalling for time, St. Denis directed skirmishes that held the Natchez advance for nine days. One at a time and in small groups, as warriors received the message from Big Leg, they came to defend the fort. Skirting the Natchez or slipping through at night, 250 fighters rallied to St. Denis's call. The Hasinai responded with a large force. The Spanish governor at Los Adaes sent 11 but for some unexplained reason they brought no guns. The Natchez dug entrenchments, threw up embankments, and built fortifications to lay siege.[4]

On October 13 the Natchez brought out a captive French woman. They tied her to a frame in full view of the fort and set a fire to burn her alive. The collected force led by St. Denis boiled out of the fort in a fury, charging into the nearest enemy with whatever weapons they had. They fought hand to hand for six days and nights. The Natchez lost seven of their leaders and asked for a truce. They began to take down their embankment and fill in their ditches, but when they thought St. Denis had lowered his guard, they renewed the battle. The fight continued for almost four more days before the Natchez began to retreat. Pursued by the Natchitoches, the Natchez retreat turned into flight that only a few survived.

The French reinforcements sent from New Orleans were still a week's march from Natchitoches when they were met by a messenger from St. Denis who described the defeat of the Natchez.[5] One hundred Cadohadachos had responded to the paper with the Big Leg drawing. The distance they had to travel made them too late for most of the action, but by answering St. Denis's call for help, the Cadohadachos proved their loyalty to a friend.

After a flood in 1735 St. Denis moved the garrison and trading post to higher ground on the west side of the Red River. With the building of a stockade, fourteen new houses, and a church, Natchitoches Post became a prospering new town. Merchandise from French ports on the Gulf arrived regularly, delivered by the relatively easy all-water route. A plentiful supply of goods flowed between traders and tribes, and St. Denis annually presented ample gifts from the government of France to the Natchitoches and Cadohadacho. The Hasinai continued to look on Los Adaes and the mission at Nacogdoches as places for the distribution of presents, but the Spanish gifts were no competition for the goods provided by French traders and Spanish trade was meager. The Spaniards' annual supplies came by caravan, carried overland for two thousand difficult miles. Even the residents of the small military settlement at Los Adaes were mostly dependent on Natchitoches for basic supplies. Their presence marking the eastern boundary of Spanish occupation was largely ignored by the Hasinais until it interfered with commerce.

Spain and Frence were unified by a compact (signed in 1733) to withstand English colonial and commercial aggression, but the dividing line between Spanish Texas and French Louisiana was still subject to the jealous interests of both nations.[6] In the spring of 1737 a French trader named Jean Legros rode out of Natchitoches leading two horses packed with gunpowder, French cloth, a flag, three muskets, axes, knives, kettles, a hat, and shirts intended for the Cadohadacho. He followed the established route from Natchitoches to the Cadohadacho villages, through Hasinai country by way of the Sabine River.[7] Twelve leagues from Nacogdoches, Legros was arrested by five soldiers and a sergeant. Accused of trying to deliver illegal goods to Hasinai villages in Spanish territory, his goods were confiscated, and he was put in stocks at the Los Adaes presidio. He was released a short time later and returned to Natchitoches.

The Hasinai were outraged by Spanish interference in their trade with the French. Fourteen angry leaders met in a council of war, then rode to consult with St. Denis at Natchitoches. Their warriors represented a formidable force; they outnumbered the Spaniards and were better armed. Their unity made it clear to the officers at Los Adaes that, although they might live in Hasinai country as friends, Spain had no authority there. The tribes could easily get rid of the Spaniards on their own; if St. Denis joined them, Spain would lose the territory to France.

St. Denis was as angry as the chiefs. As soon as Legros reported his treatment, St. Denis wrote a searing letter to the lieutenant in charge at Los Adaes:

> Perhaps we are at war, or perhaps you mean to prevent us from going to Kadodachos. What is meant that five soldiers should be sent by a sergeant to arrest one of my Frenchmen who was going to Kadodachos by the direct road? Did you know that he was sent by me? For, if you were ignorant, you should know that he was. You confiscated all his goods; on what grounds? You put him in the stocks; perhaps he is a Spaniard! You wished to ramrod him; where is your justice? You were wise that you did not do so, that's all I've got to say![8]

St. Denis demanded an immediate restoration of the trade goods and closed the letter, which he wrote in Latin, with the threat, "Otherwise I will close all commerce with you from today, and will pursue you in the name of my king even to the viceroy, or even to the king himself, if that should be necessary."[9] By the time the chiefs arrived at Natchitoches, St. Denis was able to tell them that there was no need for war—the Spaniards had made restitution, and he was satisfied.

St. Denis died in 1744. Friends and acquaintances, French and Spanish high officials, soldiers, settlers, traders, vagabonds and priests, chiefs and warriors of the tribes who had fought under him, and the entire Natchitoches nation attended his funeral. St. Denis's son, Luis, took over the role Big Leg had played in Indian relations. The transfer of authority from father to son seemed a natural one to the Natchitoches, Cadohadacho and Hasinai whose caddis descended by direct bloodline.

Luis St. Denis, raised on the frontier without the educational advantage his father had had, was not able to read or write well enough to quality for his father's official position. He never rose above the rank of lieutenant in the Natchitoches garrison, but that made little difference to the Indians who came to deal with him in the home his father had built for the family. Luis St. Denis kept their devotion and managed the trade network well. His special relationship with the Indians was officially recognized, and there were standing orders forbidding any Natchitoches commandant to tamper with it.[10]

There was a trade depot for the Cadohadachos on the site of La Harpe's old Nassonite Post above the big bend in the Red River, and there was another farther down the river at a village that the French called Petit Caddo. A third station was located at a Yatasi village near modern Shreveport. French interpreters also lived among the Hasinai and there were resident traders in the larger villages. Years of trade passed uninterrupted before the tribes were again provoked by a Spanish threat to cut off their trade with the French.

A minor disturbance was created in 1751 by an attempt to enforce the royal decree that no French entering Texas or New Mexico should be allowed to return to Louisiana. A year later the Hasinai tribes were again roused to rid themselves of Spaniards who interfered with French trade. They were alerted when a Spanish official assigned to inspect trading activities in northeast Texas came to Nacogdoches in the autumn of 1752.[11] He found ample evidence of a healthy trade with the French at Nacog-doches. The chief men openly described their trade arrangement. They told the inspector that the Spaniards would be welcome to live in their village if they supplied goods as satisfactorily as did the French.

The inspector rode on to the Hasinai-Nasoni village without incident, but his tour was brought to an abrupt halt when he headed toward the Anadarko settlement where Luis St. Denis had a trading post. Before reaching the village, the official was stopped by the Anadarko chief. The chief's message was simple: if the Spaniard valued his life, he should hurry away. The inspector wisely scurried to the presidio at Los Adaes.

Warriors were already gathering at the Anadarko village. Five hundred soon assembled. A war council of caddis and headmen discussed ridding their borders of Spaniards and decided to declare St. Denis their chief. A delegation left for Natchitoches to invite the son of Big Leg to lead them against the Spaniards.

St. Denis vehemently rejected the proposal. He told the Hasinai delegates he did not approve of exterminating the Spaniards. As skillful as his father in calming the fervor of warriors, St. Denis played on their understanding of alliances to convince the leaders that the plan was rash. He explained that his king and the king of Spain had made a pact allying their two nations and that, if Spaniards were attacked, he and the French soldiers were pledged to come to their aid.[12]

The combined strength of the Hasinai tribes and their allies was more powerful than any force the French and Spaniards could muster, but the Hasinai had no heart for forcing their French friends into a war against them. The warriors disbanded. They returned to their homes, the dust raised by their ponies' hooves settling on separate trails and clouding the collective might of the Hasinai nation.

CHAPTER 13

CHANGES

Back when the Hasinai and Cadohadacho got their first French guns, or even before, when they fought and hunted with bows and arrows, their superior weapons and skill made them powerful. They roamed hunting grounds unchecked and traveled confidently to the open range where buffalo were found. But as guns and horses came into the hands of more and more Indians outside the homeland of the friendly tribes, danger grew and there were changes.

From the time the French arrived in Louisiana, their primary goal was to open trade with the silver-rich Spaniards in Santa Fe, New Mexico. This ambition led explorer-traders to establish bases along three rivers—the Red, the Arkansas, and the Missouri—which flowed into the Mississippi from the west. St. Louis (Missouri) was the general trade center that supplied the Missouri and Arkansas River tribes, just as Natchitoches furnished merchandise for the Cadohadacho and Hasinai tribes. From each base the French widened their sphere of influence, looking for new Indian trade alliances.

When explorations west of the Mississippi began in the 1700s, the French were using an advanced musket called a fusil. It was cumbersome and often failed to fire, but it was lighter than the old matchlock, and a flint attached to the hammer struck sparks on the grooved steel of the pan to set off the priming. Osages, already guilty of hostilities against the Cadohadacho, were the first among the tribes of the lower Missouri River to be supplied with French fusils. The French made allies of the Osage because their villages on the Missouri River and on the Osage River (in modern Vernon County, Missouri) gave them "the power to open the watertradeways of the Missouri."[1]

At the same time that La Harpe was exploring west and north from his Nasoni post (1719), another Frenchman, Claude Du Tisné, was traveling southwest from the Osage River to the Arkansas River in what is now Oklahoma. La Harpe negotiated with nine bands of the Wichita Indian group and left the French flag flying at the Tawakoni village on the South Canadian River near where it flows into the Arkansas (close to the present center of Oklahoma's eastern border). Du Tisné met with other Wichita bands living farther north and west and, ignoring their objections, continued westward to a Comanche camp. The Wichitas warred with the Comanches and did not want French guns in the hands of their enemy. Du Tisné planted a flag of truce in the Comanche camp and came away convinced that the French could safely reach Santa Fe if the Wichitas and Comanches could be brought to friendly terms.[2]

Missouri, Arkansas, and Red River bases brought the French closer to Santa Fe, but Comanches effectively blocked the rest of the way along the Missouri and Arkansas Rivers and Apaches shut off the Red River route. To keep those fierce, nomadic riders of the plains confined to a range farther west, the French made it official policy to pamper the Osage and supply their warriors with guns and ammunition. Unauthorized traders, the wandering coureurs de bois, carried on less legitimate trade—exchanging guns, hatchets, knives, scrapers, fleshers, and awls for furs, slaves, and horses captured by the Osages. Legally and illegally, the Osage received arms and ammunition through trade with the French and horses and slaves through trade with or theft from other Indian nations. The Osage rode arrogantly, extending their domination south to the Arkansas River.[3]

The territorial boundaries of tribes were largely defined by rivers, mountains, and other natural barriers. The Arkansas River, flowing southeast to the Mississippi through the present states of Oklahoma and Arkansas, was such a boundary. Important markers for Cadohadacho hunting grounds were the Canadian River, a chief tributary that flowed across Oklahoma from the west and

joined the Arkansas River in east-central Oklahoma; the Red
River from the point where the Washita River flowed in from
Oklahoma; and the dense belt of woodland later called the Cross
Timbers. The Arbuckle Mountains of Oklahoma on the west and
the Ouachita Mountains of Arkansas on the east helped enclose
the vast plains that were traditional hunting grounds for the
Cadohadacho and Hasinai. A natural ford in the Red River near
the Cadohadacho settlement called Nanatsoho gave hunters easy
access to immense herds of buffalo on the plains and measureless
numbers of beaver and black bear along the Blue, Boggy, and
Kiamichi Rivers, which watered the plains before draining into
the Red River.[4]

The Cross Timbers, a famous landmark that served as a dividing line between eastern and western Indians in Oklahoma and
Texas, extended some four hundred miles in a southwesterly
direction from the Arkansas River to the Brazos River in Texas.
Except for rare breaks north of the Red River, the Cross Timbers
were continuous strips of oak, hickory, and elm that varied in
width from five to thirty miles. In some places the oaks grew large,
but most of the trees were bushy. In many places a thick under-
growth of dwarf oak tangled with grapevine and greenbrier made
the Cross Timbers virtually impenetrable.[5]

South of the Red River, in Texas, the Cross Timbers split into
two belts separated by a broad, treeless area called the Grand
Prairie. The edge of the Grand Prairie fringed by the eastern Cross
Timbers was generally recognized as the boundary of Hasinai
territory. The woodland forests surrounding Hasinai settlements
in northeast Texas merged on the west with a blackland prairie
that rolled gently toward the Trinity River and blended into the
eastern Cross Timbers. Extensive buffalo herds ranged the blackland prairie along with deer, coyotes, foxes, and rabbits, and the
Cross Timbers offered hiding places for both hunter and hunted.
The Grand Prairie supported fantastic herds of buffalo and other
large grazing animals on which the Lipan Apaches depended for
food, shelter, and clothing.[6]

As guns and horses changed and challenged the strength of
Hasinai hunters, they became increasingly cautious. They remained
concealed at the edge of woods before stepping out into a clearing.
Like discovered deer, they stood still, moving only their heads
with a slow turn so that their eyes could measure danger. They

surveyed the prairie for some time, searching for anything unusual before moving out into the open, camouflaged by branches from trees.

Apaches, driven from the north and west by gun-carrying Comanches, rampaged over the buffalo plains. Comanches got their first guns at a big peace meeting engineered by the French in the fall of 1724. The French gained passage through Comanche country to Santa Fe by negotiating an agreement that Comanches would live at peace with other French allies—Osages, Otoes, Iowas, Panismahas, Missouris, Illinois, and Kansas. Comanches won a share in the trade benefits that the French gave tribes friendly to them. The Comanches making the agreement were eager to shoot the guns carried by the French and their Indian allies, but did not know how until a Frenchman gave them lessons.[7]

Apache warriors, still fighting with bows and arrows, became desperately bold in their attempts to control the buffalo range. Roots of hatred lay undying on the buffalo plains and sprang to life each season. There is no known time when Apaches and Hasinais were not enemies. This deep enmity was shared by many tribes neighboring the Hasinai nation—"tayshas" pledged to fight Apaches with the Hasinai.[8]

Holding to the ancient policy of making peace with bordering tribes, the Cadohadacho and Hasinai continued to build and maintain a buffer zone for the core of their nation. Wichita bands, caught between Apaches on the west and Osages on the east, gave up trying to protect their people and property on the Arkansas River and its tributaries. Wichita tribes or subgroups—Tawakonis, Taovayas, Yscanis, and Wichita proper—moved south and resettled near the Trinity River in the vicinity of present-day Palestine, Texas; on the Brazos River near present-day Waco, Texas; and on the Red River, some distance west of the Cadohadacho villages. A need for strong allies and French trade drew these tribes close to the borders of Cadohadacho-Hasinai territory and made them tayshas.[9]

Nabedache lands near San Pedro Creek (a western tributary of the Neches River in what is now northwestern Houston County, Texas) were the most western occupied by the Hasinai. Because of their location the Nabedache had been the first of their nation to meet Spanish soldiers and missionaries, and for nearly half a century, as the road from San Antonio to Nacogdoches—the Camino Real de los Tejas—became well established, the Nabeda-che remained the first to observe the approach of Spaniards. In the mid-1700s Spanish officials referred to Nabedache land as San Pedro and called the Nabedache either Indians of San Pedro or Tejas Indians.[10]

Early in September 1767 another party of Spaniards crossed San Pedro Creek. At their head was the Marqués de Rubí, sent to check on military defenses along the northern frontier of the territory claimed by Spain. A capable engineer, Nicolás de Lafora, kept a diary and made a map of the districts they toured. He recorded that they crossed the Neches River and a little distance beyond, "climbed a hill on top of which there is a mound that seems to have been made by hand."[11] The mound was one of those built by the "Old People," *Keeonah wah'-wah haemay'che,* ances-tors who had settled in the Neches valley about A.D. 800.

The mound described by Lafora can still be seen twelve miles east of Alto, Texas, by anyone traveling Texas 21—a route that closely follows and sometimes covers the Old San Antonio Road followed by eighteenth- and nineteenth-century travelers.[12] The highway abuts a high, flattop mound where a temple or assembly house once stood as a center for ceremonies. Across the road a low temple mound and a burial mound rise above level ground.

Structures atop the temple mound may have housed a perpetual fire, a "sacred fire" like that the missionaries found tended by the chenesi. Six times, about every eighty years before they abandoned these mounds (no one knows why), the Old People covered destroyed temples with fresh earth and erected new temples. Six times they added layers of earth to the burial mound, raising it to a height nearly twenty feet above the base, which was ninety feet in diameter. They carried baskets filled with thirty to forty pounds of dirt to spread on the mound tops—so many baskets filled with soft earth dug from a nearby creek that a deep pit remains visible today.

A Caddo speaker today points to a drawing of a grass house sitting on a mound and calls it *nah-kuck-coh-doe-tse,* "something sitting on top of something."[13] There is no real memory of the Old People or why they created earthen mounds on the prairie fringed by the western edge of Hasinai woodlands. It was not until twentieth-century archeologists began uncovering secrets that

Hasinai descendents learned that the mounds were built up in ceremonial stages over a period of four hundred to five hundred years, beginning around A.D. 900, and were spread with a final dirt cap about A.D. 1300.

Lafora mentioned only one mound in his diary. "It was here," he recorded, "that the first Spaniards met the principal chiefs of this nation with whom they negotiated a peace observed without violation by the Indians ever since."[14] The other mounds were either too far off the road or looked the same as the rolling hills of the surrounding country.

Rubí inspected the missions of Guadalupe de los Nacogdoches and Dolores de Ais, and the Los Adaes presidio — Spain's fragile claims to northeast Texas. At the Nacogdoches mission he found two soldiers, their families, and Fray José de Calahorra y Saenz, who had lived alone and labored in hope of converting the Nacogdoches for forty-three years. No Indians were there. At the Ais mission there were two missionaries and no Indians; at Los Adaes Rubí discovered that there were two missionaries, sixty soldiers, and thirty Spanish families, but no Indians.

A need for cost cutting, not trade or French-Spanish border disputes, had caused the king of Spain to send Rubí on his tour of inspection.[15] France had fought and lost a war with England over the possession of North American colonies. The battles were waged far from the Red River, mostly around Lake Champlain on the New York–Vermont state border and Quebec, Canada. When the war ended in 1763, France lost Canada to England and ceded Louisiana to Spain; the Mississippi River became New Spain's eastern frontier.[16] Spain no longer needed to keep jealous watch on the Texas-Louisiana border, but the English lost no time in advancing toward the lower Mississippi. In Europe Spain and England were on the verge of war.

Protecting North American holdings would be costly for Spain. Louisiana had to be occupied, Gulf Coast defenses needed strengthening, and the Indians of the enormous province had to be controlled. Tribes in the Red River valley and adjacent regions in northeast Texas — the Spaniards called them *norteños*, "nations of the north" — had been under the influence of the French and were hostile to Spain.[17] Rubí's job was to assess the best allocation of the Crown's resources.

The Norteños were hostile because they believed the Spaniards had become allies of the Apaches. Lipan (eastern) Apaches had alternately terrorized and petitioned for peace at San Antonio since the beginning of that Spanish settlement. Harried by Comanches, they became friendlier, and a treaty was celebrated in San Antonio in 1749. A quarter-century of military action had failed to halt Apache depredations, and authorities were finally persuaded that missionaries could pacify the tribe. San Sabá mission for the Lipan Apaches and a presidio to protect it were built in 1757. Pursued by a multitude of enemies, the Lipans were sorely in need of a safe haven, but instead of keeping their promise to congregate at San Sabá, they used the mission as a temporary shelter. Small groups fled there following attacks on Indian camps or settlements but stayed briefly.

In March 1758 two thousand embittered Norteño warriors, at least half armed with guns, took vengeance. The mission was sacked and burned. Two priests and a half-dozen others in the compound were killed. Survivors who escaped to the presidio identified Tonkawas, Comanches, Bidais, and Tejas among the warriors. Spaniards at this time persisted in called the Hasinai tribes Tejas. Belief that Spaniards were allied with the Apaches could have caused Hasinai warriors to violate more than a half-century of friendship, but Father Calahorra, the experienced old missionary at the Nacogdoches mission, stoutly defended their Spanish loyalty, declaring, "The Tejas and Tawakonis were mortal enemies of the Apaches but not the Spaniards."[18]

Several times during the spring of 1760, a Tawakoni delegation visited Father Calahorra, seeking peace with the Spaniards. Another delegation, made up of Hasinai from San Pedro and some Nasonis, came to the Nacogdoches mission to plead for peace in the name of the Tawakoni and their northern allies. Calahorra smoothed the way for peace negotiations, but a change of officials in the Spanish government and an accompanying change of policy foiled negotiations.[19]

By the time Rubí came to check on Spain's military defenses along the northern frontier, there were observable changes in the Hasinai attitude toward Spaniards. Lafora listed tribes in the Spanish province, naming Adai, Ais, Hainai, Nacogdoches, Neches, Nasoni, Nabedache, Nacono, Tonkawa, Tawakoni, Taovaya, Yscani (who he said were farther north), and several coastal and more western tribes. "All these tribes," he said, "are allied with the

Texas [Hasinai] Indians and our safety in that province is entirely dependent upon their fidelity. They have little respect for the Spanish and we are admitted only as friends, but without any authority."[20]

Rubí blamed the Spanish for inviting the hostility of tribes allied against the Lipan Apache. In his opinion the first step toward solving the problem was "to drive the Apaches out of every Spanish mission, presidio and settlement on the frontier."[21] Having seen missions without converts, a decaying garrison without arms or uniforms, and soldiers' families clothed in tatters, he viewed Spain's possession of Hasinai country as imaginary. He said the expense of supplying the territory was a waste and recommended that it be abandoned.[22]

Near the road leading through the woods to the Nabedache settlements near San Pedro Creek, a lookout kept watch from the top of a tall tree. Hidden from sight but seeing all about, he was a guard against surprise. A few months after Rubí's tour, the lookout saw Father Gaspár José de Solís approach the village. Entering the San Pedro community, the priest found a large, thickly settled area of grass-covered, dome-shaped houses. Sent to inspect mission conditions, he gave attention to details. He noticed dogs with thin, pointed snouts and said they were known for their intelligence and cunning. Corn was abundant. Women were "pretty, being fair and very good natured." He complimented their long hair and commented on their deerskin dresses, fringed and bordered with varicolored beads, and the earrings made from long, smooth bones that some of them wore. The men he thought "not ugly"—they were well built, wore only breechclouts and a wealth of colored beads and feathers, and painted themselves with red and other colors.[23] Except for his mention of fruit orchards and flocks of young chickens and turkeys scratching about the village, probably small evidences of Spanish influence, Solís's descriptions were almost a repetition of those given by religious and secular observers from Joutel forward. Some of his other remarks, however, made the Nabedache seem quite changed from earlier times.

He said they were great thieves and drunkards and blamed these vices on whiskey and wine furnished by the French of Natchitoches. All previous accounts praised Hasinai honesty and industry. The caddis discouraged dishonesty with swift punishment, and the tammas controlled indolence by flogging.

According to Solís's description, there was a startling change in governance. "In this village," he said, "there is an Indian woman of great authority and following, whom they call Santa Adiva which means 'great lady' or 'principal lady.'" The woman, Solís said, was married to five Indian men, lived in a very large house that was divided into many rooms, and was served by many men and women, who were called "tamas conas" and were looked on as priests and captains. The rest of the nation brought presents and gifts to her. "In short," he wrote, "she is like a queen among them."[24]

Any Frenchman or Spaniard who stayed any length of time among the Hasinai said supreme authority was held by the chenesi, whose position was hereditary. Next in authority were the caddis, who also inherited their positions. The only exception to male leadership recorded before Solís's visit was Tonti's description of a Cadohadacho woman who was the leader of her village. Casañas reported that the wives of the caddis or chenesis had a special status and were treated with regard, but the highest respect and reverence were reserved for their husbands.

It is possible, but just barely, that Santa Adiva was honored as the mother of an heir too young to serve. It is probable that the epidemics decimating Hasinai villages after the coming of the missionaries or the Spanish policy of presenting the staff of leadership to an elected leader had broken the hereditary chain. With so few records available, it is a mystery that traditional leadership was so changed that Solís saw a woman treated "like a queen" in the village near San Pedro Creek.

On his way from San Pedro to Nacogdoches, Solís met a more traditional Hasinai leader. Solís identified him as "captain" of the Nabedache and said his name was Bigotes. The use of Spanish names and titles was another change brought about by Spanish influence.

Shadows thrown by the long, thin needles of pine trees feathered Solís's head and shoulders as he passed through the woods to the clearing where the mission of Guadalupe de los Nacogdoches stood carefully tended. Wooden stake fences enclosed the small adobe church and several sturdy wood houses—dwellings for the clergy, a kitchen, a granary, and soldiers' quarters. The harsh outline of the complex was softened by twining vines of medicinal herbs and roses. Peaches, blackberries, persimmons, and other fruits sweetened the site. Eighty sheep and goats; thirty or so oxen, cows, and bulls; twenty-five calves; twenty-five gentled horses; twenty gentled mules; and two droves of mares, each with its stallion, gave the mission substance, but the administrative books for the fifty-year-old mission showed only twelve baptisms, eight burials, and five marriages during its existence.

Like so many men of the church who had preceded him, Solís judged that, except for a few who were sometimes stubborn and bad, the Nacogdoches, Nabedache, Hainai, and Nasoni were peaceful, gentle, and jovial and could be congregated at the missions. Nevertheless, new generations in the Hasinai settle-ments lived much as always. Babies were born in a house specially built on the bank of a creek or river near the family home. A woman went there when she felt pangs; grasped a short, strong, forked stick that was fixed firmly in the ground; and delivered her child. The closest the infant came to baptism was when the mother walked into the flowing water to cleanse herself and her newborn.

The greatest change in the people was in their health. They suffered from smallpox, measles, typhoid fever, other unexplained fevers, bloody dysentery, blisters, and boils. Many were left looking unsightly and unclean. Solís reflected the medical opinion of his time, explaining that diseases were vices of the blood caused by diet and drink. He principally blamed ground nuts, the fruit of the medlar tree, whiskey, and sugarcane wine mixed with bear grease.

A Hasinai leader called Captain Sánchez came to visit Solís at the Nacogdoches mission. Sánchez was reputed to be capable of marshaling all the allied forces. Spanish officials spoke of him as a longtime friend who had helped Father Calahorra make peace with the Wichita bands.[25] After meeting Captain Sánchez, Solís observed, "All the Indians of this Province of Texas, of all the nations, esteem men who are handsome, brave and strong because they appoint the strongest and most valiant as captains, and they want them to be the strongest and most valiant."[26]

CHAPTER 14

TRUE CHIEFS

The name, Cadohadacho, stems from the words *caddi* and *hadachu,* which translate as "chief" and "sharp pain." Combined in the name, the words have the grander meaning of "main or true chiefs." In the 1770s history assigned a key role to two true chiefs—Tinhiouen of the Cadohadachos and Bigotes of the head Hasinai tribe, the Hainai. French, Spaniards, and other tribes called on these leaders during years that were troubled by hostility, epidemics, and snarled diplomacy.[1]

When Cadohadacho tribes learned that the king of France had transferred Louisiana to the king of Spain, they were not too concerned. French traders either lived in or regularly visited settlements in Louisiana and Texas, and friendship ties went all the way back to the elder St. Denis, the white chief they called Big Leg. His son, Luis, a trusted friend whom the tribes had known since he was a boy, still lived in Natchitoches, and Luis's brother-in-law, Athanase de Mézières, had earned their respect as a trader and as commandant of the Natchitoches Post after the death of the elder St. Denis. It seemed unlikely that the French would behave like the Spaniards, though the notion became more troubling and believable when trade goods and gifts dwindled.

The flow of goods from France to the port of New Orleans was checked after Spain took control of Louisiana, and supplies for the traders operating out of Natchitoches were minimal while Spanish officials were trying to decide how their regulations regarding trade should be applied to Louisiana. The situation was still confused when Antonio de Ulloa, the first Spanish governor of Louisiana, and Hugo O'Conor, the acting governor of Texas, issued proclamations that threatened death for any French trader found in Texas.[2]

Late in 1767, Guakan, a Yatasi chief, came for a talk with Luis St. Denis at the family cattle ranch near Natchitoches. Guakan spoke grimly, telling about a French trader named Du Buche who had left Natchitoches to bring merchandise to the Yatasis. Du Buche took the usual route traveled when going by land, but he never reached the Yatasi village because the Spaniards arrested him. Guakan said his warriors were preparing to take vengeance on the Spaniards at Los Adaes presidio. St. Denis managed to persuade the chief to call off the warriors and reported the incident to Ulloa.

Ulloa wrote O'Conor, describing how close Los Adaes had come to being ravaged. Ulloa cautioned:

> These nations have been accustomed for a long time past to this sort of trade and commerce, and any attempt that may be made to cut it off suddenly will have very evil consequences both on those fron-tiers and in this territory. . . . In view of these considerations, the method followed here [in Louisiana] to keep them peaceful and friendly is to give them presents, so that they never once come to talk without getting something, and to assure them that trade will be kept up in the same way as it has been carried on in the past. This method has succeeded with the chief Guakan.[3]

Having decided that it was in Spain's best interest to follow the French pattern for Indian relations in Louisiana—with some typically stringent Spanish regulation—the Louisiana governor appointed the most able person available to serve as lieutenant governor in Natchitoches. Luis de St. Denis might have been chosen if his formal education had matched his frontier knowl-edge. As it was, Mézières, able to write easily in French, Spanish, or Latin, eloquent of speech, liked and trusted by the natives of the district, was given the appointment in 1769.

Rumors that Osage parties raiding Cadohadacho settlements were supplied by a French trader jarred the smooth relationship long enjoyed by the Cadohadacho and the French. Tinhiouen discovered truth in the rumors when he pursued a band of Osages who had stolen some horses from his village to the well-stocked house of a French trader on the Arkansas River. Angered, Tinhiouen ordered death for the two Osage chiefs taking refuge there, but spared the merchant's life. He was deeply resentful that this trader had befriended the tribe's enemies, but the Cadohadacho had a pledge of friendship with the French, and he kept it.[4]

Mézières's instructions were to send bonded traders to the Cadohadacho, Natchitoches, and Yatasi villages and continue their annual presents. Unlicensed trade by any nationality was to be stopped, and hostile tribes, those that trafficked in stolen Spanish horses, sold Indian captives as slaves, or held Spanish captives for ransom, were to be coerced into friendship by cutting off legal trade until they proved themselves friendly to Spain. The Comanches, Tonkawas, Tawakonis, Taovayas, Yscanis, and Kichais were all labeled enemies and could have no part in trade either directly or indirectly until new orders were issued. The policy offered no specific steps for halting hostilities between the Osage and Caddo.[5]

Mézières knew Tinhiouen as a man of honor and intelligence, a chief as skillful in making peace as he was capable of making war. Mézières gave immediate and careful attention to the Cadohadachos' annual presents for 1770. The gifts were mostly the same as the items stocked for trade, but there were extras that reflected the Caddos' progressive preference for manufactured, rather than traditionally made, tools and utensils: a hat trimmed with gold-thread embroidery, an ornamented shirt, a copper kettle, forty-eight hawksbells (which were small and ball-shaped), two hundred needles, one pound of thread, two jugs of brandy, and six mirrors. The list also included twenty-five pounds of salt and ten rolls of tobacco—things the Caddos had once provided for themselves and traded to others.[6]

The Nanatsoho, Upper Nasoni, and Upper Natchitoches branches of the Cadohadacho nation lost their individual identities as shrinking population forced them to abandon their old settlements and merge with the Cadohadacho. Even the spelling of Cadohadacho shrank. Mézières and his successors referred to the two remaining Cadohadacho villages as the Grand Cado and the Petit Cado.

A hill about five miles from the principal Caddo village had been a sacred place since the time of their ancestors. It was the

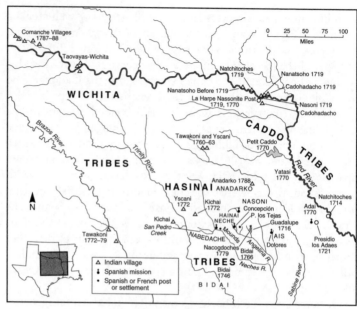

The Caddo, Hasinai, and Wichita tribes in the eighteenth century.

place where a woman called Sah-cado had appeared. She reared
the first parents and taught them how to hunt, fish, and make
houses and clothing. When all that was learned, Sah-cado disappeared. The hill was still venerated and the Cadohadacho retained respect as the progenitor of other nations.[7]

Mézières appointed three Frenchmen—Alexis Grappé, Pedro
Dupain, and Fazende Morière—as traders to the Grand Caddo,
Petit Caddo, and Yatasi villages. A merchant in Natchitoches
contracted to furnish the goods. The "List of Goods necessary for
the annual Supply of the Village of the Grand Cadaux" was long:
forty staple fusils of good caliber, sixty ells of Limbourg cloth (red
and blue), thirty woolen blankets, four hundred pounds of French
gunpowder, nine hundred pounds of bullets (caliber thirty to
thirty-two), thirty pickaxes, thirty hatchets, thirty tomahawks,
fifty shirts (half gingham and half white), one gross of hunters'
knives, one gross of pocket knives, six dozen large combs, six
dozen pairs of scissors, sixty pounds of small glass beads (sky blue,
white, and black), one thousand flints, six dozen large steels, six

dozen awls, six pounds of pure vermilion, six dozen mirrors of pliant copper, and twelve pounds of copper wire suitable for bracelets and wormscrews.

Goods for the Petit Caddo, Natchitoches, and Yatasi were practically identical, but the amounts were smaller. The Indians paid for the items with bear's fat worth twenty-five sous a pot, buffalo hides worth ten livres each, and deerskins worth thirty-five sous apiece. The prices gave the contracting merchant a 50 percent profit.[8]

Soon after January 1, 1770, Mézières invited Tinhiouen to Natchitoches to receive the annual presents, a medal, and a royal banner sent by the king of Spain to honor him. The same invitation was sent to Cocay, head chief of the Yatasi.[9] On April 21 both chiefs stood before Mézières in the assembly room at Natchitoches Post. Three other officers of the post and the commandant from Los Adaes presidio officially witnessed the ceremonial presentation. Grappé and Dupain, the traders assigned to the Cadohadacho and Yatasi villages, were interpreters.

Mézières spoke of love and loyalty, of the greatness and kindness of the Spanish king, of peace between friends and unity against enemies. He slipped the loop of ribbon from which the medal hung over the head of each chief and placed the silken folds of a Spanish flag in their hands. The face of the one-ounce shining silver medal was engraved with the royal portrait and the words "Carlos III, King of Spain and Emperor of the Indies." On the other side, between laurels, were the words "For Merit."[10] Tinhiouen and Cocay accepted their medals as distinctions showing the king's favor, the flag as proof of his protection, and the gifts as recognition of their rank. In return for the distinction, protection, and gifts, they pledged loyalty and friendship.

When he presented the king's medals to Tinhiouen and Cocay, Mézières extracted their solemn promise to arrest and bring to Natchitoches all "vagabonds" who wandered into their villages, whether French, Spanish, or black. For each such person brought in, there would be a reward of a firearm and two lengths of broadcloth. Seven years earlier some Caddos had found a Frenchman named Morvant in the forest, alone and so sick and malnourished that he was near death. They carried him home, nursed him back to health, and accepted him in their community. Tinhiouen, in keeping with his word, urged Morvant to report to Natchitoches.

Morvant claimed to be an armorer by trade. He had lived on the Arkansas River with an unsavory group of French outlaws before killing the renegades' bullying leader and fleeing to the interior country along the river. He had eked out a fugitive existence in the woods for three years until the Caddos discovered and took pity on him.

Whether or not Tinhiouen knew about Morvant's past, the chief did not expect any harm would come to the Frenchman. So when Morvant presented himself to Mézières and was promptly arrested, double handcuffed, and scheduled for trial the next day, Tinhiouen intervened. He confronted Mézières, insisting that Morvant be released to him.

Mézières explained that Morvant had broken the laws of the king. Those laws, Mézières said, were based on "the natural law (for if we are in duty bound not to do to others what we do not wish done to us, it followed that he who commits murder incurs the penalty of death, as is practiced even among the most irrational savages)."[11] Tinhiouen was saddened to hear such an intemperate interpretation of human laws, but was not moved. He told Mézières he would not leave until Morvant was released to him.

Tinhiouen was an experienced arbitrator and accustomed to making final decisions in disputed cases. He was aware that the governor in New Orleans had similar authority, and the chief used that knowledge to reinforce his position. He told Mézières that since he, Tinhiouen, was so loyal to the king of Spain, he hoped to have this favor granted by appealing to the merciful judgment of the governor. Knowing that men who led their nations should not set a path full of stumbling blocks, the Caddo chief added a promise that he would never again place himself in the way of the whites' laws. In the future, he said, if any wrongdoer asked for his help, he would order that person arrested and brought to Natchitoches.

Mézières needed Tinhiouen's help to accomplish his main mission as lieutenant governor—to bring about peaceful relations between increasingly hostile tribes and the Spanish government of Louisiana and Texas. Displeasure and distrust infected all the tribes: no frontier settlement, Indian or white, was safe from the depredations of Apache and Comanche bands; Wichita tribes had allied with Comanches to fight Apaches; and Nabedaches, thought to be friends, had recently killed two Frenchmen and a Spaniard.

The Frenchmen, illegally trading in Hasinai country, had hired the Spaniard. Even more dangerous, British agents, infiltrating west of the Mississippi, were supplying the Osage, and the Osage, out of control, were making frequent raids on the Cadohadacho. All-out tribal warfare could erupt at any time.

Considering the gravity of the situation, Mézières did not take time to forward Tinhiouen's appeal to the governor in New Orleans. Instead, he presented the problem to an assembly of the principals at Natchitoches Post. They decided it was better not to displease Tinhiouen, and Morvant was placed under the caddi's protection.[12]

Toward the end of August, Mézières learned that enemies had killed a person in the Grand Caddo village. He felt sure that if Indians from the Arkansas River district were responsible for the murder, a full-fledged war was about to break out. He wrote the Louisiana governor urging him to use his authority to curb the Osages and other tribes along the Arkansas. Then he set out to do whatever he could to appease the Caddos.[13]

In the medal ceremony Tinhiouen had accepted the role of peacemaker for the Spanish government. He formally promised to arrange a meeting between leaders of the tribes unfriendly to the Spaniards and Mézières. Mézières counted on the Caddo's influence and was not disappointed. In September Tinhiouen completed arrangements and sent three Caddo chiefs to bring Mézières to the village for a conference with the Taovayas, Tawakonis, Yscanis, and Kichais in October.[14]

Mézières left Natchitoches accompanied by the sublieutenant of the militia and five residents of the post. At Los Adaes presidio they were joined by a sergeant, four soldiers, and Fray Miguel de Santa María y Silva. Father Silva had been in charge of Texas missions for forty years, but he neither spoke nor understood the Cadohadacho language.

Bigotes and a band of the Nabedache were waiting when Mézières arrived at Los Adaes presidio. A few weeks after the ceremony honoring Tinhiouen and Cocay, Bigotes came to Natchitoches to assure Mézières that the head of the Indian who had killed the two Frenchmen and a Spaniard would be brought to him. A king's medal and a Spanish flag had already been reserved for Bigotes, and Mézières presented them to him at this time. The Hasinai chief's pleasure was evident. Phrases of gratitude burst from him. He told Mézières he would lose no time in visiting the enemies of Spain and would persuade them to beg for peace. If they did not halt their evil plans, he, Bigotes, would threaten them with war.[15]

Bigotes was on his way to Natchitoches when he met Mézières at Los Adaes. He came to report that a Nabedache man had been executed for killing the two Frenchmen and the Spaniard. The guilty man's accomplice, a Nacogdoches, had not yet been caught, but the people of his village were pursuing him to give him the same punishment.[16]

From Los Adaes Mézières followed a well-worn route through the Yatasi and Petit Caddo settlements. At both settlements the Spanish flag was hoisted, and a feast was served to honor the visitors. Yatasi and Petit Caddo chiefs and principal men then accompanied Mézières the rest of the way to Tinhiouen's Grand Caddo village on the Red River.

They arrived in the early afternoon of Friday, October 12, at the place where Alexis Grappé and some other French lived in the old fort built by La Harpe, now called San Luis. As soon as they arrived, Tinhiouen sent messengers to call all the chiefs, principal men, and elders of his district to come in for council. The Taovaya, Tawakoni, Yscani, and Kichai delegations were already camped outside the village. They were asked to appear for a council beginning Sunday morning.

Seven chiefs came into the village. The rest of their people refused to come so close. They were afraid the Spaniards would seek revenge for the destruction the tribes had taken part in. The chiefs had greater valor but no less fear. As the council began, they sat with their eyes fixed on a spot of ground, listening to what Mézières had to say.

Mézière's words were translated into Caddo by Grappé, then into the Wichita language by an interpreter named Chano Duro. Speaking sternly, Mézières told the chiefs that they must already realize that times were different from when they had help through Natchitoches in supporting their families and resisting their enemies. They had abused that help and so it was no longer given. The traders would not come to them, and there would be no gifts until there was no doubt that they would conduct themselves better. He made it clear that those in Natchitoches who had given them aid in the past had become naturalized as Spaniards; that our new and beloved monarch was the most powerful in the world [and though] they had gained the indignation of so high a prince . . . he would grant them the peace which they had come to seek if they would but show themselves constantly deserving of such a boon. . . . They should desist from robberies and hostilities . . . [or] finally, and it would not be long, they would bring upon themselves the imponderable weight of his invincible arms. . . . They should profit by the good example and inviolable fidelity of the friendly Cadodachos, whose hands, far from having been stained with our blood, have been dedicated, at the cost of their own, to the defense of our lives, when the ferocious Natches threatened them by their invasion of Natchitoches, a deed worthy of the greatest applause, and one which for all time will receive the gratitude which it merits.[17]

Tinhiouen and Cocay spoke in turn. Mézières said he was indebted to them "for at once seconding my discourse with arguments so apropos, so effective, and withal so worthy of their known loyalty, that to try to relate them would be to over-state and discredit them."[18] But even the two medal chiefs could not quiet the fear of treachery that trembled in the thoughts of the seven Wichita chiefs. The chiefs drew together for a long consultation; then one who knew the Caddo language responded that their troubles with the Spaniards had begun only recently when the Spaniards had built the fort and missions that gave aid to the Apaches and treated them as guests. Before then, said the Wichita spokesman, they could not be accused of the slightest offense. Now, he said, their anger was gone. That was the reason the Tawakoni and the Yscani had moved from their place near San Antonio after hearing the wish of the great captain of Louisiana. Now they were living off to one side, not far from the Nabedache. They would stay there, leaving the Apaches alone. He declared that they truly desired peace and had immediately obeyed the summons to come seek it. Because of that decision, the Comanches were no longer their allies and were now waging cruel war against them. Finally, trusting that the man from Natchitoches who controlled presents and trade goods was unchanged from the man they had always known, the Wichita chief asked for compassion from "their ancient protectors, the French."[19]

Mézières did not accept their promise to lead peaceful lives as sufficient proof of their goodwill. He replied:

Do not forget, that there are now no Frenchmen in these lands, and that we are all Spaniards. I have and will keep in mind your promises in order to report them to my chief, to whom they will undoubtedly be pleasing. . . . But meanwhile it is fitting, since you have committed so many insults, robberies, and homocides in San Antonio de Vexar [Bexar] and vicinity, that without loss of time you should journey to that city, with the interpreter whom I shall provide for you and two Spaniards who will accompany you, carrying a flag to protect you. There you will humble yourselves in the presence of a chief of greatest power who resides there, and whose part it is to ratify the treaty which you seek, since you have established yoruselves within his jurisdiction, and to name the light and easy conditions to which you must conform in order not to incur the misfortune of being deprived of so desirable a boon.[20]

The chiefs did not have courage enough to take that journey. They covered their fears with excuses, saying that they lacked horses, that there was too great a risk from Apaches, that the season was late, and that they had to hurry to build their winter homes before the storms came. They promised to assemble for another meeting with Mézières in the springtime and vowed they would hold themselves to peaceful occupations in the meantime. For the time being, Tinhiouen and Mézières had done all they could as peacemakers.

Communication between the Spanish governments of Louisiana and Texas was slow and frequently detoured by the official chain of command. The Texas governor, Juan María Barón de Ripperda, did not know what took place at Tinhiouen's village or what was going on among the tribes that attended the conference with Mézières. The winter months were gratefully quiet around Ripperda's headquarters in San Antonio, but renewed depredations began earlier than usual in the spring of 1771. He had by then received a copy of Mézières's report on the conference, but did not know that the governor of Louisiana had refused to allow Mézières to meet with the tribes for the promised spring peace talks.

Ripperda sought the services of two Franciscans, Fray Pedro Ramírez and Fray Francisco Sedano, to help him find out what was happening among the tribes. Both were well known to many of the tribes in the province, and they were familiar with some of the native languages. Ramírez was father president of the missions, and Sedano, a lay brother, was an especially talented linguist. Ripperda asked them to take gifts to the chiefs, especially Bigotes. He hoped the Hasinai chief would act as a mediator with the other tribes. What Ramírez and Sedano discovered was that Bigotes already had plans to mediate. Representing the Spanish government, they went with him to visit the Wichita tribes.

They were with Bigotes and his large Hasinai retinue as they rode into Natchitoches in late spring 1771. Bigotes was the proud bearer of two buffalo rugs—one white, signifying that all roads were open and free from blood; one marked with crosses, known to all the tribes as white society's venerated symbol. There were four crosses representing the Kichais, Yscanis, Tawakonis, and Taovayas. Presenting the skins to Mézières, Bigotes explained that he was the deputy of the nations represented.

Mézières recognized that the rugs and drawn symbols were as solid a contract as any paper treaty signed in ink. He forwarded them to Ripperda and called an assembly of the most prominent persons in Natchitoches. Bigotes and the Hasinais with him were given many presents, and Mézières delivered a speech describing the importance of the event in his best oratorical style.

Mézières knew that the contract these tribes had offered meant they were willing to accept the peace terms he had given them the previous fall and that a lack of immediate response would be a break of faith. However, since the governor of Louisiana had refused him permission to meet with them again, Mézières could not go in person to tell them that their decision was warmly welcomed by the "chiefs" of Louisiana and Texas. He asked Bigotes to be the official ambassador. Both he and Bigotes were delighted when Le Blanc de Villeneuve, a gifted interpreter who lived in Natchitoches, offered to go along at his own expense. Sedano, two Spanish officers, and a second Frenchman who knew Indian languages also became part of the embassy.

Before the departure of the delegation, couriers from the Tonkawa arrived in Natchitoches, bringing notice that their tribe, too, had decided to accept the treaty. Word also came from Tinhiouen that the chief of the powerful Taovayas had come to Tinhiouen's village to vouch his tribe's desire to be in harmony with the Spaniards. The Taovayas said they would attack any of the other tribes that might disrupt the treaty, and the chief had left two hostages as a pledge for his return to see Mézières in the autumn.

Late in the summer Bigotes and Le Blanc de Villeneuve escorted Kichai, Yscani, Tawakoni, and Cainione (Cahinnio) chiefs to Natchitoches to sign a peace pact.[21] The four chiefs said they also spoke for the Tonkawas. To show the unity of France, Spain, and the Norteños, Mézières sealed the customary ceremonies for signing peace treaties with an impressively symbolic act—he wrapped himself, the lieutenant from Los Adaes, two Franciscans, and the four chiefs with the royal flag of Spain.

For the chiefs the ceremony at Natchitoches was sufficient evidence of good faith, but Mézières told them they had to go to San Antonio to ratify the treaty. Again the chiefs excused themselves from doing so. This time they said that the distance was too great and that they had been called on an expedition against the Osage. Bigotes, the diplomat, went as their deputy.

His journey to the seat of Spanish government under the hot summer sun ended with a gratifying reception at the presidio of San Antonio de Bexar and the mission of San José, where Fray Ramírez had his headquarters. Bigotes covered himself with the dust of many miles while carrying on Spanish diplomacy. In San Antonio he was fitted with fine, fresh garments. Inside the coolness of adobe walls, in the presence of a portrait of the king, with uniformed troops standing at attention and all the important people from the village and mission gathered in his honor, he was decorated and given a new title. With European ceremonial flourish Governor Ripperda armed the Hasinai diplomat and declared him "Head Chief of all these Nations." Putting aside Bigotes as his name, the governor gave the chief a new name, calling him Sauto.[22]

The newly christened Sauto was given an honor guard when he left San Antonio. A captain and thirty soldiers were ordered to escort him as far as he wished them to go. He released them from duty on the second day of travel and continued on with the forty-odd Hasinais who had accompanied him on his peace missions.

The Bidai chief, Gorgoritos, and three Bidai men had joined Bigotes while he was on his way to San Antonio, and on the recommendation of the Hasinai chief, Governor Ripperda gave the Bidai chief a king's medal. The association of Bigotes and Gorgoritos was not new. They had been together when Bigotes had greeted Solís in Hasinai territory four years earlier. For some time the Bidai had acted as middlemen, supplying Apaches with arms and ammunition. It was in character for Gorgoritos to prearrange a meeting with the Apaches on the road back from San Antonio, and probably it was not happenstance that as soon as the soldier escort left, an Apache chief with more than one hundred warriors appeared.

Bigotes sent a rider to alert the soldiers, and they hurried back. The soldiers, however, had been sent only as an honor guard and were under orders to remain neutral in Indian conflicts. They stood by while Bigotes, outnumbered by the Apache throng, began to bargain. They bargained throughout the night, trading various items, then separated, each nation going its own way.

Tinhiouen, working in concert with Mézières, steadily continued to make peace, leading the Taovayas to Natchitoches for the signing of a treaty on October 27, 1771. They agreed orally to the articles of peace presented by Mézières, including one that said they would try to prevent their Comanche allies from committing hostilities and would break all ties with the Comanches if they broke the peace. The Taovayas said their Comanche friends also wanted a treaty and had asked the Taovayas to let it be known.[23]

The written document was signed with cross marks drawn by Tinhiouen and the Taovayas chiefs and the signature of Mézières as witness. The efforts of Tinhiouen, Bigotes, and Mézières had succeeded in bringing the Norteños into alliances with the Spanish government. The next step, proposed by Mézières and approved by Ripperda, was to use these new friends to campaign against their common enemy, the Apaches.

Bigotes's meeting with the Apaches on his way home from San Antonio disturbed the Spaniards' sense of security. In the summer of 1772, when it seemed certain that the Bidai and Apaches would soon form an alliance, Mézières brought Bigotes a message from Governor Ripperda. Gorgoritos was visiting Bigotes when Mézières arrived, and he had a long talk with both chiefs. He told Bigotes that the Tejas (Hasinai) must not visit San Antonio without bringing enough allies to destroy any Apaches they might meet along the way, and he warned Gorgoritos that the Spaniards would call their Indian allies to war against the Bidai if the Bidai failed to join ranks against Apaches.

Shortly after Mézières returned to Natchitoches, Bigotes heard that four Apache chiefs and their bands were on their way to trade and make treaties with the Bidai and Hasinai. He notified Mézières, who sent Grappé to call on Bigotes and Gorgoritos to prove their vowed enmity toward Apaches. The plan outlined to Bigotes and Gorgoritos was that they should pretend friendship and destroy the enemy. Bigotes's proud appointment as Sauto, head chief of all the nations, required him to take on a burden of betrayal.[24]

Bigotes and Gorgoritos mustered warriors to help trap the large number of enemies they expected. Most of the Apaches, however, stopped to hunt, and only seven leaders showed up at Bigotes's house. Bigotes received them as guests, and in the arranged attack three were killed and four escaped. Bigotes quickly dispatched a message to Ripperda, asking if he should attack the Apaches who were out hunting buffalo. Ripperda's only possible answer was no. Crown policy would not allow him to authorize an Indian offen-sive without specific permission from the viceroy, and that was a long, time-consuming process. Bigotes was left wondering about a strategy that required him to violate hospitality but forfeited the chance to catch enemies off balance.

The cries for vengeance raised by the four Apaches who had escaped the trap surged across the land like a storm wind stirring dust devils. The turbulence lasted for nearly a year—buffeting Hasinais with rumors that the Apaches planned a mass invasion to revenge the deaths of their leaders. Bigotes remained unruffled. No nation had ever dared penetrate Hasinai territory without permission. Besides, the Spaniards with their soldiers and weap-ons were his allies. He went to help fight Osages.

The sense of security offered by the Spanish was questioned in May 1773 when Ripperda came to carry out the royal decree that resulted from Rubí's tour of inspection. All Spaniards—mission-aries, soldiers, and families—were ordered to leave Hasinai coun-ty immediately and permanently. Bigotes suspended his campaign against Osages and met Ripperda at Nacogdoches. Bigotes had every right to expect that his arguments against the withdrawal would keep the Spaniards from leaving, but the medal chief's reminders of his friendship and service had no effect. Spain no longer needed the Hasinai as a bulwark against France, the missions had failed to win converts, treaties with the hostile nations of the north had been negotiated, and Ripperda had his orders.

CHAPTER 15

TWO HUNDRED YEARS LATER

Every afternoon when Iti was a very young boy, his grandfather took him down to the creek. The old man would swing his grandson onto his shoulders so that the boy's chubby legs straddled his neck and would carry him to the spot below the swimming hole where, long ago, someone had felled a big tree. There the old man would sit on the log with the child on his knee and sing the old songs. For nearly an hour he would sing, bouncing the grandson in the rhythm of a drumbeat. Then he would stop and tell the boy, "Be quiet now."[1]

They would wait in silence, and in a few minutes a rabbit would hop out of the log on which they sat. The grandfather would lift the .22 rifle he always carried with him and, aiming to miss the rabbit, trigger a single shot. The rabbit would jump from sight, and then Iti would be carried home again.

When he grew older, Iti was allowed to sit with the men in a tipi near his home where his grandfather and his father led peyote meetings. Then he listened again to some of the songs sung by his grandfather on the creek bank. Others became familiar when his family camped at the dance grounds and the drummers beat the rhythms of the songs. By the time he was seven Iti was leading the stomp dance.

Iti grew to be a large man, but some of the older people still called him by his childhood name, which means "little." Doyle Edge was now the name most people know him by. He went away for a while: to school, to serve in the army, to work for an oil company in Tulsa. He was a good athlete, played basketball and softball. He traveled across the country pitching and batting cleanup for amateur teams sponsored by firms in Chickasha and Oklahoma City. After a few years he came back home, and in 1977 he was elected chairman of the Caddo Tribe.

Caddo tribal government had been headed by a chairperson since 1938. Traditional leadership under chiefs and subchiefs or headmen ended when the tribe voted to accept the provisions of the Oklahoma Indian Welfare Act of 1936 in order to gain formal recognition for self-government. A corporate charter was issued to them as the Caddo Indian Tribe of Oklahoma, and a written constitution and by-laws were adopted. Doyle's grandfather, Stanley Edge, was a member of the tribal committee that certified the ratification vote.

The "supreme governing body" under the constitution was the Caddo Council, made up of all the members of the tribe who were twenty-one or older and who lived within the jurisdiction of the Bureau of Indian Affairs agency in Anadarko. A chair, a vice-chair, a secretary-treasurer, and two council members were named as officers to serve as the Executive Committee for four-year terms. Their election required a majority vote taken by a roll call at an annual meeting of the council. Grandfather Stanley Edge, who was sent to Carlisle Indian School as a boy and served as an interpreter for the last of the traditional chiefs, was elected to the first Executive Commitee. Later Paul Edge, Doyle's father, was a member.[2]

This form of government took some getting used to. After a few years various amendments were made to the constitution. One was to change the roll-call voice vote for the election of officers to a standing vote. Voting members met for the 1973 election in the Caddo Community House next to the dance ground, just south of the junction of U.S. highway 281, which leads south to Anadarko, with Oklahoma highway 152, which leads west to the town of Binger, five miles away. The Community House was a one-room frame building covered with asphalt shingles. The candidates were Melford Williams, who was running for reelection, and Harry Guy. Both men had strong support.[3]

It was oven hot inside the hall, and frustrations grew as hours

Thomas Wister, called Mr. Blue, and Stanley Edge (*courtesy of Western History Collections, University of Oklahoma Library*)

passed and neither man received the required majority of votes. Again and again the vote for each candidate was called for, and each time a different number of tribal members stood to be counted. People changed their allegiance; some, unable to make up their minds, may have voted for both candidates; it was impossible to get a clear count in the crowded hall; the votes would not tally. Finally, in exasperation, members were ordered outside to the dance ground and told, "All right, all of you in favor of Melford go stand on that side; all in favor of Harry go stand on *that* side." Harry won.

Daily life and tribal politics had been much simpler when the constitution was first adopted. The number of adults on the official roll was smaller. Few members lived far away from their allotted land around Binger, Gracemont, and Fort Cobb, Oklahoma. Formal recognition of status evolved as an older chief "apprenticed" a young man who showed promise. Two generations later many Caddos lived and worked in Oklahoma City or even farther away. They had experience in the use of organizations, committees, and procedures guided by *Robert's Rules of Order*. They recognized that, even patched by amendments, the original constitution had become less than effective.

A committee worked for more than a year to write a new constitution. Ratified in June 1976, it clarified eligibility for tribal membership and redefined the governing body as the Tribal Council composed of a tribal chair, a vice-chair, a secretary, a treasurer, and at least four but not more than fifteen representatives apportioned for four voting districts. The constitution specified two-year terms of office, with the tribal chair eligible for election to three consecutive terms, and it stipulated election by written secret ballot.[4]

Following the ratification of the new constitution, a second election by secret ballot confirmed Harry Guy as tribal chair. He died in 1977, and in a special election Doyle Edge was elected to fill out the term. In several ways Doyle was uniquely qualified for the office. From his grandfather, his father, and his uncle, he had learned much of the culture important to Caddo people. He grew up speaking the language, learning the dances, and participating in the practices of the Native American Church.

Six months after Doyle took office, still feeling his way in the leadership role, he talked about the language. "I've lost out on a lot of what I used to know because I didn't have anybody to talk with when I was away. Now that I'm home, it's coming back."

The same was true for the songs. At dances Doyle said he "gets out and tries to help them sing. I'm learning; I'm learning all over again. If I can just remember some of the things I've been taught, well I might be able to help somebody else learn 'em."

He talked about his own ten-year-old son, showing pride. "I think, well I know, he's above average in school. He's quite intelligent. . . . When I talk to him, he listens, and I try to tell him things, things that I know and that I learned through the years. One of the things is our religion. You know, I grew up with the Native American Church, and this is all I know. I never went to a Christian church or anything like that. I grew up worshiping in a tipi.

"Some of the people I remember being in the meeting with are Sam Wilson—he was old when I was little, but I remember him—Sam, and Francis Williams. He was my dad's first cousin, but they were close like brothers. He ran the meetings. Some of these songs my Grandpa Stanley used to sing to me, too, these peyote songs. I don't know all the songs, but if I hear 'em sung, I can sing 'em; they come back to me. I have songs that I learned, and I get along."

Since Doyle's youth, "there hasn't been that much change, but there is change. And I think it's just because things are going to change through the years, and people get new ideas and new ways, new things that they feel—and they're sincere about the things that they do, and they change things.

"When I first started going, I used to see them do different things. And now I don't see 'em do it anymore, you know? And some of these things are good things that they used to do. At the time I was just learning—I'm still learning—but at that time I wasn't experienced, I guess you might say, as I am now. And I see 'em do a lot of things now that they didn't use to do a long time ago. But that's just life.

"A long time ago, when they first went in the tipi, well, just the Road-man was the only one that smoked, see, if you prayed for everybody. Well now everybody smokes, now. And like when we have somebody passed away, there's a lot of things to that. Gettin' them ready—then things they gotta have for their journey.

"Some of these things I realize are hard to get, some of this stuff I used to see them use. Indian paint. Corn. Bow and arrows, moccasins, shirts—Indian shirts, Caddo shirts—leggings, stuff like that. These things are what I used to see them do, young as I am. Cause I'm only thirty years old. I've just been so close to these things through my father. People used to depend on him to help, and he was ready to help."

Meetings are held "when somebody's sick, and real bad needs help in getting well; we'll have a peyote meeting for them. Or a birthday, maybe a father or mother might feel good about having one on her kid's birthday, and she'll mention that she wants to have a meeting, and people come and help her worship, and they pray for her and her family . . . the person who the meeting is for.

"I've carried on myself, and I have meetings at our old home place. And up here at Binger they have them, and . . ." He named other places and continued, "Up here where the Williams—my mother's place, where her folks live, they've got a tipi down there, and they've just revived that back up in the last couple of years. I helped 'em fix that back up, too. Course they're my relatives, you know. I'm real close with my relatives."

On reflection, Doyle added, "Mostly all Caddos are kin to each other." And this, too, helped qualify him for his job. "I think that I can understand the people because I've been around them all my life. I know most of the people; most of them are kin to me, too."

Doyle's look was solemn, the tone of his voice earnest as his thoughts moved from what's past to the present. "I feel like to assume the responsibility, I need the people's support, the people's backing. We had a little conflict come up within our tribe, and our Tribal Council won out on the conflict. It not only gave me confidence in the tribe backing me and supporting me, but it just made me feel that much more, that I wanted to do these things because they voted me in and then, when a disagreement came up, they stood behind me, and all I have to do is get out and work for them!"

Friendships outside the tribe were proving valuable. "I play ball a lot, and these teams I play with, we travel quite a bit. Fairly decent teams, you know. I played for Intertribal this past year—we won the national championship." Doyle was modestly proud of his athletic ability. Teams he played for in other years "traveled all over the States. I meet a lot of people, and some of these people, later on when I got into this chairmanship, I go to Washington or some place, and I see these people. Right away I know who they are and they know me. And I tell them, 'Well, how about this one program I don't know much about. I'd like to learn more about it,' and we just sit right there and we talk about it, and then we talk about 'who you gonna play for next year' and all that, you know."

Such contacts were important to Chairman Edge because some of the programs had top priority in his mind. "We need to reach out and get some of the programs that we should have had years ago—all the other tribes had them, and we never had anything, and I've always wondered why. Now that I get a chance, I'm trying to get out and get some of these programs.

"What I'm looking forward to is some of the things that we've always needed—and never had—and all this time they're here. Like health programs, like housing. We've always needed homes. We started with this Caddo housing program, and this is good now. I mean, right now it's working real good. But there's also another part of housing that you can get a grant to help fix all these other homes up, and it's a *grant*. I'm trying to get that. If I can get that, then I can really benefit the people. But it's going to take time, and I want to do so many things."

It all goes back to the people. His confidence in them; their confidence in him. For the first time, a frown worried its way across his face. "I wish I could tell them more. I wish I knew more and could tell more to inform them. I try to inform them as much as I can already, but I wish there was things that I could reach out and I could tell 'em—this is what we'd like to have, and this is what we *are* going to have. If we can just get some of these things that'd benefit the tribe and all the people, we'd have a better way of life. This is some of the things I wish I could make them understand—that my efforts are sincere.

"I can't tell you any different. I am sincere in what I'm doing, and this is what I wish the people could understand. I think there's gonna be a time when I can talk with them, you know, like that."

Like the zinging sound of electricity surging through high-tension power lines, the office next to Doyle's hummed with energy. Office manager Gayle Cussen Satepauhoodle was the generator. A Caddo married to a Kiowa, she had six daughters, "three of them ours, three the same as ours." Because of work, her husband was usually at home only on weekends, so she often ran the household single-handed. A slender and youthful woman, she exuded a let's-get-this-thing-done-now kind of efficiency.

Her desk in the center room of the tribal office was covered with neatly sorted stacks of paper. She read through the last page of a sheaf in her hand and added it to the arrangement. At the same time she called into the outer office, "Charles, call the area office and see if we can bring this budget out for them to look over this afternoon."

There were three desks in the outer office, each with a tele-phone sitting on one corner. Charles, the accountant, lifted the receiver from his phone and dialed. At another desk, Marilyn steadily typed her way toward the completion of another set of papers. Rosie, who had been struggling with a respiratory infec-tion for several days, had gone to see a doctor. On the wall behind her desk hung the framed original design for the Caddo tribal seal and an architect's sketch of the new Caddo Community Center, now under construction.

Calvin Toho, treasurer for the tribe, came into the office to give Gayle the receipts for four bills he had paid. He lived in Binger and as one of the more experienced council members was depended on for advice.

Before the paperwork on the receipted bills could be taken care of, a telephone call interrupted. Gayle was in conversation for several minutes. Her voice sharpened. "You mean our deadline is March first? Why didn't we know about that before? That's day after tomorrow." She listened briefly, hung up the receiver not too gently, and, raising her voice, called Charles and Marilyn to her.

"We'll need to work late again tomorrow, okay?" They had all worked until nine the night before preparing the materials now on Gayle's desk. She motioned toward the typewritten sheets. "All this stuff will have to be put into final form after Doyle and I get back from that meeting in the City [Oklahoma City] tomorrow."

"This stuff" was a grant proposal for an Indian Health Speciali-zation Plan. The meeting in Oklahoma City was to review the form and content so that the proposal could be officially submit-ted to Washington. If all went well, the tribe would receive a grant allowing it to employ a specialist in health care. The job of the specialist would be to assess the facilities for health care in the Caddo community and set up a program of needed services. The people needed the program, the staff knew it, and everyone was willing to make whatever effort necessary to get the grant.

Returning her attention to Toho, Gayle talked with him about

Gayle Satepauhoodle (1978)

hiring someone to take care of some construction on a Caddo home. They agreed on a Caddo man who had done good work before.

A worried-looking woman came into the office. She had received a bill and did not have the money to pay it. She would be getting some money next week. Could Gayle or Doyle call and explain the situation for her? She was one of many people coming through the door to the tribal offices each workday. They came to get help with individual health or financial problems. They came to complain. They came to transact business or just to pay a social call. The problems often had simple solutions, but the worried individual was too timid or uninformed to handle them alone. The complaints, sometimes legitimate, sometimes rising out of jealousy—"She got a new bathroom in her house. Why can't I have one?"—were usually a result of not understanding the intricacies and limits of government-financed programs.

It was not unusual for the chair of another tribe or a representative of Indian Health Service, among others, to come by and ask for support or cooperation in various efforts. Their visits might result in meetings to coordinate Indian action to thwart a particular Bureau of Indian Affairs action that seemed detrimental to all Indians.

Non-Caddos, even non-Indians, occasionally came into the office, too. A person connected with the leasing of Caddo lands, or students looking for historical data, seeks information through the Caddo Tribal Office. The staff wryly noted that one group of people, city officials, never came into the office or asked for any kind of input. Public school personnel never visited the tribal office, either, but they cooperated when asked.

By midafternoon the budget had been approved with no changes and the last page of the proposal draft drawn from the typewriter. The reaction was immediate; everyone visibly relaxed. Gayle triumphantly waved the pages and gloated, "Do you realize that I've—*we've*—finished all our work for this week and the proposal is ready two days before the deadline!"

She had reason to feel exuberant. Budgets, grant proposals, housing projects, required expertise that few people within the Caddo Tribe had. Many programs and services that were formerly handled by Indian Agency personnel were now administered through the tribal offices. It was all part of the federal government's self-determination policy.

"We don't have anyone who really knows anything about all this," said Gayle. "Most of our young people who go away to college don't come back here. I'm one of the few, and how qualified am I," she laughs, "with a degree in French literature? Sometimes," she continued, "I think they [the federal government] couldn't get rid of us any other way so they decided to try this." An impish grin denied her words. Then she was serious again. "If we'll all get together, everybody work together for the benefit of the whole tribe, we'll do all right."

Doyle and Gayle drew attention. The *Sunday Oklahoman* for October 22, 1978, carried a feature story written by Covey Bean under the headline "Indians Raid Open Federal Purse—Throwing Money at More Money—One Way to Amass Fortunes." Following a subhead, "Caddos Rate 100 Percent," Bean wrote:

Doyle Edge, 30, is big and friendly, and drives a yellow Corvette. He is tribal chairman of the Caddo Indians. Gayle Satepauhoodle is pretty and articulate. She is tribal administrator. They make a good team. . . . The tribal offices are located in a bright new building on 37-acres of Caddo land seven miles north of Gracemont in Caddo County. It also contains a huge, almost gymnasium-sized room, where the tribe may conduct meetings and even dance on its dirt floor. A kitchen adjoins it.

The building was financed by a $254,000 grant from the federal government.

Edge and Mrs. Satepauhoodle are not experts. They struggle with the forms necessary to obtain government money, but note they've never had an application turned down. . . . "The federal grant money is marvelous and we appreciate it so much," explained Mrs. Satepauhoodle. "But there may come a time when the public will not be so generous. We don't want to depend on anybody. We want to be self-sufficient. . . ." To this end, Edge is working on a plan to lure a small industry to the area. It would be owned by the tribe and employ Caddos. . . . A center for older people is already planned. . . . Edge served one year as tribal chairman without pay. . . . He has just begun a new two-year term, and the tribal Business Committee voted him an annual salary of $9,000. . . . He works full time at his job, one of 10 persons now on the Caddo payroll. . . . "We're still going uphill," says Edge. "There's a lot of people who depend on you. You can't quit."[5]

Doyle's full term as tribal chair began with the regular election in June 1978. That year he once again pitched and batted cleanup for the Oklahoma Intertribal team, which went undefeated for the second year in a row and won the North American Indian Championship Tournament held at Calgary, Alberta.

CHAPTER 16

A PLACE FOR CRYING

✴ About five hundred Spaniards living at or near Los Adaes in 1773 were affected by their king's order to abandon northeast Texas. Some people who should have been part of the disconsolate group were missing when Governor Ripperda started the wagon train moving out of Los Adaes. They had fled to Natchitoches, hidden in the woods, or taken refuge with Indian friends. French families that had lived at Los Adaes moved nearer the Hainai, Nacogdoches, and other Hasinai villages. As soon as the winding line of cattle, horses, mules, donkeys, goats, and human beings left on June 25, bands of Indians began picking up belongings left behind, destroying houses, and digging up ammunition and presidio equipment that had been buried because there was no way to transport heavy items. Spanish families who had taken refuge returned to Los Adaes when it was safe and scavenged whatever remained.[1]

The Spaniards from Los Adaes made their first rest stop at El Lobanilla, a ranch near the abandoned mission of the Ais that had flourished for years as a trade center for the French and the Hasinai tribes. It was owned by Antonio Gil Ybarbo, a man in his early forties whose parents were both Spanish. He was born and brought up with the mixed Spanish, French, and Indian population at Los Adaes and built El Lobanilla after his marriage. Ybarbo's mother and two other members of his family were declared too sick to be moved, and he was given permission to leave a son, one family, and some servants to care for them. In all, twenty-five people remained at El Lobanilla as the exiles were straggling on toward Nacogdoches.

Bigotes, who had halted a campaign against the Osage to keep the Spaniards from leaving, was at Nacogdoches with a large group of Tejas ("tayshas") painted for war. Already embittered because the Spanish had built a mission that gave sanctuary to the Lipan Apaches and used soldiers to protect them when they fled there, the Tejas now suspected that the Spanish were fully allied with the Apaches. Why else would the soldiers withdraw and remove their women and children from Hasinai country if not to join the Apaches and bring a combined force back to annihilate the Hasinai? Ripperda had difficulty explaining, but a missionary translated for him, and he succeeded in temporarily diverting the Indians' anger. The Spaniards were going to San Antonio, he told them. Come with us, we will serve as your escort.

Bigotes said the missionaries, soldiers, and their families should stay, and he threatened bad things if they did not. To convince the powerful chief that the Spanish were not deserting the Hasinai and would come back later, Ripperda gave two families—nine people—permission to stay at Nacogdoches. Having gained that small concession, Bigotes said he would come to San Antonio with his warriors and ask the governor for the return of at least one missionary and some Spaniards to live among the Hasinai.

Trade was, as much or more than anything else, the tribes' reason for wanting the Spaniards to stay and for the Spaniards' reluctance to leave. Before the caravan led by Ripperda reached San Antonio, thirty-five Spaniards stole away and joined the small group that had been given permission to stay with Ybarbo's family at El Lobanilla. As soon as the rest reached San Antonio, two hundred of them petitioned for permission to return to Los Adaes. Ybarbo, another representative named Gil Flores, and an unnamed Indian delegate delivered the petition to the viceroy in Mexico City.

Because influential officials were still jealous and suspicious of French trade in Spanish territory, and they knew that residents of Los Adaes had fostered such trade, they would not allow the petitioners to return to their former homes so close to Natchitoches. The closest the Spaniards from Los Adaes were permitted to resettle was on the west bank of the Trinity River, about halfway between San Antonio and Los Adaes. Their new town, named Bucareli after the current viceroy, was surveyed and laid out early in 1775.[2] Illegal French traders, who had already flocked to Nacogdoches, soon made a path to Bucareli, and Texas tribes renewed active contraband trade through Gil Ybarbo.

The Indian trade network directed for the Spanish government by Mézières from Natchitoches maintained resident traders in all the principal Hasinai and Cadohadacho villages. He kept his promise to establish trade with the tribes who had made peace agreements at Tinhiouen's village and Natchitoches, and he urged them to move closer, consolidating their villages near the Cadohadachos and forming a line across the northern Red River frontier.[3]

The Grand Caddo village was the only barrier between the Osage and the European community of Natchitoches. Natchitoches and Yatasi tribal units slowly disintegrated and by January 1776 were so scattered that Mézières considered annual presents to the two tribes unnecessary. He recommended a new presidio to protect the tribes from the Osage raids and to serve as a Spanish bulwark against English traders who were penetrating the northern border. The English already kept the Osages supplied with guns and ammunition. Ripperda was enthusiastic about the idea and suggested Luis de St. Denis as the man most qualified to command the fort. Higher government officials, from far away in Mexico City, disapproved the plan.[4]

In May 1777 Osages stole a herd of horses from a Natchitoches resident who was on his way to trade with the friendly tribes. In June chiefs of the Nacogdoches and Kichai learned that a renegade was trading stolen property taken from Natchitoches to Osages on the Arkansas River. The Nacogdoches and Kichai offered to arrest the man and seize the property in his possession. Mézières accepted their service without hesitation.

By mid-1777 Tinhiouen had begun to fear that all his people would be destroyed by Osages. After five men and two women were killed in a raid on his village, the medal chief went to Natchitoches to confer with Mézières. Mézières shared the chief's concern, but could do nothing more than write his superiors another protest of the lack of control over the Osage.[5]

In July, while Tinhiouen was patrolling above the Red River, he found four French hunters who had been set on by a band of

Osages. The hunters were forced to give up their weapons and ammunition and were stripped of their clothing and other person-al belongings. Tinhiouen followed the thieves' trail, overtook them, killed five, recovered their loot, and returned it to the hunters. Tracking the path of the thieves, Tinhiouen spotted a blockhouse that English traders had built on the bank of the Arkansas River. It held a large quantity of merchandise for trading with the Indians of the district. Tinhiouen sent word of his discovery to Mézières, and a return message gave the chief leave to arrest the English and keep all the goods he found as a trophy.[6]

The Osage soon made reprisals for the punishment Tinhiouen had given their men. All joy in the Grand Caddo village was strangled by the struggle to defend lives and property. Anxiety lay barely hidden in the smiles parents exchanged with their chil-dren. Then another epidemic sickness fell on the people, and many infants never learned to laugh.

The invisible foe that preyed on the Cadohadacho struck San Antonio, Bucareli, Natchitoches, and surrounding villages in 1777. Mézières lost his wife, a son, and a daughter during one week in December. Bigotes, Gorgoritos, and the Nabedache chief all fell to the disease. The epidemic lay hidden for a while, then reappeared the following year and spread from the Nasonis to the Cadohadachos. At least three hundred Cadohadachos died.[7]

The great peacemaking medal chief, Tinhiouen, and one of his headmen died while visiting the governor in New Orleans. They were given Christian burials with full military honors. As though in compensation, nature delivered an abundant harvest to the Cadohadachos that season.[8]

Traditional hereditary succession replaced Tinhiouen with yet another trained and able Cadohadacho leader. The Hainai and Nabedache were not as fortunate. Principal men of the Hainai and Nabedache came to Mézières and asked him to appoint chiefs to replace Bigotes and the Nabedache chief who had died. Mézières told them that he did not have the rank or authority to choose their chiefs, that the Hasinai tribes were not part of his official jurisdic-tion, and that the governor of their province was in San Antonio.[9]

The Spanish government of the Texas province was reorganized in 1776, and the office of commandant general of the Interior Provinces, practically independent of the viceroy of New Spain, was created. The first commandant, Teodoro de Croix, arrived on the frontier in 1777. Croix came to office with a plan to check Apache hostilities by uniting the Indian Nations of the North, three or four hundred Louisiana woodsmen, and the soldiers of the Interior Provinces in a joint campaign. He called Governor Rip-perda, government officials, and military officers to a council of war. The council agreed that a benevolent policy had not kept the Apaches, and the Comanches who chased after them, from menac-ing Spanish frontier settlements and that there was no sense in making treaties with the Apaches because they never kept them. The council approved the plan presented by Croix and asked the governor of Louisiana to send Mézières to San Antonio to work with the governor of Texas on details for the campaign.[10]

Mézières, who was trying to cope with the effects of the epidemic and to control of the Osage bands, delayed leaving Natchitoches. When he did reach San Antonio in mid-February 1778, he found Croix's plan for checking Apache hostilities similar to his own design for a campaign against the Osage. He had proposed an offense to the Louisiana governor that would unite thirteen hundred Cadohadacho, Anadarko, Nasoni, Nabedache, Kichai, Tonkawa, Wichita, and Comanche warriors. With a few plan adjustments, he believed the Apache war could serve as a training exercise for a campaign against the Osage. He and Ripperda refined the Apache plan and decided that Mézières should initiate the support of Norteño tribes by visiting their villages.[11]

Leaving San Antonio, Mézières rode to Bucareli, where he was joined by Ybarbo, a Franciscan father, and thirteen militiamen. Together they visited the Kichai, eighteen leagues to the north; the Tonkawa, fifteen leagues west of the Kichai; a Tawakoni village sixteen leagues farther west, near present-day Waco; and a larger Tawakoni village eight leagues farther up the Brazos. Ybar-bo and the Franciscan turned back for home, and Mézières rode on, following the western edge of the Cross Timbers northward to the Red River, where he visited two Taovayas villages, one on each side of the river. The Comanches were living some distance up the Red River. Mézières sent them a message, warning them to cease their raids and to make reparation for their recent depredations. He returned to Bucareli and left from there for Natchitoches.[12]

Late in the afternoon of the day that Mézières left Bucareli, a small group of Comanches stopped to rest near the town. They were seen by some citizens, who sounded an alarm that caused so much commotion, the Indians fled in fright. The townspeople gathered at the sound of a drumbeat, noisily rounded up horses, and gave chase. They overtook the Comanches and without asking any questions opened fire, killing several Indians, wounding others, and returning victoriously to Bucareli with the Comanches' horses. Several months later the Comanches retaliated by taking 240 horses from Bucareli.[13]

Thirty Hasinais and Kichais rode to recover the stock. They trailed the stolen herd to a Taovayas village near present-day Wichita Falls, Texas; killed three Comanche guards; and headed the horses back toward Bucareli. The Comanches gathered their forces and rushed to recapture their prize. Outnumbered by the infuriated Comanches, the Hasinais and Kichais lost three of their men and were forced to leave the herd of horses behind as they sped to warn the residents at Bucareli of reprisals.

Mézières was told by trusted Indian informants that the first Comanche party discovered camping near Bucareli had come in peace. Led by the son of Evea, the principal chief, they had followed Mézières, intending to overtake him for a talk about the message he had sent them. Mézières knew that unless the Comanches could be convinced that the first attack on them was a mistake, they were likely to seek further vengeance. He called upon the Anadarko (Nadako) medal chief to go talk with the Comanche chief. Evea assured the Anadarko chief that the Bucareli horses were taken by some bands who had separated from the main body of Comanches. The Comanche chief said he was offended by the violence shown by Bucareli, but he was still firm about keeping his pledge of peace. When the Anadarko chief returned with this message, he found that the Spaniards of Bucareli, fearing Comanche reprisals, had sought refuge among the Hasinais at the abandoned Nacogdoches mission.

Croix and his war council realized that an increasingly dangerous situation was developing. The council had sent a request for military reinforcements to the king, but it would be months before any answer arrived; Ripperda had been assigned a new post and was anxious to leave, but the arrival date for the new governor of Texas was uncertain; and it appeared that all the Indian nations, those that had been considered friends and those that had never been, were inflamed with warlike intentions. To cope with the situation, Mézières was ordered to move permanently to San

Antonio de Bexar. He preferred to stay in Louisiana—he felt he could serve better at his old post in Natchitoches, where the tribes were accustomed to finding him—but the choice was not his to make. As it happened, Ripperda's replacement reached San Antonio during October 1778 and was in San Antonio almost a year before Mézières arrived.[14]

While making final preparations to leave his Natchitoches post toward the end of May 1779, Mézières learned that the new chief of the Cadohadachos was determined to go see Governor Bernardo de Gálvez in New Orleans. Diminished in numbers and distressed by repeated Osage raids, Cadohadacho defenses were weakened to the point of despair. Some of the people wanted to leave the Grand Caddo village for a more secure place to live. Before a move from the ancient village was approved, the chief felt he should personally petition the Spanish chief of Louisiana to honor the promise of protection his government had pledged to the Cadohadachos.

Mézières tried to talk the chief out of the journey, primarily because he did not want to risk having the Cadohadacho leader chance on English traders along the route down the Mississippi. When Mézières did not succeed, he sought to plant the notion that English strangers were evil and poisonous. He provided the chief with a trusted interpreter, who was told to keep feeding that idea on the way to New Orleans. Mézières wrote the governor, advising him to receive the chief and his principal men with due honor and impressive ceremony. His letter described the Cadohadacho chief as lively, vivacious, keen, and witty but did not mention his name. "I wish," wrote Mézières "that your Lordship would give audience to the chief dressed in the apparel distinctive of your position. This Indian occupies one of the most important keys to the western country."[15] Commending the chief's "inviolable fidelity to us" and his "courage which never fails," Mézières cautioned, "It is to him principally that we owe in this district a constant barrier against the incursions of the Osages; moreover, it is to the love and respect which the villages of the surrounding district show him that we owe the fact that they generally entertain the same sentiments for us."[16]

The Cadohadacho chief was welcomed in New Orleans with all the ceremony and deference that Mézières had advised. The chief wore the king's small medal, given to him before he had inherited Tinhiouen's rank. Gálvez replaced it with one of the king's large medals and, in an extra attempt to please the new chief, offered the small medal to his son. The chief, however, would not allow it. His son, said the distinguished Cadohadacho, was still young and had not yet earned the respect of the people of his nation. One of the principal men who accompanied him, said the chief, was more worthy. The governor decorated that person with the small medal.[17]

The aid that the chief sought was not given. He was told that the Osages would be made to repent their behavior, but just how or in what manner was not stated. The chief who had the love and respect of all the Indians in the district returned to his people with only presents and more promises.

Mézières started from Natchitoches, accompanied by twenty-seven veteran militiamen and sixteen other persons, on May 24, 1779. They passed the deserted grounds at Los Adaes and the desolate village where twenty Ais families lived near the Sabine River. Mézières wrote Croix from there, saying, "Their vices are without number; and the hatred which they have won from the natives and Europeans, general."[18]

At the Sabine River Mézières received an urgent appeal from Ybarbo. He had permanently moved the inhabitants of Bucareli from their village on the Trinity River to the site of the abandoned Nacogdoches mission. His dispatch to Mézières said that a Spanish party on its way to San Antonio had been attacked by Indians on the Brazos River and that it was necessary for Ybarbo to take his men to follow the attackers. This left the old men, women, and children at Nacogdoches without protection, and Mézières was asked to go to their aid. Hurrying to answer this call for help, Mézières was seriously injured in a fall from his horse. He was carried on a stretcher back to Natchitoches, where he spent three months in recovery.[19]

In August five Hasinai men came unannounced to see Don Domingo Cabello, the new governor at San Antonio de Bexar. It was obvious to him that they were important men who had come on a serious errand. The leader, called Captain Texita, was probably the same one who had gone to Mexico with Ybarbo and Flores five years earlier. Texita was articulate, had a quick intelligence, and used sensible caution in speech and action. He spoke for all the friendly nations in the region.[20]

Cabello gave the delegation special attention. Each day for five days, the five men were given a quarter of beef, a bushel and a quarter of beans, the same amount of ground corn for tortillas, roasting ears, and a box of cigars apiece. In daily talks Texita emphasized to the governor that there was a shortage of traders among all the nations. He said the treaty nations had been told by their friend Mézières—they called him "Captain Pintado"—that the Great Captain in Mexico wanted them to come together and make war on Apaches. More than one thousand warriors—Tawakonis, Taovayas, Panismahas, Tonkawas, and others—wanted to come. They expected Captain Pintado to join them with a cargo of gifts, thirty-five men from Natchitoches, and a militia captain who was his son, but they had heard he was very ill and they were uncertain when to come for the campaign. Texita had been sent to find out. The new governor knew no more, and maybe less, than the Indians did, but he asked Texita to be his emissary to the Tawakoni, Taovayas, and Panismaha villages.

A sixth day of conference was abruptly interrupted around nine in the morning when a runner from a nearby mission delivered a letter to Cabello. Texita and his companions watched while the governor read that four Lipan Apaches had arrived at the mission as advance messengers for five chiefs who were bringing many of their people to see the governor to make up their quarrel with him. Cabello showed the letter to his interpreter and told him to satisfy the curiosity of Texita and his companions by telling them that the Apache chiefs were coming, looking for a fight. Cabello then offered his startled guests a head start out of the presidio and protection for some distance while he detained the Apaches long enough for the delegation to make a safe getaway. The five men were out of the presidio by noon. They said good-bye to their Spanish escort at the Guadalupe River, expressing gratitude for the hospitality given them at San Antonio and the presents they were carrying home. That same day, August 21, Mézières rejoined his troop and led the way toward Nacogdoches.

He observed that the epidemic had left the Hainai with just eighty men. Those living near the deserted Nacogdoches mission had carefully tended the old buildings, and they were not happy with its occupation by the immigrants from Bucareli, who brought the danger of Comanche raids with them. The Hainais called the Spaniards cowards for running from their Trinity River village. They watched the Spaniards' efforts to grow crops, and when the crops failed, they put up with Spaniards wandering into Hainai homes with offers to exchange clothes for food.[21]

Mézières followed the old road from Nacogdoches to San Antonio. He crossed the rich lands of the Hainai, where the Angelina flowed, and went on to the Neches River, where he wrote a letter to Commandant General Croix. In this letter Mézières described how on one of the banks, "near the village of the Navedachos, one sees a little mound, which their ancestors erected in order to build on its summit a temple, which commanded the nearby village, and in which they worshipped their gods. It is rather a monument to the multitude than to the industry of its individuals."[22] At the time Mézières passed by, the Nabedache had been reduced to fewer than forty men.

Mézières reported for duty in San Antonio near the end of September, and on November 2, 1779, he died from the effects of his accident. Luis St. Denis had died nine years earlier.[23] As the eighteenth century drew to a close, so did the legacy of true friendship that the elder St. Denis, Big Leg, had passed to his family.

Ybarbo became captain of the militia and lieutenant governor of the Spanish settlement of Nacogdoches and was given a commission for Indian trade. He made verbal grants of land to farmers, often fifty thousand acres in one grant, and white people uninvited by the Hasinai began to lay claim to their land.[24] At Natchitoches the few remaining Indian families were already practically lost in the European population. The rest of the Natchitoches were dispersed among their Hasinai and Cadohadacho kin. The prairie adjoining the Grand Caddo village became known as the Prairie of the Enemy. Parties that went out as hunters necessarily became warriors, and the number of warriors dwindled with the loss of lives from disease and Osage weapons.[25] The Caddos clung to their ancestral homeland, succumbing to smallpox and measles, fending off the Osage, and waiting for the Spanish government to fulfill its promise to control the Osage menace.

In 1785 the governor of Louisiana called the Caddo chiefs to New Orleans to sign a treaty with the Osage. Hope in the Grand Caddo community swelled like the buds of spring, but shriveled in less than a year when the Osage broke the treaty.[26] The last of the

French families—children and grandchildren of the traders posted there by La Harpe, St. Denis, and Mézières—deserted the old Nassonite Post in 1788. The Grand Caddo village, once the center of power and population, was vacated sometime after that. No longer able to defend their exposed position, the people moved farther down the Red River, uniting with the Petit Caddo families. But neither their combined strength nor the power of a sacred place could provide enough protection for the Caddos in the last decade of the eighteenth century.

It became more and more difficult to trade the products of the hunt. Prices paid in the European market fell, and no one in Natchitoches was eager to trade for furs and hides when they brought such little profit. The Caddos' old or broken guns were not replaced or repaired, and ammunition was scarce. In 1795, five years after the consolidation of the Grand Caddo and the Petit Caddo, a surprise Osage attack devastated the village. Those who escaped massacre sought security farther down river near Tso'to Lake.[27]

At the time Caddos moved to Tso'to Lake, Europeans and Americans pronounced it Sodo. Today it is Caddo Lake. From a location fifteen miles northeast of Marshall, Texas, Caddo Lake meanders across the Texas-Louisiana border and empties into the Red River through Twelve Mile Bayou, a few miles northwest of Shreveport, Louisiana. Described as the largest natural freshwater lake in the South, today it is a nature lover's retreat where morning mists shroud a maze of shallow channels and bayous filled with the odd shapes of cypress trees. An almost eerie stillness blankets swamps where the trees are draped in Spanish moss. Surrounded by woods of tall pines, oak, and hickory that shade native plants, flowers, and wildlife, Caddo Lake has a mystique that invites people to speculate about its origin.

Geological and historical evidence supports the theory that the lake was formed by the backed-up flow of its tributaries when natural logjams in the Red River dammed the mouth of Twelve Mile Bayou sometime between 1806 and 1811. There once were claims that it was created by the upheaval of the New Madrid earthquake of 1811, when other lakes along the lower Mississippi drainage were suddenly created. Those willing to believe that the lake was formed in such a dramatic way claim that Tso'to was a Caddo place-name meaning "water thrown up into the drift along the shore by a wind," and they use the Caddo flood legend to support their theory.

The legend, remembered in the present time, is at least as old as Tso'to itself. The traditional sequence of Turkey Dance songs that relate past events includes one about two brothers who saw the creation of Sodo Lake. Several tribes were gathered for a dance when the high water came. The brothers were worried about the rising water and went to higher ground. They looked to the east and saw a ridge of land moving like a great snake. The ridge was holding back the water in the valley, blocking the stream running through, and making a lake where the people were dancing. The older brother called out to warn the dancers of the danger, and a few were saved by climbing up the hill to join him. The others paid no attention and were lost to the high water.[28] There are also story versions about what happened when the flood came.

Lillie Whitehorn was a good storyteller.[29] Her voice lifted and fell, was bright or soft, following the mood of the story. Dialogue was given an actor's inflection; explanations were asides. She sat still, only occasionally using her hands to illustrate an idea, but her face reflected the seriousness or flickering humor of her words. She recaptured the wonder of her childhood when as a girl called Sah K'un-dee-ku she had listened to the story about the high water.

"One time this old lady goes to the river, or creek, and when she got to the creek, she stayed on this side of the bank and saw another person across there from her. He was a young man. They say he was fine-looking man—built straight and tall. And she got scared of him, you know. She seen him, you know, and he spoke to her.

"He says, 'Mother, I didn't come to scare you.'

"He call her mother. He say, 'I didn't come here to scare you. I was sent over here to tell you; you go back and tell people what I have to say. You tell those people back there where you come from—they're not living right. They not doing right. They destroying that fish!'

"They get that fish out of the water," explained Lillie, "and they just waste it and just laid it around. And they were doing all kinds of evil. They were getting wicked, doing bad, some of them. They was just dancing and singing, and they weren't thinking of the Great Spirit.

"The old lady told some of those town criers, and they told her to go and tell the chiefs about it. 'Tell the head one.'

"And some of those peoples said, 'Aw, she ain't worth listening to—she just an old lady.'

"Anyway, she told that chief and them chiefs said, 'Alright. Mother here, she's telling the truth. She's an old lady.' They held council and got all the people together. 'Everybody that wants to hear come here to this place and listen to what's going to be said.' Course, some of those that believe that way, they all came.

"That Chief said, 'Everybody get your children together and just take a few belongings—just what you really have to have. And you climb that mountain.' There was a mountain somewhere. 'All you that wants to be saved, you climb that.'

"And these others, they wasn't listening. They just keep on dancing and singing and making all kinds of noise and just doing everything.

"They had their drum, these that were climbing that mountain. They took that drum with them, and they had four leaders, four of these wise men, that really could predict things, and they climb that mountain with them chiefs. They help everybody way up there.

"It was startin' to sprinkle—just little by little. And after a while it started to rain quite a bit. It just kept raining, and it rained for so many nights and days. And all that time, these four leaders, they sing them songs. I don't know what song they would be now—maybe we use them; maybe we don't. I wouldn't know that. But anyway, they got that drum, and they sung to God, singing to Almighty, using that drum.

"They said that water just *hit* that mountain, pretty near go over it. And then it goes back, you know. And them children begin to cry. And them old people, they told them, 'Keep your children quiet. And you women folks be quiet. Don't be shedding tears. Be quiet.'

"And then they sang them songs, those men. There's four of them that hits on that drum. Course, there be some others; they take turns.

"Finally they said it stop raining. It got still. It didn't rain any more. And there was *nothing* as far as you could see. It was just water. And everything was drown. And finally, they said that water, it kinda look like it was going down. And they had to stay up there so many days.

"Finally all of that went clear down, and everything was drown. All them people was drownded that didn't try to save themselves, behave themselves.

"Now that's the Caddo story of a high water. And then see, Noah — you know, the flood — it tells about that."

The flood. High water. The same? Different? Sah Gundy-coo wanted to believe. Lillie Whitehorn wanted to understand.

When the Caddos left their old home in the area of the big bend in the Red River, they first settled at a low place farther down the river. Floodwater flowed over the relocated homes and drove the Caddos farther inland, toward the west end of Tso'to. Smallpox destroyed nearly half their number during the first winter. As soon as the pox appeared on their skins, they tried to cleanse themselves by plunging into the creek. Death followed in a few hours. During their third year on Tso'to, measles broke out and more Caddos died.[30] The village on the lake became a place of crying.

Time has confused recollection of the whereabouts of Cha'kani'na, the legendary place of crying where the people emerged from the old world of darkness, and of Sha'childi'ni, their first village. The name for the old village was given to the new one by Tso'to Lake. Perhaps by calling their later village Sha'childi'ni, Timber Hill, the Caddos perpetuate the memory of their ancient home, where the old ones began a new life in the world of light.

CHAPTER 17

THE INTRUDERS

The Cadohadacho left the Red River settlements of their ancestors to save themselves from decimating Osage attacks. They built new homes, tended crops, hunted and traded, unaware of a growing new nation, the United States. American colonials were confined east of the Appalachian Mountains until they won their independence from England and the Treaty of Versailles was signed in 1783. After that their newly recognized states claimed title to the vast tract of Indian land that stretched from the Appalachians to the Mississippi River, and individual American pioneers were determined to own as much of that land as they could.

Rivers were the natural highways that led the pioneers across the Appalachians to the Mississippi. They followed the streams to places chosen for their beauty and utility, clambered onto the banks, and invested their lives in the land. Adventurers, many of them unprincipled, pressed ever farther west, and the tribes whose lands they settled on were forced to look for new hunting grounds and, eventually, new homes.

Around the time the Caddo moved to Tso'to Lake, the Spanish governor of Louisiana asked them to share their hunting grounds with the Choctaws, the largest of the southern tribes east of the Mississippi. Spanish officials hoped that the Choctaws, bitter enemies of the Osage, would help prevent the atrocities the Osage continued to commit in the Natchitoches district. Bands of Choctaws came hunting as far west as Texas. Bands of Ais and Adai attacked them, but at first there was no conflict with the Caddo, who allowed Choctaw hunters to winter with them. The Choc-taws, however, had little effect in discouraging Osage forays, and before long they proved to be only the lesser of two evils for the Spanish as well as the Caddo.[1]

Five Choctaws tried to kill a Kansa Indian living with the Caddo in 1795. The Kansa man was not home when the Choctaws attacked, but they killed his wife and a Caddo man. Soon afterwards a nephew of the Caddo chief, Bisda, was killed by the Choctaws.

Bisda and two other principal chiefs, Diortot and Chacheau, employed a French interpreter to write a letter to the commandant at Natchitoches. The letter said that since the great chief (meaning the Louisiana governor) had instructed them not to harm Indians of other nations, they had not done so, and "we believed the Choctaws when they told us they were dying of hunger in their villages for lack of finding anything to hunt, and that they were all naked and miserable and worthy of pity. We took pity on them and gave them our lands to hunt on. Now it turns out that we are the more unfortunate ones. We can not even go out without being killed because we have enemies on all sides."[2]

In conclusion the chiefs said that if the Caddo could not find justice through the French and Spanish, they would have to get it for themselves. This was not a hollow boast. Although the Caddo were reduced to about 150 warriors, their influence with allies was not diminished, and they could muster a force of more than 3,000. They were capable of uniting about 1,000 warriors from the Hainai, Anadarko, and Ais living between Natchitoches and Nacogdoches; north of Natchitoches, the Yatasi could supply close to 250; the Caddo could count on 700 Taovayas warriors to join them and 1,000 more from the Kichai, Tawakoni, Bidai, and other smaller tribes. The only weakness lay in the fact that only the Caddo had firearms, and they had very few.[3]

Other than withholding gifts and appealing to the United States to restrain Choctaws from crossing the Mississippi, there was not much Spanish government officials could do to control the Choctaws. Before time for the usual distribution of presents, they urged Choctaw chief Taboca to call a meeting of all chiefs and advise them to give the Caddo satisfaction. There was no indica-tion, however, that the murderers had been punished.

Early in 1796 the Louisiana governor agreed that Choctaws were a menace and proposed that the tribes along the Red and Arkansas Rivers ally with the Osage to keep the Choctaws on their own side of the Mississippi. The only way that could be done was for the Caddo and their allies to make peace with the Osage — an unrealistic idea. The Caddo had signed one treaty with the Osage ten years earlier, and it was followed by disaster. "About that peace you mentioned," the Caddo chiefs told the commandant of the Natchitoches Post, "we have no faith in what the Osage say. They are liars."[4]

Bands of Choctaws, up to fifty in number and well armed, frightened inhabitants in scattered settlements throughout the Red River valley. They seldom killed the Spanish or French, but they pillaged their homes, stole their horses, and slaughtered their cattle. In July 1796 Choctaws attacked two Caddos near Natchitoches, killing one, wounding the other, and riding away with their horses. Once again the Caddo, headed by a chief now old and blind, asked Spanish officials for justice.[5]

Government agents again tried to get Choctaw chief Taboca to call a tribal council to deal out justice. It is doubtful that any action was taken, but Taboca did eventually offer to settle differences with the Caddo. He proposed to come to Natchitoches and negotiate an agreement with the principal chiefs of that district in October. During the same month the offer was made (August 1796), thirteen Choctaws ambushed two Caddo men, their wives, and a child staying in a house near Natchitoches. The Choctaws waited in the early morning hours until they saw one of the women come out of the house. They watched her go to the river for water and carry it back. Just as she reached the door, they shot and killed her. They fired at the house for about an hour without killing any others, then left.

The lieutenant governor, who was in Natchitoches at the time, sent thirty militiamen and a captain to patrol the area and protect its inhabitants. He also ordered Caddo men living nearest Natchitoches Post to pursue the Choctaws. Ten Caddo men trailed the Choctaws to their camp but found them too many and too well armed to attack. The Caddo trackers returned to Natchitoches Post to report the location of the Choctaw camp and were insulted by the lieutenant governor, who said they had lost their former fighting capabilities. At the same time, however, he admitted that the Caddo had few firearms and little ammunition, while the Choctaws, like the Osage, were well supplied.

Choctaw bands traveled west in greater numbers and met increasing resistance. Choctaw chiefs, who seldom crossed the Mississippi, renewed efforts to make peace with the Caddo, but the Choctaws committing depredations in Louisiana and Texas knew little of such peace efforts. It probably would not have mattered if they had.

One hundred Choctaw hunter-warriors bypassed Natchitoches early in 1797 and entered Texas intent on winning homesites as well as hunting grounds. Violence was first reported from the Nacogdoches district, where eight peacefully occupied Hasinais were killed and others taken prisoner. The governor of Louisiana reported that Spanish homes in the neighborhood had been robbed and that "a party of the same nation [Choctaw] has assassinated the great chief of the Caddo nation, an Indian to be commended for his good conduct and affection for Spain. In the latter part of March, another band of fifty savages . . . attacked the Ayneus [Hainai] located on the Sabine River."[6] Choctaw parties return- ing from west of the Mississippi complained that the Caddo had killed twenty-five of their warriors, while they had killed only eight of the Caddo. Peace seemed impossible, but Spanish govern- ment officials in Louisiana and American Indian agents kept pursuing that illusive goal until both the Caddo and the Choctaws agreed to send representatives to a conference at Natchitoches.

The conference was scheduled for October 12, 1797, but the date was not made clear to the Caddo, and their head chief, the Grand Caddo, arrived in Natchitoches with a large contingent of Cadohadacho and Hasinai warriors in September. Finding no Choctaws present, he got angry. The commandant tried to make up for the misunderstanding with explanations and generous gifts, and the chief reluctantly agreed to return in another month.[7]

The Grand Caddo brought only eight men with him in Octo- ber. There were signs that government officials and Indian agents had bungled again. The Choctaws sent a lesser chief, the wearer of a small medal, as their representative, and it was demeaning to ask a caddi wearing the king's large medal to negotiate with one of lesser rank. The mismanaged conference lasted two days and had dubious results. White flags were exchanged, and the Caddo chief promised a permanent peace in the spring—if the Choctaws took no further hostile action. The Choctaw spokesperson said that any Choctaw who caused trouble for the Caddo would be a renegade and, if Caddos killed him, it would not prevent a peace treaty.

Nevertheless, Choctaw expeditions became bolder, especially in Texas. No attempt was made to disguise a Choctaw plan to attack Hasinai villages near Nacogdoches in the fall of 1798. The Hasinai avoided breaking the truce by temporarily evacuating their homes. The Choctaws headed back toward Louisiana, announcing to all who would listen that they were tired of searching for the Indians of Texas to make peace with them and that, if they did not find these Indians, they would return very soon with many more Choctaws to make either peace or war. A Spaniard who lived in the district and could speak the Choctaw language said they told him they would kill all the Texas Indians so that "they could live in these lands, because in their own there is not enough room."[8]

Spanish authority in Louisiana was ineffective in keeping Choctaws on the American side of the Mississippi. The intruders wandered over lower Louisiana and crossed into Texas at will. In 1803 the United States extended its boundaries beyond the Mississippi with the Louisiana Purchase, ending Spain's rule in Louisiana.[9]

Caddo and Hasinai tribes had accommodated and cooperated with French and Spanish missionaries, traders, and officials for more than a century. They had benefited from foreign tools and firearms and been laid low by foreign diseases. Neither French nor Spanish intruders, however, had hungered for their land. Americans were different.

Dehahuit was chief of the Caddo when the Americans came. Not counting rumors, all he knew about Americans was that they paid more for furs and hides. Except for a few traders who had infiltrated the district, Americans knew nothing about the natives of the Red River valley and Texas or the land they had occupied for one thousand years.

A few months after the formal ceremonies transferring Louisiana to the United States, a Caddo delegation came to meet the new commanding officer in Natchitoches. The French and Spaniards in that position had assigned traders to the tribes and showed friendship with presents. The Caddo delegation suggested this propriety to the American captain, Edward Turner, who offered a few trinkets, which the Caddo representatives accepted politely. Turner said nothing, however, about a trade agreement, and the Caddos went home wondering.[10]

The boundaries of the Louisiana Purchase were loosely defined—the United States thought they included Texas; Spain did not. Dehahuit's bonds with Hasinai tribes in Texas became obvious to U.S. officials, who were soon aware of Indian trade with the Spaniards at Nacogdoches. Captain Turner received orders to attach the Caddo people to the Americans, and $200 worth of rations and trifles were authorized as gifts for the Caddo.[11]

On the Texas side of the border, Spanish officials redeveloped an interest in the allegiance of the Hasinai tribes. By the end of 1805 the abandoned post at Los Adaes had been reoccupied, a small contingent had been positioned a short distance away on Bayou Pierre,[12] the garrison at Nacogdoches had been enlarged, and the firm of Barr and Davenport, headquartered in Nacogdoches, had been granted new Indian trade privileges.

William Barr and Samuel Davenport were Americans who had become Spanish citizens by taking an oath of allegiance to Spain. They were given exclusive rights to trade with Indians in furs and horses for a period of twelve years, and their agents, who traded between Nacogdoches and the Ouachita River (a Red River tributary flowing out of the present state of Arkansas), were authorized to introduce settlers from the Ouachita into Texas.[13]

For the U.S. government a prime source of information on Spanish border activities and Indian trade relations was Dr. John Sibley, a forty-five-year-old physician who had arrived in Louisiana in the fall of 1802. He settled in Natchitoches and became an active, unofficial government informer by corresponding regularly with Governor William C.C. Claiborne of Louisiana, President Thomas Jefferson, and Secretary of War Henry Dearborn. Both Sibley and Turner recommended that "factories" be established to divert trade with the Spaniards. Factories were American trading posts set up by the government to exchange merchandise for furs and skins brought in by Indians.[14]

Sibley's stream of communication with Washington officials paid off in December 1804, when Secretary Dearborn asked him to act occasionally as an Indian agent. He was authorized to

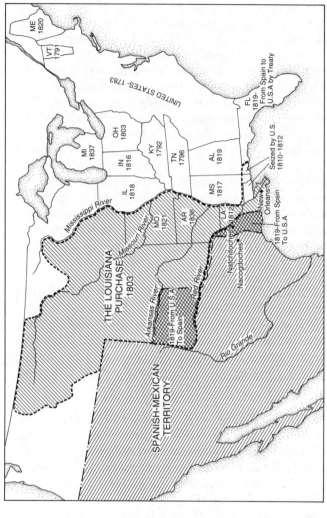

No boundaries were mentioned in the terms of the 1803 Louisiana Purchase. The boundary between Louisiana and the Spanish dominions remained uncertain until defined by the 1819 treaty negotiated by John Quincy Adams, U.S. secretary of state, and Luis de Onís, Spanish minister in Washington.

employ an interpreter, hold conferences with tribes in the vicinity of Natchitoches, and distribute some $3,000 worth of supplies and provisions. He was instructed to assure the Indians they could rely on the United States for friendship and justice if they in turn remained peaceful and friendly and broke off all relations with any other power.[15]

For his interpreter, Sibley chose François Grappé, son of Alexis Grappé, who had served until his death in 1775 as Caddo agent and interpreter for Mézières. Alexis had settled at the old La Harpe post in 1748. François was born there and lived among the Caddo for nearly thirty years. They called him Tulin (Touline). From Tulin, longtime residents of Natchitoches, and personal observation, Sibley gathered information about tribes and their terrain for a report to Secretary Dearborn.[16]

One old French gentleman told Sibley that he could remember when the Natchitoches Indian men were 600 strong. Now there were only 12 men and 19 women preserving their old dress and ways in a village some twenty-five miles above the town that bore their name. The French citizens of Natchitoches had great respect for them; many prominent families were of mixed French and Natchitoches blood. Memories of the Natchez attack on Natchitoches and their defeat by the elder St. Denis and his Indian allies remained vivid.

In reporting the nature and number of the tribes in his district, Sibley wrote:

> The whole number of what they call warriors of the ancient Caddo nation is now reduced to about one hundred, who are looked upon somewhat like Knights of Malta, or some distinguished military order. They are brave, despise danger or death, and boast that they have never shed white men's blood. Besides these, there are of old men, and strangers who live amongst them, nearly the same number; but there are forty or fifty more women than men. This nation has great influence over the Yattassees [Yatasis], Nandakoes [Anadarkos], Nabadaches [Nabedaches], Inies or Tachies [Hainais], Nacogdoches, Keychies [Kichais], Adaize [Adai], and Natchitoches, who all speak the Caddo language, look up to them as their fathers, visit and intermarry among them, and join them in all their wars.[17]

According to Sibley, the nearest route from Natchitoches to the Caddo was by land. Their homes on Sodo Creek, about 120 miles northwest of Natchitoches, were just about 35 miles west of the main branch of the Red River, but the winding, narrow, and unreliable water channels leading there were not easy to navigate.

Sibley reported about forty men, only eight of them Yatasi, and twenty-five women living in the village. He said most of the women were married to men of other tribes. Sixty to seventy miles west of the Yatasi, the Anadarkos made their homes on the Sabine River. They were reduced to forty men. The Hainai still lived on the Angelina River, about twenty-five miles west of Natchitoches. There were eighty men in their village. The same number of Nabedaches lived in their old home place, on the other side of the Angelina, opposite the Hainai.

The Kichai divided sometime during the 1770s, the greater part associating with the Caddo, others keeping their own separate village. About twenty Adais men and a larger number of women survived in their village not far from the old Adaes mission site, and remnants of the Ais, for whom the Spanish once had a mission, numbered but twenty-five total.[18]

If Sibley's figures were right, fewer than two thousand men, women, and children represented the Caddo and Hasinai families — a loss of about six thousand in 200 years.[19] Nevertheless, the total count he reported indicated a fighting strength that surprised Washington authorities. As long as the border between the United States and Spanish Texas was contested, winning and keeping the friendship of influential Caddo tribes were important.

Dearborn wrote Sibley suggesting that he prepare the Indians in his vicinity so that they would not be alarmed if surveyors for the U.S. government ran lines through their lands. Dearborn's letter stated positively, "Not an acre will be taken except with payment and treaty under the auspices of the United States and free concession on their part."[20] Dearborn's pledge was backed by President Jefferson, who wrote Governor Claiborne that "their rights and comfort would be sacredly cherished."[21]

A factory was established in Natchitoches in the fall of 1805, and Sibley was commissioned as a regular Indian agent. He was provided with trade goods and told to urge some of the principal chiefs, especially the Caddos, to visit Washington. Sibley invited Dehahuit and eight or nine other principal chiefs to go with him to meet the president. He made preparations for the trip, buying horses and mules and putting them to pasture to be readied for the journey, but Dehahuit and the other chiefs never got to meet

Jefferson. Shortly before they were to leave, the still-unresolved boundary dispute between the United States and Spanish Texas erupted, and it seemed likely that war between Spaniards and Americans would be fought on Caddo land.

Instead of visiting with President Jefferson during the summer of 1806, Dehahuit met with American explorers on the Red River and a Spanish officer camped near his own village. The explorers, Thomas Freeman and Dr. Peter Custis, commissioned by President Jefferson to explore the Red River to its source, left Natchitoches on June 2. The Spanish officer, Lieutenant Juan Ignacio Ramón, brought about 230 soldiers and four or five hundred horses and mules to camp behind the Caddo village west of Tso'to Lake toward the end of June.[22]

Freeman was a government surveyor; Custis was interested in botany and natural history. Their expedition, represented to Spanish authorities as purely scientific, left Natchitoches in two specially designed boats and five pirogues, a type of river craft made by routing out the trunk of a large bald cypress tree. Seven officers, three commissioned and four noncommissioned, and forty men accompanied Freeman and Custis. Their guides and interpreters were Tulin and a man named Talapoon, who was hired in Natchitoches. The expedition was intended to explore all the way to the upper banks of the Red River, where Panis lived. Panis was the name the French used to identify Wichita bands, including the Taovayas, Wichita, Yscanis, and Tawakoni that lived west of the Cross Timbers. Spanish officials, convinced that the expedition's scientific objectives were simply a cover for Jefferson's territorial ambition, took steps to intercept the Americans.

The boats used by Freeman and Custis were specially built to maneuver the sometimes shallow, frequently meandering Red River. Just above Natchitoches the main current was blocked by the lower end of the series of natural logjams called the Great Raft. Floating driftwood and live trees that tumbled into the Red River when rain washed away soft banks snagged on bends and sandbars and anchored on the bed of the river. Over time they compacted and formed three separate barriers, the top almost one hundred miles upstream from the lowest. As the lower end slowly rotted away, the upper end added nearly four-fifths of a mile of timber each spring.

No one knows how long the river sought ways around the Great

Raft, creating new floodplains, swamps, and lakes. When La
Harpe traveled up the river from Natchitoches almost two hundred years before Freeman and Custis, he reached "very difficult
log jams" on his second day out of Natchitoches, and five days later
he recorded:

> We found some timbers so thick that it seemed incredible to be able
> to go through them. There was on the branches of these trees an
> infinite number of snakes, upon which it was necessary for us to fire
> some musket shots from fear that they might fall into our boats. This
> route was very painful and fatigued our men extremely. We entered
> afterwards into a channel full of alligators where the currents were
> frightful. We passed through it by the tow line and by pulling
> ourselves from branch to branch.[23]

La Harpe went around the west side of the rafts, a less difficult
route than the one taken by Freeman and Custis, who went
around the east side, possibly to avoid observation by the Spaniards stationed at Bayou Pierre. The tangled mass of drifted red
cedar and bald cypress timbers approached by the Freeman-Custis
expedition soon after leaving Natchitoches stretched across the
width of the river and jutted three feet above the water. Weeds,
grass, and bushes grew on top of the mass's forty-yard thickness.
Six days later the expeditioners forced a passage through a tangle
of cottonwood, cypress, and cedar logs a hundred feet wide and
two hundred yards long. Nearing the third raft, Tulin told Freeman it was impossible to pass in boats of any kind; not even the
Indians had attempted it for fifty years. He suggested a bayou on
the east side as a way around. The Americans were told the
marshy stream was called Datche because the first Indian passing
that way had seen a bear gnawing a log and *datche* meant "a gap
eaten by a bear in a log."

The explorers paddled in deep pools and shallow water pas-
sages, winding through swampland, bending low under overhang-
ing branches, and feeling lost for fourteen days. When they at last
came out into the broad river—230 feet wide and 34 feet deep,
with a gentle current running between 10- to 12-foot-high banks—
its beauty was awesome. Tall cottonwood trees, oaks, and red
cedars bordered the banks. On the right, wooded land rose to a
height of 50 feet above the bank; on the left, rich and level land
extended as far as they could see. This was the land that became

known to frontier settlers as Caddo Prairie. It edged the western bank of the Red River for forty miles—from modern-day Shreve-port to the Arkansas state line. Westward beyond the prairie—some said fifty miles, and others said less—the principal village of the Caddo lay on the far side of Tso'to Lake. Ahead on the east bank was a Coushatta Indian village. The Caddo had given a group of Coushattas permission to live there in 1793.[24]

Soon after entry into the main flow of the Red River, a canoe paddled by Talapoon and a Caddo came in sight. Talapoon had been sent to the Caddo village with a request that Dehahuit meet the Americans at the Coushatta village. The Caddo with him was Dehahuit's messenger, sent to tell Tulin that Spaniards were camped by the Caddo village. The messenger told Tulin that Dehahuit wanted to see him and wished him to come to the Caddo village as soon as the Americans arrived at the Coushat-tas'. If Tulin could not come, Dehahuit would meet him at the Coushatta village and expected that Spanish officers would be with him. The Caddo messenger was promptly sent back to tell Dehahuit to meet Tulin at the Coushatta village *without* any Spaniards.

Freeman and Custis set up camp about a quarter of a mile below the Coushatta village. The Coushatta chief's home and large cornfield were a few miles below. He paid Freeman and Custis a brief visit, then went to prepare for the Grand Caddo's visit. A flag presented to his tribe by the Spaniards was kept at his house. He sent for it so that it could be hoisted in honor of Dehahuit. Freeman offered the Coushatta chief an American flag to raise instead of the Spanish one. Thus, when Dehahuit and forty of his young men and warriors rode into view on the opposite river bank, the flag of the United States flew from a pole in the center of the Coushatta village.

Dehahuit and his men saluted the Coushattas with an irregular firing of guns, and the Coushattas launched canoes to bring the Caddos across the river. As Dehahuit led his warriors toward the U.S. company, the Americans stood at attention and fired a salute. Dehahuit told the Coushatta chief he had never before been so respectfully received.

Dehahuit and the expedition party sat with the young Caddo men and warriors in a semicircle behind them. A brief silence was broken by Dehahuit's observation that the Americans "must have suffered a great deal of hardship in passing the great swamp," and he wondered at their success.[25] Sometime later he told Governor Claiborne, "When I saw the Spaniards on one side of me, and your people on the other, I was embarrassed. I did not know on which foot to tread."[26]

Freeman described the route he proposed to take and the distance he expected to go. He outlined the desires of the president and the American people, speaking, as instructed by Jefferson, of the respect they had for Indians of that country. The Caddo and Coushatta chiefs were told, "France for certain consideration, had sold to the United States the whole country of Louisiana together with its inhabitants, French, Spanish, and Indian and that hence-forward the People of the United States would be their fathers & friends and would protect them & supply their wants."[27]

The substance of Dehahuit's response was, "That being well treated by the French while under their Government he loved them, that under the Spanish Government he was well treated and he loved them, that now it had pleased the French (for what reason he did not know) to give them up to the Americans, and he loves them and hopes they will love and treat him as well as the French & Spanish did." He said that in the two years since coming under the U.S. government, he had not had any cause for complaints. The Supreme Being, he said, had made a difference between Ameri-cans and his people and had been pleased to endow Americans with more sense and granted them means "which they [the Caddo] were entirely destitute of." Therefore, Dehahuit said, he would look to them for protection and comfort, "to be his fathers, brothers & friends."[28]

Dehahuit said he was satisfied that the Americans had told him of their intentions, and he placed full confidence in what they said because their words showed a frankness that the Spaniards had hidden. He said the first question the Spanish commandant asked was, "Do you love the Americans?" His reply, said Dehahuit, was, "I do, but [I wonder] whether or not I think it improper for you to ask a question of the kind." Dehahuit then asked the commandant to say no more because he, Dehahuit, was not then prepared to answer any question, no matter how small.[29]

Dehahuit told Freeman and Custis that he feared the Spaniards intended to spill American blood and that "it had been a law among his Ancestors not to suffer the blood of whites ever to be spilt on their ground and he was determined while he lived not to admit of it, on his grounds, rivers, lakes, or Bayeaux." If the Spaniards wanted to fight, said the Grand Caddo, "he had not the least objection, provided they would go on their own ground."[30]

He told Freeman and Custis they had far to go "and will meet with many difficulties, but I wish you to go on. My friends, the Panis, will be glad to see you, and will take you by the hand. If you meet with any of the Huʒaa's [Wah-shush, Osages], and kill them, I will dance for a month. If they kill any of your party, I will go with my young men and warriors, and we will be avenged for you."[31]

The discussion ended. Food was served. The American soldiers and their Caddo counterparts were furnished with liquor to drink together. The soldiers were then drawn up in single file, and the Caddo warriors passed by from right to left, shaking hands and finishing in a line facing the soldiers at a distance of three paces. The principal warrior stood in front of the U.S. sergeant. He took a step forward and addressed his men, saying, "He was glad to see his new brothers had the faces of *men,* and looked like men and warriors." Turning to the sergeant, the warrior said, "Here we are, all men and warriors, shaking hands together, let us hold fast, and be friends forever."[32]

The next day Dehahuit told Freeman and Custis that he would take his people home the following morning. He explained, "He had already kept them several days from hunting: because not knowing with what intentions the Spaniards came so near: and hearing of the U.S. party, he thought it best to keep all his people together so that they could prevent hostilities in his land." Now, Dehahuit said, he had seen the U.S. party, knew its business, and had been treated well. He said he believed what Freeman and Custis told him and would hold them "fast by the hand as fathers and friends."[33]

Before leaving, Dehahuit confided that three Spanish soldiers had come to see him the day before he left his home. They had reported that their commandant had sent a messenger to Nacog-doches and that, as soon as he returned with orders from the government, they would "go to the Americans on Red River, stop them, and drive them back or take them prisoners." Dehahuit supposed the orders would arrive about the same time he got back and said he would try to find out what the Spaniards planned. If they had not already left, he would beg them "not to spill blood on his ground." He assured Freeman and Custis "that it was not fear which would make him this humble, because he did not fear man, that although his men are small and may appear to us [the Americans] like nothing, they are unacquainted with fear."[34]

Custis had already noted that the Caddo were small of stature, "without the least appearance of savage ferocity," but he knew they had some firearms and used their bow and arrow weapons "with astonishing dexterity & force."[35] Their bois d'arc bows were still prized throughout the region, and Custis had heard that Caddo hunters could send an arrow entirely through a buffalo with ease.

Dehahuit told Freeman and Custis that if the Spaniards wanted to speak to the Americans in a friendly manner, he would bring the commandant to the American camp and hear the talk of both parties. If, however, the Spaniards were determined to be hostile, he would order them to leave his grounds instantly and would not allow them to interfere with the explorers closer than 50 leagues above the Caddo village—about 450 miles above the place they were then camped.[36] He said he would send three of his best warriors to Freeman and Custis with whatever information he had learned. The Caddo chief's parting words were that the Americans would probably be attacked by the Osages and that if that happened, he would "have an opportunity to convince the American Government of his friendship." No matter how many Osages there were, he would show what his men were capable of doing, sending everyone able to bear arms.[37]

Reinforced by Dehahuit's support and three Caddos to guide and hunt, Freeman and Custis continued up the Red River. Two of the guides, Grand Osages and Cut Finger, were Dehahuit's particular friends. Grand Osages had got his name by being wounded in battle with the Osages. He had been hit by a ball fired by one of their guns.

Forty miles above the Coushatta village, the exploration party passed a beautiful bluff that rose nearly one hundred feet above the surface of the river. It stood at the mouth of the Sulphur River—called Bear River by La Harpe when he used it as a shortcut to the Nasoni village and "the lower little river" by Freeman. Another eighty-five miles of travel up the Red River brought the explorers to a lovely prairie on the northeast side. Cut

Finger and Grand Osages pointed to a hill that could be seen from the boats. There, they said, "their Old Chiefs used frequently to meet in Council." They wanted "to visit it with a bottle of liquor, that they might take a drink and talk to the great spirit!"[38]

Custis heard a Caddo version of the flood story while visiting with Caddos at the Coushatta village. He included it in his field notes because of its odd similarity to biblical accounts. Parts are like traditional tales told by Caddos long before—and long after. He did not say the hill Cut Finger and Grand Osages were eager to visit was the same as the one in the legend, but descriptions of the place sound alike. Custis recorded:

> They [the Caddo] say that a long time since a civil war broke out among them at which Enicco or the Supreme Being was so displeased as to send a great flood which destroyed all but one Family, consisting of fourteen, the Father, Mother & Children.—That this family were saved by flying to a knoll at the upper end of the Prairie, which was the only spot left uncovered; that in this knoll was a cave in which was preserved a male & female of all kinds of animals; that after the flood had continued for one moon they set at liberty a bird which they called *O-wah* which returned in a short time with a straw.—They then set out on a Raft in search of that place from whence the straw was brought, that going a west course for two leagues they came to land; that they there saw a fish which they called *Toesha* and being very much frightened at its enormous size, they all shed tears, from which circumstance they ever after called the place Chacanenah, signifying the ground upon which tears have been shed; that this fish remained there for many years after and was large enough for 30 men to encamp under.—All the Mexican [Texas] & Louisiana Indians they say are offspring of that family. I am told that some of the other Nations have a similar tradition.— That many of the tribes used to meet on a certain day in every year at the knoll upon which this family was saved and there offer up prayers and sacrifices to the Supreme Being for his singular favor of not destroying the whole race.[39]

Nearly half a century before Custis was told these things, a Spanish observer had reported that the Cadohadacho were divided into four families—"Beaver, Otter, Wolf, and Lion [panther]"—and that a hill two leagues (about five miles) from their village was held in veneration by Indians who respected the Cadohadacho "as the forefathers of the other nations."[40]

The Freeman-Custis party pulled to the bank of the Red River at the place pointed out by Cut Finger. Freeman, a trained surveyor, went with Grand Osages to examine the hill. It was about 2 miles long, 250 or 300 feet high, and narrow at the top of extremely steep sides. Freeman described it as

> an irregular mass of iron colored porous rock, in which there is a great number of small round pebbles. It has the appearance of having been in fusion at some former period. There is very little clay or soil on the surface, but a red colored gravel; it produces small scrubby Oaks and Pines only. In front of this mount lies a beautiful and rich meadow, extending from its base to the river, and downwards for about two miles. It is interspersed with small clumps of trees, and has a small lake or pond in its center. Around and near to this pond, are to be seen the vestiges of the Caddo habitations; it was the largest of their villages, and their cultivated fields extended for five or six miles from it in every direction.[41]

The expedition followed the river on around the Great Bend where Little River entered the Red. This heartland of Caddo country, from the Coushatta village to Little River, was, according to Freeman, "a distance of 162 miles" and "one of the richest and most beautiful imaginable. . . . It cannot be exceeded either in fertility or beauty, by any part of America or perhaps the world."[42]

About twenty miles past the mouth of the Little River, a stone and gravel bar crossed the width of the river. No more than fourteen inches of water covered the bar. It was the first place up the length of the Red River that could be forded throughout the year. From a height above the waterline, a half-mile of prairie stretched toward a boundary of oak and hickory woods. The prairie was wild with high grass, bushes, and briers, but in times past it had been tamed and cleared by the Caddo living there. Survivors of La Salle's expedition were welcomed there, and three years later a woman governing the settlement begged Tonti to help avenge the death of her husband. Ten Caddos lived there as late as 1773, but all that remained for Freeman and Custis to see were cedar cabin posts and some plum trees.[43]

The following day Cut Finger and Grand Osages were extraordinarily pleased to see three Caddos just ahead on the bank of the river. The two Indians had been apprehensive of Spanish attack almost every day and night they had traveled with the Americans.

The Caddos, sent by Dehahuit as promised, carried a message that would indicate if these fears were well founded.

The news was not good. The day before the messengers left home, nearly one thousand Spaniards had entered their village, cut down the pole from which the American flag flew, and carried off the flag. They insulted Dehahuit and took away two young Caddos to use as guides to a bluff on the river a few miles above the old Nasoni village.

Dehahuit's messenger advised the Americans to return. He said the commanding officer of the Spaniards was a "cross and bad man, who would do all the mischief he could to the party."[44] If Freeman and Custis decided to go ahead, Dehahuit advised that they kill the commander first. The chief sent a detailed description so they could recognize the Spaniard.

Cut Finger, Grand Osages, and the other Caddos were upset by Freeman's decision. He told them that his instructions were to proceed until stopped by a superior force, but if they wanted to turn back, they were perfectly at liberty to do so. The Caddos said they would stay with the Americans, but they were certain that none of them would ever return home.

Freeman asked how many Spanish soldiers had passed through the village and was told there were 1,050 or 1,060. He asked how far it was to the place they could expect to meet the Spaniards and was told his party would sleep twice before meeting them.

The explorers slept that night on the north riverbank. For hundreds of years the Caddos had planted corn by a lake near the opposite bank. The Caddo guides said the French had once had a small military post there, but no traces of it were visible. Freeman took a reading by astronomical observation.[45]

As predicted, the Americans and Spaniards confronted each other on the third morning. No one was killed; no prisoners were taken. But the Freeman-Custis expedition turned back, its explorations ended after three months on the Red River.

On hearing that Spanish troops numbering more than one thousand were in northeast Texas, Governor Claiborne called out the Louisiana militia and brought reinforcements from New Orleans to Natchitoches. He wrote Simón de Herrera, commander of the Spanish troops east of the Sabine River, that the treatment of Freeman's party and the cutting down of the American flag in the Caddo village were outrages. Claiborne argued that the

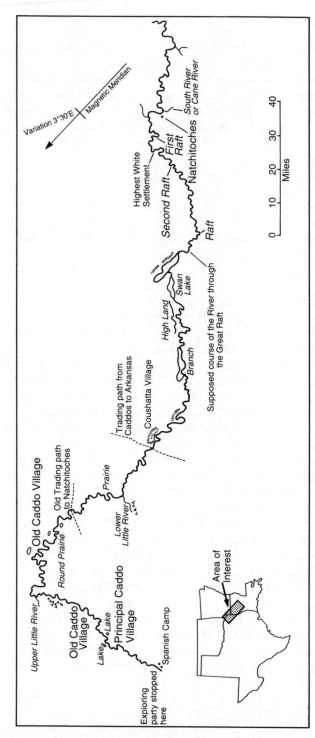

The Red River from Natchitoches to the place the 1806 Freeman-Custis exploration stopped, based on a portion of Nicholas King's map of the Red River in Louisiana. The data and reports that Freeman and Custis sent to Washington were used by King to prepare an accurate map of the 615 miles of the Red River traveled by the exploration party.

Caddo Indians were under the protection of the French government, that the French actually had a garrison established in a
Caddo village, and that the United States now owned all of what
had once belonged to France and therefore had enough authority
to display the American flag in the Caddo village.

Herrera replied, "I think as your Excellency does that all the
country which his Catholic Majesty has ceded to France belongs
to the United States, but the Caddo's nation is not upon it and on
the contrary the place which they inhabit is very far from it and
belongs to Spain."[46] Claiborne had the last word, writing, "You
have not denied, Sir, that the French when in possession of
Louisiana, had established a garrison on the Red River, far beyond
the place where Mr. Freeman and his associates were arrested on
their voyage, or that the Caddo Indians were formerly considered
as under the protection of the French Government. The silence of
your Excellency on these points, proceeds probably from a knowledge on your part of the correctness of my statements."[47]

Governor Claiborne invited Dehahuit to meet with him in
Natchitoches. Dehahuit, at the head of about a dozen men, came
on September 4. The next day Claiborne addressed them, saying
he spoke for the president of the United States, who had great
esteem and good wishes for them and other Indians. Claiborne
asked for the continued friendship of the Caddo people and
emphasized that the current disagreement between the United
States and Spain was a dispute between white people. He urged,
"Let the red man keep quiet, and join neither side."[48]

Dehahuit was cautious in reply. He told the governor:

> I have heard before the words of the President, though not from his
> own mouth. His words are always the same, but what I have this day
> heard will cause me to sleep more in peace.
>
> Your words resemble the words my forefathers have told me they
> used to receive from the French in ancient times. My ancestors from
> chief to chief were always well pleased with the French; they were
> well received and well treated by them when they met to hold talk
> together, and we can now say the same of you, our new friends.
>
> If your nation has purchased what the French formerly pos-
> sessed, you have purchased the country we occupy, and we being on
> the land of course go with it, so that we regard you in the same light
> as we did them. You request that our wars in future may be against
> the deer only, that is what we ourselves desire, and happen what

will, our hands shall never be stained with white man's blood. Your
words, which I have this day heard, shall be imprinted on my heart;
they shall never be forgotten, but shall be communicated from one to
another, till they reach the setting sun. . . .

My father was a chief; I did not succeed him till I was a man in
years. I am now in his place, and will endeavor to do my duty, and see
that not only my own nation, but other nations over whom I have
influence, shall properly conduct themselves.[49]

With these words the Grand Caddo declared the transfer of his
people's loyalty—not their land—to the Americans.

American forces massed in Natchitoches. General James Wilkinson arrived to take charge. Herrera assembled forces on the
west bank of the Sabine. Wilkinson marched out from Natchitoches and established headquarters on the east bank. Each
commander was acting under orders from a government that
regarded the other's action as an unfriendly invasion of territory.
Battle seemed unavoidable, but the two leaders confronting each
other across the Sabine were not eager to fight. They made an
agreement: until their governments settled the question of boundary, all the territory between the Sabine River and the Arroyo
Honda would be neutral ground, not to be occupied by either
one.[50] For a while at least, Dehahuit did not have to be concerned
that white men would stain his land with their blood.

Early in January 1807 a group of Caddos on their way home
from trading with the Taovaya-Wichita were attacked by an
Osage party. The Caddos suffered no injuries, but the Osages
relieved them of seventy-four horses, and they were left on foot
200 miles from home with a great deal of baggage, mostly buffalo
robes. They sent a runner to report the loss to Dehahuit, who set
out to rescue the stranded party. Dehahuit gathered the horses
remaining in the settlement and called together a strong group of
men to ride with him to punish the Osages if they could be found.
The war party returned, however, without encountering the
enemy.[51]

Another misfortune occurred while Dehahuit was away. One of
his small children, carrying fire either into or out of the house,
accidentally set the home ablaze. The timber, cane, and thatch
structure burned in a matter of minutes. The loss of the house and
everything in it was bad enough, but a greater calamity was that

the fire also consumed the corn crib where the family's entire crop was stored. The stored corn was all that could be depended on to keep hunger away during the winter months. Game was scarce in the region near the Caddo settlements, and going to hunt on the buffalo plains was almost impossible after the loss of so many horses.

Some people blamed the scarcity of game on the shortage of acorns the previous fall. A more probable reason was that the near woods and prairies were being drained of wildlife by an increasing number of hunters. Besides Choctaw bands hunting in Caddo country, numerous other Indians were migrating across the Mississippi. It was a lean winter for Dehahuit's people.

When spring came a small party of Cherokee Indians brought deerskins down the Red River to sell at Natchitoches. A brother of one of the men had been killed in Caddo country seven or eight years earlier. The present party wanted to straighten out its differences with the Caddos and stopped to visit Dehahuit before going on to Natchitoches. When Sibley met these Cherokees in Natchitoches, the brother of the slain man spoke highly of Dehahuit and did not blame the Caddos at all.

Dehahuit and fifteen of his men loaded their canoes with skins and took them to Natchitoches in April. Sibley had several special gifts waiting for them. He had bought scarlet cloth and had a regimental coat trimmed with black velvet and white buttons especially tailored for Dehahuit. He gave the son of an old Caddo chief named Carody a blue, scarlet-trimmed, half-regimental coat and a white linen shirt. Dehahuit was asked to deliver another regimental coat to Grand Osages, who was "in Major Freeman's Opinion one of the Best Indians he ever saw."[52] Cut Finger had already been presented with a blue frock coat in appreciation for the help he had given the exploration party.

A few weeks later eight Choctaws attacked some Anadarko women who were busy making salt at a saline spring above their settlement. The assault came barely three years after the May 1804 peace pact between the Caddos and Choctaws. Two Anadarko women were killed and scalped; the others were wounded. Dehahuit informed Sibley that the Anadarkos were under his protection and that he expected the Choctaws to give satisfaction. Sibley, who was depending on Dehahuit to convince the Texas tribes that the Americans were their friends, quickly sent a man to notify all Choctaw chiefs west of the Mississippi that the pact had been broken.

Three hundred alarmed Choctaws gathered at Natchitoches for protection and advice. Sibley recommended that they delegate some chiefs who were known and respected by Dehahuit and send them to him to speak in the tribe's behalf. He advised the delegation to express its indignation at the women's deaths and to convince the Caddo that the Choctaws living west of the Missis-sippi had had no part in the murders and did not approve of them. He counseled the Choctaws to make sure Dehahuit understood they wanted to preserve peace.

Sibley sent the government's interpreter, Gaspard Philebare, with the Choctaws chosen to carry the conciliatory message. The Caddos received them well. Dehahuit, who knew that the leader of the murdering party had lately been commissioned a chief by the American government, said he was willing to wait for the party leader to be given up to the Caddo or executed by the Choctaws. The Choctaw delegation returned to Natchitoches and appointed a chief to go to the Greater Choctaw Nation on the other side of the Mississippi with a request that the leader of the party responsible for killing the Anadarko women be punished. At the beginning of July everyone waited uneasily to see what would happen.

In the meeting with Governor Claiborne before the "neutral ground" agreement between Wilkinson and Herrera, Dehahuit had been asked to use his influence with tribes in Texas and bring them to Natchitoches for a council. He honored the request, arranging a council for the summer of 1807. On August 9 he announced to Sibley that about three hundred representatives of different nations were on their way to Natchitoches. Eighty Comanches arrived first. At the end of four days, ninety Caddos, thirty-four Anadarkos, sixteen Hainais, twenty-four Nacogdo-ches, forty-five Nabedaches, eighteen Tawakonis, eight Kichais, and four Chickasaws were present. Four hundred horses cropped the parched grass in the town commons.

On the final day of the council, August 18, Sibley emphasized that the United States wanted to have friendly relations with Indians, no matter where the boundary dividing the United States and Spanish territory lay. Dehahuit gave the last speech. He called the gathered tribes "my allies" and spoke of the recent attack on the Anadarko camp. He asked that the Choctaws be allowed three months to give satisfaction. During that time he would see that none of his people made mischief, but if no satisfaction was given by then, there would be no further restraints on Caddo allies. All the tribal representatives—Anadarko, Caddo, Nabedache, Kichai, Hainai, Ais, and Comanche—voiced their support.

Dehahuit and Sibley frequently had long, informal conversations. Sibley talked about world politics, wars that had been fought, the present and probable state of Spain. Dehahuit was an intelligent listener, quick to grasp major points and sometimes witty in his observations. Sibley's respect for the caddi, the unique leadership position he held, and the unswerving code of loyalty he followed increased with acquaintance. Sibley described Dehahuit in a letter to the secretary of war as "a man of more importance than Any other ten Chiefs on this Side of the Mississippi within my Agency" and added that the chief was a "Man who has a strong mind."[53]

The Caddos' strength lay in the endurance of their alliances and the extraordinary abilities of their hereditary leaders. Individually the Cadohadacho, Hasinai, and Natchitoches tribes were weakened by population decline; collectively they had the power to hold the country of their ancestors. Apaches, Osages, Chickasaws, and Choctaws stole their horses and killed or made captives of some of their people, but no tribe lived on Caddo land without permission. The French and Spanish had claimed to possess Caddo country, but neither denied tribal land rights. Dehahuit realized too late that Americans intended to dispossess his people and permanently occupy their lands.

By 1810 part of the area overseen by Dehahuit had begun to simmer like a stew pot over hot coals—ready to spill over with the least increase in heat. The Neutral Ground agreed on by Wilkinson and Herrera became a refuge for robbers, thieves, and other desperate individuals eluding the laws of the United States. They organized headquarters and outposts and generally lived off what they could get by robbing their neighbors and passing traders. A few men with families built permanent homes.

Another type of bold men and women, looking for free land and improved fortunes, became squatters on Natchitoches tribal land. Sometime between 1785 and 1792 and after the death of their chief, Tomoc, the Spanish commandant of the Natchitoches Post

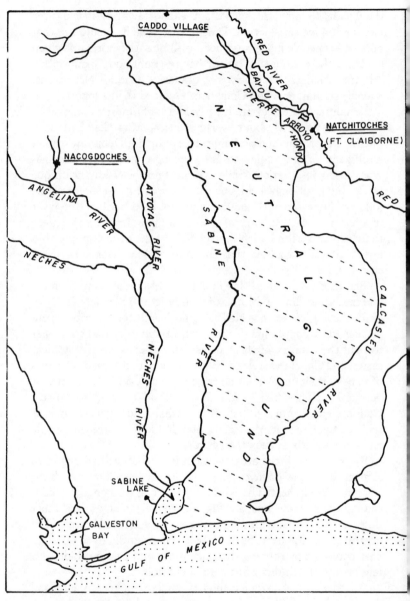

The area declared as Neutral Ground until Spain and the United States agreed on a boundary between Louisiana and Texas became the refuge of a large number of individuals eluding laws of the United States.

documented a grant of Natchitoches lands on both sides of the Red River at Lac des Muire. Their main settlement was on the west side of the Red River, about thirty miles north of the town named for them. Even after Americans took possession of Natchitoches Post and renamed it Fort Claiborne, Natchitoches land rights were generally respected; those outside the tribe who wanted land for their own use—mostly the French—bought it. In 1806 Pierre Gagnier bought 213.13 acres from John Sohano, "a civilized or Christian Indian, and other Indians of the Natchitoches village, and those claiming under the said John Sohano." Hypolite Bordelin claimed a much smaller acreage "under a purchase from an Indian chief of the Natchitoches village, by deed, bearing date the 23d of June, 1808, for the price and sum of eighty dollars."[54] Transactions like these did not prepare the Natchitoches for Americans who had little regard for Indian land rights—sturdy, land-hungry individuals who reasoned that their government had bought and paid for the whole Louisiana Territory and that it was a citizen's right, almost his duty, to pioneer its lush farmland. Any land without a fence around it was for the taking. A deed, if ever one became necessary, would come from the U.S. government.

The Natchitoches chief complained to Sibley that Americans were surrounding his village and cornfields. Sibley's solution was to survey lands the Natchitoches lived on, distinctly mark the boundaries, and then have the tribe sign a statement abandoning to the United States a claim to any more. Outlining his plan in a letter to the secretary of war on March 20, 1810, Sibley acknowledged, "When the white People first Came here in the year 1717 all the Country belonged to them [the Natchitoches] for Some hundreds of Miles & they were a powerful nation." He said the tribe was now much smaller in number and "will be content with a small quantity of lands, notwithstanding their equitable right to a great extent."[55] It was necessary, he wrote, to take care of the matter immediately to keep the Indians placid and reasonable.

Another group of unsavory intruders began collecting on the upper Red River. Most of them lived by hunting and running stock rather than farming. They were drawn to the area near the old Nanatsoho village on the Red River where a sandbar provided a crossing to fertile hunting grounds used by Caddo hunters for centuries. American squatters called their settlement Pecan Point. At this time there were not many Americans intruding on traditional Caddo-Hasinai homelands. These intruders were an unwelcome nuisance, but except for the inroads they made on the ready supply of game, they had little impact on Caddo or Hasinai tribes. If Dehahuit had made the planned journey to Washington, he might have discovered that there was a greater number of Americans than he could imagine, and he might have suspected that the first migrants to his country were the trickling sign of a coming flood.

C H A P T E R 18

FORCES BEYOND
CONTROL

In 1811 the earth shook, the rivers ran backward, and a great blazing arrow pierced the sky. An earthquake so intense that it was felt over two-thirds of the United States rolled the earth's surface like an ocean tossed by a winter storm. It created gaping troughs around its epicenter at New Madrid, Missouri, and caused the Mississippi River to appear to flow upstream. During the same year Halley's comet cut across the sky in a dazzling display. If Hasinai tribes had still depended on conas to foretell the future, they surely would have seen the rending of the earth below or the sky above as an evil portent. A century earlier the missionary Espinosa had said conas often based their forecasts on natural signs.

Other events in 1811, if they had been known and understood, could also have served to warn of bad times ahead. One was the letting of contracts to construct the first real highway leading west from states lapped by the Atlantic Ocean. Another was the passage of a steamboat down the river system from Pittsburgh to New Orleans, and effective proof it could steam back upstream against the current of the Mississippi. Both means of transportation eventually invited Americans west in greater numbers. New hostilities between Native Americans and frontier settlers that flared east of the Mississippi during 1811 practically guaranteed that white immigrants to Caddo-Hasinai country would bring with them a fear of Indians and a conviction that the races could not live side by side.[1] For a few more years, however, U.S. and Spanish officials competed to keep Caddos inside the bounds of territory claimed by their respective governments.

Louisiana left territorial status and entered the union as a state in April 1812. In the same month during one of the long talks that Sibley and Dehahuit had become accustomed to, Sibley described the limits of the new state and said they included the Caddos' village by Tso'to Lake. Six months later after a survey made to locate the northwest corner of the state of Louisiana, Sibley wrote the secretary of war, saying that both the Caddo and Anadarko towns would have been included in the state of Louisiana if the survey line had gone only half a degree higher up the Sabine River. He warned the secretary, "The Spaniards have always told them that the Country they occupied belonged to Spain & we have told them the contrary. Should the Caddos turn from us Near Twenty Other tribes will go with them." He even proposed, "If it was practicable by an Act of Congress to make a Small Alteration in Northwestern Limits of this State so as to Include the Nandaco and Caddo Tribes it is my opinion much good might Result from it. If not Much evil Avoided by it."[2]

The "good" he had in mind was Caddo allegiance in case the Spaniards ever decided to take Natchitoches. Spain was an ally of Great Britain, and a declaration of war between England and the United States was expected at any moment. Many U.S. citizens strongly believed that Texas was rightfully part of the Louisiana Purchase, and a great number of them believed, or pretended to believe, that war with England was war with Spain—a good excuse to push their nation's boundary to the Rio Grande. The Caddos and their allies would be useful if the United States decided to take Texas. The "evil" to be avoided was Indian alliance with either Spain or Great Britain.

Another view that Sibley might have considered was the use of Caddo land for an expanding white population that was sure to grow with Louisiana statehood. He wrote the secretary of war earlier in May, saying that the Caddos claimed the country on both sides of the Red River for six or seven hundred miles and that if a "space of no great extent was laid off for the Indians, they would, for a small consideration, relinquish to the United States the rest of their claim; but the longer it is postponed the more difficult it will be to effect."[3]

Samuel Davenport supplied Spanish authorities with detailed information on the location of the Caddos, their kindred, and allied tribes in 1809. Having handled Indian trade in Nacogdoches since 1798, his knowledge was possibly better than Sibley's. Davenport reported that the Caddos lived on the east bank of the Sabine River and "still numbered over two hundred braves." He fixed the location of the principal Caddo village by saying it was seventy miles or so above the Anadarkos, who lived a few miles above the Nacogdoches, whose village was about thirteen miles above the town named for them. The position he described was probably seventy-five miles from the place where Sibley said the Caddos lived.[4] If both Davenport's and Sibley's reports are correct, it would seem that there were two large Caddo communities, both inside Texas. It is probable that there were smaller Caddo communities that neither agent knew about because they were out of sight from the Red River, other waterways, or trails traveled by traders.[5]

The locations, numbers, and allegiances of the northeast Texas tribes gained added importance when the Mexican revolt against Spanish dominion jumped the Rio Grande in 1811. Revolutionists found a stronghold among the lawless adventurers in the Neutral Ground. American volunteers calling themselves "the Republican Army of the North" enlisted these white desperados along with some Indian warriors — none of them Caddo or Hasinai — and prepared to invade Texas. Their idea was to aid the Mexican revolution by conquering the Spanish province to the Rio Grande and making a republican state of it. Their plan was no secret, and it was generally understood that action would begin as soon as war was declared with England.

From the beginning of the Mexican revolt in 1810, both Spanish royalists and Mexican revolutionists tried to enlist Indians in their fight. With knowledge that an American-led invasion force stood ready to cross the Neutral Ground, the royalists made a concerted effort to win the support of the Caddos. They sent a special agent to Dehahuit in July 1812, hoping he could talk the Grand Caddo into visiting San Antonio, where he could be persuaded to bring the Caddos and their allies to the side of Spain. Dehahuit went only to Nacogdoches, where he was feasted and given many presents, but he made no commitment.[6]

News that the anticipated war between the United States and

England had been declared reached Natchitoches the last week in July. Two weeks before Sibley had asked Dehahuit to take a small party of his men and carry a "talk" to the tribes west of Natchitoches. Sibley's intent was to utilize Dehahuit's influence with the Texas tribes to keep them from taking sides with Spanish royalists and to assure them that Americans would not hurt them. Caddo and Anadarko chiefs spent several months visiting tribes living to the west in Texas and delivering Sibley's message about "the causes of the war with England, the possibility of hostilities against Spain and the probability of an American march into Texas."[7] Sibley was able to write the secretary of war on February 12, 1813, that Dehahuit could bring from three to five thousand Indian warriors into the field if the government ever had any need to call on them.[8]

Dehahuit did not underestimate the value of his services to the American government; they were an exchange for friendship and benefits. Shortly after he returned from negotiating U.S. interests, he asked Sibley to send some good man to live among his people, keep their tools in order, teach them how to plow and to manage stock. The Caddos had successfully cultivated crops for hundred of years, but Dehahuit saw the advantage of the white people's way of farming. Sibley said he was not authorized to spend as much as Dehahuit asked for but would see if he could get approval. Sibley told the secretary of war about Dehahuit's request in a letter dated May 19, 1813, saying, "Should you think proper to allow me to be at Some Small Expense to Assist him to Carry his Wishes into Effect it will give me great pleasure to do so."[9] Nothing more was done—the secretary evidently did not think the expense "proper," or perhaps he was too engaged in the war with England to be concerned with helping the Caddo farm.

As soon as Governor Manuel Salcedo of Texas heard that war had been declared, he made a last attempt to win the support of the Caddos. He sent a letter to the chiefs reminding them of the favors the king of Spain had shown their people, saying the Spaniards were their best friends and warning against the Americans, who would take their lands and drive them from their homes. Dehahuit had probably already left with Sibley's message to the Texas tribes when Salcedo wrote the letter. In August 1813 the Republican Army of the North crossed the Sabine River unopposed and was given a friendly welcome in the town of Nacogdoches.[10]

Indian warriors east of the Mississippi River were enticed to join the Americans' fight, but a faction of the Creek nation, incited by agents of Spain and Great Britain, came across the river with tobacco and war talk intended to inflame hostilities against Americans. Sibley countered by calling a council of Louisiana Alabamas and Coushattas, relatives of the Creeks, and all the other tribes in his district. Once again he counted on Dehahuit to control a difficult situation.

Caddo, Alabama, Coushatta, Yatasi, and Apalache chiefs and headmen, ninety-two in all, came to Natchitoches for Sibley's council in October 1813. Sibley reported that Dehahuit made a long speech, saying:

> it is true in such times that many false reports were Spread, they, Red People not having the Arts of Writing & Printing were more liable to be Imposed on than white people, that whenever he Visited this place the news he heard was Particularly so, that he had learned to be Very Cautious not to be led away by Idle Reports, [that] he was not a Child to Open his Ears to all he heard, that although his skin was Red he trusted he had some of the Sentiments & discretions of white people, that from the time he first Took his great Father the President of the United States by the hand, through his Brother the Agent he never had entertained but one Sentiment:—It was well known that his nation had never Injured Any white people nor Red, but in their Own defense; it was always his Instructions to his people, & himself set them the Example to be kind to white men. If they met them in the Woods, or in the Prairies to divide what they had with them, to be their Pilots & guides. If they were unable to help themselves to bring them home and feed them.
>
> He Remembered well the talk he received last Summer from his Brother the Agent which he Communicated to all the Tribes to the West & that he had great pleasure in Witnessing, that it was well Received by all of them & not one of them would throw it away. . . . He would now repeat it in behalf of all the Tribes to the West Under his Influence as well as his Own Nation, that If the United States were Invaded by an Enemy, they would all Come & fight for us as long as one Warrior Remained.[11]

Dehahuit ended by speaking directly to Sibley. "For myself," the chief said, "I will need no other notice than for you to Call upon me. . . . A long talk is not necessary truth & sincerity Can be expressed in few words. Much talking does not become Warriors, leave that to women & men like women."[12]

The next morning Dehahuit and Sibley sat alone in the agent's office. Sibley noted how many tribes were on this side of the Mississippi and how very desirable it would be for them to all understand and know one another. He said that since all the tribes looked up to Dehahuit as their older brother, had great respect for him, and knew of his visits with the western tribes the previous summer, those to the south would be much pleased by a similar visit from him. Sibley indicated that he wanted Dehahuit to come back in fifteen or twenty days and, with Sibley's interpreter and two or three other persons, be fitted out for a visit to all those tribes.

Sibley waited for Dehahuit's answer. The Grand Caddo remained silent. The agent prodded, saying "that he had made no Answer." Dehahuit "then Said I never refused you Any thing you desired of me & Am not going to do it now. I thought it was Enough for you to tell me you wished me to go. I however now tell you I will go."[13]

Dehahuit's willingness was neither naive nor totally unselfish. By strengthening friendly relations with all the tribes fringing his own country, he was practicing the caddis' centuries-old strategy of shielding their borders with allies. He obviously did not need incentives other than those given him by Sibley, but Governor Claiborne of Louisiana was worried by the possibility of a British attack on New Orleans and added his persuasion. Clairborne told Dehahuit that the English were like the Osages, who "have already robbed the hunters of all the nations, and their chiefs wage war to acquire more skins." He said that the English were not willing to fight Americans one on one. Instead, they asked for assistance from red people, telling lies and making promises they would not keep. He warned that the English would not be able to shield the Creeks, who had sent war talks to the Coushattas and other of Dehahuit's neighbors. Claiborne recalled the attack on Natchitoches by the Natchez and the Caddos' response to St. Denis's call for help. "When your father was a chief," he said to Dehahuit, "the paths from your Towns to Natchitoches was clean, and if an Indian struck the people of Natchitoches — It was the same as to strike him." Lastly, Claiborne sought to honor Dehahuit with a present, telling him, "To a chief, a man and warrior, nothing could be more acceptable than a sword. . . . I have therefore directed, that a sword be purchased at New Orleans, and forwarded to Doctor Sibley, who will present it to you (Caddo Chief) in my name."[14]

Almost a year later when the Caddos reported for service as ordered by General Andrew Jackson, Dehahuit may have been wearing a military sword. Jackson had already ordered his own troops to New Orleans when he wrote in a letter dated October 26, 1814, "The Caddo Chief with the neighboring tribes twelve in number have made a tender of their services with between 500 and a 1000 warriors to the united states. They are well armed with Rifles and I have ordered them to be enrolled and placed a[t] the disposal of the officer commanding Fort Claibourne (Natchitoches). This will afford security to that country for the present, both from external and internal enemies."[15]

It is fortunate that no emergency existed in Natchitoches. There were only about 150 warriors in camp at Natchitoches on January 10, 1815. Sibley explained, "Had they not have been dispersed in small hunting parties over an Extensive tract of Country before the receipt of Genl. Jackson's Order they would all have now been Collected. I have Sent runners in every direction. they are Coming in daily and I Expect in ten or fifteen days to have Nearly all that are Called for Collected."[16] By then they were no longer needed. Jackson had won the Battle of New Orleans on January 8.

Two weeks later Dehahuit's alliance with the United States through "his brother the Agent" was radically altered. Sibley was replaced without notice or explanation—a newly appointed agent, Thomas Gales, simply arrived to take Sibley's place. The sudden loss of a friend's authority marked the decline of Dehahuit's ability to direct the destiny of his people. Forces as far outside his control as earthquakes and comets began to gnaw at the edges of his defensive shield.

Before the War of 1812 most men who moved west came singly, seeking adventure or asylum from laws, debts, or personal misfortune. Few brought families and settled down to farm. They lived off the land by hunting, fishing, and trapping, or they became illegal Indian traders. After the war there was a rapid increase in the number of rootless white men coming up the Red River. Some of them settled at Pecan Point, near the site of the old Nanatsoho Caddo village on the south bank of the Red River. Dehahuit protested to the agent in Natchitoches, telling him that the white settlement blocked the only place for many miles that the river could be crossed to reach the Caddos' traditional hunting grounds.[17]

John Jamison was now agent—Dehahuit hardly had time to become acquainted with the man who replaced Sibley before he, too, was replaced. Soon after Jamison was appointed in 1816, he wrote the secretary of war about the Caddo chief's "disaffection" and said it came from "the want of protection."[18] In the spring of 1817 Jamison made an attempt to do his duty by using a military detachment to evict the Pecan Point squatters. He moved them to the north bank of the river, arrested unlicensed traders, and confiscated their merchandise, but these actions did little good. Two years later there were twelve families at Pecan Point and another settlement of twenty families a little farther up on the north side of the Red River at the mouth of the Kiamichi River.

Groups of hardworking Americans and new European immigrants also joined the westward movement following the War of 1812. By 1819 there were 14,273 people living between the Arkansas River and the bend in the Red River—enough to organize Arkansas Territory. Government officials, territorial and federal, seemingly agreed that west of Arkansas was not fit for white occupation but was just fine for Indians, so Arkansas Territory's western border became the eastern frontier of Indian country.[19]

Indian country between the Arkansas and Red Rivers began to fill with Creeks, Chickasaws, Cherokees, Choctaws, Seminoles, and Delawares who were bribed, tricked, or coerced into exchanging their holdings east of the Mississippi for lands west of white frontier settlements. As early as 1816 more than two thousand Cherokees were living in west Arkansas. Osage lands, almost all of the present state of Arkansas north of the Arkansas River and a large part of the present state of Missouri, had already been ceded to the United States. To protect both Indians and new white colonists, the military post that later became known as Fort Smith, Arkansas, was built in 1817. A treaty with the Quapaws in 1818 extinguished their tribal claim in Arkansas because U.S. officials thought it limited territory assigned to the Cherokees and Choctaws.

Major Stephen H. Long, commander at Fort Smith, informed the receiver in the Land Office in Missouri Territory in January

1818 that the Caddos south of the Red River "inhabited a part of the country before the cession of Louisiana to the United States, and still make some pretensions to it. — They pretended to claim all the country beginning at the Mississippi and extending west-wardly between the two Rivers above mentioned — to the north-west 'As far as they could fight off the Osages' and to the southwest, indefinitely."[20]

The next year Captain John H. Fowler, in charge of a small post established in the area where the Sulphur River forked from the Red River, wrote Jamison, saying the Caddo chief should be removed because he showed no appreciation of the gifts presented to him and was actually antigovernment in many of his views, claiming all the lands above the raft. In another letter to the superintendent of Indian trade, Fowler complained about the Caddo chief's "pretensions to land on both sides of the river, and his threats that he would drive off all the Americans settled above the raft." The captain called Dehahuit "a Mischievous Indian" and suggested that he be replaced or undermined by the appoint-ment of a second chief, which the government would recognize and deal with.[21] In nine brief years the man Sibley declared was "of more importance than Any other ten Chiefs on this Side of the Mississippi" had become in the eyes of newcomers "a Mischievous Indian." The Grand Caddo whom Governor Claiborne described to Andrew Jackson as "a man of great merit . . . brave, sensible and . . . the most influential Indian on this side of the River Grande," whose "friendship, sir, will give much security to the western frontier of Louisiana," was viewed by multiplying fron-tier Americans as a pretender. To them Dehahuit and the people he represented were simply a nuisance standing in the way of expansion.

The 1820 Choctaw Nation treaty with the United States provided for the tribe's removal to a vast area north of the Red River covering what is now part of Arkansas and southeast Oklahoma — lands including long-recognized Caddo hunting grounds and old village sites. Five thousand white settlers were already living in the part of the Red River valley extending eastward from the mouth of the Kiamichi when the Choctaw treaty was signed — Miller County, created out of this heavily populated district of Arkansas Territory in April of that year, took in the traditional Caddo heartland. One hundred fifty years later an elderly Caddo mourned, "We used to have all of Miller County."[22] The settlers of Miller County were indignant when they learned that the government of the United States had given "their" land to the Choctaws. Some of them moved to the south bank of the Red River, believing they were still within Miller County but actually crossing into Spanish Texas and deeper inside the ancient boundary of Caddo lands.[23]

Clashes between the Caddos and Osages grew with so many immigrants, both Indian and non-Indian, competing for hunting rights. Dehahuit struggled to protect his people in the old way, with strong alliances. Americans chose to misread his intent. Governor James Miller of Arkansas Territory wrote to the secretary of war that a band of Cherokees, led by The Bowle, had "left those on the Arkansas and gone to the Red River, where a banditti of outlaws are forming with whom I expect trouble. . . . This banditti consists as I am informed, of a strolling party of Cherokees, Delawares, Shawnees, Choctaws, Creeks and Coshattahs, and all backed by the Caddos, who are a very considerable tribe, and their principal chief, I am told holds a Spanish commission as colonel."[24]

The year when Arkansas Territory was organized, 1819, was also the year that the United States and Spain finally signed a treaty agreeing on the Sabine River as a boundary between Louisiana and Texas. Surveyors immediately appeared with their sticks and chains to measure lines running through Caddo country in Louisiana, but the international boundary remained unmarked for more than twenty years—the final wooden post with "U S" carved on the east side and "T" on the west was not erected until 1841.[25] One reason for the long delay was unstable government on the Spanish side of the Sabine.

The Caddo stayed sturdily neutral while the battles of the Mexican revolution shifted power back and forth between Spanish royalists and Mexican republicans below the Rio Grande. Few, if any, Spanish or Mexican families lived farther north in Texas than San Antonio. Royalists defeated the American-assisted revolutionists, who entered Texas across the Neutral Ground in 1812. The non-Indian population of Nacogdoches, about one thousand people, abandoned the town and scattered. Americans continued to claim that Texas justly belonged to the United States, and when the 1819 treaty was signed, they accused the U.S. negotiators of bartering it away. During June 1819 another force of American volunteers invaded the province, set up a provisional government in Nacogdoches, and proclaimed Texas a free and independent republic. John Sibley was a member of the governing council for this short-lived republic. Invading Americans were again routed by royal Spanish forces, but the threat of territorial loss to Americans or Mexican revolutionists made it necessary for the Spanish government to find means to defend the frontier.[26]

Juan Antonio Padilla was sent to gather information on the Indians of Texas for the Spanish. Padilla's descriptions of the Caddo and Hasinai tribes in 1820 were not far different from those written one hundred years earlier. He said the Caddos were perhaps the most civilized of all the Indians. They farmed and hunted, built well-constructed houses with straw or wood, believed in an idea of God as the origin of all creation, gave thanks and celebrated with dances and festivities, and cured the sick and wounded with herbs and magic. He said they married by contract "with ridiculous ceremonies," and when a man's wife died, he remarried. They enjoyed visiting, were hospitable, disliked theft, depended on trading for whatever they wanted or needed and could not supply for themselves, and were faithful in keeping their contracts. Their ordinary dress was made of deerskins, but they also wore skirts made of chintz or flowered material. Certain classes of men shaved a part of their heads and painted their faces with vermilion and charcoal in the old way. In earlier times men had worn shell or colored stone ornaments in pierced ears and noses; when Padilla visited the custom was to wear a silver pendant hung from a nose ring.[27]

Padilla discovered that a large number of the Caddo had learned French, the result of "the commerce they have with foreigners," and that a few knew Spanish, which, he said, they pronounced poorly. Like all Spanish observers, Padilla frowned on Indian trade with "foreigners," and he noted that the Caddo carried large supplies of bear, deer, beaver, otter, and other animal furs to Natchitoches, where they traded for "carbines, munitions, merchandise, tobacco, and firewater, of which they are very fond." He said the Nadacos (Anadarkos), who ordinarily went on hunting trips with the Caddo and had a close friendship with them, were also "given to the use of firewater because of their extensive trade with foreigners." The Nacogdoches were much given to drunkenness and poorer because of it. According to him, the other two Hasinai tribes, the Nabedache and Hainai—Padilla called them San Pedro and Texas, as Spaniards had for many years—rarely went to Natchitoches and were "but little addicted to firewater."[28]

Another piece of information that Padilla reported was either the result of his bias against French and Americans or a reflection of changes brought about by trade. About the Caddo he wrote, "At their dances, they drink great quantities of firewater—some of them drinking until they tumble over. In these gatherings there are never lacking some disorders resulting in personal injuries because of their drunkenness." It is possible, however, that instead of the sort of drunkenness Padilla thought he saw, he actually witnessed ancient initiation rites for young men tutored in the mysteries of healing and prophesy. Espinosa had said that drinks and tobacco consumed by prospective conas during initiation ceremonies caused them "to fall upon the ground like drunken men" and remain there in a state of trance for twenty-four hours before awaking to "relate what they have dreamed."[29] If Padilla was accurate in his descriptions of drunkenness, then easily acquired liquor consumed with abandon had replaced potent drinks brewed for restricted ceremonial use.

From the time of the missionaries forward, Spanish reports recorded that all of the tribes that lived in the wooded region between the Trinity River and the frontier of the United States lived in perfect harmony and together preserved an inviolable peace. Padilla made the same observation, and unlike American officials who complained that Dehahuit was a pretender, he reported that all the friendly nations recognized the superiority of the leader of the Caddos, that they called him "Gran Cado," and that his office was usually hereditary. "At the present time," Padilla said, "they [the Caddo] are in the Neutral Ground."[30]

The Spanish governor of Monterrey sent a message inviting the Caddos to move to Mexican land. A deputation of eighty-three Caddos went to hear what he proposed in August 1821. The governor offered good pay to any white man who would conduct the Caddos to Monterrey, and two men who farmed around Natchitoches and had known the Caddo for many years, Pierre Rublo and Joseph Valentin, accompanied them. In conference with the governor, the Caddos said they were willing to accept a good tract of land on the Guadalupe River, beginning where the upper road from San Antonio to Nacogdoches crossed and running to the river's source. According to Valentín, the only reason they did not make any immediate move was that one of their respected elders was ill, and they did not want to leave him behind.[31]

The Caddo delegation barely had time enough to return home before the government of Mexico changed. Mexico won its independence, and a treaty with Spain was signed August 24. Augustín de Iturbide was declared emperor of the Mexican Empire; Gaspár López became commandant general of the eastern Interior Provinces—Texas. On November 3, López issued a proclamation that was sent to all tribal chiefs or headmen. It announced the change of government and asked the tribes to unite with the empire, promising them equal rights and privileges as citizens, a liberal system of government, and protection. Iturbide sent a sergeant and three soldiers to deliver letters and documents to the Grand Caddo, addressing him with the Spanish spelling of his name, Dia Juyn. The carriers left San Antonio the last week of November.[32]

The trip from San Antonio to Nacogdoches was never an easy one. The poor condition of the couriers' horses made it ever more difficult. They had to walk part of the way and did not deliver the papers until mid-January. Dehahuit wrote Iturbide on January 22, saying he had received the letters and documents but would not be able to have council with the other chiefs before spring.

Dehahuit had time to study the letters and documents before responding on March 4, 1822. His letter to Iturbide said that he was glad to hear of the change of government, that he was well satisfied, and that he had been suspicious of Arrendondo, the former Spanish commandant general, but had great confidence in López. Dehahuit offered the support of all the Caddo nations if Iturbide decided to make war against the Comanches and stated that the only way to deal with them was with "strong blows." As for the proposed treaty, Dehahuit was willing to swear his allegiance to Iturbide as father and chief but said he could not accept Article Four, "to accept the Catholic Religion and exclude all others, because one cannot speak their opinions for a people, especially concerning their Religions."[33]

The Cherokees, led by The Bowle and backed, according to the governor of Arkansas Territory, by the Caddos, built a village north of the deserted town of Nacogdoches. Their chiefs, head-men, and interpreters proceeded to Mexico to treat with Iturbide for rights to the land. Moses Austin was there at the same time, petitioning for the first land grant to colonize Americans in Texas. The Cherokees were promised title to the land they were living on and given a written agreement guaranteeing that "until the agreement of the Supreme Government is obtained," they could continue to enjoy their free and peaceful right to cultivate their crops on the lands they had settled in common. The Cherokee agreement was confirmed by Iturbide in April 1823. Austin's grant had been confirmed the previous month.[34]

By 1825 so many Americans had made improper claims to Caddo land in Louisiana that Dehahuit asked their agent, who was then George Grey, to designate Caddo territory within the United States by natural boundaries or some other way that would be recognized by all. Grey had relocated the agency in 1821, moving up the Red River from Natchitoches to Sulphur Fork. Four years later he had moved again, to Caddo Prairie. Instead of winding his way through the labyrinth of waterways to Natch-itoches, Dehahuit only needed to ferry across Tso'to Lake to reach the agency. Grey's instructions were to strictly enforce the act of Congress regulating trade and intercourse with Indian tribes. He was informed by the secretary of war that white persons trespassing on Indian land were liable to prosecution, fines, and imprisonment. Like Jamison, Grey had authority to detail soldiers from the nearest military post to remove trespassers by force if necessary.[35] Nevertheless, Grey's duty to keep white persons off Indian land was almost impossible. Dehahuit's request for the designation of recognizable boundaries seemed like a solution. He proposed a "line commencing at mouth of Sulphur Fork, thence, meandering, the old channel of Red River to its junction with the Cypress Bayou on the east and the Cypress Bayou on the south east, Sulphur Fork on the west, and the Spanish line on the south west, those lines are natural ones and generally understood as the boundary of the Caddoan lands by both Indians and whites."[36]

In 1826 the Quapaws arrived in Caddo country. When they ceded the last of their lands in Arkansas Territory to the United States, they were unfairly given the impression that lands had been purchased for them from the Caddos. The surprised Caddos agreed to let them stay, and with Dehahuit's consent the Quapaws selected a place to settle near the agency. But there was soon dissatisfaction in both tribes.[37]

A short time later Grey told the Caddo chief that the government also wished to settle the small bands of Indians living elsewhere in Louisiana on his lands. The chief again cooperated, saying that since it was the wish of the government, he had no objection. But game and other resources in his country were becoming increasingly burdened not only by the intrusion of white people but also by the number of Indians seeking refuge there. Dehahuit felt the government was stretching the limit of what it should ask and expressed this sentiment, telling Grey "that he had never sold lands to the Government, but had permitted the Quapaws, and other Indians that had sold their lands, to reside amongst his people; and he thinks the Government should give him a small annuity, for which he would be very thankful."[38] An annuity of $50 was granted.

Grey at least made an effort to keep white intruders off Caddo territory inside the United States. There was no control protecting Caddo-Hasinai lands across the border. The great Anglo-American immigration to Texas came in 1825. First a slow trickle of newcomers repopulated Nacogdoches. Then a revolt led by General Antonio López de Santa Anna forced Emperor Iturbide to abdicate, and new colonization laws brought hundreds of settlers to the rich, rolling land, luxuriant woodlands and mild climate of Texas. An official line between Mexico and the United States had not yet been drawn, and a treaty with Santa Anna's government provided for the immediate definition of the border. A Mexican boundary commission headed by General Manuel Mier y Terán was sent to determine the location in the region of the Sabine and Red Rivers.

General Terán, Lieutenant José María Sánchez y Tapía, and a seven-man escort crossed the Trinity River and rode toward Nacogdoches on May 29, 1828. The next afternoon, near the Nadaco village of twenty-nine homes, they met with chiefs of the Ais, Texas (Hainai), and Nadacos (Anadarkos). Sánchez said, "All of them expressed great vexation at the admission into this territory of tribes coming from the North, and stated that if they had more men in their tribes, they would, doubtless declare war upon them, so great is the jealousy they feel toward the newcomers."[39] By then there were Choctaw, Coushatta, Cherokee,

Quapaw, Shawnee, Delaware, and Kickapoo villages in Caddo-Hasinai territory.

At night the Anadarkos held a dance. A drummer placed himself in the center of the dance circle with a kettle drum—drums were made either of an iron pot half-filled with water and covered with a stretched deerskin or a gourd covered the same way. Dancers formed a circle around the drummer, and an unappreciative Sánchez said they spent "the whole night jumping, singing, and yelling. Their songs are monotonous, but although the singers sing in unison, not one gives a false note or loses the time during the whole night."[40]

Terán and his party went on to the town of Nacogdoches. Including troops of the garrison, not quite seven hundred Spaniards, French, Americans, and free blacks were settled there. Indians from all the tribes in the region often came to trade or visit in the town. After Terán arrived, Caddo, Hasinai, and immigrant tribes sent delegations to confer with him on definite assignments of land and assurance that white people would not be allowed to take Indian land.

The Caddo men, dressed for a state occasion, wore spectacular ornaments. Small figures of horses, crescents, large disks, or several rings made of silver or tin hung from metal clips that pierced the septum of their noses. Some of the ornaments were large enough to cover their mouths or even their chins. They wore earrings more than two inches in diameter. Small silver rings and tubes or tubes of bright glass were fixed along the entire outer rim of their ears, and turkey feathers were placed behind their ears. Some wore dried bird skulls instead of metal ornaments. They carried little looking glasses that reflected the vermilion painted around their eyes. Men of a certain rank shaved most of the hair on their heads, leaving an uneven crest along the center. On either side, from the crest down to the neck, they painted wavy vermilion streaks.[41]

Lieutenant Sánchez, who was a cartographer and an artist, made sketches of a Caddo couple. The woman wore a calf-length cloth coat over a skirt and long blouse. Her blouse had a ruffled collar and was pinned on the front with silver disks, graduating in size from the largest at the top. Her hair was nearly hidden by a turban; she wore moccasins and cloth leggings. The Caddo man wore a long cloth shirt with ruffles at the cuffs and a V neck. His leggings were buckskin, and garters of ribbon or yarn were tied below his knees. His head was covered by a flat-topped hat with a ribbon-bound crown and a broad brim. His face was painted with charcoal, and he wore a gleaming nose ornament.

Another sketch captured a man and woman of the Yowani Choctaw band, which had been united with the Caddo for a half-century. The Yowani woman's blouse pins and ear pendants were like the ones worn by the Caddo woman. Her hair was tied back and bound by an array of ribbons with long streamers that fluttered from behind her like bands from a bright rainbow.[42]

Tribal delegates who conferred with Terán assured him that, although they lived on the border and traveled back and forth over the Red River, they wanted to be thought of as Mexicans. The general specifically asked the Grand Caddo whether his people's lands lay in Mexico or in the United States. After making sure he understood what was asked, the chief's firm answer was that "he was neither on Mexican nor United States Territory, but on his own land which belonged to nobody but him."[43]

CHAPTER 19

BREAKING THE HEART

The Red River artery of Caddo heartland was
partially protected by the Great Raft. The top raft, which had
forced Freeman and Custis to detour through a great swamp
before coming back to the free-flowing river along Caddo Prairie,
grew to connect with the high east bank, completely blocking the
river on that side. When spring rains raised the water level, the
raft turned all the flow toward the west bank and flooded Caddo
Prairie.[1]

Before the 1830s it was believed impossible to remove the
logjams that blocked the navigation of the Red River above
Natchitoches. Steamboats navigated the river to Natchitoches as
early as 1820, but even canoes or keel boats had difficulty
penetrating beyond. Congress appropriated funds to cut a route
through in 1829, but first attempts were unsuccessful. The river,
more expert at construction than humans were at demolition,
built on to the top end faster than debris could be hacked through
and carried away at the bottom. It was obvious that greater force
than muscle power would be required to destroy the rafts. Jeheil
Brooks, appointed Caddo agent in 1830, arrived with the knowledge that the removal of the Great Raft had been authorized and
that Captain Henry Shreve had invented a battering-ram steamboat that could do the job.[2]

In the meantime Brooks planned to build a new agency, below
the Caddo villages on Tso'to Lake. His earliest correspondence

with officials in Washington described the deplorable condition of the agency house on the Caddo Prairie, brought about by annual flooding, and predicted that the "once dry and beautiful prairie will be transformed into a Lake as the Lakes below it have been formed in regular succession, as the raft has advanced up the river, in its annual accumulation."[3] He sent an estimate of cost for new agency buildings and a statement signed by Larkin Edwards, the Caddo interpreter for many years; his son John W. Edwards who was the Quapaw interpreter; and his sons-in-law James Shenich and Jacob Irwin, the agency's gunsmith and blacksmith. They certified that the river had risen four feet above the grounds and flooded the buildings in the springs of 1826, 1827, and 1830.[4] All three men knew the country well. Larkin Edwards had lived in Louisiana for a long time, perhaps since 1803 and certainly before 1820, and was married to a Caddo woman, who was the mother of John Edwards.[5]

It was drought, not flood, that troubled the Caddos the first summer and fall that Brooks was their agent. Their crops were scanty or nonexistent. The river level dropped so that trade goods and supplies for the tribes could not be shipped upriver from New Orleans before the hunting season. Game, once plentiful near Caddo villages, was scarce, overhunted since practically all the small Louisiana bands of Indians taken in by the Caddo had come to live between the Red and Sabine Rivers.

In November Dehahuit, whose age by then caused him to be referred to as the old chief, led almost every able-bodied man on a four-month hunt that took them to the valleys of the Blue, Boggy, and Washita Rivers of Oklahoma and even farther northwest. Long before they returned, those left in the village—women, children, and men too old, ill, or disabled to travel—had been rendered destitute.

The Anadarko and Hainai, victims of the same circumstance, came to the Caddos for food. They shared their meager stores, but in a short time all were going hungry. Brooks, showing little compassion, reported in January that they were chiefly subsisting by begging and stealing from neighboring whites. He said the white settlers expected him to remedy the situation and complained that the commanding officer of the frontier refused to send military aid. It seems implausible that he wanted to use troops against starving tribes that had befriended Americans for more than a quarter of a century, but Brooks saw only the present. He catered to the intolerance of imminent white immigrants, and was indignant that his authority was usurped. "I did suppose," he wrote the secretary of war on January 17, 1831,

> prior to the event above alluded to [the rejection of his request for military aid], that if it should become necessary to the safety of the frontier, on account of Indian insurrection, or any other movement of Indians falling under my superintendance prejudicial to the safety or welfare of American citizens, that it would be my duty not only to report the same to the nearest military command, but to indicate the number of troops requisite, and, if required to act within the Indian Territory, to designate this direction of station therein.[6]

Although Brooks had wanted soldiers to solve his problem, he evidently felt some sense of duty toward the Indians in his charge. In mid-February he wrote that he had "long since exhausted the provisions allowed them for the last year in fairly preventing these miserable beings from starvation," and he requested an extra allowance. In the same communication he again lobbied for a new agency situated on a bluff on the Bayou Pierre channel of the Red River about fifty miles below Caddo Prairie. In addition to other reasons given for the location, he argued that it would "protect the Indians from the continued complaints and mumerings of the frontier Whites which would be certain to follow were the Indians necessitated to pass through or amongst them."[7]

Brooks's new agency buildings were built where he wanted them, near the site of modern Shreveport. During the next year, 1832, James Cane and William Bennett established a trading post on the bluff that became the actual townsite. Shreve starting work on the river in May 1833, using two battering-ram-type steam vessels. He removed seventy-one miles of the lower raft and was opposite the new agency in a year's time. Brooks wrote the commissioner of Indian affairs:

> I am informed that persons are engaged at Natchitoches taking the depositions of every old resident from this quarter, to prove that the Caddo nation have no right to the country they occupy. . . . This matter is already exciting unfriendly feeling among the Caddoes, who are instigated, by some of the parties concerned, to lay the blame entirely on me.

Thus, between the Indians on the one hand, and the evil minded whites on the other, I consider my present situation quite embarrassing.[8]

Neither the Caddo nor other tribes in the vicinity had confidence in Brooks. Dehahuit expressed their lack of trust in a letter to the president of the United States, written on behalf of all of the tribes within the agency area. Dehahuit requested a new agent and a new interpreter of their choice and asked why tribal allowances had been stopped. Even more revealing, he asked the president to send a reply, not to Brooks, but to John Sibley, who was still a Natchitoches resident.[9]

Dehahuit's judgment of Brooks may have been intuitive, but there is evidence that he was correct in his feeling. In a letter to the commissioner of Indian affairs on March 20, 1834, Brooks wrote:

Since the practicability of removing the obstructions to the navigation of Red river has been established, much excitement has been manifested respecting the *river lands* throughout the region of the raft, embracing a considerable scope of the Caddo territory and is already a fruitful source of trouble to me and uneasiness to the nation. This state of things was anticipated by me from the first, and was the occasion of my suggesting to the President, when last at Washington, the necessity of extinguishing the Indian title to all such land prior to the removal of the raft. . . .

As there are frequent attempts of late to encroach upon them, I have felt it my duty to apprise the register of lands for this district of the occurrences, and now take leave to renew the suggestion, through you, whether it would not be best to negotiate for these lands at once, before the further progress of the work shall open the eyes of the tribe, as to their importance to the whites, or before their true interest shall be surrendered to the cupidity of the evil advisors who surround them.[10]

Dehahuit died in 1833, the year Captain Shreve started work on removing the raft. Other than the year, little is known about the passing of the great leader. About 1870 James Shenich, son-in-law of former Caddo interpreter Larkin Edwards, discovered a burial washed out on Stormy Point overlooking Tso'to Lake. A silver crown and copper epaulets exposed by erosion may have been part of the burial dress of the Grand Caddo, Dehahuit.[11]

The project to open the Red River attracted land speculators looking for profits as naturally as a wounded animal draws a circle of buzzards. Once the raft was removed, acres of fertile land would lay ready to produce riches. Cotton planters coveted the rich Red River valley soil. Merchants craved the wealth that river traffic would bring. The easiest, cheapest way for these groups to gain title was to convince the Caddos to cede their lands to the government so that they could be legally purchased by white businessmen and farmers.

If the U.S. government had seen fit to give the Caddo the agricultural tools and training that Dehahuit had requested twenty years earlier, the Caddo might have become prosperous farmers, and there would have been a different story. As it was, Caddo farmers lacked the tools to support themselves with agriculture, and to supplement their food supply with game, they had to travel ever-farther distances.

By 1833 the Choctaws were occupying the Caddos' traditional hunting grounds on the north side of the Red River above the ancient villages where the bones of their ancestors lay in graves. A story still repeated in southeast Oklahoma concerns a battle between the Choctaws and Caddos at a place named Caddo Hills. The Caddo Hills stand between the Boggy and Blue Rivers, near the present small town of Caddo. Over the years various storytellers have given different dates for the fight. One version says it took place in 1845; another, 1832. Still others say it was earlier than that or give no date at all. According to one published story, a large band of Caddos was almost annihilated by roving Choctaws from east of the Mississippi in 1832.[12] A later version says the battle took place after the Choctaws were well established in their new western home. In this tale, "some four hundred Caddo Indians from the western plains country on a marauding expedition arrived near the western border of the Choctaw country and pitched their teepees and began to make raids on the neighboring prairies." The Choctaws called out their well-trained soldiers, who shot with rifles and killed all four hundred Caddos.[13] In the 1970s old-timers still told of picking up bleached bones and arrowheads left from the battle at the Caddo Hills.

Three years after ratification of the 1834 treaty that required the Choctaw removal to Indian Territory, 7,000 Choctaws lived north of Red River and east of the Kiamichi River. Another 2,000 lived west of the Kiamichi. Wisely, they wanted to make peace with the Plains tribes farther west—Wichitas, Comanches, and Kiowas. They proposed that their agent furnish them with a leader in whom they had confidence, and they would send a large, well-armed group of Choctaws to pose as a hunting party and make contact with the Plains tribes. Instead of that plan, the Choctaw agent suggested that since the Caddo usually hunted on the western prairies and knew the Indians who lived there, the Choctaws should ask a number of Caddos and their agent to go along. The Caddos might have been expected to refuse, but they did not. The government furnished the peace party with provisions and a troop headed by Colonel Henry Dodge. Thirty-three Caddo men led them to a conference with the western Indians.[14]

Continued service to the U.S. government earned nothing for the Caddo. From the time of Dehahuit's first meeting with American officials through the first year or so of Brooks' tenure as agent, the Caddos were urged to stay within the boundary of the United States, and their loyalty to that government was courted. After that Americans seemed determined to be rid of them. Brooks used ruthless persuasion and finally, in 1835, assisted Caddo leaders in addressing a memorial to President Andrew Jackson, saying:

> The memorial of the undersigned, chiefs and head men of the Caddo nation of Indians.
> HUMBLY REPRESENTS:
> That they are now the same nation of people they were, and inhabit the same country and villages they did, when first invited to hold council with their new brothers, the Americans, thirty years (sixty Caddo years) ago; and our traditions inform us that our villages have been established where they now stand ever since the first Caddo was created, before the Americans owned Louisiana; the French, and afterwards the Spaniards, always treated us as friends and brothers. No white man ever settled on our lands, and we were assured they never should. We were told the same things by the Americans in our first council at Natchitoches, and that we could not sell our lands to any body but our great father the President. Our two last agents, Captain Grey and Colonel Brooks, have driven a great many bad white people off from our lands; but now our last-named agent tells us that he is no longer our agent, and

that we no longer have a gun smith nor blacksmith, and says he does not know what will be done with us or for us.

This heavy news has put us in great trouble; we have held a great council, and finally come to the sorrowful resolution of offering all our lands to you which lie within the boundary of the United States, for sale, at such price as we can agree upon in council one with the other. These lands are bounded on the one side by the Red river, on another side by bayou Pascagoula, bayou and Lake Wallace, and the bayou Cypress; and on the other side by Texas.

We have never consented to any reservation but one, to be taken out of these lands, and that was made many years ago. The Caddo nation then gave to their greatest and best friend, called by them Touline, but known to all the white people by the name of Francois Grappe, and to his three sons then born, one league of land each, which was to be laid off commencing at the lowest corner of our lands on the Red river, (as above described,) and running up the river four leagues, and one league from that line back, so as to make four leagues of land. We went with our friend and brother Touline (otherwise Grappe) before the Spanish authority, and saw it put down in writing, and gave our consent in writing, and the Spanish authority ratified our gift in writing. But, before the Americans came, our brother's house was burned, and the writings we have mentioned were consumed in it. Touline (otherwise Grappe) was a half-blood Caddo; his father was a Frenchman, and had done good things for his son while a boy; but when he grew to be a man, he returned among us, and continued near to us till he died. He was our French, Spanish, and American interpreter, for a great many years; our brother is now dead, but his sons live.

We, therefore, the chiefs and head men of the Caddo nation, pray that the United States will guaranty to the sons now living of our good brother, deceased, Touline, (otherwise Grappe) the whole of our original gift—four leagues to him and to them. And your memorialists further pray, that your excellency will take speedy measures to treat with us for the purchase of the residue or our lands, as above described, so that we may obtain some relief from our pressing necessities. . . .[15]

Touline had served as agent and interpreter for the Caddo until his death in 1825. It was he who acquainted Sibley with the Caddo's Red River territory, guided Freeman and Custis, and acted as their interpreter. He indiscriminately served both the Spanish and Americans during the same time period but always kept his relationship with the Caddos close. They valued his friendship and trusted his advice.[16] Brooks was probably the author of such a formal document, but part of the Caddo message to the president seemed to reflect their sentiments. Tarshar, identified as head chief, and twenty-three other chiefs placed marks beside their names. The signatures of witnesses were as follows: "Larkin Edwards, *late Caddo Interpreter*; John W. Edwards, *late Quapaw Interpreter*; J. C. McLeod, and J. Brooks, *late Indian Agent*."[17]

President Andrew Jackson endorsed the memorial on January 28, 1835, and passed it on to the secretary of war with comments recommending that a commissioner be appointed to obtain a complete cession of Caddo lands to the United States and that care be taken in his instructions to ensure that the treaty contained no reservations.[18] Evidently no one in official Washington considered that the United States had any obligation to honor the pledges made in the name of President Jefferson — that Americans would protect the Caddos, supply their wants, and respect the extent of their rightful land claim. Past promises to an Indian nation no longer useful were of no consequence.

Colonel James B. Many, in command of Fort Smith on the Arkansas frontier, was asked to report on the Caddo Indians, their condition and position, and the extent and boundaries of the country they held or claimed. He did not know enough to make the report and went to Indian country to get the information. His findings were that the Caddo used to live in the vicinity of the "Kio Michie," but were driven from there by the Osage "upwards of thirty years since" and settled where they now lived; and that while Grey was agent, he had assigned the Caddo a tract of country on the Red River between the Sulphur Fork and Cypress Bayou, extending to the sources of those streams and from there to the Sabine. Many wrote that except for the fact the Caddo had lived there for thirty years, "they have no other claim to them [the lands] that I can learn." Many's opinion was that only a small portion of the tract assigned by Grey was within the United States, that Caddos were willing to sell it, and that it could be bought "cheap." He emphasized that the quality of the land was first-rate, mentioned that a Frenchman had a grant from the Mexican government for eleven square leagues on the lower side of Tso'to Lake, but thought the grant would be within the United States when the borderline was run. Colonel Many concluded:

The Caddo Indians are a poor and indolent people, who will not work; and, as the game is becoming very scarce, they plunder the inhabitants of their cattle and hogs to a great extent, of which the citizens complain much. The Caddo villages are from twenty to twenty-five miles from the white settlements, and will, in all probability, be on the Mexican side of the line, when run. I have understood, from good authority, that they have a Mexican grant of lands, and that a number of them have gone into that country to settle. I have been informed, and have no doubt of the truth of the information, that these Indians are more attached to the Spaniards than to the Americans; and that the only thing that has kept them from going over to the Spaniards for some time past was the few presents they have received, and the work that has been done for them by the gunsmith furnished by the United States. The com-merce of these people is inconsiderable. Their whole number, men, women and children, I have been informed by the best authority, cannot exceed six hundred.[19]

Colonel Many clearly learned nothing about the Caddo's past status, their service to the United States, or the role played by the government in bringing them to their present state. Showing no respect for Caddo land rights, his attitude was typical for the time.

Many's report was dated January 6, 1835. Brooks was in-structed on March 25, 1835, to procure the Caddo land in Louisiana. On June 3 he employed Larkin Edwards to visit the Caddo villages with a message that he was at the agency ready to negotiate with them. Almost all—close to five hundred Caddo men, women, and children—assembled at the agency house on June 25. At noon the next day head chief Tarshar, underchief Tsauninot, and twenty-three chosen councilors met with their former agent.

A pipe was lit and passed. Then without further ceremony, Brooks explained that the president was pleased to hear they were willing to sell their lands and had delegated him to arrange this council to complete the sale, provided they could agree on the price and method of payment. He said if they came to an agree-ment, the land would be purchased for white settlers, and the Caddos would have to move. Addressing them as "Brothers," he said:

Knowing your wants, from a residence among you, I come prepared to alleviate them, and to place you in a state of independence, when compared with your present destitution, if you will but make use of a little prudence. But I am told you have changed your minds, and do not intend now to part with this country. And, although I know you have received such advice from many who fain would have you consider them as your exclusive friends, still I do not believe that you are so blind to your true interest as to follow such advisers, who cannot, if they would, supply your wants, but whose only aim is to deceive, that they may yet a little longer rob you of the little you, from time to time, accumulate by the chase. On the other hand, I have never deceived you, and you know it; and am again sent, as your friend, to obtain that from you which is of no manner of use to yourselves, and which the whites will soon deprive you of, right or wrong, and am ready to give you for it what you cannot otherwise obtain, or long exist without, in this or any other country. I am instructed to deal liberally with you, which coincides with my own feelings and wishes. Brothers, I am done, my business is stated; I await your answer.[20]

Exactly who had advised the Caddos is not recorded. The tribe was certainly protected from outside influence during the negotiations. Brooks had forty U.S. troops from Fort Jesup, Louisiana, posted for this event. Three men the Caddos had asked to attend the treaty negotiations—Manuel Flores, Francis Bark, and Joseph Valentin—were first detained by the soldiers and then evicted. The Caddo hid Flores, later condemned as a Mexican agent, under some blankets until he could escape Brooks's men. Documents of the proceedings described Bark as an old Frenchman, hostile to Anglo-Americans, who had spent the greater part of his life with the Caddos.[21] Valentin was one of the men who had accompanied the Caddos to Monterrey, Mexico, when they were given a land grant on the Guadalupe River.

Brooks's speech to the Caddo chiefs and headmen offered no hope that the government would provide protection for their lands and interests if they chose to stay. His emphasis was on what they already knew—they had lost their means of subsistence. His goal has been previously stated—to negotiate for Caddo lands "before the further progress of the work [removing the Great Raft] shall open the eyes of the tribe, as to their importance to the whites."[22] If the removal of the raft was going to bring benefits, they would go to the Americans, not to the Caddos.

Tsauninot, underchief of the Caddos, responded to Brooks's demand for an answer:

We are in great want, and have been expecting you to bring us relief; for you told us, before you departed last fall, that you had no doubt our great father would treat with us for our country, and would supply us with things of much more value to us than these lands, which yield no game. . . . It is true that we have been advised by many not to make a treaty at all; that we would be cheated out of our land, and then driven away like dogs; and we have been promised a great deal if we refused to meet you in council. But we have placed no reliance on the advice and promises of these men, because we know what they want, and what they will do; and we have warned our people, from time to time, not to heed such tales, but wait and see what our great father would do for us. We now know his wishes, and believe he will deal justly with us. We will therefore go and consult together, and let you know tomorrow morning what we are willing to do.[23]

Later, Tsauninot told Brooks that they were expecting him to make an offer and that they did not know how to fix a price. He said the Caddo had been advised to ask for $200 per mile—$100 in currency, $100 in goods—but Brooks said it was impossible to make that sort of agreement because the number of miles were not known and would not be until the survey of the western line was run.[24]

Toward the end of the first day's formal meeting, Brooks passed out presents, telling the council they were tokens of friendship and had nothing to do with the bargain for land that he wished to make. After adjournment, he brought out samples of the goods intended for the Caddo if they agreed to the treaty.

The main body of the Caddo spent the day waiting to hear what happened at council, speculating on what help the government would offer. When the people heard Brooks's words repeated, any hope for survival in the heart of their homeland vanished. Tarshar spoke to their bowed heads, saying:

My Children: For what do you mourn? Are you not starving in the midst of this land? And do you not travel far from it in quest of food? The game we live on is going further off, and the white man is coming nearer to us; and is not our condition getting worse daily? Then why lament for the loss of that which yields us nothing but misery? Let us be wise, then, and get all we can for it, and not wait till the white man steals it away, little by little, and then gives us nothing.[25]

The people lifted their heads, rose to their feet, threw back their shoulders, and consented to the sale.

The treaty was concluded July 1, 1835. The Caddo leaders signed with an X:[26]

Tarshar	his X mark	Tiohtow	his X mark
Tsauninot	his X mark	Tehowahinno	his X mark
Satiownhown	his X mark	Tooeksoach	his X mark
Tennehinun	his X mark	Tehowainia	his X mark
Oat	his X mark	Sauninow	his X mark
Tinnowin	his X mark	Saunivoat	his X mark
Chowabah	his X mark	Highahidock	his X mark
Kianhoon	his X mark	Mattan	his X mark
Tiatesun	his X mark	Towabinneh	his X mark
Tehowawinow	his X mark	Aach	his X mark
Tewinnun	his X mark	Sookiantow	his X mark
Kardy	his X mark	Sohone	his X mark
		Ossinse	his X mark

With those marks, the Caddo cut away their Red River heartland. The treaty bound them to move outside the borders of the United States within one year of the signing and never to return to live on their ancestral land as a nation, tribe, or community of people. The United States agreed to immediately pay the Caddo $30,000 in goods and horses and, beginning one year from September, to pay $10,000 in cash every year for five years. The Caddo did very little bargaining other than asking for authority to appoint an agent or attorney who was a resident within the United States to receive the annuities for them.

According to Brooks, the Caddo asked him to make two reservations that were added to the treaty as supplementary articles. These supplementary articles spelled out an agreement to reserve two tracts from the land ceded to the United States. A four-square-league tract bordering the Red River in the southeast corner of the Caddo's territory and given by the Caddo to François Grappé (Touline) and three of his sons in 1801 was reserved and assigned to the legal representatives of Touline, his three sons, and their heirs. The second reservation was for Larkin Edwards, who "has resided for many years to the present time in the Caddo nation, was a long time their true and faithful interpreter, and though poor he had never sent the red man away from his door hungry: he is now old, and unable to support himself by manual labor, since his employment as their interpreter has ceased, possesses no adequate means of which to live."[27] The agreement gave Edwards the right to select a section of land, 640 acres, anywhere within the ceded Caddo territory.

Larkin Edwards refused to interpret for the treaty. His son, John Edwards, served in his place. Larkin may or may not have been influenced by the reservation of land made to him. His reason for refusing was not recorded. An official witness to the proceedings, Lieutenant J. Bonnell from Ft. Jesup, later described John Edwards as a weak man who had poor health and was subject to fits. Bonnell also said he felt uneasy that a treaty so important to the Caddo had been carried through in only six days. He said that he had attempted to read the supplementary articles but was stopped by Brooks and that he had signed as a witness *"only* as one who touches pen to paper, not as one who had read what he has signed."[28]

The U.S. Senate ratified the Caddo treaty on January 26, 1836. President Andrew Jackson signed it on February 2, 1836, and possession of approximately one million acres of Caddo land passed to the United States.

CHAPTER 20

WHERE WE COME FROM

At the same time that the Louisiana Caddos were planning their move, Texans were designing a republic independent of Mexico. Indeed, the American population of Texas had reached twenty thousand by 1834. Nacogdoches thrived as a seat of government with thirty-five hundred citizens; San Augustine de los Ais, on the road from Nacogdoches to Natchitoches, had twenty-five hundred; and Johnsburg, on the Red River thirty-two miles from Pecan Point, numbered two thousand. There were small community centers on the east bank of the Neches River at its junction with the Angelina, on the Neches about forty miles from Nacogdoches, and on a creek about thirty-five miles northeast of Nacogdoches.[1]

Both single individuals and families set up homesteads. They crowded and surrounded Hasinai villages and fields that had stood along the streams of the Neches and Angelina long before the time of De Soto; they nudged the boundaries of the Cherokee village north of Nacogdoches and pressed against the settlements of other tribes that had emigrated and settled with Caddo-Hasinai permission. Then these homesteaders complained that their lands were almost encircled by Indians.

The Texans' revolt against Mexico began in October 1835, four months after the negotiation of the Caddo treaty. All Texas towns, precincts, and jurisdictions had already formed committees of safety, and in September the committees at San Augustine and

Nacogdoches sent a joint deputation to soothe any disquiet among the east Texas Indians. Sam Houston and Thomas Rusk were members of the delegation that assured the tribes that the committees of San Augustine and Nacogdoches did not intend that any white person should intrude on their lands and that surveyors had been ordered to keep away from their lands and not to make any marks on them.[2]

The first governing body recognized by Texans was a "permanent council" organized to direct the revolution. Representatives from the committees of safety throughout Texas met and established the provisional government on November 13, 1835. On the day of organization, each representative signed a declaration pledging

> that the Cherokee Indians, and their associate bands, twelve tribes in number, . . . have derived their just claims to lands included within the bounds hereinafter mentioned from the government of Mexico, from whom we have also derived our rights to the soil by grant and occupancy. . . .
>
> We solemnly declare, that the governor and general council, immediately on its organization, shall appoint commissioners to treat with said Indians, to establish the definite boundary of their territory, and secure their confidence and friendship.
>
> We solemnly declare, that we will guarantee to them peaceable enjoyment of their rights to their lands, as we do to our own.[3]

The declaration was transcribed into the language of a formal treaty, which Houston and two agents appointed by the governor and the council entered into with "the Cherokee, and their associate Bands now residing in Texas . . . to wit: Shawnee, Delaware, Kickapoo, Quapaw, Choctaw, Biloxi, Ioni, Alabama, Choushatta, Caddo of the Nechez, Tahocullake, and Mataquo," on February 23, 1836.[4]

An estimated 14,200 Indians lived in the fledgling republic of Texas; of these, 8,000 to 9,000 had their homes in agricultural villages in the northeast corner.[5] Houston fully recognized the difference in danger represented by tribes in northeast Texas versus Plains tribes such as the Comanches, Apaches, and Tonkawas. He was a particular friend of the Cherokees and consistently followed a policy of peace in Indian relations during his terms as commander of the troops in east Texas, commander in chief of the

Texans' army, and first constitutional president of Texas. Too many Texans, however, saw no difference between one Indian and another. Their fear of an Indian uprising approached paranoia, and rumors that Mexican agents were inciting the tribes led to further distortions.

The day the provisional government was organized was also the day General Santa Anna and his Mexican forces approached San Antonio. Exhilaration built on victories won by the Texas army in the first battles of the revolution was extinguished by the fall of the Alamo on March 6. A division of the Mexican army began a march toward Nacogdoches on March 24, and the terrible fear that Mexican soldiers would be joined by Indian allies vividly colored everything the citizens of Nacogdoches heard or saw. The town's Committee of Safety again sent agents to visit the Indians in their district. These agents returned with a report that the Cherokees were hostile; that they were drying beef, preparing meal, and sending off their women and children; that they had murdered an American trader; that a large body of Caddos, Kichais, Hainais, Tawokanis, Wacos, and Comanches were expected to attack the American settlements; that the Cherokees gave every indication of joining the attack; that an estimated seventeen hundred warriors were concentrated on the Trinity River; and that The Bowle, chief of the Cherokees, had advised the agents to leave the country because it was dangerous. The Bowle, they said, had visited the Shawnee, Delaware, and Kickapoos tribes and urged them to take up arms against the Americans. Citizens of Nacogdoches did not doubt that a combined force of Mexicans and Indians was within a few miles of their town.[6]

As the Caddos were preparing to move out of Louisiana, their long-valued reputation for influence with tribes in Texas proved a detriment. Convinced that the Caddos intended to lead massive Indian assaults engineered by Mexico, Texans were determined to keep the tribe from crossing Louisiana's western border. Soon after the fall of the Alamo, John T. Mason of Nacogdoches wrote the commander at Fort Jesup near Natchitoches, saying:

An apprehension of a serious character exists here that the Indians are assembling to fall upon this frontier, particularly those from the United States. . . . Is it not in your power to send a messenger to them, particularly the Caddoes, to make them keep quiet? To the extent of your authority, every principle of humanity and safety to the inhabitants of both borders requires an exertion of your powers to avert the disaster of an Indian war; and I have no doubt you will exert all your energies to that end.[7]

General Edmond P. Gaines, in command of the southwestern military division of the United States, immediately sent Lieutenant Bonnell to persuade the Caddo to remain peacefully in their villages. On his return, the lieutenant reported that he had visited two Caddo villages, where the chief and warriors informed him through his interpreter that a Mexican agent named Manuel Flores had been among them trying to persuade them to go with him to Texas to kill the white inhabitants and plunder their settlements. Bonnell said he had found only two or three women and a few children at the first village; the warriors had gone to the prairies because Flores had told them that the Americans were going to kill them. He said he found a few warriors in the neighborhood and assured them that the Americans were their friends and wanted them to return to their villages, to live in peace, and to hunt on their own grounds as usual. These men declared that Flores had not changed their loyalty but that they had heard so many reports they did not know what to believe and were glad now to know the truth.[8]

At the second Caddo village, twelve miles beyond the first, Bonnell had talked with several warriors and a chief named Cortes. Cortes had told him that the Caddos were friendly to the whites when leaving to hunt on the prairies. He promised to send the hunters a message that sounded like Dehahuit's words echoing through the years: if the Caddo saw the Americans and Spaniards fighting, they should refuse to take part on either side.

Passing through the first village again, Bonnell was told by one Indian that if Flores had not told lies, the Caddos would have long since returned to plant their corn. He said his tribe would not wage war against the whites but admitted that Flores went with the Caddos who were hunting on the prairies. He said because the Mexican agent had not been able to persuade the Caddo to go with him, he had gone with the Caddo.

The combined Mexican and Indian forces rumored to be advancing on Nacogdoches never materialized. Texas independence was won in the Battle of San Jacinto fought on April 21, 1836. Mexican agents, however, did not stop their efforts to rouse Indian hostility toward Americans in Texas.

U.S. Army Major B. Riley was sent to make a thorough investigation of the Caddo villages. After visiting four Caddo settlements and talking with the head chief, Tarshar, he wrote General Gaines that Flores had been trying to persuade the Caddo to move to Texas but the head chief, Tarshar, refused to go. Riley's opinion was that the 120 to 130 men he saw in the four Caddo villages were a peaceably inclined, "poor, miserable people, incapable of the smallest exertion either as it regards living, or anything else except liquor."[9]

Larkin Edwards described the pressure put on the tribe in a letter to Gaines on May 13, 1836:

> A Mexican or Frenchman named Manuel Flores, an emissary of the Mexican Government, has been for some time past residing among the Caddo Indians, and by promises of large sums of money attempted to embroil the Indians in the war between the Mexican Government and Texas. This I know to be the fact, as he is commissioned by the Mexican Government for the purpose of exciting the Caddoes to war against the Texians. . . . The emissary, Manuel Flores, informed them that the American Government intended to exterminate them. . . . The Cherokees of Texas, they [the Caddo] also inform me, have attempted to make them a part with them against the Texians.[10]

According to the Caddo treaty, the deadline for leaving Louisiana was July 1, 1836. General Gaines, however, insisted that the Caddos stay. They were still in the area when the payment date for the second installment of their annuity drew near. Brooks arrived by steamboat and paid the captain $100 an hour to wait for him.

Ten boxes of merchandise, each box marked $1,000, were presented as payment of the $10,000 due, but Brooks refused to allow the boxes to be opened until the Caddo had signed a receipt for payment in full. They refused for several days, and Brooks finally left after promising $500 to John C. McLeod if he could get a receipt in full from the Caddo. McLeod was a merchant and knew that the contents of the boxes were worth no more than $1,500. Nevertheless, he earned his bonus. Doing as Brooks had instructed, he told the Caddo that if they did not take what was offered, they would have nothing. Within a few days he succeeded in getting a receipt for $10,000 and made delivery. The content of one of the boxes was thirty to thirty-five rifles of a very common quality. The other nine held blankets, strouds, domestic goods, and some trinkets.[11]

Embittered, impotent, and impoverished, the Caddos began to leave the land of their Louisiana ancestors. A band under Cissany stayed in Louisiana for several years, but a large group led by Tarshar left immediately, moving to the most western fringe of Hasinai country. Others followed different paths.[12]

A few months after Brooks negotiated the Caddo treaty, he wrote the secretary of war, saying he was enclosing a paper "which I obtained from the Caddo chief, purporting to be, as I am told, a grant of land to the Caddo nation of Indians from a former Governor at St. Antonio. As I have promised to return the paper to them, please return the same to me and you shall have done with it."[13] What happened to the document afterward is not known.

Almost ninety years after the signing of the treaty, Mary Inkanish, the oldest living member of the Caddo tribe, was asked to recall that time. C. Ross Hume, attorney for the Caddo tribe, conducted the interview in the home of Harry Edge, a Caddo and the son-in-law of Mary Inkanish. Henry Inkanish, a son, acted as interpreter. Two more sons, one daughter, three grandchildren, and one great-great-grandson were also present.[14]

Hume first asked Mary Inkanish if she remembered the year of the "Falling Stars"—the calendar year 1833. She said she "did not remember the Falling Stars but was told about them by Te-wan-tut. He was a young man when the event occurred and told her about them after he was old. Te-wan-tut was a Cadodacho."[15]

Asked where she was living at her first memory, Mary Inkanish remembered

> things that happened at and during the Treaty of 1835. At the Council the Indians were asked for an amount of land large enough to be covered by a hide. After the bargain the hide was cut into thin strips and stretched around a large plot of land and claimed as per agreement.
>
> She related that the whites raided the Indians, drove them from their villages and took a portion of their crops. After the treaty a

Mary Inkanish, her son Grover, and granddaughter Cynthia Williams (*courtesy of Western History Collections, University of Oklahoma Library*)

part of the money was paid, but a part never was paid. Afterwards her people and fourteen other families went to old Mexico. Texas then was a part of Mexico. . . . They crossed a large river near where another flowed into it, and there the water boiled and was of a red color. It appeared as a dream. She could not remember much before she was seven or eight years old.

In answer to Hume's question "Did the Caddo tribe divide?" she said,

The tribe divided, and a part went among the Choctaws and a part went into Texas. They did not separate as to gens or tribes, but went in groups made up of members of the different tribes. Some Hai-nai, Cado-dacho, Nadarko and others in the same group. Her group went to Mexico, led by Mon-won or Mon-well, a chief. . . . They started to Mexico in the spring. They stopped along the way to make crops. During the late summer of the second year small-pox caused the death of several of their number. The graves covered a large area.

This created a fear among the group and the greater part of them returned to Texas and Indian Territory. Those who returned to Texas went to Big Arbor, the place from which they left to go into Mexico. . . .[16] The Mexican Government set aside a large plain of land watered by beautiful streams for the Indians, and the Mexican Officials told the Caddoes that if the Whites abused them that they could come to Mexico. . . . They made two crops. After two years they moved to another town named "Navia." The third year they went to another place and made another crop. Here she had the smallpox. Then they drifted back to Texas. She went to school at Navia. . . . The town was small and her people had to cross a river and ditches in going to the school. When they got ready to start back she jumped up and left her books and ran away from the school so she could be with her people. . . . The biggest stream was caled Veda. They crossed many rivers, crossed a large stream near a fork where another river flowed into it.

Hume wanted to know the names of rivers they crossed and asked about the Pecos. She said Pecos sounded like one of the names. They passed many rivers, but she did not know their names. They called one stream Cattle Creek; another was called in Spanish Pecan River. She remembered that there was a river called No-aces.

Hume asked if they came into contact with other tribes or people on the trip. Mary Inkanish said they did not. She also described how "they returned and settled near the Big Arbor in which the tribes held council before making the trip to Mexico. . . . The arbor was close to the Brazos, south of Waco. They came to the Arbor in the fall and those camped there had plenty of food and corn."

Hume wanted to know if, while they were near the Brazos, they exchanged visits with the Caddo in the Choctaw Nation. Henry Inkanish "answered yes, they visited back and forth. I asked her that last night. At about that time there was fighting between the White people and the Mexicans."

Hume next asked Mary Inkanish, "Did her people fight with the Mexicans or the whites?" He was told, "No they did not fight with the whites or the Mexicans, but the whites and the Mexicans fought to see who should take care of the Indians. . . . They had councils with both parties the whites and the Mexicans, but she did not remember the particulars as the chiefs would not permit the children to mix in the council proceedings."

Reports circulated in Texas that a large body of Caddos, recently well armed by the payment of their annuity, had entered the republic intent on plunder and murder. Texans contended that Flores's stay among the Caddos and his promises of gold had incited them to hostile acts against the settlers. Even before the first annuity was paid, the Caddo were charged with violence.

A man named James Dunn testified in June 1836 that he and two companions had been attacked by about fifty Indians, about half of them Caddo. He said he knew they were Caddo because Caddos wore shirts that other tribes living in Texas did not and they had a distinctive way of wearing their hair, cut closely on both sides of the head and leaving a "topknot," which they generally wore in a silver tube. They also "had silver in their noses." Dunn said he recognized a Caddo chief named Douchey among the Indians attacking him. Dunn also said the Indians killed a companion's horse, wounded the man, killed many of their cattle, and drove the rest away before going on another mile and one-half to attack other settlers, killing two of them. Dunn's testimony was sent to General Gaines with a letter urging, "If the facts as stated will justify your march against the Caddoes, the country, we trust, will shortly be relieved from Indian hostility."[17]

That winter, January 1837, Captain George Erath, commanding fourteen Texas Rangers, encountered more than one hundred Caddos at Elm Creek west of the Brazos. Texas Rangers were an irregular body first authorized in 1835 to protect the frontier, primarily from Indians, while the regular army and the militia carried on the revolution. Rangers were volunteers required to furnish their own horses, equipment, guns, and ammunition.[18] Erath's personal account was that he and his men

> came in full view of the Indians less than a hundred yards distance, all well dressed, a number of them with hats on, busy breaking brush and gathering wood to make fires. We dodged back to the low ground to keep out of sight as quick as possible, but advanced, it not being broad day light. . . . They were camped in a small horse shoe bend. We took a position at a point under the bank of the creek. It was not light enough to see the sight of the guns. Our distance from them we thought to be fifty yards but it proved to be not more than twenty-five after the battle. We fired and some of them fell about the

burning brush. Most of them stooped to grab their guns and immediately took posts behind trees beyond the fire from us, commencing a yell, and to return our shots and flanked out from both sides to get into the creek where they could see our strength, especially on our right wing, where the creek was wider and opened down to where they were. Half of us jumped on the bank. If we all had had pistols or the six shooters of the present day we could have charged them and kept them running, but as it was we had to keep our position to reload our guns. By this time the Indians commenced opening a heavy fire with their rifles. Their powder out cracked ours. If a shot gun was heard it was but once or twice out of the five or six hundred shots. No bows and arrows were seen among them.[19]

The Rangers lost the battle. Two of their men were killed, several injured, and "still another one missing, whom we all knew had not been injured, but had taken advantage to get out of the way while the others were covering his retreat." Even though his men had been defeated, Erath boasted that ten Caddo warriors had been killed and that his attack was justified because eight miles away, in the home of a white settler, "women and children left in a great measure by themselves, would have been killed next day, perhaps, if we had not attacked the Indians."[20]

Accusations against Caddos, true or not, multiplied. It was claimed that they murdered a Captain Beaston and several persons with him on the Guadalupe River; that they murdered an old man, his wife, and several children about thirty miles north of the community of Nashville on the Brazos River; and that they killed two men who belonged to the Rangers in that region.[21] The Texas secretary of state wrote the minister plenipotentiary of the Republic of Texas in Washington, D.C.:

The line of the Sabine and Red River frontier is not the scene of the depredations of the Cadoes; *their* acts of violence are perpetrated on the Trinity, Brazos, Colorado, Guadalupe etc. far distant from the places of their ordinary abode. In almost every skirmish that occurs on our western frontier Cadoes are recognized. They have in several instances, been shot in the act of stealing horses and murdering the Texians.

They are not formidable on account of number, but from their influence with the prairie Tribes.

This information we derive from officers in the ranging service, and citizens living on the frontiers.[22]

There was credible information that Mexican agents were actively attempting to incite various tribes in 1837. They visited all the Indians on the frontier during the spring, promising arms, ammunition, plunder, and prisoners if they became active in the Mexican cause. These agents guaranteed the tribes title to their lands and possession of their hunting grounds and said that if Texans were successful in declaring an independent state, they would take all the lands occupied by Indians and drive them from the country. A man named Anthony Butler claimed he secured information that about eighty Cherokee, Delaware, Kickapoo, and Caddo warriors went to Matamoros, Mexico, and were issued rations and given arms, ammunition, and clothing. He said that, as soon as the trees put out leaves in 1837, the Indians were supposed to rendezvous north of the road leading from San Antonio to Nacogdoches and be joined there by a force of 5,000 Mexicans. The supposed Mexican-Indian plan to exterminate or drive off the settlers in the spring of 1837 was not carried out, but Texans could not forget the possibility.[23]

It was easy for the Indians to believe what the Mexicans said about Texans taking over Indian lands and driving the tribes away. Their own eyes told them it was so. Immigration to Texas was heavy in 1837, and land locators and surveyors were seen at work throughout the woods and clearings in northeast Texas.

Early in October 1837 the Standing Committee on Indian Affairs for the Republic of Texas presented the results of its study of the Indian problem. In describing the different tribes, their locality, and probable feeling toward the government, the committee reported:

The Caddo, Ioni [Hainai], Anadarko, Abadoche [Nabedache] among whom are dispersed the Ais and Nacogdoches Indians speak a similar language are descended from the old Caddo nation and with the exception of the Caddo are natives of this Country—They all understand and speak the Castilian [Spanish] Language. They are about 225 in number and previous to their late Hostilities live in the County of Nacogdoches, some have returned to their old homes but most of them are still with their squaws and Children on the Praries [sic] united with the Hostile tribes that dwell there; about one half of these Indians are good marksmen all of them Hunt for a living and are on intimate terms with all the tribes of the Prairies. They are thought to be the greatest rogues and the most treacherous Indians on our frontier.[24]

The committee addressed the possible claims that tribes had "on soil of Texas" and concluded that the only ones with any rights at all were "natives of the country" and that their rights were occupancy, not ownership. Dishonoring the pledges of the first governing body during the early days of the revolution, the Senate of the Republic of Texas refused to ratify the treaty that Sam Houston and John Forbes had concluded with the Cherokees and associate bands in February 1836. Caddo of the Neches was one of the associate bands specified in the treaty. The Senate did "consent to ratification of a treaty entered into between T J Rusk and K H Douglass on the Part of the Republick of Texas and the Chiefs of the Ioni and Anadarko Tribes of Indians on the 21 day of August 1837." Strangely, the treaty with the Hainai and Anadarko was lost from the files and never found.[25]

Representatives of the United States were hardly more faithful than Texans in honoring their government's pledges. John G. Green, acting as the agent appointed to receive the Caddo annuity in 1837, went to Washington and received the funds but never accounted for the money. Green's name is one of several coupled in a curious tangle of events that tie directly or indirectly to the Caddo treaty supplementary articles that granted land to Larkin Edwards and François Grappé. Schemes connecting the founding of the town that became Shreveport with articles of the Caddo treaty twine through records like the string of a cat's cradle. The signatures of Green, Angus McNeil, and Charles A. Sewall appear on documents of dubious legality.

Two deeds binding the sale of the 640 acres granted Larkin Edwards were recorded. The first, to McNeil for the sum of $5,000, carried the signatures of Green and Sewall as witnesses. It was dated January 24, 1835 — six months and twenty-four days *before* the treaty — and was signed by Edwards but not by McNeil. Green took the deed to be recorded by Judge Graneaux in Natchitoches on February 3, 1836. Six months later McNeil appeared before Judge Charles E. Graneaux and signed a notarized statement saying that at the time the deed from Larkin Edwards was passed to him, he was not aware that it was necessary for him to sign it, and to remedy this defect, "he does by the presents accept of the said sale in all its clauses, stipulations and conditions."[26]

The second deed, binding the sale of Edwards's grant to members of Shreve Town Company for $5,000, was dated February 13, 1837, and recorded by Judge Graneaux on the same day. The document said that the January 1835 date on the first deed was an error and that it should have been January 1836.[27]

McNeil was president of the Shreve Town Company formed with eight partners on May 27, 1836. The partnership agreement specified the name Shreve Town and bound each partner to contribute a proportionate share to the purchase of a site located on Bennett and Cane's Bluff. The bluff overlooking the Red River was the site of a trading post operated by Bennett and Cane for a number of years.[28] Once the Shreve Town Company gained clear title to the Edwards grant, which, according to treaty, could be located any place within the ceded Caddo territory, they began to lay out the town on Bennett and Cane's Bluff.

Less than a year after the Caddo treaty was signed, Henry Shreve accused Jeheil Brooks of fraud in connection with the Grappé claim. In a letter to President Jackson dated April 29, 1836, Shreve wrote:

> SIR: I have understood, from a source that can be relied upon, that an extensive fraud has been practiced on the United States by the agent of the Government making a treaty with the Caddo Indians in this vicinity in July last. Believing it to be my duty to give information in such cases, I relate the facts to you as I have them; they are as follows: The interpreter officiating in making the treaty was sworn to secrecy. This fact I have from the interpreter himself, (John Edwards;) a reserve was made of four leagues of land, commencing at the Pascagoula bayou, running up the river for quantity, including all the land between the bayou Pierre and Red river. By the meanders of the river, it will include a front of about thirty-six miles, and contain not less than 34,500 acres of the best lands on Red river. . . . The reserve was made to a half-breed Caddo, or to his heirs, without any knowledge on their part of the transaction, until after the ratification of the treaty, when the agent came direct from Washington to Camplé, the residence of the half-breed's heirs, and bought from them the whole of the reserve at $6,000. . . . I am also informed that the principal chiefs of the Caddoes did not understand that such a reserve had been made. The witnesses to the treaty were also ignorant of such a clause having been in it.[29]

Shreve's letter to the president had no immediate effect, and his motive for writing it was probably self-serving, but his accusation was supported later by a document addressed to the U.S. Senate. Tarshar, Tsauniot, and nineteen other Caddos marked X's by their names on a statement declaring that

> they have, this 19th day of September, 1837, heard the treaty read and interpreted to them by a white man, who understands and speaks their language well, . . . that they discover that the bounds and limits of the treaty are not such as they understood at the time of the treaty; . . . that they, the said chiefs, head men, and warriors, of the said Caddo Indians, never made any reserve to any person in the treaty aforesaid except to Mr. Larkin Edwards, an old white man that lived among them a long time; that Mr. Brooks, the Indian agent, told them that they could give Larkin Edwards a small piece of land if they wished to do so; that they then told Mr. Edwards that they would give him a small piece of land any where he wanted it in their lands. The said chiefs, head men, and warriors, would further represent unto your honorable body . . . that they never made any reserve to Francois Grappe, or any of his heirs or representatives, by the treaty, within the limits of land they claimed or sold to the United States.[30]

The names of André Valentin, Charles Rebin, P. Poissot, and Cesair Lafitte were listed as interpreters for this document. An endorsement by twenty-six other men certified that the contents were truly interpreted; that the document was written, interpreted, and signed in public; and that there was no undue influence used to gain the assent and signatures of the Indians. Some years later the courts confirmed Brooks's title to the Grappé claim.[31]

Shreve Town was laid off with eight streets running in each direction. The northernmost street was named Caddo; other streets were named after heroes of the Texas revolution, Fanin and Travis. The founders had no reason to be dissatisfied with their profits as settlers were quick in coming and the town lots were soon sold off. Shreve Town was renamed Shreveport after the first steamboat docked there. The *Nick Biddle,* first boat to identify the port, brought 248 bales of cotton down to New Orleans from "Shreveport" on January 8, 1837.[32]

In 1838 Green gave his power of attorney as agent for the Caddos to Thomas T. Williamson, but when Williamson arrived in Washington, D.C., to collect the funds, he was not permitted to receive them on Green's power of attorney. To ensure that the $10,000 annuity would be faithfully paid to the Caddos in 1838, the U.S. Department of Indian Affairs required Williamson to pay a security. Williamson did so and notified his partner in a mercantile business in Shreveport. His partner was Charles A. Sewall, one of the witnesses who had signed the first Edwards-McNeil deed.

After hearing from Williamson, Sewall sent a messenger to the Caddo chiefs. How many there were or where they were located was not recorded, but 156 men, women, and children assembled in Shreveport around the beginning of October. They agreed to appoint Sewall their agent not only to receive their annuity for 1838 but also to compel Green to arrange the payment of the $10,000 he had received for 1837.[33]

In a letter to the commissioner of Indian affairs, Sewall wrote that "the Indians have been paid their year's annuity by me in a manner most highly satisfactory to them, and they declare they have never had an agent with whom they have been so well pleased and in whom they have placed so much confidence."[34] He sent copies of the Caddos' letter of attorney and receipts for the amounts paid them with this letter and stated he would file suit against Green if necessary.

The single most expensive item on Sewall's list of receipts from the Caddos was $100 for a horse; the least, 12¢ for a cup and saucer. More than $1,300 were paid in groceries. About $1,000 of the annuity money were paid with dry goods—cloth, clothing, and shoes. There were purchases of fry pans, brass kettles, coffeepots, tin cups, and kitchen knives and forks; scissors, needles, and thread; razors and combs (some listed as fine ivory); horse combs, bridles, stirrup irons, saddles, and saddlebags. Eight half-kegs of powder, two 500-pound kegs of lead, eighteen pistols, and seventeen rifles were furnished.[35] The Caddos sold six of their pistols and seven rifles to residents of Shreveport.

Sewall's account showed that the Caddo received most of these goods on October 22. The total worth of distributions to the Caddo before the end of the month was listed as $6,201.77. Of this amount, the only cash accounted as received by the Caddo was $4. Twenty dollars was paid "Francis Co.," and someone named Ted Valentine was paid $79. Ted Graves was paid $60, and L. Edwards was paid $50, probably for acting as Caddo interpreter.[36]

Two days before the Caddo started to leave, people in Shreve-port began to hear stories about two homesteading families that had been menaced, it was supposed, by Indians. The day after the Caddo left town, the neighborhood was alarmed by more rumors and reports of murders. A group of citizens hurried to bring back the Caddo, who were camped five miles away. Three days later a large party of "protectors," self-appointed Texas Rangers, came into Shreveport armed and determined not to let the newly armed Indians escape. Several Louisiana farmers who lived some dis-tance north of the town were with the Texans. Having heard all sorts of stories about Indian atrocities, they were willing to escort the Caddos to the Texas line and hand them over.

The townspeople explained the facts—the Caddo had been in Shreveport when the supposed atrocities had taken place, and respectable citizens of the town had pledged themselves to keep them from going near the white settlements. The Louisianans were satisfied and went back home.

Shreveport residents were intolerant of the insolent Texans who came into their town armed and, they believed, prepared to rob and murder the Caddos. The Texans were denounced for disrupting the peace, and the self-styled protectors went away vowing vengeance against the town. Just across the Louisiana borderline, they made camp at a place called Scotts.[37]

People in Shreveport advised the Caddo to stay within the limits of the United States until peace was restored in Texas. Sewall suggested they take up winter quarters on a large island in the Red River about twelve miles from Shreveport and well inside the territory of the United States. He said the island had two advantages: it supplied plenty of game and water, and it was completely separated from whites.[38]

Isolated on the island, the Caddo kept watch on the side facing Texas. Only a short distance and shallow water separated the island and the riverbank. Three weeks passed without threat. Then seventy men led by General T. J. Rusk rode into sight. The Caddo had only thirty-two men who could in any way qualify as warriors, but they went for what guns they had and fired. A Mexican who spoke the Caddo language scouted a little in advance of the troops, and when the general ordered his men to dismount and prepare to charge, the Mexican told him that the

Indians said they did not wish to fight—they wanted to hold a talk.

General Rusk told the Caddo that Texas was at war with part of their tribe and that they had to surrender their arms. The chief said that without their arms, his people could not feed themselves; they would starve. The general replied that the arms would be deposited at Shreveport until the war was over and that the Caddo should not cross the Texas line until then. He maintained that the government of Texas would support the Caddo, and the chief agreed to the surrender. They exchanged hostages: one of the principal Caddo men stayed with Rusk, and one of Rusk's officers went with the Caddos.[39]

The Caddos brought their small arsenal into Shreveport the next day. General Rusk arrived at noon, took possession of a vacant square in the city, posted sentinels, and encamped for the next twenty-four hours. Sewall requested troops from the commanding officer at Fort Jesup. A Shreveport citizen described what happened next:

> The citizens of the Parish of the neighborhood hearing of the capture of Shreveport promptly came to our assistance, and Genl. Rusk to prevent the occurrence of any unpleasant affair and the effusion of blood ordered his troops to march to Port Caddo and they returned over the same road by which they had advanced the day previous.
>
> That evening a large number of the citizens of the Parish assembled who were much incensed at his conduct. Genl. Rusk made a speech, by which he attempted to justify his cause by assigning as a reason for his marching into our territory that he should thus be the means of saving the lives of women and children as we were already convinced alike of the weakness and friendship of the few Caddos left his reasoning by no means satisfactory nor do we deem him in the slightest degree justified in crossing the borders and taking possession of our town.
>
> In pursuance with his original plan he concluded his treaty (if such it can be done) with the Indians. They . . . are now living as the charges of Genl. Rusk himself, no one now being willing to take the security of the Texas Government.[40]

Texas had no money, no banks, and shaky credit. The Caddo, to sustain themselves, had to draw on their annuity from Sewall—$32.90 for tobacco, sugar, meat, rice, a vest, a pocketbook, a curry comb, and a coffee mill in November. Without weapons for hunting, and with a weakening hope that life would become better, the Caddo waited to be released from the river's island. Almost all of their purchases in December were for gin and brandy.[41]

Between November and April 9, 1838, Sewall accounted for nearly $7,500. The amount included $3,803.69 "to Scott in Cash for his Claim."[42] It was at Scott's place that the Texans camped while waiting for Rusk and his troop.

On November 29, 1838, the secretary of state for the Republic of Texas, R. A. Irion, wrote the "Minister Plenipotentiary of the Rep. of Texas, [in] Washington City, D.C.":

> The President is gratified to learn that the ratifications of the Treaty of Limits between Texas and the United States have been ex-changed. . . . The Cadoes, numbering about 300 efficient and expe-rienced Warriors, shortly after the sale of their lands to the Govern-ment of the United States in 1834, without asking the consent of the authorities of this country, removed to it and associated themselves with the prairie indians; and have been ever since, with the excep-tion of a few short intevals, committing depredations on our frontier settlements; and are at this time combined with them and jointly waging an active marauding warfare against us. . . . It is reasonable to suppose that the Mexicans, finding that they are unable to reconquer Texas, . . . would willingly see it desolated, and again fall into the hands of savages. . . . The fine hunting grounds afforded by the Colorado, Brazos, Trinity, and Red rivers and their tributaries, present strong allurements to the bold, enterprising and somewhat civilized indians. . . . Those hunting grounds are now being sur-veyed out under the authorities of the Republic, which frequently occasions serious collisions between the surveyors and indians. . . . With regard to the Cadoes I am directed by the President to instruct you to . . . request the adoption of such measures as will lead to their entire expulsion from Texas. Since they came to Texas their perfidious actions present a continuous catalogue of depreda-tions on the most exposed and defenseless settlements of the country.
>
> The injuries which they have inflicted, severe it is true, are small when compared with the consequences which will necessarily follow should they be allowed to remain among the wild indians. The latter when the former went among them, carrying rifles, powder and lead in abundance, . . . were but little acquainted with the use of fire arms. Since then by the facilities afforded them by the Cadoes they have become tolerable hunters and are much more efficient in war.[43]

In laying the blame for Indian problems in Texas on the Caddos, Irion either chose not to know or was ignorant of the fact that Comanches were given their first lessons in how to shoot a gun in 1724 and that neither the Wichita bands nor other so-called wild Indians lacked experience with firearms.

Mirabeau B. Lamar became the second president of the republic on December 10, 1838, and launched a campaign to rid Texas of all Indians. He addressed the Congress of the republic, saying, "The whiteman and the red man cannot dwell in harmony together. Nature forbids it." He said the two races were separated by the strongest hatreds of color and ways of thinking and that "knowing these things, I experience no difficulty in deciding on the proper policy to be pursued towards them. It is to push a rigorous war against them to their hiding places without mitigation or compassion, until they shall be made to feel that flight from our borders without hope of return, is preferable to the scourges of war."[44]

In the spring of 1839 two companies of Texas militia were ordered to occupy the Neches Saline to watch the Cherokees and cut off contact with the prairie Indians. Chief Bowle of the Cherokees notified the major in charge that he would use force to prevent any such occupation. Because the major's force was not strong enough to carry out his orders, he established his force on the west bank of the Neches, outside Cherokee land.

General Rusk moved to the edge of Cherokee country with the Nacogdoches regiment; a force of 400 men under a Colonel Burleson reached the east bank of the Neches on July 14 and was joined by an east Texas regiment. Commissioners were sent to arrange a peaceful removal of the Cherokees. These negotiators asked the Cherokees to surrender their guns and move to Arkansas, where the majority of the tribe now lived. An offer was made to pay for improvements they had made on the land in Texas but not for the land itself. The Cherokees refused to agree, and the Texas forces were put in motion.

The battle began a little before sunset on July 15. It lasted until dark and began again the next day. Chief Bowle was killed, and probably one hundred other Cherokees were either killed or wounded. The Texas militia followed survivors for several days, cutting down cornfields and burning houses in any Indian village the troops passed through. Brigadier General K. H. Douglass, in charge of the entire force, reported to the Texas secretary of war,

"The Cherokees, Delawares, Shawnees, Caddoes, Kickapoos, Bi-
loxies, Creeks, Ouchies, Muskogees, and some Seminoles, had
established during the past spring and summer many villages, and
cleared and planted extensive fields of corn, beans, peas, &c.,
preparing evidently for an efficient co-operation with the Mexicans in a war with this country." He observed that the country
through which he marched "in point of richness of soil, and the
beauty of situation, water, and productions, it would vie with the
best portions of Texas."[45] The Caddo, Hasinai, and other tribes
they had invited into their rich country fled like frightened
woodland creatures escaping smoke and flame.

CHAPTER 21

THE BITTER YEARS

The Trinity River was the traditional western
boundary for Hasinai territory. Toward the sunset beyond that
natural boundary—between the Trinity and the Brazos Rivers
and north of a line running roughly from below Nacogdoches to
south of where the town of Waco came to be—the Hasinai shared
hunting grounds with other tribes, annually setting up camps in
the fall. It was in that familiar region within the natural boundaries of rivers and the Cross Timbers that surviving members of
the Hasinai tribes and the Caddo led by Tarshar tried to find
peace. Moving right along with them were the surveyors they had
learned to hate because white settlers always followed, claiming
the land.

The chief of the Nadako tribe, usually called Anadarko after
1835, rose as the principal leader of the Hasinai tribes that settled
along the north forks of the Trinity River after being pushed out of
northeast Texas. His name among his people was Aasch (also
spelled Aisch and Iesh), but Mexicans and Americans called him
José Maria. Aasch was probably born around 1800 in an Anadarko village on the east bank of the Angelina River or on the
Sabine River—he was christened José Maria by the Spanish
missionary who was serving the mission of Guadalupe de
Nacogdoches.[1]

Aasch was one of the names on the 1835 treaty. It is possible
that the Anadarko chief was there. What is known for certain is

that José Maria was still a young man when Texans began repeating tales about him.

Texas historian Kenneth F. Neighbours included some of the stories in a biography of the Anadarko chief published in 1967. One of the less believable is an account told by a man named Taylor. Taylor said he was with a four-man survey party when they met José Maria, his second chief, and some young men hunting buffalo on the prairie a few miles southeast of present-day Waco. The surveyors were captured, and the under chief was eager to permanently remove them from locating land for white settlers. José Maria argued with the subchief about what should be done, and Taylor, who was a master Mason, claimed that while his fate was being decided, he made a Masonic sign that José Maria immediately understood. He said the chief saw the sign, spoke briefly with him in English, then returned to his discussion with his hunter-warriors, who finally unstrung their bows. Taylor said he later asked José Maria where he had learned Masonry, and the famous chief replied that he was a master Mason in a French lodge in Canada. "Inquiry in Canada," reported Neighbours, "failed to disclose any further information on this lead."[2]

The atrocities that the Caddo were accused of were often exaggerated, and evidence against them was faulty, but vicious crimes were committed by Indians against settlers entering north Texas. The Morgans and the Marlins, families with married children, built homes on the east side of the Brazos River, some above and some below the present-day town of Marlin. One night in January 1839 some members of the families were spending the night at Morgan's Point, six miles above Marlin; the remaining family members were at John Marlin's house below. Indians entered the house at Morgan's Point and killed George Morgan, his wife, their grandson, another Mrs. Morgan, and one of Marlin's daughters. The victims were scalped, and the house was plundered. Three children who were playing in the yard at the time of the attack hid until the Indians left and then ran to the Marlins' house.

Ten days later seventy Indians attacked the Marlin home. John Marlin and his son, with the help of a visiting man and his son, managed to drive them off. The next morning forty-eight men commanded by Benjamin Bryant pursued the Indians. They followed a trail to the Brazos and crossed where it entered the river.

On the other side they found a recently deserted camp. About one mile beyond the camp they found a fresh trail leading back toward the river and counted sixty-four horse tracks, plus a great number of moccasin prints. After recrossing the river where the trail entered, one of the men spotted smoke rising from a prairie fire. Thinking Marlin's house was burning, Bryant's party hurried there, only to discover they were mistaken. The next morning they started after the Indians again.

In an open post-oak woods near a dry ravine, they met José Maria riding in the lead of his men. As the story was later told, José Maria turned his horse "with calm composure" and rode to the rear of his band, where he halted and removed his "gauntlets." He took up his gun, deliberately aimed, and cut the coat sleeve of one of Bryant's men with a bullet. Bryant ordered a charge. José Maria was struck in the breast by a shot, and his horse fell. But he was not so seriously wounded that he could not direct his warriors. The Indians fired one volley and fell back to the ravine. The Texans followed, firing on the Indians from the bank. José Maria's men retreated down the ravine toward some bottom timber. Bryant's men flanked them and took a position below. The Indians returned to their original position, and the Texans became over-confident. They broke rank, "every man acting as his own captain and fighting on his own hook." Three of them were killed, and "the shrewd old Indian chief, observing this state of affairs, suddenly sprang from the ravine at the head of his men and opened a terrible and unexpected fire on them. This threw the Texans into some confusion, and their commander seeing how matters stood, ordered his men to retreat to a point some two hundred yards distant where he intended to reform them, and then charge the enemy again." Some of the men thought Bryant ordered a full retreat. Most of them bolted away in panic. Several fell from their horses; one ran into a tree with his horse. José and his warriors were in full charge, circling and chasing the disordered Texans for four miles. Ten of Bryant's men were killed and five wounded in their wild retreat. "José Maria visited Bryant's station years afterwards and offered Bryant his pipe to smoke. Bryant insisted that José Maria should smoke first as he had won the fight, and the old chief proudly followed the suggestion."[3]

Around the time José Maria led the fight against Bryant's men, Charles Sewall, still acting as agent to the Louisiana Caddos, heard that T. G. Scott had been appointed agent for the Caddo tribe. Scott—the Texan whose place was headquarters for those of Rusk's Rangers who entered Shreveport—claimed a power of attorney marked by members of the Caddo tribe in Texas. Sewall protested to the commissioner of Indian affairs. He admitted to the commissioner that some of the Caddos were split from those near Shreveport and were living in Texas, but he objected to the power of attorney given Scott, saying that most of the Caddos in Texas had no connection with the tribe proper and that, although Scott occasionally resided in Louisiana, his principal interests and property were all in Texas, where he lived at Port Caddo.[4]

The treaty of 1835 had given the Caddo the right to appoint a U.S. resident as the agent to receive their annual annuity, but this was a power that circumstances did not permit the tribe to handle well. Divided by distance and broken communication, the Caddo were prey for unscrupulous agents who coveted control of the $10,000 they were awarded yearly. To know what terms they accepted when they scratched Xs by their names, the Caddos had to trust an interpreter and the white men with whom they contracted.

The commissioner of Indian affairs took the precaution of sending the money appropriated for the Caddo annuity due in September 1839 to Captain William Armstrong, who was the western superintendent. Armstrong was instructed to send a special agent to the Caddos to determine if they understood the power of attorney and wanted Sewall to receive the money. Armstrong sent H. G. Rind to hold council with the Caddos near Shreveport. In February 1840 Rind reported:

> Having proceeded to the residence of the Caddo Indians near Shreveport, La. I informed them that I had been sent by you to know something of their situation and whether they understood the power of attorney given by them to Charles A. Sewall. I read your letter to them, also the power of attorney. I asked the[m] concerning the balance of the tribe, they informed me that their head chief and a number of their warriors had left them two years ago with a determination never to return any more, having been defrauded out of their annuity by their attorney John G. Green. The young Chief died sometime back. Those that are residing near Shreveport told me that they had given the power of attorney to Mr. Sewall, and that they understood all about it. They number about one hundred and

sixty, forty or forty-five men the rest are women and children.

The Chief told me that their interpreter Larkin Edwards Jr. had been offered five hundred dollars to misinterpret for T. G. H. Scott. After the papers had been read by me and the articles which accompany this, had been signed by the Chief and others of the tribe a protest against the proceedings was served on me from T. G. H. Scott, which also accompanies this letter.

From what I could see and learn from the Caddoans, they have the utmost confidence in C. A. Sewall who they say has befriended them in all their difficulties.[5]

Although Rind's report was favorable for Sewall, Armstrong delayed paying out the annuity, waiting to receive further instructions from the commissioner of Indian affairs. Sewall's clerks certified that his accounts were accurate, that the Caddo had received their full annuity for 1838, and that they had not been furnished with any arms or ammunition of war. Prominent Shreveport citizens wrote to members of Congress vouching for Sewall. Sewall's partner in business, T. T. Williamson, wrote on February 24, 1840, saying that a proposition had been made to the Caddo that they change the way their next annuity would be paid and that they had been advised to accept, provided they were given a home among the Creek or Choctaw in what was then Indian Territory and now Oklahoma. Williamson added that he did not think either the Creek or Choctaw would take the Caddo on terms they could accept.[6]

In July 1840 the "Chief, Headmen and Warriors of the Nation of the Caddo Indians, residing near Shreveport, Caddo Parish, La." signed a statement that their "faithful Interpreter Larkin Edwards, Senior" had "read, interpreted and explained" to them Armstrong's letter and the power of attorney they had given Sewall. They acknowledged "the same to be understood by us, and to be our wish. We furthermore say, that we believe ourselves to have been fairly dealt with by said Charles A. Sewall." X's were marked by fifteen names. The name Tsauninot was on both the 1835 treaty and Sewall's power of attorney. Only two other names marked on the treaty were also on the power of attorney. Following the signatures of thirteen witnesses was the statement "I was present during the interpretation and signing of the within, and as far as I could understand it was faithfully done," signed H. G. Rind.[7]

The 1835 treaty had stipulated that the Caddo would receive:

Thirty thousand dollars to be paid in goods and horses, as agreed upon, to be delivered on the signing of this treaty.

Ten thousand dollars in money, to be paid within one year from the first day of September next [1836].

Ten thousand dollars per annum in money, for the four years next following [1837, 1838, 1839, 1840] so as to make the whole sum paid and payable eighty thousand dollars.

The U.S. Department of Indian Affairs' *Report of the Commissioner,* showed that no money was disbursed to the Caddo between September 30, 1839, and September 30, 1840. The amount appropriated for the Caddo in the hands of agents but unexpended was $20,000, and the balance not yet drawn from the Treasury was $10,000.[8]

Early in 1841 Armstrong wrote the commissioner of Indian affairs:

The Caddoans in Texas, who have not participated, in the annuity, and constitutes, at least, two thirds, or three fourths of the tribe, had sent a delegation of their people to me, accompanied by the Son of Tarshaw [Tarshar], the Chief of the tribe, soliciting that this their last annuity should be paid them at Fort Towson or on the Boggy, in the Choctaw Nation. . . . I have been advised a few days ago, by Pitman Colbert a Chickasaw . . . that he had seen Tarshaw the Chief [of the Caddo], in the cross timbers, who showed my letter and stated that they would be in, in the Spring, to receive the money; and hoped that the Shreveport Indians would not be participants in the ensuing annuity. My object in making this communication, is, to place you in possession of the facts. I am aware, that if I pay the annuity it will give me great trouble and responsibility but I do not hesitate to say that the Indians have been speculated upon; and I know that the Majority of the tribe has not received even the small amount, that the Indians about Shreveport have. A requisition for the money was issued in my favor, if it is to be paid on the power of attorney, I would prefer to have nothing to do with it.[9]

A year later, in the spring of 1842, Colonel A. M. M. Upshaw, agent for the Chickasaw, observed that there were only about 250 Caddo Indians left and that 167 were refugees in Choctaw country. "The last annuity due them was paid them this year," he said, "and now they are without a country and without an annuity and are living here by sufferance of the Choctaws."[10]

More than sixty thousand Choctaws, Cherokees, Chickasaws, Seminoles, and Creeks were relocated in Indian Territory between 1830 and 1840. Law-abiding people who had adopted many white customs, they were called the "Five Civilized Tribes." They had been pushed and in part forcibly removed from their farms in southern states east of the Mississippi and were no better prepared than white people to become neighbors of western Indians fighting for supremacy on the plains.[11] The Osage did not easily relinquish hunting grounds within Indian Territory; Kickapoo bands roamed wherever they wished; Comanches and Kiowas threatened peace and order in western Indian Territory; and Pawnee horse thieves raided on the north. Forts Gibson, Towson, Coffee, Wayne, and Washita were erected at strategic locations in Indian Territory and staffed by U.S. troops for the protection of the Five Tribes.

Applying a theory that conciliation works better than coercion, the Creek Chiefs called a "Grand Council" of tribes in May 1842. They hosted a great body of delegates from the Choctaw, Chickasaw, Seminole, Delaware, Shawnee, Quapaw, Seneca, Pawnee, Osage, Kickapoo, Wichita, Kichai, Piankashaw, Tawakoni, and Caddo tribes. Representatives of the U.S. Army and agents and clerks for the Creek and Seminole observed while the Indian delegates solemnly discussed ways and means to keep peace among the tribes.[12]

Impressed by the apparent influence of the Creeks and their contacts with the government, Caddo chief Red Bear wrote the Creek chiefs for advice on ways to go about bringing peace to Texas. The Creek chiefs replied on July 20, 1842:

> We this day received a letter sent to us from one of your people. . . . We were aware sometime back from information which we received of many difficulties and troubles that your people have had with the Texians, but after an interval of time we heard no more and supposed you doing well but from your statements we find that you are again about to be molested by the Texian Army—we further understand from your letter that you are about to abandon your Crops—that your old Women and children have tried to raise and leave it to itself again—your letter mentions of various tribes, neighbors to your people, are in the habit of entering Texas and bringing away from that Country Cattle and horses which they having robbed with Scalps of people that they have destroyed—at

the General Council which was held in our Country not a great while ago where we met in Council tribes of many nations there we held out to them good talks and endeavored to impress upon their minds good feelings and friendship and told the men who attended that Council that they must all on reaching home give to their young people and others our talks that we sent for them which talks were good—from your letter we suppose they never have told this to their people what we said, we wish you to notify should it lay in your power—who are the people that are in the habit of committing depredations upon the people of Texas after you inform them that our talk to them is to quit all such practices that they are guilty of and if they should not abandon such robbery and murder then inform us who are the principal ones that partake in this design.[13]

The Creek chiefs advised Red Bear that Texans and Mexicans "are furnished with Ammunition and Guns, and the Indians being poor have none—Therefore in order that your children may not be affrighted have nothing to do in their wars and combine all other Indians the same as one, and not meddle in no way with either side." The Creeks also said they had written to some of the U.S. agents who had been at the council to ask them to tell the people of Texas not to cross into Caddo country or "interrupt" the Caddo. The Creeks indicated that they would send Red Bear's letter with one of their own to Captain William Armstrong and tell him about the condition the Caddos were in because they had followed the advice of the Indian council. Armstrong was U.S. superintendent for Indian affairs for Western Territory. The Creek chiefs offered hope that the Caddo "may some day have good people that will come to your houses and men that will be of service to you."[14]

Red Bear also wrote to an influential Choctaw, Robert M. Jones. Jones was intelligent, educated, and rich; owned many slaves; and used their labor to cultivate extensive tracts of land. Because he was also associated with two white men in a successful Indian trade company at Boggy Depot in the Chickasaw Nation, Jones had excellent contacts with government officials. Red Bear asked him to intercede with Texas for the peace desired by the Caddo.

Two days after Red Bear's letter was delivered to Jones, three newly appointed Texas Indian agents came to Boggy Depot. Sam Houston, serving his second term as Texas president and working to rebuild his Indian peace policy, appointed Henry E. Scott,

Ethen Stroud, Joseph Durst, and Leonard Williams to "treat with any and all Indians on the frontiers of Texas."[15] Jones wrote to Red Bear, "I send you a medal and some tobacco and white beads as an emblem of the long friendship between your people and the Choctaws and Chickasaws, and Col. Stroud has sent you, the Ironeyes [Hainai] and Madargoes [Anadarkos], tobacco in token of his favorable reception of your request for peace."[16] Jones also counseled the Caddo to separate from the Kichai, the Waco, and other Indians unless they could be induced to make peace.

Stroud, Williams, and Durst talked with Red Bear's letter carrier and through him arranged a meeting with

> four of the principle chiefs with other head men and warriors of four different tribes at a small Caddo village above the Chickasaw . . . and concluded a treaty with Said tribes. . . . In addition to Said treaty the Said chiefs headmen and warriors entered into Stipula-tions with the commissioners to visit with presents the hostile Indians twenty tribes in number and to assemble the said hostile Indians for the purpose of meeting the commissioners with the President for the purpose of entering into a treaty at the Waco Village on the Brazos the 25th of Oct. next.[17]

October and cold, brutal winter months came and went with-out a meeting at the Waco village, but on a bright spring day in March 1843, a council was held at Tehuacana Creek, near the Brazos River, seven miles below the present town of Waco. The council grounds were very old—intertribal councils had taken place under a big arbor there long before Texans came to claim the land. Nine tribes were represented in the 1843 council. Chiefs of the Caddo, Hainai, Anadarko, Kichai, Waco, Delaware, Shaw-nee, Tawakoni, and Wichita sat with Texas commissioners. The Cherokee agent, Pierce M. Butler, and a military escort from Fort Gibson, were sent to witness the proceedings. Speeches, inter-pretations and responses took up three days. The commissioners pledged peace and promised the Indians land to live on, trading houses to buy goods from, and agents to represent them. The commissioners said that President Houston wanted the chiefs to visit him and receive presents from him and that he would meet them or send men to make them presents once every year. Butler spoke, urging peace among the tribes as well as between the Indians and whites.

On March 28 a treaty was signed. Bintah, Chowa, and Had-da-bah (Ha-de-bah) drew their marks as chiefs of the Caddo and Hainai, José Maria as Anadarko chief.[18] Except for trade privileges at a trading house on the Brazos River, the agreement pledged nothing more than a truce until some future date when "a permanent line shall be established between Texas and Indians" and a grand council would settle a definite and permanent treaty of peace "between the Republic of Texas and all the Indian tribes, residing within or near the limits of Texas."[19]

Torrey's Trading House was established about four miles below the big arbor where the council had been held. President Houston and a frontier settler named George Barnard were stockholders in the company organized for Indian trade by the Torrey brothers, John, David, and Thomas. Their Post Number Two—six or seven log houses for storing pelts, a house for the company agent and helpers, and the trading house proper—was built near the mouth of Tawakoni (Tehuacana) Creek in 1843. For a while it was a marker separating the white settlements below from the Indian homes above.[20]

The chiefs and headmen who signed the treaty in 1843 accepted President Houston's invitation to visit the Texas capital, which at that time was Washington City. Eighty-five years later the widow of another Caddo chief, White Bread, turned two carefully kept documents over to the tribal attorney. Both were signed by President Houston and were identical except one named Bintah a chief of the Caddo, and the other named José Maria a chief of the An-na-dah-kos. Bintah's read:

> To all to whom these presents shall come: Know ye, that BINTAH, a Chief of the Caddo, is one of the signers of the treaty lately concluded with various border tribes of Indians, and therefore is entitled to the friendship and protection of the whites, so long as he shall continue to walk in the path he has helped to make. When he returns to his tribe, he will give them the talk of peace, and keep all his warriors and the warriors of his friends from mischief, from stealing horses and from war. We wish and expect a firm and lasting peace; but if mischief is done, trouble will grow out of it. He will give counsel to all of his red brothers of all tribes to make peace. This is the talk of a friend to peace and a brother. He will be expected at the Great Council in August when we will again shake hands.[21]

The great seal of the Republic of Texas with the Lone Star embossed in the center was set on white, blue, and green ribbons in the lower right corner of the document. "The White," said Houston, "denoted peace; the blue was like the sky, unchangeable; the green, like the grass and trees, existing as long as the world stands."[22]

In the spring of 1843 José Maria and his people were living north of a landmark called Comanche Peak on the western branch of the Trinity about eight miles from the main river.[23] An American artist, J. M. Stanley, visited them there and made portraits of José Maria and six other Caddos. The portraits were later destroyed in a fire, but a catalog listed his subjects by name and briefly described them. The seven portraits were of

> Bintah, the Wounded Man. Principal Chief of the Caddoes. He derived his name from the fact of his having been wounded in the breast by an Osage; he wears a piece of silver suspended from his nose, as an ornament; Ah-de-bah [Ha-de-bah], or Tall Man. Second or Assistant Chief of the Caddoes. Painted in the act of striking the drum; Se-hia-ah-di-you, the Singing Bird, (painted June, 1843). . Wife of Ah-de-bah, seated in her tent. A view of Tiwocanny Creek, Texas; Ha-doon-cote-sah. A Caddo Warrior; José Maria. Principal chief of the Anandarkoes. This chief is known to the Mexicans by the name of José Maria, and to the Caddoes as Iesh. He has fought many battles with the Texans, and was severely wounded in the breast in a skirmish with them; Cho-wee, or the Bow. Principal Chief of the Natchitoches. This man had a brother killed by the Texans, some four of five years since, while on a hunting expedition, whose death he afterwards avenged by taking the scalps of six Texans.[24]

Despite peacemaking efforts, it was evident that the Caddo, Anadarko, and other peace-seeking tribes in Texas would continue to be blamed for the hostile acts of other tribes and that the war between Indians and Texans could not end until Comanche, Wichita, and other belligerent bands agreed to make peace. The problem was to locate roving Comanches and somehow persuade them to come to the grand council, where President Houston and peace commissioners might make a treaty with them. Houston thought he found the solution to the problem when he talked with three Delaware men who came to Washington City with the chiefs and headmen after the signing of the treaty at Tehuacana

Creek. These three men—Jim Shaw, John Connor, and Jim Second Eye—spoke English as well as the languages of the prairie tribes, and they readily accepted appointments as commissioners of peace. The president also commissioned Joseph C. Eldredge to carry out the mission with the three Delawares. Eldredge was instructed to go immediately to the Comanches and bring their chiefs to the grand council set for August 10, 1843, at Bird's Fort.

A collection of Cherokees, Seminoles, Kickapoos, Shawnees, Wacos, and Caddos had once lived at the site of Bird's Fort, near the mouth of Village Creek, between Dallas and Fort Worth. Driven from east Texas, they fled to that vicinity and eked out an existence until they were attacked by an expedition of some seventy men led by Edward H. Tarrant on May 24, 1841. Tarrant and his followers did a great deal of damage but were outnumbered and forced to withdraw. Returning with a larger force in July, Tarrant found the place empty. Later that summer he commissioned Jonathan Bird to take troops and settlers to the place. About nineteen families, including about twenty-five men, erected a blockhouse and several cabins. They stayed only a few months, but Bird's Fort remained in use as a frontier gathering place.[25]

On the way to meet with Comanches toward the end of May 1843, the peace commissioners made camp near José Maria's village. They sent a runner to let José Maria know they were close and their reason for being there. "On the morning of the 28th," wrote Eldredge, "we were notified of the approach of the chief. He shortly appeared escorted by thirty of his warriors splendidly mounted presenting an exciting novel and interesting sight from their unequalled horsemanship, fanciful costumes and paint."[26] José told Eldredge that a number of tribes were hunting on the prairies and that runners had been sent to bring them in for talks. Delegates from eleven small tribes came in, but no one seemed to know where the Comanches could be found.[27]

Commissioners for the Republic of Texas and the chiefs of nine tribes—Delaware, Chickasaw, Waco, Tawakoni, Kichai, Biloxi, Cherokee, Anadarko, and Hainai—concluded a treaty of peace and friendship at Bird's Fort on September 29, 1843. The Cherokees were the survivors of the battle at The Bowle's village who had fled to Mexico and only recently returned. Caddo chiefs Red Bear, Binchah (Bintah), and Had-dah-bah (Ha-de-bah); Anadarko chief José Maria; and Ioni (Hainai) chief Towaash placed X's by their names. President Houston was not present as promised. He had arrived for the date set for the council, August 10, and had waited a disappointing month for Eldredge and the Comanches before going back to the Texas capital.

The treaty at Bird's Fort incorporated the principles of Houston's peace policy:

- Warriors should make war only on other warriors, not on women and children or unarmed persons.
- Indians should never unite with the enemies of Texas; if proposals for unity came to the Indians, they would immediately notify an agent of the president.
- Agents would be appointed by the government of Texas to communicate the president's orders and wishes, hear Indian complaints, and see that justice was done between Indians and whites.
- Traders would be licensed.
- Stolen property would be returned by whites and Indians.
- A white man who committed a crime against an Indian would be punished by the laws of Texas in the same manner as he would be if he committed a crime against a white man; an Indian who committed a crime against a white man would be punished by Indians in the presence of an agent.
- A geographical line of demarcation would be drawn between the two races, which neither would cross without authorization.
- Chiefs and headmen would control their young men and warriors, compelling them to keep peace.
- Prisoners and stolen property would be surrendered.
- The president could send blacksmiths and other mechanics, schoolmasters, and families among the Indians to instruct them in the English language and Christian religion.
- As soon as the Indians showed they would keep the treaty—by not making war on the whites or stealing horses from them—the president would authorize the traders of Texas to sell them powder, lead, guns, spears and other arms, "such as they may need for the purpose of killing game."
- The Indians would receive annual presents from the government of Texas.

Following the policy of the republic, the commissioners were careful not to include recognition of the Indians' right to possess land.[28]

A ledger sheet of gifts to Indians for 1843 listed $55 for wire, bed-tick, sheeting, knives, and paint for the Caddo tribe and two blankets, two red strouding flaps, tobacco, and knives for Bintah and Red Bear. The Anadarko and Hainai were given wire, blue drilling, bed-tick, sheeting, and knives worth $50; the chief received a blanket, red strouding flap, and tobacco. Chiefs also received a kettle and a hatchet. Best of all were hoes — seventeen to the Anadarko and Hainai, fifteen to the Caddo; and small, medium, and large axes — fifteen to the Anadarko and Hainai, thirteen to the Caddo. Tin cups and pans, powder, and lead filled out the gift list.

Although the Waco and the Tawakoni signed the Bird's Fort treaty, some of them kept on stealing horses. The Waco chief Acaquash made efforts to control his warriors, but a band of young men led by another chief, Narhashtowey (Lame Arm), continued to raid. When pursued, they sometimes passed through An-adarko, Caddo, and Hainai villages on trails that led from white settlements to the villages of the Waco, Kichai, Tawehash, and Tawakoni (all Wichita bands).

One day Lame Arm, dressed for war but riding alone, came through the Anadarko village and by accident met José Maria. He asked the Waco chief why he appeared there in such dress. Lame Arm replied that he had just returned from the "Spanish war," meaning raids along the border of Mexico. If so, asked José Maria, where were his warriors? When he went to war, said the An-adarko chief, "I lead my men; I am found in the front; if you did the same how do I find you here by yourself alone? You speak with forked tongue; follow me."[29]

José Maria took Lame Arm to John Connor, one of the Dela-wares assigned to Houston's peace commission who happened to be in the Anadarko village at the time. At Connor's camp Lame Arm told the truth: he had started out to make war on the Mexicans but had been sidetracked into stealing horses. The whites followed and overtook the raiding party, but he escaped and took the nearest way to the Anadarko village.

At the next grand council, on the Tawakoni Creek grounds in early May 1844, the errant Wacos and Tawakonis were rebuked and urged to live in peace. Red Bear said:

> Sometimes the young captains get mad, but they had better turn aside and look at the white path. Now, today, the Big Spirit will look

down, with pleasure, to see what the white people are trying to do
for us: tomorrow or the next day, our young men will hear and listen
to good counsel, and the chiefs must lead the young men to the
Council to hear good talk. . . . That is the way with chiefs who love
their women and children, and those who listen to it will do well.
You, Waco and Tawakoni captains and chiefs, if you love your
women and children, do the same. all the rest of the tribes you see
here are as brothers united. all the other nations are friendly but you.
you steal horses, which you should not. if you chiefs try to do right
the horses will be given up to the chiefs to whom they belong—
tomorrow or the next day, you will hear a talk from our white
brothers: after them other chiefs will talk, and all will be glad to
hear you talk. This is all I have now to say.[30]

On the next day the Texas commissioners called a council for
the purpose of naming a line to divide white settlements and land
inhabited by Indians, regaining horses stolen from the white
settlements, and distributing presents. The spokesman for the
commissioners had some stern remarks about "bad Red men" and
"bad White men." He told the Indian delegates that the whites
punished their bad men and that Indians should do the same. He
said that chiefs should watch bad men and make them follow good
counsel and that if a chief counseled bad or did bad, he should be
put down. The commissioner said that some good white men had
been killed and many horses stolen and that the commissioners
wanted the chiefs there to tell all they knew about these matters.

Acaquash said he would do his best with his young warriors.
He revealed that he knew that "some of my white brothers may
think I tell a lie, but I speak the truth." He did not like to see his
young men steal white men's horses.[31]

The Tawakoni chief demanded to know where the white men
had been killed, saying that he had not heard of the murders until
now. The commissioners told him the men had been killed eighteen or twenty miles east of Austin about twelve days before. The
chief claimed that no Tawakonis had been out to war since the
previous spring and so were unlikely to have been the murderers.
But he could not vouch for what had taken place since his party's
departure sixteen days before.

Red Bear said that at the time he had first met with the
commissioners on the Red River, he lived at the Tawehash (Wichita) village and that he and the Delawares talked very little with

white people and made few friends. Now, he said, they talked much with white people and made many friends:

> I do not like to see guns firing and blood spilled, for I am a friend of peace. I am one of the oldest of my tribe. all the red men and all of my other brothers know me well: they know I want to travel on in the white road. . . . my hands are clean and I like to see others the same. . . . I live upon the Brazos: José Maria the Anadarko chief is my neighbor. when our brothers steal horses and take them through our towns the whites blame us for it. Some Caddo, Ioni, Anadarko live with the Tawehash. I saw nine going to war and told them to turn back, yet they went on; if red captains talk of peace and go to war their words are nothing. Why do the captains and chiefs leave the council house? such conduct is not good. . . . I fear if the Tawehash or other indians take horses from the whites and I try to get them away, that they will kill me. This is all I have to say. my hands are bloody only from killing deer.[32]

Red Bear's last statement caused a great laugh to swell in the Indian audience — he had never been known to kill game of any kind.

Bintah spoke first in the next day of council, telling the young captains to stick to what they heard their chiefs say so that all could become like one, sitting close together.

The Caddo chief Ha-de-bah spoke, saying:

> . . . You have heard what the old chiefs have said; I want you now to hear me, a young man speak. . . . I want you to hold strong to their talk. we are not talking here to children: our talk is strong and we all want you should hear it. Your warriors by living as we would wish them to, would be happy, and your wives and children see no danger. Captains and you, young warriors, I want you all to stop going to war: 'tis all I have to say to you.[33]

José Maria seldom had spoken in the earlier councils. This time he took his turn, saying:

> As I am myself, small in size, my words to fit me, shall be few. long talks admit of lies; my talk shall be short but true. Captains and chiefs, listen to me. The Great Spirit has given to us a good day, and we have listened to many good talks. Captains I want you now to listen unto me. the Big Spirit, above, is watching all now here. young men you all look happy. Captains, if you love your children, advise them not bad, but good; and show to them the white path. . . . we

are all made alike, all look alike and are one people, which you must recollect. The Great Spirit our father, and our mother, the earth, sees and hears all we say in council. You have here listened to none but good talk. I hold the white path in my hands, (a string of wampum beads) given by our white brothers. look at it: see, it is all fair. To you, Waco and Tawakoni captains and warriors I give it. stop going to war with the white people. they, the white people, gave it unto me: I give it now to you: use it as I have done and your women and children will be happy, and sleep free of danger. I give to you this piece of tobacco to smoke, and consider of the white path. when you return to your village, then smoke this tobacco, think of my words and obey them.[34]

Lame Arm remained silent until the commissioners called on him. He then confessed that he had acted badly but that now his heart was like Houston's; he had taken the white path and wished to keep it. Afraid he might lose the presents he hoped to receive at the council and knowing that the Texans were eager to bring the Comanche in to make a treaty, he said, "Look at us, we came here poor, having nothing; now if we go back and the Comanche see we have presents they will believe whatever we say is true; but if we go back without they will not believe, but think we lie. We are with the Comanche friendly, the same as you, chiefs, say you are with the white people. we all mix in together the same as one people. When they make peace it will be a good one. we all talk one way."[35]

On the last day of the council, the commissioners presented a list of horses stolen since the treaty at Bird's Fort. They reported the white people had seen Indians they thought were Waco, Tawakoni, and Kichai and killed some of them. Acaquash retorted that none of his people had ever stolen a horse from the whites and the atmosphere of the council became as charged as air during a midsummer thunderstorm.

Jim Ned of the Delawares said that the Wacos and Tawakonis had stolen horses from the whites and that everybody knew it. Red Bear pointed to a man who had come into Red Bear's village with ten others and eleven horses. "The animals were all fat and greasy, like those fed in salt and corn. . . . The Waco chief Narhashtowey [Lame Arm] is getting mad; he need not be, for I am speaking the truth."[36]

"We wish you to stop and talk no more," announced Lame Arm.

"If the horses are in the possession of the Waco or Tawakoni you shall have them soon: if with the Tawehash it will take us some time longer."[37]

Acaquash became defensive. He said his people had been accused, but they knew of two Hainais who had stolen three horses on the Colorado River at one time the previous winter and three at another time. A Hainai was named and brought before the council.

Red Bear protested, "This young man is an Ioni, who lives with the Tawehash, and has now a wife among the Tawehash people. This spring as he was leading his young men to war he came to my village. I told him his people had made peace with the whites, and he was doing wrong and that we were coming in to the council. he said he did not know it, he had never heard of a council; never been to one. but he would come to this and steal no more. That he had now a one eyed Bay horse at the Tawehash village . . . which he was willing to give up."[38]

The council was almost finished when Bedi, a Hainai chief, gave a short, emphatic talk:

> Hear all: an Ioni [Hainai] now speaks; red brothers listen. I am an Ioni, and we are now but few. our old chiefs have all gone. I have no chief. I am about to speak to you as my brothers have. I have seen Houston and talked with him. I remained near him a day and a night. he gave me a paper, but that I left at home. My body, only, I brought here. I don't talk much, the old people of my race are all dead and I stand here the oldest. I have heard my white and red brothers all speak and I feel like them. Houston has said we must all both red and white be brothers. we can hunt and find plenty of game. by so doing we shall have plenty to eat, and be glad.[39]

The straight talk of the chiefs had no lasting effect on the young men of the Waco, Kichai, and Tawakoni. By fall Red Bear felt compelled to take charge of matters and punish the culprits. He sent messengers to José Maria's village to raise men for war against the Wacos. The warriors intended to go to the white settlements and ask the Texans to join with them against the Wacos. If the whites did not want to fight, they would be asked to witness the punishment of the Wacos.

Delawares Jim Connor and Jim Shaw were in the Anadarko village when Red Bear's messengers arrived. At Houston's request they were on their way to bring the Comanches in for the grand council scheduled for mid-September. Persuading the messengers to wait, Connor and Shaw rushed to Red Bear's village and advised the Caddos not to fight until after the council.

The council began October 7. President Houston was there to meet representatives from the Comanche, Kichai, Waco, Tawako-ni, Lipan, Cherokee, Delaware, Shawnee, Anadarko, Hainai, and Caddo. A treaty very like that made at Bird's Fort was concluded on October 9, and presents were distributed to all but the Wacos, who were told they could not receive theirs until they brought in the stolen horses in their possession.

In January 1845 José Maria presented the longest talk recorded for him in official documents. Wild talk and rumors of whites' deceit had spread throughout the Indian villages. Honoring his treaty commitment, he reported them to the Indian agents who lived at Torrey's Trading House. The Anadarko chief's talk was endorsed by Bintah and Red Bear. José Maria said:

My young men have left me and gone around because they have heard bad talk, but I do not believe this bad talk, and this is the reason I wish to hold council. That my young men may be convinced that the talk they have heard is false and the talk of bad men.

When I went out on my hunt, I got a passport from the agent, and did not meet any trouble until I got nearly back to this place. When I met this bad news.

When Col. Williams [an Indian agent] went up into our country last summer, I was told that the object of his mission was to get all the women and children in to the council in the fall, and that the whites were then to fall upon them and kill them. The waggons with the goods were to stop below and the troops from the United States were to assist in killing them. At the last Council all of the Captains said the old men with grey beards would not tell lies. — My beard is not yet grey. I am a young man, but I speak truth. For myself I believe that these stories I have heard are lies. . . . For my own part I am not afraid, but my people say I am a fool for staying so near the whites, as so soon as the corn gets fit to eat they intend to raise and kill them all and that the reason these goods were put here was to cheat our people out of their hunts to pay for the good white men they have killed.

I have understood also that if we did not go with the whites and help kill the Waco that the whites would think we were friends to the Waco, and kill us. — The Waco say that if we do not move out, away from the whites they will steal our horses, so you see we are between two fires. What shall we do? I know that it is the desire of the whites to make peace with all, but it is impossible. The whites have done their best to make peace, but the Waco and others will not be friends.

Two nights ago news was brought me that the Waco had stolen all the horses from 5 of my men, and that the men had left their families and pursued the Waco, and I have not heard of them since and do not know whether they are killed or not.

The Waco also stole some horses from some Lipan a short time since. . . . They have also stolen all the horses from Bintah's son, and he has followed them. . . . I come in to see you and give you my talk so that it can be sent to your *Chief* as I do not wish to go around like my young men have done but come straight to the white path, and pursue it. Our women and children are naturally scary. but myself and men are not afraid.

Brothers my talk is done.[40]

José Maria and his people had about 150 acres of some of the finest corn ever seen in Texas in the summer of 1845. Their gardens were green with plump watermelons, beans, peas, and pumpkins yellowed on vines. Texas finally signed an armistice with Mexico, and they were no longer plagued with accusations of conspiring with the enemy.

In the general council held at the Tehuacana Creek grounds that fall, José Maria and Bintah spoke once more of their hopes that the white path would be maintained. Towaash, chief of the Hainai, told the council:

The Great Spirit made the day fair and bright so that we can see a long distance — See the path we have made white, and all walk in it as Brothers. the President thinks now that all his people are not afraid, for the path has no brush in it, and his heart is glad, because his women and children know that all is peace. Our women and children are not afraid now of the white warriors, all is good. I hope we may always be at peace, and not let the wind blow away our friendship. . . . I know what I promised at the first Treaty, and I have done as I said. The President then gave us powder and Lead, and told us to go home and shoot deer and buffalo, and raise corn, for our women and children, so that in the cold rainy weather they would not cry for bread and meat. We have done so and found that it is good. All that he told us was true, and now I can go home to my people and tell them that all is still good, that they can eat and sleep in safety and feel no more afraid.[41]

The Caddos living outside of Texas in Indian Territory, still homeless and struggling to support themselves, depended mostly on hunting to feed their families. Conflicts persisted throughout Indian country, and the Creeks hosted another intertribal council near the present town of Eufaula, Oklahoma, in 1845. Eight Caddo chiefs attended. Chief Chowawhana was their spokesman. Pierce Butler, who represented the United States, noted in his journal:

> The talk of the Caddo chief was of deep interest. He was a striking man of great personal beauty and commanding appearance. Small in stature, yet beautiful and attractive features, dressed in what would be called Indian magnificence, feathers, turbans, and silver bands. His speech was looked for with interest and was very well received. Approving the council, deploring the past and probable future fate of the red man, had been gloomy. future prospects worse, hostility among themselves, destruction of their race and ruin of their children. His people honest and true to the objects of this council. Would, when he got home assemble the people and tell them the talk. The same as though they were present. . . . Creek chiefs, made long speeches in good taste and temper promising peace and good will to the effect that their brothers the Caddos had agreed to become the messengers of this tobacco and beads to the Comanches and the Osages.[42]

Tribal delegates formed a circle at the end of the council. Each tribe's representatives, one group at a time, walked the circumference shaking hands, except for the Caddos, who made their leave-taking with the traditional embrace of their tribe, "a real lover's embrace — warm, affectionate and delightfully intimate."[43]

Peaceful relations among tribes in Texas were still tenuous when Texas's annexation to the United States was approved in February 1846 and the Stars and Stripes took the place of the Lone Star flag. As a state, Texas reserved rights to all its public lands, assumed no responsibility for Indians, and charged the federal government with the right and duty to defend the state's frontiers. In other words, the United States had political control of the Indians, but the state controlled the land they lived on. Texas would be for Texans, and the United States would have to remove Indians as quickly as Texans were ready to move onto Indian lands.

CHAPTER 22

TAYSHAS

★ The United States sent Pierce M. Butler and
M. S. Lewis to negotiate a treaty with the Texas Indians in May
1846. Butler knew most of the Caddo chiefs, but he became ill, and
Lewis, who was less experienced and competent, took charge.
Lewis collected the Indian signatures on separate sheets of paper
but did not identify them by tribe. Later it was disclosed that
Lewis actually wrote the treaty between "commissioners on the
part of the United States" and the "undersigned chiefs, counsel-
lors and warriors of the Comanche, I-on-i, Ana-da-ca, Cadoe,
Lepan, Long-wha, Keechy, Tah-wa-carro, Wi-chita, and Wacoe
tribes of Indians, and their associate bands" after returning to
Washington.[1]

Following the 1846 treaty council, Butler and Lewis took a
delegation of chiefs to Washington, D.C. The trip was intended to
impress the Indian leaders with living conditions in the United
States, the workings of the nation's government, and its power.
Major Robert S. Neighbors, newly appointed special agent for the
Indians of Texas, accompanied the delegates. To allow more
freedom for the chiefs to move about and to draw less attention
from crowds of curious urbanites, the Indians were given quarters
outside Washington. Nevertheless, the chiefs grew restless, and
some became ill. They were eager to return home. As a bonus for
their long, tiring trip Major Neighbors gave the chiefs the horses
they rode on arrival back in Texas.[2]

José Maria returned to his village, sixteen miles west of the present town of Hillsboro, between Fort Worth and Waco. A second Anadarko-Hainai village below Kimball's Bend was not far off. The chief brought from Washington another document that was proudly protected through several generations. Signed by James K. Polk, it proclaimed:

KNOW ALL MEN BY THESE PRESENTS. that *José Maria* a Chief of the Ano-dah-kos and the tribe to which he belongs are by Treaty, on terms of Peace and Friendship with the United States of American.

José Maria has in person visited Washington City, the seat of Government of the United States and conducted himself according to the terms of the treaty to which he was a party.

This paper is given in testimony of the Friendship existing between the two countries.

Done at the City of Washington this twenty fifth day of July one thousand eight hundred and forty six.[3]

For more than 150 years after the first white man came to live within Hasinai territory, there were peaceful, friendly relations. It was only when the American population began to outnumber that of the tribes and white settlers began to overrun the land that the relationship became fragile and distrust destroyed the peace. Building peace, however, was ingrained in Caddo-Hasinai leaders. Even after they were pushed off their homelands and did not know if they would be allowed to stay in one place long enough to gather the corn they had planted, José Maria formed friendships with good Texans all along the Brazos River. He often visited them, and their stories about him are the stuff of legend.

Among the tales collected by Neighbours is one about José Maria's friendship with the Barkley family. He and Square Barkley became good friends while the Anadarkos lived on Big Creek east of Marlin. One of the many young Barkleys was chronically ill with malarial chills. Hoping the child's health could be improved, Square Barkley entrusted him to José Maria's care. At winter camp near the Falls of the Brazos, young Barkley slept in the chief's shelter, and about four o'clock every morning, no matter how cold the weather was, José Maria carried the boy to the river, held him close, and plunged him head first into the dark, chill water. Bounding directly back out, he briskly rubbed the boy dry. After this age-old Hasinai treatment had been administered for a while, the Barkley boy was cured. He walked with the hunters when they went out for bear, shared the closeness of the campfire, and developed an unbounded respect for José Maria and his people.[4]

Another kind of Texan, one with a bad reputation, accused José Maria's people of stealing hogs and threatened the chief with a gun. José gathered some warriors and chased the man, who fled to the Barkleys for refuge. After a talk with Barkley, José Maria withdrew, but the troublemaking settler soon tried to raise a force to kill José Maria's entire band. Barkley told the chief that it would be wise to move his people. José Maria followed his friend's advice and moved his village to a place on the Navasota River in Limestone County.[5]

Violence on the Texas frontier did not cease with the signing of Indian treaties. Rangers killed a Wichita in 1848, and the Wichitas retaliated by killing three surveyors. Returning from burying the surveyors, the Rangers met the sixteen-year-old nephew of Caddo chief Ha-de-bah and killed him. The Rangers had no excuse—they knew the young man, he had supplied their post with game, and he gave them no cause to kill him. José Maria had a hard time controlling his people's anger but managed to convince them that they should keep to the treaty and let the agent handle justice. Major Neighbors persuaded them that the murderers would be arrested and tried by the laws of the state. He reached an agreement with the chiefs: they would forgive and forget, and the government would pay the tribe $500.[6]

Neighbors recommended another move, and José Maria again relocated his people, this time farther northwest near a well-known landmark (in present Hood County) called Comanche Peak. Two years later the Anadarko, Caddo, and Hainai were living in Palo Pinto County. Their villages were separate, but José Maria was recognized as their head chief.

American immigration to Texas slowed between 1846 and 1848, but in 1849 the surge toward cheap land in Texas was almost as great as the rush toward gold in California. In 1849 U.S. Army captain Randolph B. Marcy, at the head of an expedition from Fort Smith, Arkansas, to Santa Fe, New Mexico, discovered a route through west Texas that provided a shorter southern link to California. In November of that year more than five thousand Texas-bound Americans crossed the Arkansas River at Little

Rock. The *Northern Standard* newspaper in Clarksville, twenty miles below Red River in northeast Texas, observed on November 2, 1850, "For the last two weeks scarcely a day has passed that a dozen or more mover's wagons have not passed through our town. Most of the immigrants we have seen appear to be well prepared to meet the hardship, expense and inconvenience attending the establishment of new homes in the wilderness."[7]

A month later the same newspaper reported, "Day after day it comes increasingly. Whenever we step to the doors or south windows of our office, looking out upon the square, we see trains of wagons halted, until supplies are purchased and inquiries made about the country and the roads. . . . Upon the southern line of travel through the state, as we hear, there is the same ceaseless stream, ever moving westward."[8] The spread of settlers beyond central Texas made the invisible line separating Indian villages and white settlers useless.

A *Report of the Commissioner of Indian Affairs* in 1849 said that José Maria was the leader of twelve hundred people. Caddos who had gone to Mexico returned during the summer of 1844, and fragments of some other tribes joined the Hasinai. The report inaccurately stated that the Anadarko and Hainai as well as the Caddo had migrated from Louisiana. Texans in 1849 commonly chose to forget or did not know that the Anadarko and Hainai had lived in northeast Texas for hundreds of years before the first white people arrived.

Neighbors's service as agent for the Indians of Texas was interrupted in 1849 when a new administration in Washington, D.C., terminated his appointment. He was succeeded by J. H. Rollins from Mississippi. Rollins rarely left his office, and the Indians suffered two years of neglect before two active subagents, Jesse Stemm and John A. Rogers, were appointed.[9]

Jesse Stemm visited José Maria, Towaash, and the principal men of the Caddo, Anadarko, and Hainai near their villages on the Brazos, about twenty miles below the Waco village. In Stemm's report for 1851 he quoted José Maria as saying, "That now there was a line below which the Indians were not allowed to go; but the white people came above it, marked trees, surveyed lands in their hunting grounds, and near their villages, and soon they would claim the lands; if the Indians went below they were threatened with death; that this was not just."[10]

Stemm was sympathetic and reported:

> These tribes are more fixed in their location, and more advanced in
> the arts and comforts of civilization, (slight as they are,) than any
> other of the Indians in Texas. They are making very creditable
> efforts at raising Indian corn, beans, pumpkins, and melons; their
> lodges are made of a frame or net-work of sticks, thatched with
> coarse grass, and are large, warm, and comfortable. Their corn fields
> looked well, and were comparatively well cultivated.
>   They have no farming instruments but hoes, most of which they
> said they had bought. They wanted some light ploughs and plough
> harness, and more hoes.[11]

Stemm went around to look at the cornfields, promised some
ploughs and harnesses and more hoes in the fall, and said he would
try to provide some seed potatoes and other seeds next spring.

Believing it was important to know exactly how many Indians
there were, Stemm asked the chiefs for a count. He said the tribes
"enumerated only with their fingers, or by means of bundles of
sticks. They brought me a bundle of sticks for each tribe."[12] The
final count, which Stemm considered very accurate, was Caddos,
161; Anadarkos, 202; Hainais, 113 — a total of 476 people, with 161
of them identified as warriors. He was told that about 80 warriors
from the Caddo, Waco, and Kichai had left within the previous
two years and were now living in the Wichita Mountains north of
the Red River. Still living in Texas, with or near the Caddo and
Anadarko, were Tawakonis numbering 171; Wacos, 114, and
Kichais, 38. Sixty-three Delawares and 70 Shawnees were also
counted.

At the time Stemm enumerated these tribes, 300 Caddos were
living on Wild Horse Creek near the site selected for a new fort
named Arbuckle in Indian Territory. The Choctaw and Chickasaw, whose treaties with the United States gave them lands in
that section of the territory, tolerated the Caddos, but for how
much longer was uncertain.[13]

A few months after Stemm made his 1851 report, he observed
that Fort Belknap had been established on the Clear Fork of the
Brazos beyond the Indian villages on the Brazos. He said the
military post extended "the location and settlement of the adven-
turous citizens of this State on the hunting grounds, and perhaps
upon the corn fields, and in villages of these Indians, . . . [who]

have built up villages, cleared off corn fields, and established homes, which they are forced to yield up without compensation; already have several of these tribes been compelled to yield up homes thus established."[14]

The Caddo and Hasinai had lived with uncertainty for fifteen years. Stemm pled their cause in his 1852 report, saying:

> With the constant anticipation that the fields which they have subjugated, the warm lodges they have erected, the clear cold springs they had discovered, are to be given up to the adventurous white man, whose surveys have already enclosed and surrounded their villages and "marked their trees," they have no courage for vigorous and hopeful effort.
>
> José Maria, after the close of his "winter hunt," would not go back to his old village on the Brazos. His lands had been surveyed, (a subject about which he has been extremely sensitive), and perhaps he feared interruption. The consequence has been that, upon new land, the corn-crop of his people (limited at best) has been unusually small; and their frail and imperfect lodges failing to afford the accustomed protection, they have experienced an unusual amount of sickness and mortality. I have adverted in my former reports to the obvious policy of the general government, in connection with the State of Texas, assigning some territory to those tribes in Texas who have manifested a desire to establish homes for themselves, and to cultivate the arts of civilization.[15]

Stemm resigned in the spring of 1853 and was murdered by Kickapoo Indians on February 12, 1854.[16] A week before his death the Texas legislature reacted to the pressure of citizens who demanded a protective line between themselves and the Indians and passed an act providing for Indian reserves. The act (approved February 6, 1854) gave the federal government authority to select twelve leagues of land for the reservations so long as no reserve was placed farther than twenty miles within the line of military posts intended to separate Indian range from white settlements. Captain Randolph B. Marcy and Major Neighbors, who was brought back as special supervising Agent in 1852, were appointed to locate and survey lands.

Much of the vast unpopulated area Marcy first crossed in 1849 had since been occupied. Isolated farmhouses and small communities framed his route from the time he crossed the Red River, just above the present town of Denison, Texas, until he reached a cluster of four or five log cabins whose residents boasted they were a town named Gainesville. From that point on to Fort Belknap—more than one hundred miles—nothing foreign sat on the rolling plains.

Arriving at Fort Belknap, Marcy recorded:

> Major Neighbors and myself called the chiefs of the small tribes together, and held a council with them concerning the settlement upon the new reservations.
>
> The Ionies and Anadahkas were represented by their chief José Maria, who has the blood of both tribes in his veins. He was a fine specimen of his race, about sixty years of age, with an erect, elastic carriage, and a dignified and commanding demeanor.
>
> A young and very intelligent chief, named Tiner, who commands that portion of his tribe living upon the Brazos River, appeared for the Caddos.[17]

José Maria was beginning to feel old. He had attended too many councils with too many white men to have faith that this one would have any truer meaning than the others. In this council his words were the product of many crushed hopes:

> I know our Great Father has power to do with us as he pleases; we have been driven from our homes several times by the whites, and all we want is a permanent location, where we shall be free from further molestation. . . . Heretofore we have had our enemies, the whites on one side, and the Camanches on the other, and of the two evils, we prefer the former, as they allow us to eat what we raise, whilst the Camanches take everything, and if we are to be killed, we should much rather die with full bellies; we would therefore prefer taking our chances on the Brazos, where we can be near the whites.[18]

W. B. Parker was with Marcy in no official capacity—just to make the trip. He had a wide-ranging curiosity, and the notes he made of his experiences showed an appreciation of Indian character. While Marcy and Neighbors surveyed land for the reservation, he visited with the interpreter for the council who "was *Bear Head*, a famous Delaware, employed by the Indian agent for these tribes as guide and interpreter. His American name was Jim Shaw. He had been adopted into the Caddo tribe, and became a chief among them."[19] Parker said that Shaw

led a Gypsy life, with his wife and two children, living entirely in tents, but providing many comforts for them unknown or unthought of by other Indians.

I visited his camp several times, and was surprised to find some domestic appendages which I did not expect to see with them, moving as they did from place to place, viz., two cats and some barn-yard fowls.

He seemed very fond of his family, and anxious that his children might go to school, and that he might soon be settled on the Reserve, and have his farm and permanent home. He had provided his wife with an excellent side saddle, and in her tent I saw a *musquito* bar, a luxury scarcely to be expected in an Indian Camp.[20]

Parker's description of the Caddo village is so like that written by Joutel in 1690, it could almost be a carbon copy. Parker counted about 150 lodges, which

were constructed by erecting a frame-work of poles, placed in a circle in the ground, the tops united in an oval form, strongly bound with withes, and thatched with long grass. They were about twenty-five feet in diameter at the base and twenty feet high, making a very comfortable shelter, and looking in the distance like hay or grain stacks.

Each person had a bunk raised from the ground and covered with skins, as a couch, and the fire was built in the centre, the smoke escaping from the apex of the cone.[21]

Marcy and Neighbors found a vacant tract of country below the junction of the Clear Fork with the Brazos River. The Brazos was very crooked there, the water was very bitter, and the streambed was quicksand. However, the river divided two equal sections of four leagues and thus made a boundary for the use of two separate tribes. Twenty-six miles of river frontage assured water throughout the seasons, and there were also several freshwater streams fed by springs. The valley land on either side of the stream was fertile, and mesquite uplands bordered both sides. Gramma grasses grew luxuriantly, making good pasturage. A range of mountains covered with oak timber offered a natural east-west boundary.

A lower reserve of 37,152 acres for the Anadarko, Caddo, Waco, Kichai, Delaware, Tawakoni, and Tonkowa tribes was situated on the main branch a few miles below Fort Belknap in the territory that became Young County. An upper reserve of 18,576 acres set aside for the southern branch of the Comanche was located on the Clear Fork of the Brazos in what are now Shack-elford and Throckmorton Counties. To protect the Brazos agency Indians as well as frontier settlers, the federal government sta-tioned two companies of mounted soldiers and two companies of infantry (about 850 men) at nearby Fort Belknap in the fall of 1854.

As soon as the reservation was opened for settlement in 1855, the Caddo and Anadarko began to move. They gathered in March, eager to select a place to break the tough prairie-grass sod and plant their fields in ground they could call their own. It was a dry spring in west Texas; there had been no rain for nine months. By the time the fields were prepared, it was late in the season. Four hundred acres were planted, but the corn, dropped late into dry earth, did not yield enough to make the effort worthwhile.

In the second week of September, 205 Anadarkos and 188 Caddos were settled in villages next to the dried-up fields. Hainais were counted with the Anadarkos. In two years they had neat cabins and gardens full of vegetables and melons in the villages. The Caddo built seven good log houses in 1857 and had 130 acres in corn, 20 in wheat. The Anadarko built ten log homes that year and had 115 acres of corn and 20 acres of wheat. Men of the tribes gave particular attention to raising stock, and the number of horses, cattle, and hogs steadily increased. The women milked and made butter.

There was a grove of mesquite trees in the middle of the reserve. The agency buildings — a kitchen, a storeroom, a blacksmith shop, and three houses, one for the agent and two for other employees — were located there. G. W. Hill was the agent during the first months; then Captain Shapley Prince Ross became the agent for the lower reserve. Major Neighbors kept his headquarters in San Antonio. The chiefs of the reserve Indians, Neighbors, Hill, and Ross worked together to organize law and order. A government farmer lived at the agency and worked with the tribes to develop their fields and stock. A resident blacksmith took care of tools and weapons. Finally, a schoolhouse was built. The teacher, Z. E. Coombes, came in June 1858. He soon had sixty pupils who spoke only their native language; Jim Shaw was hired as an interpreter to assist Coombes.

When Marcy and Neighbors surveyed the boundaries for the

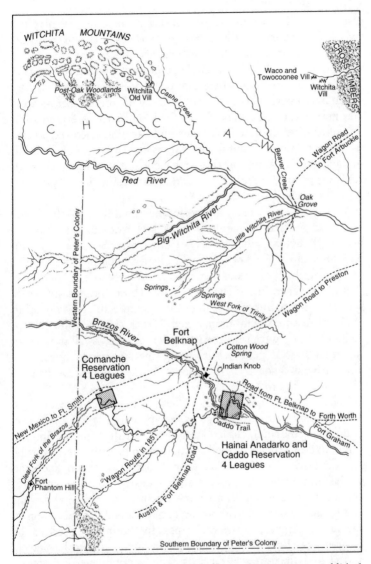

The Caddo reservation on the Brazos River, the Comanche reservation, established routes, and geographical markings redrawn and adapted from a section of Captain R. B. Marcy's *Map of the Country upon the Brazos and Big Wichita Rivers Explored in 1854, Embracing the Lands Appropriated by the State of Texas for the Use of Indians*, reproduced in W. Eugene Hollow, *Beyond the Cross Timbers: The Travels of Randolph B. Marcy*.

reserves, leaving a wide stretch of mesquite-dotted country be-tween the settlers and the Indians, they thought they were locat-ing far away from the white settlements. But in less than three years, while the Caddo, Anadarko, and Hainai on the reservation built and planted, the surrounding landscape changed. Stage-coach lines operated over the trail Marcy had blazed across west and northwest Texas. The Butterfield Southern Overland Mail line of coaches departed St. Louis and San Francisco six times a week, and "from the first its operations had the effect of advertis-ing and greatly aiding in the settlement of the country through which it passed, notably Fort Belknap and Young County, which it put on something of a boom."[22]

When the last treaty between the republic and the Texas Indian tribes had been signed, President Sam Houston had ex-plained the color symbolism of the ribbons attached to the seal and had counseled, "Our hearts ought always to be pure and white and never change, and as the grass is ever green our friendship should be ever fresh."[23] The sky remained blue, the grass and trees remained green, but pure white hearts jaundiced. Texas historian Walter Prescott Webb summarized, "Texas, the Republic, had an Indian policy—with Houston it was peace, with Lamar it was war, in either case a policy; but Texas, the state, had none. The alternative was gone. *There could be no peace; there must be war. The Indian had to go.*"[24]

Texans complained that the federal government provided too little protection. Small groups of self-appointed protectors, many of dubious character, chased after "horse-stealing, murdering red skins" and mostly succeeded in stirring up hostility between the races. A leading troublemaker, John R. Baylor, had been dismissed as the first agent for the Comanches on the upper reserve. He claimed that his former charges were responsible for depredations and blamed Major Neighbors, Agent Ross, and his successor on the upper reserve, Mathew Leeper, for failing to confine the Comanches. Baylor's inflammatory remarks in public letters and at mass meetings of citizens excited prejudices and roused emotions.

Late in January 1858 Governor H. R. Runnels gave J. S. Ford command of volunteer troops in the service of the state of Texas and authorized him to organize 100 additional men—Texas Rangers. Ford's orders were to "follow any and all trails of hostile or

suspected hostile Indians you may discover, and if possible, overtake and chastise them, if unfriendly."[25]

Ford brought Rangers to the Brazos reserve on March 19 and,
with the cooperation of Ross, called the chiefs into council to
enlist their help in a war against their old enemies, the Comanches.
One hundred thirteen Brazos Reserve Indians led by Ross crossed
the Red River with Ford's 102 men on April 29.[26] On May 12 Ford
directed an attack on unsuspecting Comanches camped near the
Canadian River. A running battle covering over six miles began
about seven in the morning and lasted until Ford declared a
victory about two in the afternoon. He counted 76 dead Comanches and 18 prisoners (mostly women and children) and took
more than three hundred horses. Two Texans were killed, 2
wounded. The first and last men wounded were a Shawnee guide
and an Anadarko captain, Jim Pockmark. In a report to the
governor of Texas, Ford commended Ross for his leadership of the
reserve Indians and gave the Indian captains his highest praise,
saying, "They behaved under fire in a gallant and soldier-like
manner and I think they have fully vindicated their right to be
recognized as Texas Rangers of the old stamp."[27]

The Comanches were far from intimidated by the defeat of one
of their bands. They replaced their lost mounts in raids on Texas
frontier settlements, made an easily followed trail to the lower
Brazos reserve, then scattered so there was no visible trail beyond.
Texas frontier settlers, ready to believe the worst about any
Indian, concluded that all their troubles were caused by reserve
Indians.

In the fall of 1858, 125 Anadarko, Caddo, and other Brazos
reserve warriors again cooperated in another campaign against the
northern Comanches. This time they were led by L. S. (Sul) Ross,
the agent's son. Young Ross's Indian brigade supported 400 U.S.
cavalry led by Major Earl Van Dorn. A little after daybreak on
October 1, they charged a camp near the Wichita Mountains in
what is now Oklahoma. After a battle that lasted only thirty
minutes, 56 Comanches were dead, all the lodges were burned,
and 300 horses were captured.

Texas historian Webb observed:

> When Ford and Van Dorn pursued the Comanches beyond the Red
> River and practically annihilated those they found in what is now

Oklahoma, they turned a page in the story of the Texas frontier. The Indians never again attacked the people of the Texas frontier with the confidence which they had exhibited hitherto, because they had learned that they had no retreat safe from the Rangers or from the United States soldiers south of the Red. But before Texans were free from Indians who were their avowed enemies, they turned on those left in the state who had professed friendship and proved it by joining expeditions against Comanches.[28]

CHAPTER 23

CHOCTAW TOM

★ Tom was a Choctaw Indian married to an Anadarko woman. They lived among white people for twenty years before the Brazos reserve was established, and their large family was known and respected by whites who settled near the reservation. In fact, when someone was sick in one of the settler's homes, the women of Choctaw Tom's family were often called on as nurses.

Toward the end of 1858 Ross gave Tom permission to take his wife, some of his children and grandchildren, and other family connections a few miles below the reserve where there was good grass for grazing. Altogether there were twenty-seven people—eight men, eight women, and eleven children—enough for five camps. The young men of the party had just returned from serving with Major Van Dorn on his expedition against the Comanches. The major had asked that they accompany him again on his spring campaign, and they planned to do so, but for now their horses needed rest and fattening. The place they camped was above Golconda, the seat of Palo Pinto County at that time.

Days in the family camp went by without counting. Late fall eased into early winter—the hunting season. Although game was not as plentiful as it used to be, bears still came down into the area when their food supply grew scarce farther north. Several white men came to ask Tom's family to go with them on a hunt, and the family agreed, moving its camp to the edge of a small creek about fifteen miles below the reservation. The bear hunting plans were interrupted when Tom learned that a man who lived nearby had a cart and yoke of oxen for sale. He bought the cart and team and set out to drive them back to the reservation. The other family members were supposed to bring the horses and camp equipment back to their village by a different, shorter route, but after Tom left, bear signs were sighted, and the white people living near the campsite talked these family members into staying a few days longer.

Eight nights later all of Tom's family was asleep in camp. Near daylight, before anyone was awake, gunshots pierced the tents. Choctaw Tom's wife, another Anadarko woman, three Anadarko men, and a Caddo man and woman were killed. Six died instantly. The seventh, one of the men whose wife was dead, was shot on his bed but was able to reach his gun and crawl through the tent flap before he died. José Maria's nephew, Little John, who had served with Van Dorn, was one of the young men killed.

One of Tom's daughters had a thumb shot off her hand. Another woman and three men had severe wounds. Eight children were injured, three seriously. One young boy was not expected to live.

When the survivors brought the wounded home to the reserva- tion, a turmoil of grief, anger, and panic stirred the tribes. There were cries for immediate vengeance, but José Maria urged the friends and family of the murdered to hold back. He reminded them that Ross had promised he would not see them wronged and asked them to wait while he and Tinah, the Caddo chief, went to the agency to see what Ross had to say.

Ross was away, attending U.S. District Court in Austin, and J. J. Sturm, the government farmer for the Brazos reserve, was in charge. José Maria spoke to him, saying that he had been a friend to white men and looked on them as brothers, but now that they had murdered his people, he did not know how to meet them. He said his young men wanted to leave right away to punish the murderers, but he would wait until the agent could get back to the reservation.

Sturm wrote a brief account of what had happened and sent it off to Ross. Then with four other white men and nearly thirty Indians, he left to investigate the place where Choctaw Tom had camped. The starkness of the circumstances pressed on them as they entered the neighborhood of the campsite. Houses along the way were empty; all the settlers were gone. The Indian riders stared darkly at the vacant homes—guilty people ran away. Past the deserted homes, by the edge of the creek in the bend of the river, they found a man and a woman in each of two camp tents and a single person in each of three others. Except for the man who lay at the entry of his tent, all the dead were on their beds, with their eyes closed as though sleeping.

The sun was half-hidden below the western horizon. Because no tools had been brought for digging graves, the Caddos and Anadarkos covered the bodies of their relatives with brush and stones. While the dead were being cared for, Sturm and one of the Indians searched around the encampment. They found the place where the gunmen had lain in darkness, waiting for early light to aid the accuracy of their aim.

It was dark again when the burial party left the campsite. The party stopped for the night about five miles from Golconda. Townsmen came out early the next morning, and from them Sturm learned the names of seven of the murderers—they were white men who had made no secret of their identities.

Back at the reservation, Sturm tried to make sure that there was no misunderstanding among the Indians, who, fearing further attacks, had all gathered about the agency for protection. Using an interpreter, Sturm explained that the people who lived in the vicinity of the camp were not guilty; they had left their homes because they were afraid they would be blamed and retaliated against. José Maria and Tinah responded that they were not wild Indians and would not harm the innocent. Sturm should send someone to tell those settlers to return to their homes and take care of their farms. The Caddo and Anadarko did not blame them—both tribes had been told that the men who killed members of their families would be caught and punished according to the white man's law, and that was the way it should be.[1]

But that was not the way it was. Rumors, developing naturally or deliberately, claimed that Indians from the Brazos reserve were going to attack white settlements. Agitators played on Texans' hatred and contempt for horse thieves. A rash of sworn statements accused the "rascally Reserve Indians" in general and José Maria in particular of stealing livestock. Speeches made at public meetings roused citizens to take action intended to break up the reservation. Inflammatory remarks were printed in newspapers.

The men who had participated in the massacre of Choctaw

Tom's family justified their action in a long "Open Letter to the People of Texas" published in the Palo Pinto newspaper:

We, the undersigned, are the individuals who composed the company that attacked and killed a party of Indians (from the lower reservation) in this county, on the morning of the 27th of December, and felt it due to ourselves to make known the causes that led to this act, and all the attending circumstances, in order that the public mind may be enabled to form a just opinion of our conduct, from a correct acknowledgment of the facts. We do this, not from any disposition to evade any responsibility that may attach to our acts, but a proper regard to an impartial public sentiment.

Facts and circumstances, dating as far back as last winter, all connected, produced the opinion among ourselves and the community, that it was the reserve Indians, and them alone, that have committed the depredations in our section of country. These circumstances are too numerous to give them all, and yet they all form an important link in the chain. . . . Still, many of our citizens, [were] willing to make some allowance for irregularities among a people changing, or, it would be more proper to say, which it is claimed are changing, from a savage to a civilized state, and we hoped our suspicions might prove groundless. . . . This fall our red neighbors from the reservation began to come down among us in hunting parties. We immediately had our apprehensions excited. Some of our number . . . went to a party above Robert Martin's Esq. . . . and firmly but kindly told them they must return to the reservation; that the people could not nor would not permit them to hunt through the settlements; that they claimed to be friends and good Indians, but that our people could not distinguish one tribe from another, and they did not intend them to stay; that if they were good Indians, they would show it by returning to the reservation, and, if they did not do it, they would raise men and kill them. The Indians promised to go the next morning early, and also promised to go by and notify some other parties that were in the country. The next day, Judge Motheral, while horse hunting, met with two men of this same party near the same place. He again warned them of their danger, and they openly laughed in his face at the warning; and he replied to them that they might laugh, but if they did not heed it, they would find it but too true when, perhaps, it was too late. . . . These warnings were made intelligible to the Indians, and repeated till satisfied; and one who spoke the English language said he understood it. . . . Other parties were warned, all to no purpose. They would move their camps two or three miles, but would not leave the settlements.

After these repeated warnings, and the failure of the Indians to obey, six horses were stolen from off the Palo Pinto. . . . A party of citizens from Palo Pinto and Erath counties, numbering from forty to fifty, assembled . . . to take into consideration the best course to rid ourselves of horse thieves, either red or white, or both, as we had reasons to believe that there were a few white men in collusion with Indians. A committee, composed of a large number, was appointed. They organized the company composed of the undersigned, and they were ordered by the committee, and it was sanctioned by the meeting unanimously, that we should kill any Indians found this side of Cedar creek, and arrest certain white men, and warn others to leave the State. We failed to find the white men we were ordered to arrest, but notified the others to leave the State, which they promised to do. We then, in pursuance of our orders, went in pursuit of the Indians that had been encamped on the waters of the Palo Pinto, and who, we learned, were still in the county of Palo Pinto. . . . We pursued the trail made by the Indians . . . with a conscientious feeling of duty to ourselves and our country, until we came on a camp, early on the morning of the 27th of December, when we charged the camp, and killed all the men we saw, and, unfortunately and unintentionally, for it was positively against orders and our intention, to molest the women, still, from the situation of the men, being in the tents, it being early in the morning and raining, two women and one child were killed. It was unfortunate, as we knew it will be made a frightful theme for denunciation against us by the sickly sentimentalists who are ready to plead the cause of the poor Indians. . . . We have testimony to prove that a warrior made the first effort to shoot; but candor and truth, and that spirit that dictates this narrative, require us to say, that our charging his camp was sufficient to atone and cause his resistance, and that it had no influence on our course. It is proper, also, that we should say, that the hostile demonstration made towards Mr. Vernay by José Maria, the principal chief on the lower reservation, and his son, was made known to us before we made the attack . . . and, in conclusion, will only add, that we honestly believe that we only anticipated the Indians; that when we reflect that they were scattered over the country, from the lower reservation to Paluxy, a distance of eighty miles, and the insulting manner with which they acted, and the depredations actually committed many minor ones we have not detailed, such as killing cattle—and it leaves no doubt in our minds but that they, after making their hunt and spying out our horses, would have left a sufficient number to have driven off our stock and, killed many unfortunate citizens happening in their way, and it

would, as usual, have been charged to the Comanches, and the
reserve Indians ready in the spring to have led our troops to avenge
themselves upon an enemy of theirs, but who, we do not honestly
believe have done us any harm. That we have had wool pulled over
our eyes in this way long enough, is about a unanimous opinion. We
have no apology to offer for what we have done. We are sustained by
hundreds of our fellow citizens. We are well known in the country
in which we live, and have ever been men obedient to the law.[2]

The letter was signed by "Peter Garland, captain," and eighteen
others.

Word reached the Brazos reserve that a large body of armed
settlers was advancing to "clean up" the place. Agent Ross had not
yet returned, and Sturm was still in charge. He called for help
from Fort Belknap, and Captain T. N. Palmer arrived at the
agency with a detachment of thirty-four men on January 5. They
returned to Fort Belknap after four days. Palmer's report, written
on January 10, said that three men appointed to make arrangements for a peaceful solution to "the existing difficulties" came to
the agency and were satisfied that the citizens they represented
were in no danger. "As far as I can learn," he reported, "the Indians
never had any idea of retaliating for the murder of their people."
He said the people assembled below the reservation returned to
their homes and quoted their commissioners as saying they "did
not pretend to excuse the outrage of the 27th December; that
affair is condemned by the good people as a cold-blooded, cow-
ardly affair."[3]

Minutes of a meeting held by the group camped below the
reservation gave a different account of what took place. They said
that 200 men from five counties assembled and appointed an
executive committee and 3 commissioners "whose duty it would
be to repair to the agency, and make known our situation, and
demand that the Indians should remain on the reservation; and
that they should be made to understand that the late killing of
their people was caused by their leaving the reservation; and that
they could expect nothing better in future, if they were found
down in the settlements, &c."[4] While the commissioners proceeded with their mission, the assembly formed a military organization and drilled. The commissioners reported back on January
13, saying that they had sat in councils with the chiefs for the
tribes on the Brazos reserve and that the chiefs had agreed to the

demands of the assembly. José Maria, Sturm, the interpreter, and—except for the 3 commissioners—all those present during the discussion at the agency, vowed they never heard of or made any such an agreement.

Agent Ross and Major Neighbors reacted promptly when they received Sturm's account of the massacre. Both men hurried to the Brazos reserve. Neighbors stopped only to inform Governor Runnels, who assured him "that energetic measures will be taken to arrest the murderers and abate the evil."[5]

The governor issued a proclamation warning "all persons against joining or otherwise engaging or assisting in such unlawful expedition and hostilities" and directing "all civil authorities and peace officers of the State to use all legal means in their power to arrest all offenders in the premises (in order that they may be dealt with according to law) and to prevent the carrying out of the aforesaid unlawful plans and purposes."[6] The proclamation was printed as an "extra" in the *Southerner,* a newspaper published in Waco, Texas, on January 15.

Neighbors, on his way to the reservation, arrived in Waco the day the governor's proclamation was published. He made the necessary affidavits, and the district judge issued writs for the arrest of Garland and all his band whose names were known. Captain John S. (Rip) Ford, as commander of the state troops, was notified to arrest and bring them in. Neighbors took the additional precaution of employing an attorney to represent the Indians in court during preliminary investigations.

Ross got back to the reservation on January 14. He found most of those wounded during the massacre recovering, but two were still in a condition so serious that he placed them in the care of the surgeon at Fort Belknap. Choctaw Tom, his daughter and son who were wounded, and several other Caddos and Anadarkos had left the reservation to live with relatives across the Red River. Ross could not determine how many had left because of the upheaval on the Brazos reserve.

Immediately after the attack on Tom's camp, the tribes prepared to defend their families. Farms, which were mostly located near the outer boundaries of the reservation, were vacated, and everyone gathered around the centrally located agency buildings. The people remained there for better protection, leaving horses, cattle, hogs, poultry, and crops unattended. Ross read and explained the governor's proclamation and encouraged them to return to their homes. The chiefs said they would accept the decision made by the whites' law if the ones who murdered their people were promptly arrested and judged. Ross told them that Major Neighbors had already taken steps to see that would happen and that proper action would be taken by state authorities. With these assurances for their safety, families began to return to their farms and villages.

Ross was actually far from confident that their lives and property would be protected. He addressed a letter to Neighbors on January 26, 1859, saying that if the U.S. Department of Indian Affairs expected to keep the reservation, it needed to provide laws and the means of enforcing them so that the Indians settled there would have their lives and property protected as granted by treaty. If not, he said, the sooner the Indians placed on the Brazos reserve were moved to "other United States Indian territory, north of Red river, and protected from the numerous marauding bands of whites and Indians that are now infesting this frontier, the better it will be, both for the good citizens and the Indians themselves."[7]

Neighbors agreed with Ross and predicted that if the murderers were not arrested and punished, the Indians of the reservation would "disband and seek satisfaction." Information he had gathered in Waco, Dallas, Weatherford, and frontier counties he had passed through on his way to the reservation had convinced him that John R. Baylor and his cohorts (Allison Nelson, Garland and his party, and a man identified as Mr. Alexander) had formed an organized conspiracy for the purpose of breaking up the reservations. The only encouraging news given Neighbors or Ross was that "numbers of the best citizens of the adjoining counties" disapproved the attack on the Caddos and Anadarkos.[8]

An official examination of the murders was scheduled to take place in Waco, and Neighbors expected the men identified as the party that attacked Choctaw Tom's camp to be arrested by that time. He told Ross to furnish supplies and transportation so that the wounded Indians who were able to travel and other competent witnesses from the reservation could attend. The witnesses left on January 31, accompanied by J. J. Sturm.

No arrests were made. Captain Ford had in fact refused, saying that as a military officer he was not required to follow the orders of civil officials. The district judge issued new orders for the sheriff to make the arrests, but they were not followed. The grand jury described the Brazos reserve as a nuisance, stating that the Indians there were doing all the mischief and concluding, "It is now the prevailing sentiment that we must abandon our homes and take up arms against the reserve Indians."[9] Instead of finding Garland and his company guilty of murder, the jury found José Maria guilty of stealing a mule. It was well known, said Neighbors, that the mule belonged to a citizen of the reservation and was legally taken by the Anadarko chief and that any attempt to arrest José Maria was sure to bring about conflict. Having waited for justice as it should be, the Anadarko chief returned to the reservation on February 14, sick in body and spirit.

It was time to prepare ground for planting early corn. The tribes started repairing fences and cleaning fields but did little else. Oxen used to pull plows grazed outside the reserve and were not brought in because the Indians were afraid to leave the reserve. They were further disheartened near the end of February when Comanches stole eighty horses from the Caddo — about the last of some five hundred head that they and the Anadarko had had three months earlier.

When Ross notified Captain Ford that Comanches had taken the horses from the Caddo and some citizens' horses as well, the commander of the Texas troops responded promptly. He was unwilling to arrest Garland and his crew but quite willing to chase Comanche horse thieves. He arrived at the agency within a few hours, bringing thirty Rangers, who were joined in a pursuit of the Comanches by thirty reserve Indians. Before they returned, Ross was alerted that parties meeting in Jack, Palo Pinto, and Erath Counties had set March 20 as the date to drive both Indians and whites off the Brazos reserve.

The absence of the thirty warriors left the reserve more vulnerable than usual, and the troops had recently been withdrawn from Fort Balknap. Ross believed these facts influenced the timing for the attack. He asked for assistance from Major G. H. Thomas, in command of the cavalry at Camp Cooper near the upper reserve; wrote Neighbors, who was in San Antonio, that his presence was needed; and sent a letter to the governor. Then Ross called a council of the chiefs.[10]

Troops arrived from Camp Cooper, and March 20 passed without incident, but everyone knew that Baylor's followers were massing about twelve miles below. The reservation remained in a nervous state of readiness. The U.S. Office of Indian Affairs had slowly realized that the Texas reservations had to be abandoned and the Indians moved to a place where they could be protected from lawless violence. Neighbors was notified in late March that the only place the tribes could be permanently located was a section of Indian Territory between the 98th and 100th parallels of west longitude that the government had leased from the Choctaws and Chickasaws. However, that part of the country was practically unknown, and Neighbors was told that the move had to be delayed, probably until fall or winter, so that preparations could be made—location of a site for the agency, erection of buildings to accommodate the agent, and establishment of a military post at the proper point. Official notice of the government's intent to remove the Indians from the Brazos reserves was sent to the governor and published in Texas newspapers on April 15. Neighbors, Ross, and Leeper (the agent for the Comanches on the upper reserve) fervently hoped that Texans bent on ridding themselves of Indians would be pacified by the announcement.

Baylor's crowd was not satisfied—it only tried harder to bring about hostilities. Lieutenant William Burnet wrote his father from the Brazos reserve on May 9:

> The people say they have lost a thousand head of horses in the last year. This Reserve consists of only eight leagues; and as they have the right to come and look for their horses at any time, it would be easy to find some of them within so small a space, if there were any there; but none have ever been found. . . . We kept on our guard, but nothing happened until the day before yesterday, when a party of Indians (who had been carrying an express from this to Fort Arbuckle, and were returning with despatches from that Fort,) came into camp very much excited and stated that they had been attacked by about 20 men (there were seven Indians in the party) some nine miles from here.[11]

Burnet led 100 Indians, 2 soldiers, and Sturm to find the missing express rider, the government papers, and five stolen horses. They easily found the place where the attack had taken place and after searching for some time found the missing Indian's tracks. Concluding that he had been taken prisoner, they followed his trail for about one and one-half miles and came to a house, one of the stations on the mail route to California. A man at the mail station told Burnet that fifteen men from Jack County called themselves the Jacksboro Rangers had been there eating and grazing their horses when they saw the Indian express riders and started after them. The Indians thought they were safe carrying government mail and did not try to escape until shots were fired at them.

The first shot did no harm, but a second shot brought down one of their horses. They dropped the reins of the five horses and scattered. All except the one whose horse was shot got back to the Brazos reserve. The man at the mail station said the Jacksboro Rangers returned to his place, bringing an Indian, six horses, two rifles, and a Colt pistol. They broke open the saddlebags and read some documents and a letter from the agent in Indian Territory addressed to Ross. The rangers cursed the Indian, telling him he had no business with the papers and no right to be there, then started on the road to Jacksboro. Twelve miles along the road, Burnet found the body of the Indian shot through the chest and scalped.

Burnet said, "The sun had just set. The Indians gathered around the dead man, and each looked at him, but no one spoke a word. There was a brother and a cousin of the murdered man in the party. They wrapped him in a blanket, and carried him to a small ravine hard by and covered him with with boughs—the others stood by their horse but said nothing."[12] The name of the dead dispatch carrier was Fox. He had served as a scout for both the Ford and Van Dorn expeditions.

Burnet led his Indian troops on to Jacksboro and stationed them about one hundred yards from the first house while he made an unsuccessful search of the town. The search for the men who had killed Fox was then given up. But by leading 100 Indians to the edge of a white settlement in search of Texas citizens, the lieutenant gave agitators all the ammunition they needed to ignite the frontier.

An infantry company under Captain Charles C. Gilbert reinforced the guard already posted at the Brazos agency. Neighbors urged the Office of Indian Affairs to authorize immediate removal of the tribes to a temporary location north of the Red River at Fort Arbuckle. He argued on May 12, "I am certain that the Indians cannot be controlled or confined to their present narrow limits with the present threats against their lives; and, unless prompt measures are taken, they will abandon the reserve and take the chances for self-defense and a subsistence."[13] On May 23 Baylor led 250 men onto the lower reserve.

Baylor and his company drew their mounts up in a single line of battle within 600 yards of the agency building. Captain Joseph B. Plummer, in command of the guard, sent an officer with fifty men to meet Baylor and ask what he wanted. Baylor said that he had come to fight Indians, not whites, but that if the troops fired on his men, they would fight back. He said he would wait forty-five minutes for a reply from Captain Plummer.[14]

Plummer sent Lieutenant Burnet to say that his orders were to protect the Indians on this reserve from the attacks of armed bands of citizens and that he would do so to the best of his ability. He warned Baylor in the name of the government of the United States to leave the reservation. Baylor replied that the warning did not alter his determination to attack the Indians on the reservation and that he would take care of his own leaving. He said he regretted "the necessity of coming in collision with the United States troops, but he had determined to destroy the Indians on this and the upper reserve, if it cost the life of every man in his command."[15]

The Indians and soldiers were prepared for action. Mounted Indians followed the movements of Baylor and his men, watching from under cover. Baylor started a retreat. A short distance from the agency buildings, an old Indian man motioned to Baylor with friendly gestures. The old man was a Tonkawa chief past eighty years old who had fought with whites against Indians but never with Indians against whites. When he approached Baylor's men, they tied a rope around his neck, dragged him a short way, then killed and scalped him. Passing an old woman working in her garden, they killed her, too. The mounted Indians left their cover, and a running fight began—50 Indians exchanging gunfire with 250 whites over an eight-mile course that led to William Marlin's place. There Baylor and his men took cover, firing through cracks in the house and outbuildings. Fearing that Mrs. Marlin or children might be hurt, the Indians did not shoot into the home. Jim Pockmark, second chief of the Anadarkos, rode up to the house and called for Baylor to come out and fight him face to face. Baylor declined. Three of Baylor's men firing from behind fences and outbuildings were seriously wounded, and two were killed before daylight faded and the Indians returned to the reservation. One Indian, Caddo John, was killed. Baylor dispersed his men with orders to return in six days with more recruits.

Major Neighbors pushed harder for Indian removal in his report to the commissioner of Indian affairs after Baylor's attack. Writing that he could begin the removal on a day's notice, Neighbors insisted, "It is impossible to keep the Indians here, as the ball is already in motion."[16] Ross disagreed with Neighbors on the need for immediate removal. He said the agency defense was good, and he believed the tribes could protect themselves. He pointed out that the Indians had property that could not be moved at that time without great loss. He was speaking mainly of the tribes' cattle, which habitually grazed off the reservation on open range. Such grazing was common in Texas, but because of the danger posed by Baylor's men, the Indians could not safely collect their stock.

Neighbors's assessment of their position was more realistic. U.S. troops had orders to protect lives and property *only on the reservation*. State troops offered no help outside. The governor, more interested in his political career than the welfare of the Indians, was most anxious to avoid a collision of Texas citizens with U.S. troops. His solution was to send John Henry Brown at the head of 100 men to police the reservation. Brown placed a guard "to prevent Indians from leaving before they are finally removed" and "at the same time preventing hostile assaults upon the Reserves." Any Indian found off the reservation unaccompanied by an agent "or some responsible white man" was to be treated as hostile.[17]

By June 10 two lieutenants and eighty men of the Second Cavalry had been posted at the Brazos agency. Conditions inside the crowded defense enclosure where families stayed for protection were so poor that many were sick. There were three or four deaths daily, and a serious epidemic was feared. At the insistence of the military, the Indians were sent to camp near pure water. They were more vulnerable to attack there but less endangered by disease. Neighbors continued to press for permission to take them across the Red River. Finally, on June 11, instructions were written—pack up and move.

Neighbors's counterpart, Elias Rector, superintendent of the southern superintendency, was given responsibility for the tribes after removal. He and Neighbors were to select locations for reserves in the leased district, the western section of Choctaw and Chickasaw lands that the government had already set aside for the settlement of Wichita bands.

Rector left his headquarters in Fort Smith, Arkansas, and traveled across the present state of Oklahoma to inspect the Wichita Mountain area that the War Department had selected as the site of a fort to protect the Indians of the Wichita agency. He employed Caddo chief Fai-o-tun as a guide and Chim-ma-sha as a Caddo interpreter. A Delaware interpreter, other Delawares, the chief and war chief of the Wichitas, and Samuel A. Blain, agent for the Wichita, accompanied him on his tour of inspection.[18]

Rector and his party arrived at Fort Arbuckle, near present-day Pauls Valley, Oklahoma, in mid-June. Bands of the Wichita and the Caddo who had come across from Louisiana without ever living in Texas were camped eighteen miles from the post on Caddo Creek. Rector said, "They are peaceable and obedient, but of course doing nothing whatever, having come in temporarily . . . through fear of the Comanches. . . . Those now here are armed with bows and arrows and spears alone. I earnestly advise that each warrior be at once furnished with a rifle and a moderate supply of ammunition, which are equally indispensable with the implements of agriculture in my possession to be delivered to them."[19] Both the Caddo and the Wichita were destitute and eager to have a permanent home where they could provide for themselves.

Rector found much of the country he traveled through uninhab-itable—no water, no trees, no fertile soil—but the valley of the Washita River, near the future town of Anadarko, was wide, fertile, and covered with a thick growth of timber. Sugar Tree Creek flowed into the Washita River from the northwest. The creek took its name from the sugar maple trees that grew farther up in the hills. The Caddos and Delawares told Rector before leaving Fort Arbuckle that they wanted to settle there. After seeing the terrain, he consented and selected a site for the agency on the south side of the Washita River near an old, abandoned Kichai village. He proposed to place the Texas Indians on the south side of the river unless they chose to settle with the Caddos and Delawares on the north side.

Neighbors and the headmen of the Texas reserves arrived at Fort Arbuckle the day Rector returned from his exploration. A council was held for all the bands, those that had been living in Indian Territory and those that were from Texas. Rector said he and Neighbors "explained to them the great pain and regret felt by the government at being compelled so hastily to remove those in Texas to another country; but assured them that they would be paid for all losses thus incurred, and that after removal, they would occupy a country belonging to the United States, and not within any State, where none could intrude upon them and they would remain, they and their children, as long as the waters should run, protected from all harm by the United States." The Caddos who came across Indian Territory from Louisiana; the Caddo, Anadarko, and associated tribes from the lower Brazos reserve; the Comanche from the upper reserve in Texas; the Delaware; and the Wichita were advised "to become acquainted with each other, and to prepare to live near each other as friends and neighbors."[20]

CHAPTER 24

THE REMOVAL

★ They started moving on the first day of August. For the past month the thermometer reading had averaged 106 degrees from midmorning until five in the evening. The gauge was no different that Monday morning when the removal began at eight o'clock. The Anadarko, Caddo, Hainai, and associated bands that lived on the Brazos reserve started over a trail that led nearly two hundred miles through searing heat and dust to evening camps where water seldom satisfied their thirst.

Some, old and infirm, rode; a few, still weak from the July sickness, were given a place to ride; others, young and small, were carried; most walked. All knew that the Rangers, whose policing had prevented the gathering of livestock, were riding close. The whereabouts of Baylor and his mob was not known, but it was possible that they would try to carry out their threat to kill all the Indians as soon as they were off the reservation. The refugees left behind their houses, gardens, almost all their stock, and, except for what they could carry, all their other possessions. Fear they took with them.

Major Neighbors had planned, bullied, and pushed authorities to provision and protect the Indians in their flight from the reserve. Teams of oxen driven by agency employees pulled wagons and carts holding twenty days' rations for the immigrants. Ross, Sturm, and a blacksmith with tools and equipment were part of the train. So were all the other employees. No one wanted to be left

behind at the deserted agency. All the buildings were emptied—
even the glass-pane window sashes of the schoolhouse were carted
away. Major Neighbors sold the whole stock of hogs belonging to
the Indians and placed a respectable citizen in charge of the
agency buildings. He also made an arrangement with "several of
the stock-raisers in the vicinity, to gather up the Indian cattle, a
large portion of which they were unable to collect, on account of
the hostile attitude assumed by the State troops and a portion of
the citizens, one Indian having already been killed in trying to
gather his stock, as heretofore reported."[1]

Two companies of cavalry and one of infantry served as a
protective escort. Wagons carried military provisions for five
months. Lieutenant Burnet, quartermaster and commissary of the
expedition, had estimated, "The entire Command will number
about 2500 Persons of all sorts and sizes and conditions and about
the same number of Stock Horses, Mules, Oxen and Cattle."[2]

The wagon train covered ten miles before making an uneasy
camp the first day. Sisters and aunts took turns carrying José
Maria's infant grandson. The feet of an old sow trotting along
with one family began to bleed; it was lifted into the lap of a
grandmother riding in one of the wagons.[3]

The next morning at seven o'clock the refugees started toward
the next water source, Conin Wood Spring. They found the spring
dry and had to go on to the west fork of the Trinity River. The
water there was drinkable but low—they had traveled twenty-one
miles to find water that was hardly enough to moisten throats. Major
Neighbors ordered some beef butchered and issued sacks of flour.

They started at eight on the third morning and marched another
twenty-two miles to the Little Wichita River. A heavy rain broke
the heat but did nothing to make the distance less difficult. The
stream of the Little Wichita carried sufficient water, and a layover
was called for the next day.

From there on the pace slowed: six miles to Frog Pond, August
5; twelve miles to a creek of unknown name, August 6; eighteen
miles to a good spring on the bank of the Red River, August 7. The
next day the Red River was crossed, and Major Neighbors wrote
his wife:

> I have this day crossed all the Indians out of the heathen land of
> "Texas" and am now, "out of the land of the Philistines."

If you want to have a full description of our Exodus out of Texas—Read the Bible where the children of Israel crossed the Red Sea. We have had about the same show, only our enemies did not follow us to R River. If they had—The Indians would have—in all probability sent them back—without the interposition of Divine providence.

. . . I have just received your letter and only have one hour to write—It is now 3 o.c. and I have been in the saddle since 6 this morning. . . .

Yesterday . . . we traveled twenty five miles with our Trains—and it was my day to bring up the rear—I did not get into Camp until 8 at night—after being on horseback 13 hours—

Col. Leeper and family are now with us—they joined us this morning—with the Comanches [from the upper reserve]. . . . They crossed Red River while I was crossing the Train. (one hundred waggons)—and about 1500 Indians).[4]

It was a relief to cross the Red River and leave Texas behind. The week of strenuous marches brought the tribes away from the threat of attack. Three miles above the Red River they stopped for the night and stayed there all the next day. The water was barely fit for their needs, but both the people and the animals needed rest. The teams, particularly the oxen, suffered from the heat and lack of water; many died before they reached the Washita.

Briefly rested, the Indians and their escort broke camp on August 10 and traveled twelve miles to the main branch of Beaver Creek. The creek water was good, and they used its branches as campsites the following two nights. At the third evening's camp on Beaver Creek, some cattle were slaughtered for fresh meat, and more flour was given out. Now within two or three days' march of his destination, Major Neighbors sent four Indian riders to find Samuel Blain in his camp on the Washita River. He gave the riders a letter to be delivered to Superintendent Rector through Agent Blain. With plenty of water and good grazing available at the camp on Beaver Creek, Neighbors called for another day's rest.

Before the day's end the sense of refuge that came with crossing into Indian Territory vanished. First, Major Thomas, in charge of the troops, received orders recalling the military escort. The uneasiness created by the recall was intensified when the Indians sent to contact Blain returned saying that they had been attacked by a group of Kiowas.

The riders had safely reached Blain's camp the day before and stayed overnight. Three men who came from Fort Arbuckle with the group of Caddos and Wichitas led by Blain joined them when they started back early in the morning. By afternoon they were within eight or ten miles of the Beaver Creek camp and stopped at a pool to rest and water their horses. The Kiowas surprised them there, seriously wounding one Caddo man and taking all the horses. Five of the Indians attacked by the Kiowas brought the wounded Caddo into Neighbors's camp that night. Another man, also injured when an arrow struck his arm, reported back to Blain, who concluded that the attackers were Comanches. Whether they were Comanches or Kiowas, danger was again close, and the refugees from the Texas reserves were about to lose their protec- tive escort.

Major Thomas delayed long enough for the cavalry to lead the column out the next morning. The day was very hot, and after ten miles of travel camp was made at the large spring that fed Beaver Creek. There was some comfort in the knowledge that Thomas's cavalry was camped two miles above. Major Neighbors again gave an order to butcher some cattle and distribute flour. Rations were running low, but he fully expected that supplies for the tribes under his protection would be waiting at the new agency on the Washita.

Early next morning the soldiers and the Indians passed each other traveling in opposite directions: the cavalry toward Texas, the Indians toward the Washita River. Only eight miles' progress was made toward the Washita that day. A death slowed travel. One of the agency employees unintentionally discharged his rifle, and the bullet struck and killed a Caddo of the Hainai band.

Covering seventeen and one-half miles the next day, the immi- grants arrived on the banks of the Washita River. Blain and the Caddo, Delaware, Kichai, and Wichita bands with him were camped five miles away, but Superintendent Rector had not yet arrived, and no one had authority to take charge in his place. A site for the new agency had not yet been designated, and no provision had been made to furnish the Indians from Texas with rations.

The Caddo, Anadarko, and Hainai camped on the banks of the Washita that night—their first night in the region of their new home—but it did not appear much more hospitable than the area

they had fled. Angry, unsettled Plains Indians roamed this country, where the water tasted of gypsum, and the only shelter in sight
was a fringe of cottonwood trees on the bank of the Washita River.
The next ten days were grim. The last of the rations brought from
Texas was issued, and even the weather conspired to make conditions miserable. The camp by the Washita was lashed by torrents
of rain driven by gale-force south winds.

Several months later Lieutenant Burnet, who had had the
experience of living in this country, deemed it unfit for anything
he could imagine. "Except a few places on the River, the land is not
fit to cultivate and there is no winter range for cattle, and the
winters are too servere [sic] for them to live without shelter. The
soil is poor, light sand; the grass coarse and, in winter dryed
up. . . . In summer, it is hot and sultry—and in winter, cold—with
piercing winds blowing constantly."[5]

During the days spent waiting for Major Rector, chiefs and
headmen rode out with Major Neighbors, Ross, and Leeper to
inspect the country for miles around. They found heavy grass in
valleys on both sides of the Washita and a number of good cold-
water springs. Post oak grew on the hills, and black walnut, burr
oak, and red cedar stood along the river and creek bottoms.
Several families liked what they saw and chose locations for their
farms.

After ten days of waiting, Major Neighbors was notified that
Rector would not be coming. In truth, Blain had written the
superintendent, warning him that hostile Indians were moving in
the area and advising him to travel with sufficient protection.
Whether for this or some other reason, Rector decided not to come
in person and sent word for Blain to act as his deputy.

Blain selected a place to build the agency on the south side of
the Washita River near a small stream later named Leeper Creek.
On September 1 Neighbors turned over all the government property he had brought with him across the Red River and discharged
the employees of the abandoned Brazos agencies. He returned the
Indians' individual property, which had been in his care, and gave
certified census rolls to Blain.

Neighbors's census list for the Anadarko and Caddo tribes
(Hainais were not listed separately) showed Anadarko men over
twelve years, 78; boys under twelve years, 27; women over twelve
years, 81; girls under twelve years, 32; total Anadarko, 218; Caddo

men over twelve years, 78; boys under twelve years, 41; women over twelve years, 83; girls under twelve years, 42; total Caddo, 244. A notation recorded that one Indian had died during the flight from Texas and that one had been born.[6]

The responsibility Major Neighbors felt for the Caddo and Anadarko he had struggled to protect did not end there. He sent Rector estimates for the support of the Texas Indians on their new reserve through June 1861. The estimates did not include houses, but in a final report to the commissioner of Indian affairs, Neighbors reminded Commissioner A. B. Greenwood that the subject had been called to his attention earlier:

> With the invoices you will find a list of the number and value of the houses abandoned at the two reserves in Texas, and their estimated value. It is deemed but an act of justice that the Indians here should be assisted to the same extent, as this country is much further north, and the winters will prove more severe.
>
> Early attention should be given to the preparation of lands for cultivation. For that purpose, I have estimated for funds for breaking up six hundred acres of land this fall; and the Indians evince a commendable desire to settle down again and cultivate the soil. They are well pleased with the country, and, with reasonable encouragement and protection, will be able to furnish their own bread before the end of next year.[7]

Major Neighbors left the Washita on September 6. A week later he camped overnight on the Brazos River. The next day he crossed the river, walked into the town of Belknap, and was fatally shot by a white man who hated him for being a friend of the Indians.[8]

After nearly a quarter-century of displacement, the Caddo, Hainai, and Anadarko came together north of the Washita River in Indian Territory. They left the bones of their ancestors in the mother earth of their Red River heartland, in the prairies and along the rivers and streams of Arkansas, Louisiana, and Texas, but brought with them traditions and a sense of being that enabled them to survive as the Caddo Nation of Oklahoma.

CHAPTER 25

JULIA

There are few trees and no tall buildings in
Anadarko. This west-central Oklahoma community lies on level
ground, a town flat-ironed by the sun. It began as a crude
collection of wood structures built by the federal government on
the bank of the Washita River to house the agency for the
Wichita, Caddo, and affiliated bands of Indians in 1871. One of
the traders at that time, William Shirley, was married to Habunista, a member of the Anadarko tribe of Caddo Indians. Shirley
applied for a post office and, when asked to supply a name,
suggested Anadarko to honor Habunista's tribe.[1]

One hundred years later the agency offices were in a single-
story, brick-and-concrete structure squatting on a corner of North
Main Street. Cars parked in an unshaded gravel lot beside the
building radiated heat. Lettering on the building's plate glass
entry doors read, "Kiowa-Wichita-Caddo Agency, Hours Monday
thru Friday, 8:00 AM–4:30 PM."

Inside, the wide, drab-walled corridor was crowded. People
stood in small groups or sat on the straight-backed, goverment-
gray chairs that lined the walls between doors. Signs identified the
offices—superintendent, social services, education, housing, leases
and real property management, accounting. Central air-condition-
ing labored to cool the windowless building. Women stirred the
air with fans; men used high-crown straw hats to move the tired

air back and forth across their faces. Children, sticky with heat, leaned against adults or squirmed on their laps.

Conversations rose and fell in a confusion of languages — Caddo, Kiowa, Apache, Comanche, American English. The mingled sounds were good-humored, angry, complaining, joking, bewildered. Small pockets of silence surrounded some individuals, whose faces reflected a resignation learned from years of waiting for official attention. The movement of the crowd shifted as people entered and left the offices.

A few blocks away Julia was holding court at "her place," a chair at a long table in the back room at Joe's Cafe.[2] She was there by eight o'clock every morning; the "regulars" reported to her there. Sipping steaming cups of coffee before going to work, they bantered with Julia, knowing they would never win the verbal game. Occasionally one of the young people received a dressing down, quietly, yet firmly delivered. When that happened, they all laughed and teased, but there was no doubt that they respected "Aunt Julie." "She's wise," said one. "She's had a lot of experience. She's old, but she thinks young."

At seventy-eight Julia was a matriarch. She expected her family to attend her, and generally they did. This morning, however, there was a grandson seated at the table who had failed to meet her expectations. He sat, staring into his half-empty coffee cup, contritely subject to her accusations. "You were in such a hurry—you just dump me there, and then you go off with all my things." Her words were so low that only very attentive ears could hear. "I didn't have my shawl—you said you bring them."

"Grandma, I was sick. Honest."

Some of the regulars left for work; some lingered. Two women, near contemporaries of Julia, took a chair at the table just long enough to eat breakfast or drink a cup of coffee. As her grandson started to leave, she issued an order: "You come get me. I've got to go to the bank."

"What time you want to go?"

"Oh, I don't know. After while, before noon."

"Okay, Grandma. I'll be back."

Smoke from her cigarette veiled her face. She did not look at him when he got up from his chair to leave but gave the cigarette a punctuating double tap against the edge of a tray. "That one . . . "

she began, but left the rest of the sentence—"He can't be depended on."—unspoken.

Julia was more cross than usual on this Monday morning in
August—all because of the grandson's behavior the previous
Thursday. He had been responsible for taking her to the grounds
where Caddos were having a dance celebrating Veterans Day. It
had taken careful planning to get ready for the weekend; Julia
expected many people, family and friends, to be guests at her
table. She had gathered all she needed for her camp: clothes and
bedding, pots, pans, soap, towels, dishes, napkins, knives, forks,
spoons, coffee, flour, cornmeal, and canned goods. She had ordered
a side of beef from a butcher and twelve pies from Joe's Cafe.

The grandson loaded many boxes and bags into his truck when
he came to pick her up at her house in Anadarko. And, as she had
wished, Julia was the first person to arrive in camp. Her camp, in
sight of the dance circle, was a permanent arbor built of sturdy
poles supporting a canvas cover. It was well shaded by tall cedar
and oak trees. Members of her family had already cleaned the
hard-packed dirt floor and cleared the immediate area. But there
was still a lot to be done.

The grandson unloaded supplies, and Julia discovered that a
few things were missing. The most important was her shawl. A
proper Caddo woman entering the dance circle wore a shawl
about her shoulders or carried folded over her left arm. For this
important dance, Julia had ordered a special one made from a nice
blue cloth and bordered with white fringe. A design like the
Louisiana state seal with a pelican in the center was embroidered
on the back. Stitched in the outer ring of the seal, instead of the
name of the state, was the name Caddo people called themselves—
Hasinai. The twelve pies ordered from Joe's Cafe had also been
left behind.

Yes, he would remember to pick up the pies, said the grandson,
and yes, he understood which shawl she wanted, and yes, he
understood where to find it at home. He would be back. He had
left, forgetting to take the suitcase packed with Julia's clothes from
the cab of the truck, and he had not returned.

"You stayed out there alone Thursday night," asked one of the
women at the table. "Weren't you afraid?"

"No, I know this place. I can walk it in the dark."

"This place" was Whitebead's. Julia's grandmother on her

Julia Edge, her grandson, and Joe outside Joe's Cafe in Anadarko (1973).

mother's side was a Whitebead. At dusk Julia had taken a walk alongside Boggy Creek, where she used to play as a girl. She had come back to camp and had sat in the soft darkness listening to the sounds of summer insects, watching the white moonlight cover the surface of the empty dance circle. Then she had slept.

Others began to arrive the next morning. Julia's daughter, Pauline, came early. Together they washed down the tables, chairs, and bed frames; cleaned the old refrigerator standing in the center and plugged it in to cool; set up the pole forks and crossbar next to the fire pit by the side of the arbor. Other families were busy arranging their camps, and the refreshment stand behind the dance circle was being prepared to serve hamburgers, hot dogs, chili, candy, and cold pop.

By midday, with everything in her camp in order, Julia was sitting at ease in the shade of the arbor. Family and friends came and went, stopping to chat a while before returning to their own chores. A light, hot breeze barely stirred the leaves of the trees. The sounds of summer locusts — repetitive, briefly sustained dry rasps — vibrated monotonously throughout the afternoon.

When the sun was lingering over the western horizon, Julia leaned forward, her elbows placed on the ends of the chair arms. With slow, deliberate motion, she lifted her cigarette and drew on it. Through the smoke she looked with narrowed eyes out on the dance circle, which was half-shadowed by tall trees and empty except for three or four children playing tag. The Turkey Dance should be starting, but no drum was in sight.

The way Julia had learned, the way it was done when she was brought up, was that the Turkey Dance was to begin "when you got shade. They start way anytime after dinner" (the midday meal). "When you got no shade, you have to wait for cool."

In those days, too, women entered the dance circle differently. When the drum beat began, and the drummers started to sing, the women immediately stopped whatever they were doing, wherever they were in camp, and started to move toward the dance circle in step with music. "When I started, this one came in here," Julia pointed her forefinger down to indicate a place, then moved it forward, "and this one." She repeated the movement with her opposite hand to show a beginning from a different point. If "someone's got dough in their hands, they leave that dough and

Julia Edge (1978)

they're dancin'," hands still covered with flour. "That's the way they used to do."

Now "they dress up and get pretty. They line up, follow this hoop. That's why—I see them now—so when I come, I start from where I can go. I'm kinda crippled, but I try to on account of them old ancestors. I want to be right there with them.

"Turkey Dance—you know they talking in that—it's got some meaning in it. It was meant to tell what's what. It's like War Dance," she said, explaining what she meant with a rhythm in her words like a drumbeat, "where they *fought* and when they *fought* and when they come *back* and when they *kill* and how they *act*."

The dances celebrate Caddo survival. Thinking about times when Caddos were forced to fight off their enemies, Julia spoke with a hurt like that of an aching old wound. "You know, it's pitiful in a way, in the way they met—where they *jump* on—*attack* them—for *nothing*—as they travel."

A public address system had been set up, and a speaker began to talk about custom and tradition and the need to preserve them. The Veterans Dance, held each year, honored all those who fought "for our homes," all those who "served in the Armed Forces or are presently serving." The drummers, now in place around the drum in the center of the circle, began the Turkey Dance.

Julia is Cadohadacho. Her people, the "Whitebead bunch," "came across." They never lived on the reservation in Texas. When they left their homelands in Louisiana sometime after the 1835 treaty, "they came across this way—just like you cut through the pasture. They didn't follow the road. They angled like, follow this creek, they call it Washita—today, Washita—from up there, from Red River." She paused a moment, thinking about the Caddo's old home along the bend in the Red River where the river lost its easterly direction and curved to the south. "We had the whole county of Miller County," said Julia, speaking of that territory above the Red River where early white settlers organized a vast area spreading from west Arkansas into a political unit they named Miller County.[3]

The way Julia heard it, the Cadohadacho started out three times. "One group got lost in the mountains"; two groups came across. "Two groups, I just know them. Might be more, but, see, I just know them two."

The family of Melford Williams, the former Caddo tribal chair to be commemorated during the Veterans Dance this weekend, also "came across." Julia says they belonged to the Kiamichi band. "Kia-may-che. Means 'water running into the—the stream running into the big river.'" The stream, still called Kiamichi, flows through the Kiamichi Mountains in a part of southeast Oklahoma—Miller County back then—and empties into the Red River. Julia's mother's people stopped there, and then "just the Whitebeads, they stopped round what you call Pauls Valley. They got two cemeteries over there." For at least a part of that journey, "old lady Whitebead," Julia's "mother's-father's-mother's-mother," led the group across.

The next morning Pauline drove Julia to a community a few miles down the road, where she bought two plastic washbasins and a change of underclothes at a general store. Then they went to the butcher's to pick up the side of beef.

The grounds had filled with people by the time they got back. A friend, Hubert Halfmoon, carried the beef from the car to a wooden table under Julia's arbor, and the two of them set to work slicing it into thin strips. Some were hung to be smoked on a crossbar over the camp fire. Strips to make the favored beef dish *ha-bush-ko* were put in a big black kettle on a grate over the fire. There was plenty of time for the meat to simmer in its own juices before being served for dinner.

Just after noon a recording of the Flag Song played through the loudspeaker system stilled all activity throughout the family camps. It was an old recording, but the voices of the men singing were full and strong. The beat was steady and regular, like marching feet. It was an old song that had no words until they were added during World War II. A male voice, through the loudspeaker, explained that the words meant something like

> People, everybody look to the flag.
> They're raising the flag.
> They are raising it.
> The reason they are raising it is
> Because of our boys
> Of our boys and girls
> Who are in the Armed Services.
> Some of them are still Overseas.
> Some of them are here.
> Wherever they are
> We want them to be blessed.

The speaker, Jesse Adunko, welcomed guests, including a troop of Boy Scouts from Texas, and began a dedication: "This being a Veterans Day, we all have to . . . " He faltered; there were tears in his eyes. "Excuse me. I can't talk. Just can't help it."

There was a long pause before Adunko cleared his throat and tried again. "We should honor and dedicate this day," his voice strengthened, "for the Caddo Tribe, and Indians, and regardless of what tribe—or nationality, we honor all of them because if it hadn't been for all these veterans from World War I back this way, we probably wouldn't been able to gather here with freedom of speech and worship. . . .

"One of the members of our tribe, who was a leader, Mr. Melford Williams, this day is set aside for him and the rest of the veterans, to honor." The U.S. flag flying over the Dance Grounds had belonged to Melford Williams. Jesse Adunko asked that time and thought be given especially to veterans in hospitals and children in orphanages. He called for the election of federal officials, "those who make the rules and regulations," who would care about the needs and hardships of veterans. He spoke in English for close to seven minutes. Then in the Caddo language, he prayed for a blessing.

Each camp contributed food for a shared meal laid out on a long, cloth-covered table near the dance circle. A water container was set at the head. All who were there—Caddo families, Indian and white friends, visiting strangers—were served. Everyone received a small paper cup full of water before passing around the table to have a plate filled. "Because," said Julia, "water, we use it for everything. It comes first. We need water to live. For everything. So then when we're through with the prayer, we use water."

The meal was eaten leisurely at tables under the shade of family camps. Afterward there was little movement; talk was dilatory, with long pauses between comments and responses. For the most part, people sat quietly, waiting out the heavy heat of the August afternoon.

Slowly shade began to spread toward the center of the dance circle from the grove of trees at the edge. The drum was carried in, and the drummers sat around it, their drumsticks poised. They hit the drum and commenced the call to the Turkey Dance. The camps emptied as everyone began to gather at the dance circle. Some carried folding chairs to set around the outer edge. Women and girls ringed the inside of the circle and started the stately movement of the first dance.

The dance circle was like the lens of a kaleidoscope. Reds, blues, greens—shades from pale to dark—the ankle-length skirts of the dancers swayed with their steps. Their skirts had rows of ribbon in contrasting colors stitched around the hems. Their blouses, patterned with full gathers stitched to wide yokes, matched their skirts in color. The yokes were either squared and flat or rounded full and ruffled to look like small capes. Some of the women pinned the closing of their blouses with silver disks. Some wore multiple strands of tiny beads. All wore full-length aprons tied around their waists. Varicolored ribbon streamers rippled down their backs from their heads to the hems of their dresses. The ribbons hung from a flat, hour-glass-shaped ornament made of a stiff black material and decorated with silver studs. It was fastened to the hair so that it covered the back of the head from below the crown to the nape. Small mirrors and tiny glass or silver beads sewn to a wide center ribbon in the headdresses caught the last rays of sunlight.

The dancers changed steps with the differing rhythms of the Turkey Dance songs. Near the end, when the song signaled, the women chose men for partners. Even the Boy Scouts were urged into the dance. Shy and awkward at first, most of the young men watched the feet of their partners until they were enthusiastically moving with the beat of the drum.

At sunset the Turkey Dance ended. Everyone stood in solemn respect while the drummers played and sang the Flag Song and the flag was lowered. The dark hours that followed were filled with talk and laughter and light-spirited social dances. By midnight the Boy Scouts and most of the other guests had left. Many of the Caddo families were packed and ready to leave. Children who were still awake were subdued by sleepiness.

The hauntingly beautiful Bell Dance songs, sung without the drum, penetrated the quiet outside the dance circle. Men and women dancers sang in unison, following a leader who carried a ring of small bells. At the end of the songs in this cycle, he paused, lifted the ring, and shook it so that the clear tinkle of the bells greeted earth's four directions.

Julia was tired. She lay on her cot and listened. The drum again began to pulse. She drifted into sleep, the sound of the drum like her own heartbeat.

NOTES

CHAPTER 1
THE ARCHEOLOGISTS

1. Standard equipment for each participant in an archaeological field school includes a metric measuring tape, a sharpened trowel, black ink permanent marking pens, two buckets, a dustpan, a whisk broom, a clipboard, and ballpoint pens. To these may be added string and a line level; a small, soft brush; shears for cutting roots; and a shovel. The description of the archeological activity at Caddo Gap is based on personal experience while enrolled in the Arkansas Archeological Society and Survey Training and Certification Program at Caddo Gap, June 22–July 4, 1975.
2. The term Caddoan refers to cultural ancestors of the historic Caddos.
3. "Caddo Valley Archeological Project, 1975"; *An Introduction to Caddo Gap,* prepared for the Survey-Society training program held in Caddo Gap, Montgomery County, Ark., June 16–July 4, 1976; "The Standridge Site: a Review and Preview," *Field Notes: Monthly Newsletter of the Arkansas Archeological Society* 135 (March 1976): 2–3.
4. Early, "Turquoise Beads."
5. Early, Burnett, and Wolfman, *Standridge,* 163.
6. Archeologists trace the root of Caddo culture to an antecedent culture, which they term Early Ceramic or Fourche Maline. Fourche Maline culture dominated southwest Arkansas from about 400 B.C. to about A.D. 800 and has been identified at locations in northeast Texas. (Wyckoff, "Caddoan Cultural Area"; Schambach, "Archeology of Great Bend," 5; Clarence H. Webb, interview by author, tape recording, Shreveport, Louisiana, July 1, 1975.)
7. Robert W. Neuman, "Archaeological and Historical Assessment," 10.
8. Webb, "Changing Archeological Methods," 41.

9. Webb interview.

10. Ann Early, personal communication, July 26, 1991.

11. Webb interview.

12. The largest surviving Caddo mound is Battle Mound in Lafayette County, Arkansas. Most of the mound was constructed A.D. 1200 to 1400. The Cren-shaw site, situated on some twenty acres of Red River bottomland in Miller Country, Arkansas, contains six mounds, four cemetery areas, and evidence of an extensive village area. Other representative multiple-mound centers identi-fied as Caddoan and dating from the earliest time are the George C. Davis site (3 mounds) in the Neches River valley, Cherokee County, Texas, and the Gaha-gan (3 mounds) and Mounds Plantation (9 or 10 mounds) in the Louisiana Red River valley. A farming-oriented, sedentary village was functioning at the Davis site about A.D. 800, and evidence for an associated village has been found at Gahagan. (Wyckoff, "Caddoan Cultural Area," 107–108, 69–83).

CHAPTER 2
THE EXPLORERS

1. Swanton, *Indians of Southeastern United States*, 55. As the 400th anniversa-ry of the De Soto expedition approached, the U.S. Congress appointed a commission to study De Soto's route. Swanton, a prominent ethnohistorian, was chair. The results of the study were published in U.S. Congress, *Final Report of the United States De Soto Expedition Commission*, 76th Cong., 1st sess., H. Doc. 71. The De Soto chronicles are narratives by Rodrigo Ranjel, Luýs Hernández de Biedma, and a "Gentleman of Elvas" and an account written by Garcilaso de la Vega.

2. In 1988 Charles Hudson of the University of Georgia offered a revised version of the extreme western end of De Soto's route that is strongly supported by Arkansas archeology. His arguments for the new reconstruction were sup-ported by Morse and Morse, "Spanish Exploration," 197–209; and Scham-bach, "End of the Trail," 27/28:10–13.

According to the De Soto chronicles, the Spaniards left the place they had been staying and encountered the Tula after traveling one and one-half Indian days southward and up a river. Equating the distance traveled in one Indian day to about thirty miles, Dan and Phyllis Morse determined that De Soto left from a location on the Arkansas River and by traveling southward reached the Fourche La Fave River. This distance and direction would bring the expedition to site 3YE15, some thirty-five to forty miles southwest of an archeologically defined location on the Arkansas River. The Morses concluded that the Tula "were Caddo Indians and site 3YE15 was a Caddo mound center" (204–205). See also Charles Hudson, "Reconstructing," 146–148.

3. Swanton, *Source Material*, 7–8.

4. Elvas, "Narrative," 224.

Swanton believed that the final stage of the Spaniards' route led from Arkansas into Louisiana, then west across north Louisiana to the Red River Valley and east Texas. Hudson traced the Spaniards across southwest Arkan-sas to the Red River. Schambach, "End of the Trail," offered archeological evidence in reconstructing the extreme western end of the route through southwest Arkansas and east Texas.

5. Schambach, "End of the Trail," 17.

6. Ibid., 20. There is scholarly consensus regarding the approximate location of Naguatex in the Great Bend of Red River but some debate on its ethnohistorical identification. Swanton, *Source Material*, 8, listed names mentioned in the De Soto documents which he said undoubtedly represented Caddo tribes. In identifying these names, he said, "Naguatex, or as we should pronounce it, Nawataysh, signifies 'place of salt' and the people so designated may be set down as a branch of that [Caddo] tribe later known as Namidish."

   A more recent study of the names listed by Swanton was made by Wallace Chafe ("Caddo Names," 222–225), a linguist at the University of Santa Barbara, who specializes in the Caddo language family. Chafe explained that *gu* written by a Spaniard would sound like *w* written by an English speaker; *x*, like *sh*. With the addition of the Caddo prefix *na* (used to designate "place of" or "the people of") the resulting name was Nawidish, a derivative from *widish*, the Caddo word for "salt." Chafe also pointed out that the name Nawidish is known to Caddo people today and that "there appears to have been a Caddo dialect in which *w* was replaced by *m*" (223).

   Schambach cited archeological and historical evidence that a single great Caddo settlement, within the area identified in the De Soto documents as the province of Naguatex, had persisted from about A.D. 1400 through 1788 to 1790 and that ruins of compounds in that settlement were observed and identified by members of the Freeman-Custis expedition in 1806 as the last village of the Kadohadacho. Admitting that the interpretation of the term Naguatex presents some problems, Schambach's position ("End of the Trail," 21) was that "it [Naguatex] is generally considered a place name so it does not contravene my identification of the people of Naguatex as the Kadohadacho (Cadohadacho)."

7. Ibid., 20. The mound, part of the site archeologically designated as the Battle site, is about one-half mile east of the Red River in Lafayette County, Arkansas. Schambach gave the measurements as 592 feet long, 157 feet wide, and 33 feet high.

   Other sources have given the mound's measurements as 672 feet long, 320 feet wide, and 34 feet high. See Wyckoff, "Caddoan Cultural Area," 108; Hoffman, "Archaeological and Historical Assessment," 163.

8. Swanton, *Source Material*, 6.

9. Elvas, "Narrative," 240.

10. Ibid., 241.

11. Ibid., 242.

12. De Soto documents named the areas the Spaniards marched through after leaving Naguatex in this order: Nissohone, Lacane, Nondacao, Soacatineo (or Xaucatino or Xacatin), Aays (or Hais), Guasco, Naquiscoça, Naçacahoz. Of those Nissohone and Nondacao can be recognized as tribes later known as Nasoni and Anadarko. Early in the eighteenth century there were the Upper Nasoni associated with the Cadohadacho and the Lower Nasoni in Hasinai territory. Schambach ("End of the Trail," 25) commented, "Except for the Hasinai themselves, the names of every group in the Hasinai confederacy begin with N (Nabedache, Nacogdoche, Nasoni, Neche, Nacono, Nechaui, Nacao, and Nadaco). Early in the seventeenth century, the northeastern-most Hasinai

group (probably the first group the Spaniards would have encountered) were the Nadaco [Nondacao]." Chafe ("Caddo Names," 222–225) equates Non-dacao with the source name for Anadarko, which is the Caddo word *daakuh*, meaning "bumblebee." Aays or Hais (in some later records spelled Ais, Haish, or Eyeish) is a name still familiar to Caddo people, but Griffith (*Hasinai Indians,* 88) said they were not friends of the Hasinai.

13. De Soto narratives gave Daycao as the name of the river that Moscoso reached before turning back. Although scholars have generally agreed that Daycao was the Trinity River, it has been argued that Daycao was the Navasota, the Brazos, or the Colorado River.

14. Schambach, "End of the Trail," fig. 2, p. 12.

15. Cavelier, "Cavelier's Account," 268–285; Douay, "Narrative," 1:222–247. Most of the documents in Cox, *Journeys of La Salle,* are abridged versions of those in the primary source edited by Margry, *Découvertes et établissements.* An unpublished English translation of Margry's full text, privately commis-sioned, is in the Detroit Public Library, Burton Historical Collection. Also on microfilm, it is available for reading but has not been released for publication.

16. Parkman, *La Salle,* 291–294, 305–306.

17. Bolton, "Location of La Salle's Colony."

18. Douay, "Narrative," 1:231.

19. The Douay narrative (1:232) says: "It is at least twenty leagues long." The distance of a league varies according to country and time. The French league equivalent of 2.49 miles is used here.

20. Ibid., 1:233. Jumanos have never been clearly identified as a tribe. Newcomb, *Indians of Texas,* 226, offered a definition: "*Jumano* is an Indian word of unknown meaning in Hispaniolized form. . . . It has come to be commonly applied to the Indians of southwestern Texas and parts of northern Chi-huahua, Mexico."

21. Douay, "Narrative," 1:234.

22. Joutel, "Relation de Henri Joutel," in Margry, ed., *Découvertes et établisse-ments,* English trans., Burton Collection, Detroit Public Library, 3:296–297.

23. Joutel, "Joutel's Journal," 133. Unless otherwise noted, the remainder of this chapter is based on this work.

24. Ibid., 136.

25. Ibid., 137. The identity of the Cannokantimos (Kanoatinos) is in doubt. Newcomb, *Indians of Texas,* 286, said parenthetically that they were "proba-bly the Wichitas."

26. Joutel, "Relation," in Swanton, *Source Material,* 184–185. The material in the following two paragraphs is from this same source. Swanton made his own translation of "Relation de Henri Joutel," in Margry, *Découvertes et établisse-ments* 3:95–534.

27. Joutel, "Joutel's Journal," 161.

28. Ibid., 162–165.

29. Joutel, "Relation," in Swanton, *Source Material,* 186–187.

30. Recent work within the Caddo Tribe to transcribe and translate Turkey Dance songs is scheduled for completion in 1995.

31. *Sah* is a Caddo-language prefix used with women's names in the way Ms. is an honorific in English.

32. Weller interview by Beals.

33. Leon Carter interview by author, tape recording, July 1974.

34. See note 12 above.

35. Joutel, "Joutel's Journal," 172.

36. Assony, Nathosos, Nachitos, and Cadodaquio are the spellings used in Joutel, "Joutel's Journal." The Nasoni associated with the Cadohadacho grouping are generally referred to as Upper Nasoni to differentiate them from the Hasinai Nasoni. In the same manner, the Natchitoches associated with the Cadohadacho are called Upper Natchitoches to differentiate them from the Natchitoches lower down on the Red River.

37. Swanton, *Source Material,* 7, said the Cahinnio had an independent status and "were, it is believed, closely connected with the Kadohadacho, with whom they undoubtedly ultimately united." Arkansas archeology links Caddo occupation in the vicinity of Arkadelphia with the historic Cahinnio.

38. Joutel, "Joutel's Journal," 188.

39. Williams, "Aboriginal Location," 235–236.

40. Joutel, "Relation," in Margry, *Découvertes et établissements,* English trans., 3:406.

CHAPTER 3
THE SEARCHERS

1. McGimsey, "Indians of Arkansas," 35–36. McGimsey said that Tonti established Arkansas Post on the north bank of the Arkansas River and that it was probably located on the southern edge of the Grand Prairie just downstream from the present Arkansas Post National Museum. A few hunters lived there until about 1700, and a major settlement established nearby in 1721 was officially abandoned in 1723. Arkansas Post was reestablished by the French in 1731, and the area was continuously occupied after that date, first by the French, then by the Spanish, and then, after 1803, by Americans.

2. Parkman, *La Salle,* 339; Tonti, "Memoir," 41. The remainder of the material concerning Tonti in this chapter is based on the latter text, 41–50.

3. Parkman, *La Salle,* 341–342; Tonti, "Memoir," 42.

4. Tonti, "Memoir," 43–44.

5. Tonti arrived at a place below the bend in the Red River near the present city of Natchitoches, Louisiana, "which is in the midst of the three villages called Nachitoches, Ouasita and Capiché" (ibid., 45). The Natchitoches who came to see Joutel were part of the Cadohadacho group from a separate, upper Natchitoches village.

Swanton, *Source Material,* 12–13, said the "Ouasita" had moved down from the lower Ouachita River (near the south Arkansas–northeast Louisiana border), and that when Tonti spoke of a tribe called Capiché, "it may be assumed that the tribe intended was the Doustioni."

6. Tonti, "Memoir," 45.

7. Ibid.

8. Ibid., 46.

9. ibid., 48.

10. Bolton, *Original Narratives,* 347–348.

11. Weddle, *Wilderness Manhunt,* 189–190.

12. León, "Itinerary of Expedition," 388–404 (hereafter León, "Itinerary"). Unless otherwise noted, this is the source for descriptions of the De León expedition in this chapter.
13. Bolton, "Native Tribes," 249–251.
14. De León to the Viceroy, Coahuila, May 16, 1689; quoted in Weddle, *Wilderness Manhunt*, 199.
15. Massanet, letter to Don Carlos de Sigüenza, 1690, 363–364.
16. Bolton, "Native Tribes," 263.
17. Report of the Bishop of Guadalajara, as quoted in Bolton, "Spanish Occupation," 16.

CHAPTER 4

THE MISSIONARIES

1. Unless otherwise noted, material for this chapter is taken from Massanet's letter to Don Carlos de Sigüenza, 1690, 353–387 (hereafter Massanet to Sigüenza), and León, "Itinerary," 405–423.
2. Massanet to Sigüenza, 378.
3. Ibid., 379.
4. Ibid., 380.
5. León, "Itinerary," 416.
6. Massanet to Sigüenza, 364.
7. Ibid., 380–381.
8. Ibid.
9. María de Agreda was fifteen years old when her father entered a monastery and she, her mother, and her sister converted their home into a Franciscan convent. She was elected abbess when she was twenty-five. In 1620, as Mother María de Jesús, she told her confessor that while apparently lying rigid on her bed in the convent in Spain, she was "transported in ecstacy" to work among the people of a distant country. Reports of her experience reached the archbishop of Mexico, who made inquiries, and in 1629 Jumano Indians told a missionary in northeast Mexico about a white woman who had appeared to them. In the same year Father Alonso de Benavides, former supervisor of the missions in New Mexico, returned to Spain and visited Sister María de Jesús at her convent in Agreda. She wore the Franciscan habit of a brown sackcloth covered by a white one, a blue cloth cloak, and a black veil. She told Benavides that she had instructed the Jumanos and commanded them to call on the friars. Benavides said she gave him all the Jumanos' signs and knew a one-eyed Jumano chief well enough to describe his personal characteristics. She also told him she had appeared to people she called Titlas and had talked to them in Spanish, but they understood her as though she used their language. In 1670, five years after her death, her book *Mística ciudad de Dios* ("Mystical City of God") was published and was read by Franciscans like Massanet (Carter and Carter, *Doomed Road*, 31–34).
10. Massanet to Sigüenza, 382.
11. John, *Storms Brewed*, chaps. 1 and 2, gave an account of the Indian and Spanish experiences that led to the 1680 Pueblo Revolt. The Jumano Indian traders who brought items from New Mexico to trade with the Hasinais in all probability also brought reports on the exploitation of Indian labor by secular

authorities and the demands for work and worship in the mission programs that were the root of grievances resulting in the Pueblo Revolt.

12. Report of the Bishop of Guadalajara; quoted in Bolton, "Spanish Occupation," 16.

13. Weddle, *Wilderness Manhunt,* 210–211.

14. Casañas de Jesús María to the viceroy of Mexico, August 15, 1691, "Descriptions of the Tejas or Asinai Indians," pt. 1, trans. Mattie Austin Hatcher, *Southwestern Historical Quarterly,* 30 (January 1927):207 n. 2. The remaining material in this chapter is based on this translation (hereafter Casañas, "Descriptions").

Casañas's biographer was Fray Isidro Felís de Espinosa.

15. Casañas, "Descriptions," 215–216. Casañas named nine subject tribes and briefly described their locations: "The first is the Nabadacho [Nabedache] who are also called *Ineci.* Within the bounds of this tribe is located the mission of Nuestro Padre San Francisco, as well as the mission I have founded in your Excellency's name, called Santíssima Nombre de María. The second tribe is the Necha [Neches]. It is separated from the first tribe by the river Archangel San Miguel [now the Neches River]. These two tribes are located toward the northeast. To the south east is the Nechavi tribe. Another tribe, located about a half a league away is the Nacono. To the north of the boundary of the Nechavi is a tribe called Nacachau. Between this tribe and one called Nazadachotizi [Nacogdoches]—which is located toward the east on the road to the home of the grand *xinesi,* about half way between the tribes is another called Cachae [Hainai]. Their boundary begins at the home of the grand *xinesi.* Northward of the boundary of this tribe are the Nabiti. Adjoining and to the eastward are the Nasayaha Indians. These nine tribes occupy about thirty-five leagues and they are all subject to the grand *xinesi.*"

16. The beginning of the Caddo people as told here is drawn from three accounts: Dorsey, *Traditions,* 7–12; Newkumet and Meredith, *Hasinai,* 4–6; and Mooney, *Ghost-dance Religion,* 1093.

17. The story told to Dorsey, in *Traditions,* 7–13, by Chief White Bread sometime between 1903 and 1905 says that Moon later disgraced himself by sexually abusing his sister and "Great Father Above took him away and placed him far above, where the people could see him and the shame-marks on his forehead." In White Bread's story Moon foretold the birth of Medicine Screech Owl, who grew to have more and stronger powers than Moon and was selected by the people to succeed Moon. Dorsey recorded several tales about Medicine Screech Owl (Ha-coo-shoo Cah-e-tsi) told by different storytellers. Some present-day Caddo people say a screech owl is a bad omen.

18. Casañas, "Descriptions," 213.

19. Ibid., 284.

20. Ibid., 216.

21. Ibid.

22. Bolton, "Native Tribes," 260–261. The nine Hasinai tribes named by Casañas did not include the Hainai (see n. 15 above) but after correlating documents with geographic and topographic data to locate and identify Hasinai tribes, Bolton concluded, "Considering with these facts the probability that Jesus Maria would hardly have left the head tribe unmentioned in so formal a

description as is his, and the fact that the Hainai is clearly the head tribe, it seems reasonably certain that the Cachae and the Hainai were identical."

23. *Ayo* = *hayo*, "above"; *aymay* = *haemay*, "great." Present-day Caddo speakers pray to Ah-ah (father) Ha'-yo (above). Various sources give different spellings (*caninisi, cononicis, coneneses, cononicis*) but similar identifications for the two children: Casañas, "two children"; Espinosa, "boys or small children whom their great captain sent from the cachao ayo, or the sky, for the purpose of discussing their problems"; Hidalgo, "children from God whom they call in their language coneneses 'the little ones'"; Morfí, "children who were sent from heaven by their Great Captain, to be consulted when in doubt."

As in the time of Casañas, a cona (*kuna*) is a "doctor" or "healer," a person who can cure sickness and may have the power to predict things or to keep bad things from happening. Since the Caddo suffix for little is *iti* or *itsi*, it is tempting to think that the chenesi's little ones were small healers—*cono* plus *itsi*—or small moon healers, a contraction of *cona* (healer), *nici* or *nishe* (moon), and *itsi* (little or small). However, the general word for children is *ha nin*, and *ha nin itse* could easily have been heard and transcribed in the early writings as *ca nin isi*.

A story recorded by Dorsey, *Traditions*, tells of two boys who are brothers. One receives the power of thunder; the other, the power of lightning. They join in adventures and kill monsters until their parents die and they decide to leave the world and go up in the sky. The word for thunder is *adihanin*.

24. Casañas, "Descriptions," 292–293.
25. Ibid., 296.

CHAPTER 5
"GOD MUST BE ANGRY"

1. Casañas, "Descriptions," 288.
2. Ibid., 300.
3. Ibid., 285.
4. Ibid., 299.
5. Ibid., 299–300.
6. Ibid., 298–299.
7. Ibid., 294.
8. Ibid., 297–298.
9. Ibid., 296–298.
10. Ibid., 295.
11. Ibid., 214–215.
12. I recorded the Pole Song as Grace Akins sang it during a car trip from her home to the Stovall Museum (Oklahoma Museum of Natural History) on the campus of the University of Oklahoma, February 23, 1978. Her recollections of the origin and use of the pole come from tape-recorded conversations with her between 1976 and 1978.
13. The standard source on the Ghost Dance among the Caddos as well as other tribes is Mooney, *Ghost-dance Religion*.
14. Parsons, *Notes on the Caddo*, 49, listed the seven men's names given by Michael Martin (White Moon or Silver Moon), a Caddo artist who cooper-

ated with Parsons in recording data while he was living in New York City during the winter of 1921–1922. She said the last four named were still living in 1921.

The seven men named by Grace included three of those named by Martin: Mr. Blue (Thomas Wister or Wooster), T'amo' or Tompmo (Joe Hainai, who was married to my great-grandmother), and Squirrel (Shewah). The other four recalled by Grace were different: Billy Bean, Strongman (Hah dus kats), Buzzard (Su ka tee), and Billy Spybuck.

15. Dances are still held at the dance grounds below the hill where Chief White Bread made his home, north of Anadarko between the communities of Gracemont and Binger. The grounds, known as the Murrow Dance Grounds, still are tended by members of Grace's family.

16. Castaneda, *Our Catholic Heritage*, vol. 1, *Finding of Texas*, 366–376. Unless otherwise noted, this is the source for the remainder of this chapter.

17. Castaneda, *Our Catholic Heritage*, vol. 2, *Winning of Texas*, 29 n. 71; Weddle, *Wilderness Manhunt*, 228.

18. Castaneda, *Finding of Texas*, 373.

CHAPTER 6
THE FRENCH

1. Ross Phares, *Cavalier*, 184.

2. Giraud, *History of French Louisiana*, vol. 1, *Reign of Louis XIV*, 52; Charlevoix, *History and General Description*, 124–125 n. 1. According to the note, Iberville began the fort on January 10, 1700, and "it is said to have been at Poverty Point, 38 miles below New Orleans. . . . It was abandoned the next year."

Delisle's map of 1703 shows a fort on the east bank of the Mississippi near the mouth, and his 1718 map shows the same location labeled "Vieu Fort." Charlevoix (6:12) gave 1705 as the date when the Mississippi fort was abandoned, and Giraud (216) gave the date of abandonment as the end of 1706 or the beginning of 1707.

3. Charlevoix, *History and General Description*, 5:125; Giraud, *Reign of Louis XIV*, 35.

4. Weedle, *Wilderness Manhunt*, 253; Weedle, ed., *La Salle*, 215–216.

5. Weedle, *La Salle*, 238–239, 255.

6. Giraud, *Reign of Louis XIV*, 35.

7. Swanton, *Source Material*, 188, 161. They left the river near the Taensa village, which was located about where Newellton, Louisiana, is now.

8. Ibid., 51. Swanton said the 1702 date is implied by contemporary events, particularly the participation of Natchitoches and Acolapissa warriors in an expedition against the Chitimachas, which St. Denis led in 1702.

9. Giraud, *Reign of Louis XIV*, 97, 100, 167.

10. Penicaut, *Fleur de Lys*, 107. Penicaut wrote a narrative of his experiences after he returned to France in 1722. It was designed to capture the attention of patrons and impress them into rewarding his service in Louisiana.

11. Penicaut, *Fleur de Lys and Calumet*, 109.

12. Clark, "Louis Juchereau de Saint-Denis," 6–10.

13. Weddle, *Wilderness Manhunt*, 264; Clark, "Louis Juchereau de Saint-Denis," 12.

14. Ramon to Hidalgo, July 22, 1714; quoted in Weddle, *Wilderness Manhunt,* 264. Ramon's letter identifies St. Denis, the two Talons, and Medar as the four Frenchmen who arrived at the garrison. Penicaut claimed to have been with St. Denis throughout this expedition, but Weddle said, "Their [the Talons'] part in this important episode generally has been obscured, thanks to the mixing of fact and fiction by one Andre Penicaut, with emphasis on the latter" (262). Weddle further discredited Penicaut: "This letter [Ramon's], so many times overlooked by writers on the St. Denis expedition, shatters the illusion that the glib Penicaut had any part in it, placing in his stead the Talon brothers" (264).

Swanton, *Source Material,* also questioned the credibility of Penicaut. Before quoting Penicaut's description of Hasinai warfare, Swanton cautioned, "Penicaut, who accompanied St. Denis across the Hasinai country in 1714, gives another picture of warfare among these people in which none of the gruesome details are spared, though, from his tendency not to overwork truth where a good story is to be extracted, it should be treated with some caution" (188). Penicaut's account (*Fleur de Lys,* 153–156) gave the Hasinais a reputation for cannibalism that dismays the Caddo people today.

Joutel ("Joutel's Journal," 163) described a victorious Hasinai war party that divided the flesh of a captive and forced other captives to eat portions. Casañas briefly mentioned the eating of flesh, observing, "It may be said that these Indians practice no greater cruelty than their enemies do" ("Descriptions," 217).

CHAPTER 7

NEW MISSIONS

1. Castaneda, *Winning of Texas,* 46 n. 22; Clark, "Spanish Occupation," 28–30; Phares, *Cavalier,* said the total was seventy-five to eighty people.
2. Espinosa, "Ramon's Expedition," 357.
3. Morfí, *History,* pt. 1, chap. 1, n. 75, and chap. 4, n. 66; Bolton, "Texas," 10–13.
4. Castaneda, *Winning of Texas,* 66–67; Morfí, *History,* 187.
5. Espinosa, *Crónica de la Provincia Franciscana de los Apóstoles San Pedro de Michoacán,* pt. 4 of "Descriptions of the Tejas or Asinai Indians 1691–1722," trans. Mattie Austin Hatcher, *Southwestern Historical Quarterly,* 31 (October 1927): 152, 175, 178 (hereafter Espinosa, *Crónica*). Espinosa's account of his service among the Hasinai from 1716 to 1719 furnishes the details used to describe customs and ceremonies throughout this chapter.
6. The exact rank of the caddi's councilors is uncertain. Espinosa called them *caziques,* but the meaning of this term is unclear. Griffith, *Hasinai Indians,* 64, cited Espinosa in saying that a single cazique was designated as a mentor. Griffith commented, "Inferior to the caddices, but men of rank in the tribal aristocracy, were certain individuals variously designated as 'captain,' 'caziques,' 'noblest men,' 'principal men,' or 'old men,' who were called upon for counsel and for other important service" (65–66). Griffith also noted, "Lack of uniformity in nomenclature among the sources, inconsistency in terminology within the same source, and meager evidence on the basis of which identification by function might be practicable, make it impossible either to establish accurately the identity of these groups or to distinguish among them" (66 n. 48).
7. Espinosa, *Crónica,* 178.

8. Ibid., 179.
9. Ibid., 177.
10. Casañas, "Descriptions," 296.
11. Bolton, *Hasinais*, 38. Bolton located the chenesi's house "about three leagues from the mission of La Concepción and apparently west of the Angelina River." Here 2.65 miles is equivalent to 1 league.
12. Espinosa, *Crónica*, 161, 169.
13. Lillie Whitehorn told me this while I was visiting in her home one winter day in 1978. She agreed to have our conversation tape-recorded and related the story about the Snow King, another about Kuna Cahdee, and one about the Flood. The stories were told to her by her father, Enoch Hoag, who was the last traditional chief of the Caddos. His grandfather was Aash (José Maria), who was well known as the head chief of the Hasinai tribes in Texas during the 1840s and 1850s. Lillie said her father was taken to council meetings beginning when he was a baby, and when the chief before him knew that it was time to name another chief, he called Enoch the rightful chief, telling the council that Aash's grandson should have held the position in his place and that the time had come to recognize him. Enoch Hoag became the principal leader in 1896, when he was about forty-five years old, and served the tribe until his death in 1929. He was given a traditional burial at his home place, but after the grave was vandalized by unknown individuals, he was reinterred in the public cemetery in Anadarko.
14. Espinosa, *Crónica*, 169.

CHAPTER 8
HA-COO-DOOH (WINTER)

1. Morfí, *History*, 230, n. 9.
2. Espinosa, *Crónica*, 167.
3. Ibid., 167. Espinosa's condemnation of dances during the initiation of conas was extended to the entire Hasinai nation by Hidalgo, who reported November 4, 1716, "The whole nation is idolatrous. . . . They are very perverted and in their dances they have the Indian braves or the Indian women who get drunk on *peyote* or *frixolillo*, which they make for the occasion, and the people believe everything these persons tell them they have seen" ("Descriptions," 31 [July 1927]:55–56).
4. Espinosa, *Crónica*, 166.
5. Parsons, *Notes on the Caddo*, 33–34. Parsons visited with the Caddos in Oklahoma in 1927 and added to the data collected from Martin in 1921–1922. Her informant in 1927 said that sickness might be caused by a witch and that witches might turn into a *cah-e-tsi* (kaietsi); *nee-hee* (nihi') was sometimes a supernatural partner or helper who had the power to predict and brought messages or warnings to his human partner. *Cah-e-tsi* is a screech owl; *nee-hee*, a white owl. Contemporary Caddos may joke that owls seen around someone's house are an omen of death or bad luck, but for some the belief has not totally vanished.
6. Espinosa, *Crónica*, 162.
7. Ibid.
8. Ibid.

9. Parsons, *Notes on the Caddo,* 37–38; Fallis Elkins, personal communication, Apache, Oklahoma, 1972.

10. Other contemporary sources say that faces were painted with certain designs so that a person would be recognized by those who had gone before and that moccasins had to be slit to allow water to flow through and keep the person from drowning when crossing the river between this life and the next.

11. Pat Carter conversation, taped July 1978, Anadarko, Oklahoma.

12. Shelby, "St. Denis's Declaration," 172.; Bolton, "Native Tribes," 255.

CHAPTER 9

SPRING

1. "Tsa-cup-bee" is a spelling that approximates the way the name is pronounced by contemporary Caddos. Espinosa's spelling of the name by which the Hasinais called "the month or moon of February" was "scabbi" (*Crónica,* 168).

2. Lillie Whitehorn sang this song for me during February 1978. She told me it was a song her sister liked to sing when she was a little girl. I have attempted to transcribe the Caddo words in English syllables; the loose translation is Whitehorn's.

3. Espinosa, *Crónica,* 168.

4. Ibid., 176.

5. Ibid.

6. Ibid., 174.

7. Ibid., 163–164.

8. The description here is based on recall and notes made immediately after a memorial dinner at the Caddo Community Center, Binger, Oklahoma, February 1978.

9. Espinosa, *Crónica,* 180. A baton symbolized authority and was presented to tribal leaders whom the Spaniards recognized through investiture as "chiefs" or "governors." It is sometimes referred to as a "staff." Here Hatcher's translation of the extract from *Crónica* uses the word *cane.* The Spanish term is *bastón.*

10. Espinosa, *Crónica,* 180.

11. Swanton, *Source Material,* 56.

CHAPTER 10

THE TRADERS, 1719

1. La Harpe, "Account of Journey of Bénard de la Harpe: Discovery Made by Him of Several Nations Situated in the West," trans. Ralph A. Smith, *Southwestern Historical Quarterly* 62 (July 1958): 85. Unless otherwise noted, the Smith translation is the source for this chapter.

2. The Natchitoches branch referred to here is the upper Natchitoches, separate from the Natchitoches lower down the Red River where St. Denis established the French post.

3. La Harpe, "Account of Journey," 75; Santos, *Aguayo Expedition,* 112 n. 16.
   The "province of Texas" referred to was the northeast Texas territory occupied and controlled by the Hasinai. The Kingdom of New León included most of what is now Texas.

4. Jean Baptiste Le Moyne de Bienville, brother of the founder of Louisiana,

Pierre Le Moyne d'Iberville, moved the capital of Louisiana from Mobile to New Orleans soon after being appointed governor in 1718. The port at New Orleans was better situated to receive shiploads of settlers and merchandise for the development of concessions.

5. La Harpe, "Account of Journey," 250. Sulphur River begins in Fannin County in northeast Texas. Translator Smith said the route taken by La Harpe was probably a short distance up the Sulphur River. He located the Nasoni village on the north side of the Red River opposite present-day New Boston in Bowie County, Texas.

6. Ibid., 252. According to Smith, "one of these soldiers," probably referred to La Salle, but it is not certain that the Naouydiches mentioned by La Harpe were Nabedaches. If the chief did mean that the Hasinai Nabedache band was once an enemy of the Cadohadacho, this would contradict earlier indications that the Hasinai and Cadohadacho tribes were allied kindred. Given Caddo syntax and problems in translating from Caddo to French to English, "their village" could refer to the Nabedache, not the Nasoni, village. In that case, "other wild tribes" made peace with the Nabedache after a French soldier arrived in the Nabedache village.

Swanton, *Source Material,* 11–12, discussed the puzzle of identifying the Naouydiches, who he said may have been related to but not necessarily identical with the Nabedaches of the Hasinai nation. He said there seemed to be a family relationship among the names Nabiti, Naviti, Nabiri, Namidis, Noadiche, and Naouydiche recorded in various French and Spanish records and concluded, "Undoubtedly we have two tribes called Nabedache and Namidi or Namidish distinguished at a very early period, and it must always remain doubtful whether they stemmed from one original group or whether the resemblance in their names is purely accidental." La Harpe, "Account of Journey," later found a band he called Naouydiches a good distance north of the Red River in what is now Oklahoma.

7. Tanner, "Territory" 40–41. Tanner, whose ethnohistorical report concerning the aboriginal territory of the Caddo Tribe of Oklahoma was presented as Plaintiff's Exhibit T-212 for the Indian Claims Commission Docket 226, stated that 1 French land league in the 1700s was roughly equivalent to 2.65 English miles. She identified the vicinity of present-day Ogden, Arkansas, as La Harpe's base point where "the Nassonites" lived.

8. La Harpe, "Account of Journey," 253.

9. Ibid., 255.

10. Ibid.

11. Ibid., 254–255. A dedicated group of nine amateur archeologists worked for fifteen years to locate and identify La Harpe's post. Their conclusion, in Miroir et al., *Bernard de La Harpe,* 163, was that journals left by La Harpe in 1719 and by the Freeman-Custis expedition of 1806 made possible "the tentative identification of the Rosebrough Lake Site (41 BW 5) in Bowie County, Texas, as the site where La Harpe established the Nassonite Post (Ft. St. Louis de Kadohadacho) in 1719." Eighteenth-century artifacts found at the site substantiated their hypothesis and Rosebrough Lake is still considered the primary site of the French trading post and garrison. See also Schambach, "Archaeology of the Great Bend Region," 93.

12. La Harpe, "Account of Journey," 255.
13. Ibid., 156.
14. Ibid., 257.
15. Ibid., 259.
16. Castaneda, *Winning of Texas,* 115–119. The mission and presidio were established in 1718.

CHAPTER 11
THE RETURN

1. Santos, *Aguayo Expedition.* Unless otherwise noted, this text is the source for the account of Aguayo's expedition used in this chapter.
2. Ibid., 54.
3. Ibid.
4. Ibid., 56. The measurements given were thirty-two varas long and four and one-half wide. One Mexican vara equals thirty-three inches. The bridge proved so stable that it was given the blessing of the church.
5. Ibid.
6. Morfí, *History,* 188; Castaneda, *Winning of Texas,* 141.
7. Corbin, "Retracing the Camino." Archeological research has identified the locations of the missions of San Miguel, Dolores de Ais, and San José de los Nasones; the Presidio de los Adaes; and the civil settlement of Los Adaes. The exact locations of the other three missions have not been found, but Corbin has developed strong evidence for mapping the route followed by the Spaniards.
8. Santos, *Aguayo Expedition,* 63.
9. Ibid., 59.
10. Buckley, "Aguayo Expedition," 49–50.
11. Ibid., 52; Castaneda, *Winning of Texas,* 159.
12. Swanton, *Source Material,* 63. Rivera's report was dated March 23, 1728.

CHAPTER 12
BIG LEG

1. Le Page du Pratz, *History of Louisiana,* 167–168; Phares, *Cavalier,* 189. Unless another source is noted, this section is based on the latter text.
2. Yoakum, *History of Texas,* 1:76–79.
3. Swanton, *Indians of Southeastern United States,* 73, 77–78, 159–160; Charlevoix, *History and General Description,* 6:88–117.
4. Charlevoix, *History and General Description,* 6:118 n. 1, cited a report that said there were 400 Hasinais and 14 Spaniards. According to Phares, there were 16 Spanish soldiers.
5. Charlevoix, 6:118.
6. Bolton, *Texas,* 32–33.
7. Ibid., 35–38.
8. St. Denis to Ybiricú, April 1737; quoted in Bolton, *Texas,* 37.
9. Ibid.
10. John, *Storms Brewed,* 343–344.
11. The investigator was Don Manuel Antonio de Soto Vermúdez, second in command to the newly appointed governor of Texas, Jacinto de Barrios y Jáuregui.
12. John, *Storms Brewed,* 344–345; Bolton, *Texas,* 70.

CHAPTER 13
CHANGES

1. Mathews, *Osages*, 127, 138.
2. John, *Storms Brewed*, 213–218; Hyde, *Pawnee Indians*, 32–101. According to John, four of the bands named by La Harpe can be identified with eighteenth-century bands known as the Taovaya, the Tawakoni, the Wichita, and the Yscani. Hyde traced the migrations of the various bands that formed a "very mixed tribe which late in the eighteenth century was termed Tawehash, Taovaya, Pani, Pani Pique, and—after 1850—became known as the Wichitas" (97). He gave attention to the effect that French trade had on the Wichita, Caddo, Osage, Comanche, and Apache tribes.
3. Mathews, *Osages*, 138; Bolton, *Texas*, 66.
4. Tanner, "Territory," 63–81; Foreman, *Indians and Pioneers*, 138, 286. Utilizing maps and historical data, Tanner concluded that territorial borders encompassing the villages and hunting grounds of the Caddo confederacy formed "somewhat of a square, with the four 'corners' near Hot Springs, Arkansas; Colfax, Louisiana; Bedias, west of Huntsville, Texas; and Paul's Valley, Oklahoma" (77). Foreman located Nanatsoho on the south bank of the Red River, across from the present community of Kullituklo, which is a short distance east of Idabel in McCurtain County, Oklahoma.
5. This Cross Timbers description is taken from one written by Josiah Gregg and quoted in Hollow, *Beyond the Cross Timbers*, 63. Gregg blazed a trail from Van Buren, Arkansas, to Santa Fe, New Mexico. His journal, *Commerce of the Prairies*, was published in 1844.
6. Tanner, "Territory," 71–73; Newcomb, *Indians of Texas*, 96–97, 104, 112; Richner and Bagot, *Reconnaissance Survey*, 29, 42–43.
7. John, *Storms Brewed*, 219–220.
8. Bolton, *Hasinais*, 61–64.
9. Bolton, ed., *Athanase de Mézières*, 1:95–99, 283–330.
10. Ibid., 1:163.
11. Nicolás de Lafora, "Relación del Viaje Que de orden del Excelentísimo Señor Virrey Marques de Cruillas hizo"; quoted in Castaneda, *Passing of Missions*, 230.
12. Corbin, "Retracing the Camino," 191–219.
13. Randlett Edmonds, a fluent Caddo speaker, and I were discussing the meaning of Caddo place names such as Nacogdoches when he made the drawing to illustrate.
14. *Caddoan Mounds.* La Fora quoted in Castaneda, *Passing of Missions*, 230.
15. Castaneda, *Passing of Missions*, 223–230.
16. The war between France and England, fought with Indian allies on both sides, is known in America as the French and Indian War (1756–1763). Battles in North America began the Seven Years' War.
17. Bolton, *Texas*, 4, 102–103.
18. Castaneda, *Passing of Missions*, 33.
19. Ibid., 140; John, *Storms Brewed*, 355–374.
20. Nicolas de La Fora, *The Frontiers of New Spain*; quoted in Tanner, "Territory," 62.
21. Castaneda, *Passing of Missions*, 257.

22. Bolton, *Texas,* 378–380.
23. Solís, "Diary," 69–70. Details given in the remainder of this chapter are based on this source.
24. Ibid., 61.
25. John, *Storms Brewed,* 372.
26. Solís, "Diary," 70.

CHAPTER 14
TRUE CHIEFS

1. "Historical Introduction," in Bolton, ed., *Athanase de Mézières,* 1:74. Unless otherwise noted, all references in this chapter are in Bolton, ed., *Athanase de Mézierès,* and are noted by volume and page number only.
2. Ibid., 1:88.
3. Ulloa to O'Conor, 1768, 1:128–129.
4. Mézières to Unzaga y Amezaga, November 19, 1770, in 1:193–195.
5. "Historical Introduction," in 1:71; Instructions for the Traders of the Cadaux d'Acquious and Hiatasses Nations, February 4, 1770, in 1:148–150.
6. "List of the Effects Which Should Be Given to the Three Indian Nations of the Post of Natchitoches, Copied from the Instruction Drawn by the Most Excellent Senor Conde de Orreilli," in 1:132–134.
7. Morfí, *History,* pt. 1, 88. Morfí cited a letter from a Caballero Macarti to Governor Angel Martos de Navarrete, November 17, 1763. The letter, written in Natchitoches, contained a description of the "Cadodachos" that named the family divisions and recounted the legend of a woman, called Zacado, who appeared on the hill. Since the pronunciation was probably the Caddo-language female prefix *sah* plus *cado,* I have used that spelling.
8. Contract of Juan Piseros with Mézières, Natchitoches, February 3, 1770, in 1:145–146.
9. The spelling of native names by French, Spanish, and English speakers is a continual problem, especially since different letters are often used for the same sound. The Yatasi chief Cocay could be either Guakan, who came to see St. Denis three years earlier, or his successor.
10. Report by Mézières of the Expedition to Cadodachos, October 29, 1770, in 1:211 n. 310.
11. Mézières to Unzaga y Amezaga, May 15, 1770, in 1:162.
12. Ibid., 1:160–163.
13. Mézières to Unzaga y Amezaga, August 21, 1770, in 1:182; Mézières to Unzaga y Amezaga, October 23, 1770, in 1:186.
14. Bolton said the Tawakoni, Yscani, and Taovaya were classed as "subdivisions of the Wichita group, of which the Wichita tribe was a rather minor one in Texas, notwithstanding the fact that it gave its name to the group." The Kichai were a separate tribe that had long lived in Texas (in 1:215 n. 316).
15. Mézières to Unzaga y Amezaga, June 10, 1770, in 1:175.
16. Mézières to Unzaga y Amezaga, October 23, 1770, in 1:186.
17. Report by Mézières of the Expedition to Cadodachos, October 29, 1770, in 1:210.
18. Ibid., 1:211.
19. Ibid., 1:211–212.

20. Ibid., 1:212–213.
21. The Cainiones were probably the Cahinnios that Joutel had known of in 1678 (in 1:93–94 n. 115).
22. Ripperda to Unzaga y Amezaga, December 31, 1771, in 1:262–268.
23. Treaty with the Taovayas, in 1:256–260.
24. "Historical Introduction," in 1:99; Mézières to Unzaga y Amezaga, August 20, 1772, in 1:337–338; La Peña to Unzaga y Amezaga, September 14, 1772, in 2:16, 23.

CHAPTER 15
TWO HUNDRED YEARS LATER

1. This chapter is based on observation and tape-recorded interviews with Doyle Edge and Gayle Cussen Satepauhoodle in the Caddo Tribal Office, Brown Building, Anadarko, Oklahoma, February 21, 1978.
2. Information on Caddo tribal government (1938–1978) is from the Tribal Charter, Constitution, and By-laws (1938 and 1976) and minutes of council meetings. Files in the Caddo tribal office are incomplete. Minutes of many meetings are missing or were never recorded. Some that are in the files are written in pencil and faintly legible; some are not dated.
3. Minutes of the 1973 election referred to in this chapter and the reference for the number of votes taken to elect the chair were found in the files. The method for the final count was told to me by so many Caddo people that I cannot remember the name of my original source. Everyone, however, told the same story.
4. Shirley French, who chaired the Constitutional Committee that drafted the 1976 revised constitution, furnished me with draft copies and background information. "Chairman" and "Vice-chairman" are named as officers in both the 1938 Constitution and the revised 1976 Constitution, but women may fill these positions. Except for restrictions having to do with age, residency, commission of a felony, or delinquent indebtedness to the tribe, eligible candidates are defined as "all members of the Caddo Indian Tribe," and women have been elected.
5. Bean, "Indians Raid Open Federal Purse."

CHAPTER 16
A PLACE FOR CRYING

1. Castaneda, *Passing of Missions*, 295–343; Bolton, *Texas*, 387–446. The description of the Spaniards' removal from Los Adaes through their permanent settlement of Nacogdoches in this chapter is based on more detailed accounts in these two sources.
2. Castaneda, *Passing of Missions*, 313, identified the location of Bucareli as the Tobbin's Ferry crossing on the Trinity at the "old village of Randolph in Madison County."
3. Bolton, "Historical Introduction," in 1:95–97.
4. Ibid., 97.
5. Mézières to Unzaga y Amezaga, May 2, 1777, in Bolton, ed., *Athanase de Mézières*, 2:130.
6. Ibid., 2:130, n. 150, 2:141; Mézières to Gálvez, September 14, 1777, in Bolton,

ed., *Athanase de Mézières*, 2:141.

7. Mézières to Croix, November 15, 1778, in Bolton, ed., *Athanase de Mézières*, 2:231–232.

8. Ibid.; John, *Storms Brewed*, 523; Mézières to Bernardo de Gálvez, May [?], 1779, in Bolton, ed., *Athanase de Mézières*, 2:248, 250. Exactly when Tinhiouen died is uncertain. The last letter that referred to Tinhiouen by name was written September 14, 1777 (2:141–143). In it Mézières reported that he gave Tinhiouen permission to dislodge English traders from a store-house on the Arkansas. In a letter to Governor Gálvez, May 1779 (2:250), Mézières did not name "their [the Caddos'] medal chief [who] died a Christian at the Capital and was buried with military honors," but it is believed that he was referring to Tinhiouen.

9. Mézières to Croix, August 26, 1779, in Bolton, ed., *Athanase de Mézières*, 2:263.

10. Croix to Gálvez, September 10, 1778, in Bolton, ed., *Athanase de Mézières*, 2:218–219.

11. Mézières to Gálvez, September 14, 1777; Report of Council at San Antonio de Bexar; and Mézières to the Viceroy, February 20, 1778, all in Bolton, ed., *Athanase de Mézières*, 2:143–147, 168–169, and 172–186, respectively.

12. Mézières to Croix, March 23, 1778; Mézières to Croix, March 28, 1778; Mézières to Croix, April 5, 1778; Mézières to Croix, April 7, 1778; Mézières to Croix, April 18, 1778; and Mézières to Croix, April 19, 1778, all in Bolton, ed., *Athanase de Mézières*, 2:190–192, 192–193, 193–196, 196–197, 201–204, and 212–214, respectively.

13. Mézières to Croix, November 15, 1778; Mézières to Croix, August 23, 1779; and Mézières to Croix, September 30, 1779; all in Bolton, *Athanase de Mézières*, 2:232–233, 260–262, and 289–291, respectively, cover this incident and the steps Mézières took to cool the situation. See also Bolton, *Texas*, 432–438; and Castaneda, *Passing of Missions*, 326–332.

14. Croix to Mézières, September 10, 1778; and Mézières to Gálvez, February 7, 1779, both in Bolton, ed., *Athanase de Mézières*, 2:216–217 and 239–240, respectively.

15. Mézières to Gálvez, May [?], 1779, in Bolton, ed., *Athanase de Mézières*, 2:253. In another letter written before the chief's visit, Mézières to Gálvez, May [?], 1779, in Bolton, ed., *Athanase de Mézières*, 2:250, Mézières traced the new chief's lineage from "their [the Caddos'] medal chief [who] died a Christian at the capital and was buried with military honors; that of which his father was likewise worthy; and finally, that which he merits himself, as a worthy successor of these good and valorous chiefs." It is probable that the new chief's father was Tinhiouen (see n. 8 above).

16. Ibid., 248.

17. Gálvez to Mézières, June 1, 1779, in Bolton, ed., *Athanase de Mézières*, 2:253–254.

18. Mézières to Croix, May 27, 1779, in Bolton, ed., *Athanase de Mézières*, 2:256–257.

19. Mézières to Croix, August 21, 1779, in Bolton, ed., *Athanase de Mézières*, 2:258–260.

20. John, *Storms Brewed*, 537–539.

21. Mézières to Croix, August 23, 1779, in Bolton, ed., *Athanase de Mézières*, 2:260.

22. Mézières to Croix, August 26, 1779, in Bolton, ed., *Athanase de Mézières*, 2:263.

23. Bolton, ed., *Athanase de Mézières*, 1:128 n. 155.

24. Blake, "Captain Antonio Gil Y'Barbo." According to Blake, Gil YBarbo's informal method of making "verbal grants of land to many of the farmers at that time" was the only one that could be employed because no legal machinery was set up, but he was severely censured "for thus illegally granting lands, often fifty thousand acres in one grant, without any record made of it; and it is probable that the report of conditions made to the governor, together with the report of clandestine traffic with the French, caused the dismissal of Y'barbo from his official status in 1794." (22).

25. Gaignard, "Journal," 2:83. Gaignard reported ninety warriors in the Grand Caddo village, sixty in the Petit Caddo, and ten living in the Prairie of the Enemy vicinity.

26. Tanner, "Territory," 56.

27. With both Louisiana and Texas under Spanish government, Caddo movements were given less attention and records pertaining to their moves are sparse. The old villages were still occupied when J. Gaignard traveled up the Red River in 1773. Leaving Natchitoches, he arrived at the Yatasi settlement in the vicinity of modern-day Shreveport three days later, and six days after that he "arrived at the village of the Petit Cadosdagos, who are twenty-five leagues from the Natasee." In five more days he was at the Prairie of the Enemy and found about ten Caddos living in the vicinity. Nine more days placed him "at the village of the Great Cados, who are thirty leagues distant from the Petit Cados" (Gaignard, "Journal," 2:83).

An indication that the Grand Caddo village was deserted in 1788 and that consolidation with the Petit Caddo village came in 1790 is found in a letter the commandant at Natchitoches, Luis de Blanc, wrote Governor Esteban Miró. Blanc's letter, written March 27, 1790, said, "The Great Caddo tribe of Indians found itself obliged two years ago to change the location of its village on account of the continual war being waged on them by the Osage tribe. Being persecuted incessantly by their enemies, these Indians were obliged last month to take refuge in the village of the Little Caddo" (Kinnard, ed., *Spain in the Mississippi Valley*, 3:316). John Sibley, who became the first American Indian agent in Natchitoches, indicated that this move was made about 1791. In an 1805 report submitted to the secretary of war, General Henry Dearborn (Sibley, "Historical Sketches," 1832, 721–725) stated that the Caddos "live about thirty-five miles west of the main branch of Red River, on a bayou or creek, called, by them, Sodo . . . distant from Natchitoches about 120 miles, the nearest route by land, and in nearly a northwest direction." He added that they had lived there only five years, having "formerly lived on the south bank of the river, by the course of the river 375 miles higher up, at a beautiful prairie, . . . which has been the residence of their ancestors from time immemorial. . . . The Indians left it about fourteen years ago, on account of a dreadful sickness that visited them" (quoted in Swanton, *Source Material*, 74; Lange, "Report on Data," 216–217). According to this information from Sibley, the Caddos moved from the Grand Caddo village around 1791 and came to Tso'to Lake in 1800. Peter Custis, however, understood from talks with Dehahuit and Caddo Indian guides in 1806 that the Caddos had left their village near the bend in the Red River after a surprise Osage attack in 1795 and had lived at Tso'to Lake for eleven years (Flores, *Freeman-Custis Accounts,* 168, 184).

28. Gleason, *Caddo,* 66–69; Torma, "Caddo Lake State Park," 20–29; Flores, ed., *Freeman-Custis Accounts,* 168 n. 12. Swanton, *Source Material,* 16, gave "water thrown up into the drift along the shore by a wind" as the Caddo meaning of the place name Tso'to.

29. The following story was tape-recorded as it was told to me by Lillie White-horn, Anadarko, Oklahoma, February 1978.

30. Sibley, "Historical Sketches," quoted in Swanton, *Source Material,* 74.

CHAPTER 17
THE INTRUDERS

1. Kinnaird and Kinnaird, "Choctaws." This is the principal source of informa-tion on Choctaw-Caddo relationships used in this chapter.

2. Caddo chiefs to Commandant of Natchitoches, April 28, 1795; quoted in Kinnaird and Kinnaird, "Choctaws," 354. The commandant at Natchitoches in 1789, Césaire de Blanc de Neuveville, wrote the governor of Louisiana, Esteban Miró, saying that he had "caused the man named Bicheda [Bisda] to be recognized as chief of the Great [Grand] Caddo. I delivered to him Your Lordship's commission with the large medal of merit, the banner, and uni-forms" (De Blanc to Miró, September 30, 1789, in Kinnard, ed., *Spain in the Mississippi Valley,* 281). Diortot was possibly the Caddo chief whose name is spelled Dehahuit in other documents; Chacheau was possibly the Yatasi chief whose name was spelled Cocay elsewhere.

3. Kinnaird and Kinnaird, "Choctaws," 359–360, gave this information about the strength of the tribes summarized by Carlos Grand Pré, lieutenant governor of lower Louisiana, in a letter to the governor, Baron de Carondelet, in September 1796.

4. Caddo chiefs to Commandant of Natchitoches, April 28, 1795; quoted in Kinnaird and Kinnaird, "Choctaws," 357 n 18.

5. Castaneda, *End of Spanish Regime,* 119. The old chief is not identified by name. He is probably the one who succeeded Tinhiouen (see chap. 16, nn. 8, 15).

6. Carondelet to Delavillebeuvre, April 19, 1797; quoted in Kinnaird and Kinnaird, "Choctaws," 365.

7. Kinnaird and Kinnaird, "Choctaws," 367. Since the old chief had been assassinated a few months earlier, this was probably his son. When the old chief went to New Orleans for a visit with Governor Gálvez in May 1779, he was given a large medal. Gálvez wrote to Mézières, "With respect to the small one which he had and which you thought proper to give to his son, the father has had the contrary opinion, thinking that he does not deserve it, and saying that because he is young and as the people of his nation have as yet no respect for him, it would be better to give it to another Indian who was with him, worthy of it because of his fidelity, constancy, and love for us, and for the valor which he has shown on the occasions which have arisen" (Bolton, ed.,

Athanase de Mézières, 2:253–254). The chronology indicates that the young son was Dehahuit.

8. Guardiana to Lemos, December 3, 1798; quoted in Kinnaird and Kinnaird, "Choctaws," 369.

9. Treaty arrangements for the Louisiana Purchase were signed in May 1803. The ceremony for the transfer to the United States took place on December 20 of that year.

10. Cox, "Louisiana-Texas Frontier II," 155–156; Glover, "History of the Caddo," 889–900.

11. Ibid.

12. Castaneda, *End of Spanish Regime,* 257, 263; Flores, *Freeman-Custis Accounts,* 68 nn. 107–108. According to Flores, remnants of the Natchitoches tribe may have fled to Bayou Pierre and joined the Yatasis there during the 1730s. A number of French families moved there during the same decade, but the Spanish maintained the place was not officially settled until 1783. The Spanish refused to let go of Bayou Pierre following their cession of Louisiana, and it was the center for Spanish activities east of the Sabine River in 1806. According to the first U.S. Indian agent, John Sibley, about forty families, most of them French, lived there. Located on the banks of a creek named Bayou Pierre about ten miles northeast of present-day Mansfield, Louisiana, the community was called Bayou Pierre by the French, Las Piedas by the Spanish, and Stoney Creek by American frontier settlers.

13. Haggard, "House of Barr and Davenport," 73–74; Cox, "Louisiana-Texas Frontier," 158. Cox reported that Barr and Davenport sent agents to ply their trade between Nacogdoches and the Washita and to introduce settlers from the Washita into Texas. Two rivers flowing from the north into the Red River were called Washita: a lower tributary entering from the present state of Arkansas and another entering from the present state of Oklahoma several hundred miles upstream. Wright, "Some Geographic Names," 193, explained that French explorers distinguished the two by calling the Arkansas stream the Washita and the tributary farther west the Faux Ouachita. The Oklahoma tributary was still called the False Washita as late as the Civil War, but today's geographies label the Oklahoma river the Washita and the Arkansas river the Ouachita. There were settlers on the Ouachita in the first half of the nineteenth century but none on the Washita.

14. Garrett, "Doctor John Sibley," 45 (January, 1942): 286–288.

15. Cox, "Louisiana-Texas Frontier," 17 (October 1913): 160–161; Garrett, "Doctor John Sibley," 45:287–289.

16. Sibley, "Historical Sketches," in *American State Papers,* class 2, *Indian Affairs,* vol. 1, 725–731; extracts in Hume Collection. See also Cox, "Louisiana-Texas Frontier," 161, 165.

17. Sibley, "Historical Sketches"; quoted in Swanton, *Source Material,* 74. Intermarriage has blurred unmixed indentification, but most twentieth-century Caddos say their grandparents were Anadarko, Hainai, Natchitoches, or Caddo. Some older Caddos recall the Yatasi and Kichai as affiliated tribes. Nabedache is a name that only a few recognize today. Except among those familiar with historical documents or ethnological accounts, the Adai were lost to memory.

18. Morfí, *History*, 89; Bolton, *Athanase de Mézières*, 2:191; Tanner, "Territory," 158–161.

19. Swanton, *Source Material*, 16–25.

20. Dearborn to Sibley, May 23, 1805; quoted in Cox, "Louisiana-Texas Frontier," 17 (October 1913): 162.

21. Jefferson Papers; quoted in Cox, "Louisiana-Texas Frontier," 17 (October 1913): 163.

22. Flores, *Freeman-Custis Accounts*, 146 n. 37.

23. La Harpe, "Account of Journey," 246–247.

24. Flores, *Freeman-Custis Accounts*, 149; Swanton, *Indians of Southeastern United States*, 145. Flores indicated that the Coushatta chief lived in the vicinity of Carolina Bluffs, Bossier Parish. According to Swanton, a section of the Koasati (Coushatta) migrated to the Red River, Louisiana, between 1793 and 1795 and occupied several different places. The name of one place is preserved near present-day Coushatta, Louisiana, forty-six miles southeast of Shreveport.

25. Flores, *Freeman-Custis Accounts*, 161.

26. Speech of Governor Claiborne, and the reply of Dehahuit, the Grand Chief of the Caddo Nation, delivered at Natchitoches, September 5, 1806, *Mississippi Messenger*, September 30, 1806.

27. Flores, *Freeman-Custis Accounts*, 162–163.

28. Ibid.

29. Ibid., 163–164.

30. Ibid., 164.

31. Ibid., 165.

32. Ibid.

33. Ibid., 166.

34. Ibid.

35. Ibid., 169.

36. Ibid., 168 n. 11. The 450 miles that Custis said Dehahuit gave as the distance seems too far. Flores, who traveled the river route, said the distance might have been an estimate based on the winding course of the Red River. He said the old Caddo village was probably the original Upper Nasoni village where La Harpe located his post, and seventy-five or more miles upriver from there "was the site of the most westerly Caddo confederacy village, at Pecan Point, long since abandoned by the Nanatsoho division. But the Spaniards undoubtedly regard the more recently occupied site as the perimeter of the Caddo country."

37. Ibid., 168.

38. Ibid., 184.

39. Ibid., 170–172.

40. Morfí, 88. The observer, Caballero Macarti, wrote Governor Angel Martos de Navarrete from Natchitoches, November 17, 1763. The Caddo family division mentioned in this letter seems to indicate a clan system. Swanton (*Source Material*, 163–166) discussed the possibility of Caddo clans and concluded that there was doubt that a normal clan system existed. If the Caddo ever had a true clan system, it has not survived.

41. Flores, 186–188; Schambach, "Archeology of the Great Bend," 10. Flores said the lake in this description was probably Clear Lake, shown on the USGS

Boyd Hill (Ark.) Quadrangle. He identified the village as the Lower (Petit) Kadohadacho village that most of the Caddos fled to in 1790. The area has drawn the interest of archeologists since early in the twentieth century, but there has been no confirmation that the village was there. Flooding and cultivation have probably erased any evidence of the village site, but Flores maintained that Freeman's topographical description and astronomical observations, coupled with map work and on-site investigation, fix the locations. He also pointed out that the site answers to the description of the mythical location where the Caddos emerged from "Old-Home-in-the-Darkness" and built their first village called "Tall-Timber-on-Top-of-the-Hill."

Schambach said that 115 archaeological sites in the alluvial valley subregion of the Great Bend region had been recorded by 1979. The archaeological finds represent periods from Paleo-Indian (before 8000 B.C.) through early historic European times (after A.D. 1800). Excavation and analysis of residential sites in 1979–1980 suggested that many of the units of a single settlement were located on a stretch of the river 10 to 20 kilometers (6.25–12.5 mi.) downstream from Boyd Hill. Schambach offered these explanations for a discrepancy between the site documented by Freeman-Custis and the distance (6.25–14.4 mi.) of known archaeological sites: some sites are now gone or have not been located; and the Freeman-Custis group "succumbed to the tendency to shorten the distance between a point of interest and a nearby landmark"—they perhaps saw some farmsteads at the north end of the village but missed the main body downstream.

See also Schambach et al., "Test Excavations"; and Hemmings, "Spirit Lake." Hemmings associated Battle Mound, the largest artificially constructed mound in the Caddoan area, and Spirit Lake sites with a prairie shown on an 1848 map as Chickaninny Prairie and on late-nineteenth-century maps of the Red River as Chicanini or Chicanina Landing. All three names seem to derive from cha-ka-ni-na (Caddo for "the place they cried") and are near Battle Mound.

42. Flores, *Freeman-Custis Accounts*, 175–176.

43. Ibid., 192 n. 24.

44. Ibid., 194.

45. The site just east of Rosebrough Lake in Bowie County, Texas, was excavated by a team of archeologists from Dallas led by R. King Harris (see chap. 10, n. 11). The archeologists used Freeman's account and his celestial readings to help identify the La Harpe Post–Nasoni village location.

46. Official Letter Books of William C. Claiborne, 1801–1816; quoted in Glover, "History of the Caddo," 903.

47. Ibid.

48. Claiborne's Address to the Caddo Chief, *Mississippi Messenger*, September 5, 1806.

49. Caddo chief's reply to Claiborne's address, *Mississippi Messenger*, September 5, 1806. Lange, "Report on Data," 63, supported the opinion "that the terminology referring to land was simply a figure of speech, signifying loyalty rather than actual transfer of ownership and usage rights. This interpretation is substantiated by statements made by Sibley to a delegation comprising the headmen of seven Indian nations who gathered at Natchitoches, August 18,

1807, for a 'Grand Council.'"

50. Arroyo Honda was considered the boundary in St. Denis's time.

51. Sibley to Dearborn, January 10, 1807, in Garrett, "Doctor John Sibley," 45 (January 1942): 294.

52. Sibley, "Report from Natchitoches in 1807," 21.

53. Sibley to Eustis, January 30, 1810, in Garrett, "Doctor John Sibley," 47 (April 1944): 389.

54. American State Papers, Public Lands, 1834, vol. 3, 83; quoted in Swanton, Source Material, 83–84.

55. Sibley to Eustis, March 20, 1810, in Garrett, "Doctor John Sibley," 47 (April 1944): 390.

CHAPTER 18
FORCES BEYOND CONTROL

1. Paxson, History of American Frontier, 130–166.

2. Sibley to Eustis, November 28, 1812, in Garrett, "Doctor John Sibley," 49 (July 1945):417–418.

3. Sibley to Eustis, May 18, 1812; quoted in Lange, "Report on Data," 232–233.

4. This information from Davenport's 1809 report to Mexican authorities is quoted in Castaneda, End of Spanish Regime, 404–405, and summarized in Tanner, "Territory," 77. Davenport also reported 100 Nabedache warriors and their families living west of the Neches River (near present-day Slocum, Texas) and 60 Hainai warriors and their families who still had homes on the bank of the Angelina River in the vicinity of present-day Rusk, Texas. Counting the Caddo and Hasinai along with the Yatasi, Adai, Bidai, and Kichai, Davenport estimated a population of 3,300.

5. Working from descriptions like Sibley's and Davenport's and maps like the one drawn by U.S. surveyor William Darby in 1816, amateur archeologist Claude McCrocklin of Shreveport believed he found the Caddo village in 1991. Artifacts he collected, recorded, and reported have stirred interest, but professional archeologists have not confirmed the site as that of the Caddo villages. Claude McCrocklin, letter to author, March 25, 1992.

6. Castaneda, Transition Period, 48–52, 56.

7. Ibid., 81.

8. Sibley to Eustis, February 12, 1813, in Garrett, "Doctor John Sibley," 49 (January 1946): 421–422.

9. Sibley to Eustis, May 29, 1813, in Garrett, "Doctor John Sibley," 49 (January 1946): 427.

10. Sibley to Eustis, February 12, 1813, in Garrett, "Doctor John Sibley," 49 (January 1946): 421–422.

11. Sibley to Armstrong, October 6, 1813, in Garrett, "Doctor John Sibley," 49 (April 1946): 602–603.

12. Ibid., 603.

13. Ibid.

14. A talk between William C.C. Claiborne and the great chief of the Caddo Nation, October 18, 1813; quoted in Glover, "History of the Caddo," 906.

15. Jackson to Secretary Monroe, October 26, 1814, in Correspondence of Andrew Jackson, 83.

16. Sibley to Monroe, secretary of war, January 10, 1815, in Garrett, "Doctor John Sibley," 69 (April 1946): 611.

17. Foreman, *Indians and Pioneers,* 137–138.

18. Jamison to secretary of war, March 31, 1817; quoted in Lange, "Report on Data," 240.

19. Discussions of the westward movement, its effect on eastern Indian tribes, and the opening of new territories are found in Paxson, *History of American Frontier,* chaps. 7–21; and Foreman, *Indians and Pioneers,* chaps. 3–5.

20. Long to Smith, receiver in the Land Office at Franklin, Missouri Territory, January 30, 1818; quoted in Lange, "Report on Data," 242.

21. Fowler to Colonel John Jamison, April 16, 1819, and Fowler to T. L. McKenney, June 14, 1819; quoted in Lange, "Report on Data," 242–243.

22. Julia Edge, conversation with author, Anadarko, Oklahoma, August 1973.

23. Foreman, *Indians and Pioneers,* 142–149. The Choctaw treaty at Doaks Stand was signed October 18, 1820.

24. Miller to secretary of war, June 30, 1820; quoted in Foreman, *Indians and Pioneers,* 175.

25. Hardin, "Outline of Shreveport," 837.

26. Yoakum, *History of Texas,* 1:198–208.

27. Padilla, "Texas in 1820," 47–48.

28. Ibid., 51–53.

29. Ibid., 48; Espinosa, *Crónica,* 167.

30. Padilla, "Report," 47.

31. Glover, "History of the Caddo," 913–914.

32. McElhannon, "Imperial Mexico," 129.

33. McElhannon, "Imperial Mexico," 129.

34. Winfrey, "Chief Bowles," 32; Yoakum, *History of Texas,* 1:216, 218.

35. Glover, "History of the Caddo," 908.

36. Grey to McKenney, superintendent of Indian affairs, September 30, 1825; quoted in Lange, "Report on Data," 248.

37. The Quapaw were unhappy with the location given them: it was subject to floods caused by the Raft, and they were never accepted into the family of Caddo tribes. After a few years they moved, small groups at a time, back to the Arkansas River area (Lange, "Report on Data," 249–250; Glover, "History of the Caddo," 912–913).

38. Grey to secretary of war, *American State Papers, Indian Affairs,* 1834; quoted in Lange, "Report on Data," 249.

39. Sánchez, "A Trip to Texas," 279.

40. Ibid.

41. Berlandier, *Indians of Texas,* 52, 107.

42. Ibid., 127 n. 175. According to editor Ewers, the Yowani Choctaw band lived on the Chickasawhay River in Mississippi until about 1764, when they separated from their main clan and emigrated to Louisiana, where the band united with the Caddo. (See also Kniffen, Gregory, and Stokes, *Historic Indian Tribes,* 85–89.) Watercolors signed by Lino Sánchez y Tapía, designated after originals by Lieutenant Jose María Sánchez y Tapía, are reproduced in Berlandier, *Indians of Texas.* Plate 7 shows the Caddo couple; plate 8, the Yowani. A headdress with ribbon streamers is part of the dance costume

worn by modern-day Caddo women.

43. Berlandier, *Indians of Texas*, 107.

CHAPTER 19
BREAKING THE HEART

1. Hardin, "Outline of Shreveport," 845–847.
2. Grey was succeeded as agent by Thomas Griffith, who served from 1828 to 1830.
3. Brooks to John H. Eaton, secretary of war, October 23, 1830, copy in Hume Collection.
4. Certification of Larkin Edwards, James Shenich, John W. Edwards, and Jacob Irwin, January 31, 1831, Hume Collection, box 1; also reprinted in Hardin, "Outline of Shreveport," 784–785.
5. Hardin, "Outline of Shreveport," 812.
6. Brooks to Eaton, secretary of war, January 17, 1831, copy in Hume Collection.
7. Brooks to Eaton, February 16, 1831, copy in Hume Collection.
8. Brooks to Judge E. Herring, April 9, 1833; quoted in Glover, "History of the Caddo," 910–911. In 1832 Congress created the Bureau of Indian Affairs in the War Department under a commissioner, whose duty it was to care for Indian wards.
9. Tanner, "Territory," 98.
10. Brooks to Herring, March 20, 1834; quoted in Lange, "Report on Data," 251–252.
11. Webb and Gregory, *Caddo Indians*, 32; Flores, *Freeman-Custis*, "Epilogue," 308 n. 39.
12. Morrison, "Across Oklahoma," 336.
13. Culberson, "Indian Against Indian," 165–167.
14. Foreman, *Advancing the Frontier*, 127, 130–131.
15. House, *Report*, no. 1035, 27th Congress, 2nd sess., 1842, quoted in Lange, "Report on Data," 260–262.
16. Lee, "François Grappé." Lee said that, although many people, including the Caddos, have assumed that the mother of François Grappé was Caddo, "evidence suggests that his mother, Louise Marguerite Guedon, was half Chitimacha" (53).
17. Ibid.; italics added.
18. Lange, "Report on Data," 263.
19. Many to Kurtz, acting commissioner of Indian affairs, January 6, 1835; quoted in Lange, "Report on Data," 264–266.
20. House *Report*, 1842; quoted in Lange, "Report on Data," 268.
21. Lee, "François Grappé," 62; Hardin, "Outline of Shreveport," 776, 794; Glover, "History of the Caddo," 920 n. 31.
22. Brooks to Herring, March 20, 1834; quoted in Lange, "Report on Data," 251–252.
23. Glover, "History of the Caddo," 918–919.
24. Lange, "Report on Data," 272.
25. Glover, "History of the Caddo," 919.
26. Articles of a treaty made at the agency-house, in the Caddo Nation and State of Louisiana, in Hardin, "Outline of Shreveport," 792–796; and Lange, "Report

on Data," 274–281.

27. Hardin, 795; Lange, 279.

28. Deposition of Captain J. Bonnell, Juanita Henry Collection, Archives Division, Eugene P. Watson Memorial Library, Northwestern State University, Natchitoches, Louisiana. Copy of depositions related to the Grappé claim, presented before the Twenty-seventh Cong., 2d sess., House of Representatives, 1842; quoted in Lee, "François Grappé," 62. Bonnell evidently received a promotion sometime between 1835 and 1842.

CHAPTER 20
WHERE WE COME FROM

1. Almonte, "Statistical Report," 206.

2. Yoakum, *History of Texas,* 1:358, 377.

3. Declaration of the Consultation meeting at San Felipe, November 13, 1835, in Winfrey, "Chief Bowles," 34.

4. Treaty Between Texas and the Cherokee Indians, in Winfrey and Day, *Indian Papers,* 1:13–17. All except three of these tribes—Ioni, Tahocullake, and Mataquo—are identifiable by name. Ioni is a frequently used variant spelling of Hainai, but in other copies of the treaty this tribal name is spelled Iawahies, which editor Ewers (in Berlandier, *Indians of Texas,* 103, n. 120), and Hyde (*Pawnee Indians,* 33) said was Awahe, the old Caddo and Wichita name for the Skidi, or Wolf, Pawnee. Tahocullake and Mataquo are undetermined.

5. Yoakum, *History of Texas,* 2:197.

6. Ibid., 2:127.

7. Mason to Nelson, March 20, 1836; quoted in Glover, "History of the Caddo," 924.

8. Ibid., 926–927.

9. Yoakum, *History of Texas,* 2:168; Glover, "History of the Caddo," 930. Several documents spell the chief's name "Tarshar," but Caddo words do not end with an *r* sound. It is likely that the chief's name was Ta'sha, the word for "wolf" or "coyote."

10. Edwards to Gaines, May 13, 1836, in Glover, "History of the Caddo," 928.

11. Account compiled from testimony of Charles Sewall, December 15, 1840, and testimony of Larkin Edwards, December 16, 1840, recorded as part of the Brooks case, House *Report,* 1842; quoted in Lange, "Report on Data," 299–302.

12. Webb and Gregory, *Caddo Indians,* 22.

13. Brooks to Cass, secretary of war, November 9, 1835; quoted in Lange, "Report on Data," 297–298.

14. Statement of Mary Inkanish, August 25, 1929, Hume Collection, Box 2. The following quotes are from this statement.

15. Ross Hume identified 1833 as the "year of the Falling Stars" in a set of informal notes.

16. An intertribal council ground, called Big Arbor, was located near the present town of Waco, Texas.

17. Glover, "History of the Caddo," 928–929.

18. Webb, *Texas Rangers,* 23–30.

19. Erath, "Captain Erath's Fight," 248–253.

20. Ibid., 253, 254.

21. Henderson to Wharton and Hunt, Jan. 21st, 1837, in Garrison, ed., *Diplomatic Correspondence of the Republic of Texas,* 2:178.

22. Irion to Hunt, September 20, 1837, in Garrison, ed., *Diplomatic Correspondence,* 1:260.

23. Yoakum, *History of Texas,* 2:227, 241, 248; Foreman, *Advancing the Frontier,* 165 n. 7; Ann Muckleroy, "Indian Policy," 26: 27; Webb, *TexasRangers,* 49.

24. Report of Standing Committee on Indian Affairs, October 1837, in Winfrey and Day, *Indian Papers,* 1:23.

25. The reasons given for refusing ratification of the Cherokee treaty included a denial that such a community as the "Associate Bands" recognized in the 1835 declaration ever existed; a denial that the rights mentioned ever existed or were ever granted; and a statement that some of the tribes listed as being represented by the Cherokees "have been the most savage and ruthless of our frontier enemies ever since and even at the very date of the signing of this [the 1836] Treaty; an opinion that the People of Texas at the time of the Declaration were acknowledged to be citizens of Mexico and therefore had no authority to pass an act which obligated either the Mexican government or the present Texas government"; and a finding that the territory mentioned in the declaration and treaty was part of the "soil granted to David G. Burnet Esq. for the purposes of Colonization and which Colony was filled or nearly so Prior to this Declaration Many of the titles Being completed and others commenced and now in progress" (Winfrey and Day, *Indian Papers,* 1:25–26).

   Burnet, who was elected president of the ad interim government that filled the void between the Texans' declaration of independence and their adoption of constitutional government, received his land grant in 1826, at least six years after Chief Bowles had led his band of Cherokees into northeast Texas. Tanner, "Territory," 100, gave the information that the treaty with the Hainais and Anadarkos was lost.

26. First Deed from Larkin Edwards to Angus McNeil Covering the Site of Shreveport, Parish of Natchitoches, January 24, 1835, in Hardin, "Outline of Shreveport," 797.

27. Second Deed from Larkin Edwards to Members of the Shreve Town Company Covering the Site of Shreveport, in Hardin, "Outline of Shreveport," 798–801.

28. First Agreement of the Shreve Town Company, in Hardin, "Outline of Shreveport," 801–802. McNeil's partners were Bushrod Jenkins, James Huntington Cane, William Smith Bennett, Henry M. Shreve, Sturgis Sprague, Thomas Taylor Williamson, and James Belton Pickett. All were well established in the area before the Caddo treaty of cession. The names Bennett and Cane were listed by George Grey in 1825 when he notified the War Department that certain persons were making improper claims to Caddo lands.

29. Shreve to Jackson, April 19, 1836, *House Reports,* 1842, 96–97; quoted in Lange, "Report on Data," 284–295. Hardin, "Outline of Shreveport," 776, gave the boundaries of the Grappé claim and detailed proof of the Agency House location.

30. Quoted in Lange, "Report on Data," 286–287.

31. Ibid., 288–289. On February 6, 1840, charges of fraud were brought against Brooks by Samuel Norris, an inhabitant of Rush Island, on which the

reservation in favor of the Grappés was located. The Committee on Indian Affairs decided that the question of fraud was one for the courts. When the case of the *United States* v. *Brooks* was heard in the Circuit Court of the United States for the District of Louisiana, the charges were judged unwar-ranted, and Brooks's title to the lands he had got from the Grappés was confirmed. The case was carried to the Supreme Court, which upheld the judgment of the Louisiana court in 1850. (See Lange, "Report on Data," 289–293.)

32. Shreve Town officially became Shreveport in 1839, when the Louisiana legislature created present Caddo Parish out of Natchitoches Parish and granted a charter to the town of Shreveport, making it the seat of justice for Caddo Parish (Hardin, "Outline of Shreveport," 789–791, 847).

33. Sewall to the commissioner of Indian affairs, January 8, 1839, Hume Collec-tion; Frost, Statement of facts notarized by W. Jenkins, Caddo Parish Judge, January 8, 1839, typewritten copy, Hume Collection.

34. Sewall to the Commissioner of Indian Affairs, January 8, 1839, Charles A. Sewall Papers, Correspondence, and Agency Records, 1829–1841, typewrit-ten copy, Hume Collection.

35. Sewall, list identified as "Caddo Indians, Apr 1838 & 9, A & G (B)," typewritten copy, Hume Collection.

36. Ibid.

37. The account of this incident is taken from Statement of the Citizens, January 8, 1839, Charles A. Sewall Papers, typewritten copy, Hume Collection.

38. Frost, Statement, January 8, 1839.

39. Rusk to secretary of war, December 1, 1838, typewritten copy, Hume Col-lection.

40. Frost, Statement, January 8, 1839.

41. Sewall List, Caddo Indians, Apr 1838 & 9, typewritten copy, Hume Col-lection.

42. Ibid.

43. Irion to Jones, November 29, 1838, in Garrison, ed., *Diplomatic Correspon-dence,* 2:350–353.

44. *Journals of the Fourth Congress of the Republic of Texas, 1829–1840,* 1:14–15; quoted in Webb, *Texas Rangers,* 31.

45. General K. H. Douglass, Report to Secretary of War, November 1839; quoted in Yoakum, *History of Texas,* 2:270.

CHAPTER 21
THE BITTER YEARS

1. Neighbours, "José Maria," 255.

2. Ibid., 256.

3. Wilbarger, *Indian Depredations,* 361–367.

4. Sewall to the Commissioner of Indian Affairs, January 8, 1839, typewritten copy, Hume Collection.

5. Rind to Armstrong, February 5, 1840, typewritten copy, Hume Collection. The young chief who was killed was probably Tarshar, who led the large Caddo band into Texas. His name was one of those marked on the 1835 treaty and on the memorial addressed the U.S. Senate in 1837, but his name was not

among those of the chiefs, headmen, and warriors on the power of attorney given Sewall on October 11, 1838. The names of Tsauninot—subchief at the treaty signing—and seven others who signed the treaty were on the power of attorney.

6. Frost, Statement, January 8, 1839; R. Garland to J. R. Poinsett, January 25, 1839; Certification of Accounts by I. B. Dorrance, L. K. Person, J. M. Lewis, April 3, 1839; W. North to Hon A. K. Paris, February 24, 1840; H. T. Williamson, February 24, 1840; all in Charles A. Sewall Papers, Correspondence, and Agency Records, 1829–1841, typewritten copies, Hume Collection.

7. Statement of the Chief, Headmen & Warriors, Shreveport, La., July 23, 1840, ibid.

8. U.S. Department of Indian Affairs, *Report of the Commissioner,* 1840, 288–289.

9. Armstrong to Commissioner of Indian Affairs, March 5, 1841, typewritten copy, Hume Collection.

10. Foreman, ed., *Traveler in Indian Territory,* 181, 183.

11. Foreman, *Advancing the Frontier,* preface.

12. Ibid., 201.

13. Letter to the Chiefs of the Caddo from Jim Marthler Mieed, Hopochthli Yoholo, Tuscoomah Harge, and Jim Boy, July 20, 1842, in Winfrey and Day, eds., *Indian Papers,* 1:137–138.

14. Ibid.

15. Appointment of Henry E. Scott, Indian commissioner, by Sam Houston, July 5, 1842, in Winfrey and Day, eds., *Indian Papers,* 1:136.

16. Webb, "Last Treaty," 152–153.

17. Ethen Stroud, Leonard Williams, and Joseph Durst to Sam Houston, September 4, 1842, in Winfrey and Day, eds., *Indian Papers,* 1:139. The letter implies that the four tribes were Caddo. If so, they would be the Caddos living in Indian Territory, and the Anadarkos, the Hainais, and the Caddos in Texas. The Chickasaws arrived in Indian Territory in 1838 and settled in the valleys of the Blue, Washita, and Boggy Rivers in the southern part of the country assigned to them.

18. Minutes of Indian Council at Tehuacana Creek, March 28, 1843, in Winfrey and Day, eds., *Indian Papers,* 1:149–156.

19. Ibid., 1:153–154.

20. Richardson, *Frontier of Northwest Texas,* 54–55.

21. These and other documents preserved by the tribe were certified by C. Ross Hume and deposited with the Oklahoma State Historical Society in 1929.

22. Winfrey and Day, eds., *Indian Papers,* 1:109.

23. J. C. Eldredge to Sam Houston, December 8, 1843, in Winfrey and Day, eds., *Indian Papers,* 1:256.

24. "Portraits of North American Indians, with sketches of scenery, etc., painted by J. M. Stanley"; quoted in Swanton, *Source Material,* 96.

25. Richardson, *Frontier of Northwest Texas,* 45–46.

26. J. C. Eldredge to Sam Houston, December 8, 1843, Winfrey and Day, eds., *Indian Papers,* 1:254.

27. Eldredge to Houston, June 2, 1843, in Winfrey and Day, eds., *Indian Papers,* 1:211–212; John Henry Brown, "The Thrilling Mission of Commissioner

Joseph C. Eldridge to the Wild Tribes in 1843, by Authority of President Houston—Hamilton P. Bee, Thomas Torrey—The three Delawares, Jim Shaw, John Connor and Jim Second Eye—The Treaty," Winfrey and Day, eds., *Indian Wars*, 95. According to Brown, there were delegations from "Wacos, Anadarcos, Towdashes [Tawehash, a Wichita band], Caddos, Keechis [Kichais], Tehuacanos [Tawakoni], Delawares, Bedais [Bedis], Boluxies [Biloxis], Ionies [Hainai], and one or two others."

28. Proclamation by Sam Houston, September 29, 1843, in Winfrey and Day, eds., *Indian Papers*, 1:241–246; Muckleroy, "Indian Policy," 26: 193–196; Brown, *Indian Wars*, 99–100. The treaty was ratified January 31, 1844.

29. Statement of Luís Sánchez as taken by Winn, May 1844, in Winfrey and Day, eds., *Indian Papers*, 2:65.

30. Minutes of a Council at Tehuacana Creek, in Winfrey and Day, eds., *Indian Papers*, 2:33–34.

31. Ibid., 39.

32. Ibid., 42.

33. Ibid., 44.

34. Ibid., 44–45.

35. Ibid., 46–47.

36. Minutes of Final Day of Council at Tehuacana Creek, May 15, 1844, in Winfrey and Day, eds., *Indian Papers*, 2:52–53.

37. Ibid., 53.

38. Ibid.

39. Ibid., 55.

40. Webb, "Last Treaty," 162–164.

41. Minutes of Council at Tehuacana, August 1845, in Winfrey and Day, eds., *Indian Papers*, 2:341–342.

42. Gibson, "Indian Territory," 408–409.

43. Ibid., 413.

CHAPTER 22
TAYSHAS

1. Tanner, "Territory," 102.

2. Neighbours, "José Maria," 264–266.

3. This is another of the documents placed in the hands of C. Ross Hume, tribal attorney, in 1929. The original was deposited with the Oklahoma Historical Society. A photostatic copy is in the Hume Collection, University of Oklahoma Library.

4. Neighbours, "José Maria," 256.

5. Ibid., 257.

6. Koch, "Federal Indian Policy," 275.

7. Holden, "Development of Agriculture," 170–172.

8. Ibid.

9. Neighbours, *Indian Exodus*, 64–65, 79–80.

10. U.S. Department of Indian Affairs, *Report of the Commissioner*, 1851, 260–261; quoted in Swanton, *Source Material*, 100.

11. Ibid.

12. Ibid.

13. Foreman, *Five Civilized Tribes*, 128.
14. Stem letter, November 1, 1851; quoted in Swanton, *Source Material*, 101.
15. Report to the Commissioner of Indian Affairs, 1852; quoted in Swanton, *Source Material*, 101–102.
16. Mayhall, *Indian Wars*, 85–99.
17. Marcy, *Thirty Years*, 171–172.
18. Parker, *Notes*, 213–214.
19. Parker, Ibid., 214.
20. Ibid., 218–219.
21. Ibid., 218.
22. Crane, "Some Aspects," 588.
23. Minutes of Council at the Falls of the Brazos, in Winfrey and Day, eds., *Indian Papers*, 2:109.
24. Webb, "Last Treaty," 172.
25. H. R. Runnels to J. S. Ford, January 28, 1858, in Winfrey and Day, eds., *Indian Papers*, 3:272–273.
26. Ford to Runnels, March 31, 1858, in Winfrey and Day, eds., *Indian Papers*, 3:279–281; Webb, *Texas Rangers*, 154–155.
27. Webb, *Texas Rangers*, 158. In Webb's account of this battle Captain Shapley P. Ross was a "son of the agent." Actually, Shapley P. Ross led the reserve Indians who fought with Ford, and Ross's son, Lawrence Sullivan Ross, led the reserve Indian company in its support of Major Earl Van Dorn's campaign against the Comanches in October 1858. Lawrence Sullivan Ross was later governor of Texas. Biographies of both men are included in Brown, *Indian Wars*, 315–318.
28. Webb, *Texas Rangers*, 161.

CHAPTER 23
CHOCTAW TOM

1. This account of the attack on Choctaw Tom's family was gathered from the letters of J. J. Sturm to S. P. Ross, December 23 and December 30, 1858, and January 15, 1859; S. P. Ross to R. S. Neighbors, January 26, 1859; Affidavit of Wm T. Sengle, Assist. Surg., U.S.A., January 25, 1859, in U.S. Department of Indian Affairs, *Report of the Commissioner . . . for the Year 1859*, 220–222, 230–232, 228–230, 235.
2. "To the People of Texas," *Southern Democrat* (Palo Pinto, Texas), January 27, 1859.
3. T. N. Palmer, Captain Second Cavalry, January 10, 1859, in U.S. Department of Indian Affairs, *Report of the Commissioner . . . for the Year 1859*, 233–234.
4. Minutes of assembly, Camp Palo Pinto, January 6, 1859, in U.S. Department of Indian Affairs, *Report of the Commissioner . . . for the Year 1859*, 245–246.
5. Neighbors to J. W. Denver, Commissioner Indian Affairs, Washington, D.C., January 10, 1859, in U.S. Department of Indian Affairs, *Report of the Commissioner . . . for the Year 1859*, 220.
6. Proclamation by H. R. Runnels, January 10, 1859, in Winfrey and Day, eds., *Indian Papers*, 3:312.
7. Ross to Neighbors, January 26, 1859, in U.S. Department of Indian Affairs, *Report of the Commissioner . . . for the Year 1859*, 229.

8. Neighbors to Denver, January 30, 1859, in U.S. Department of Indian Affairs, *Report of the Commissioner . . . for the Year 1859*, 227.

9. E. J. Gurley to Maj. R. S. Neighbors, May 5, 1859, in U.S. Department of Indian Affairs, *Report of the Commissioner . . . for the Year 1859*, 275.

10. Ross to Neighbors, March 5, 1859, in U.S. Department of Indian Affairs, *Report of the Commissioner . . . for the Year 1859*, 261.

11. Burnet, "Letters," 38:296, 298. Burnet is spelled with two *t*'s in the title of part 1 of the "Letters" series but is correctly spelled with one *t* in the text and in the titles of parts 2 and 3. The Lieutenant's father, David G. Burnet, was the first president of the Republic of Texas, serving during the period of *ad interim* government from adoption of the constitution by the Texas convention, March 16, 1836, and ratification of the constitution by popular vote September 5, 1836.

12. Ibid., 299.

13. Neighbors to Charles E. Mix, May 12, 1859, in U.S. Department of Indian Affairs, *Report of the Commissioner . . . for the Year 1859*, 270.

14. Accounts of Baylor's attack on the Brazos reserve are given in Burnet's "Letters," to his father dated May 23, 1859, and May 26, 1859, 38:302–306; and correspondence in *Report of Commissioner* as follows: J. B. Plummer to Assistant Adjutant General, May 23, 1859, 276–277; Ross to Neighbors, May 26, 1859, 277–278.

15. J. B. Plummer to Assistant Adjutant General, May 23, 1849, in U.S. Department of Indian Affairs, *Report of the Commissioner . . . for the Year 1859*, 276–277. The year 1849 printed in this report is an obvious error.

16. Neighbors to Mix, May 27, 1859, in U.S. Department of Indian Affairs, *Report of the Commissioner . . . for the Year 1859*, 275.

17. J. H. Brown to R.S. Neighbors, in Winfrey and Day, eds., *Indian Papers*, 3:334.

18. Elias Rector, Superintendent Indian Affairs, to A. B. Greenwood, Commissioner of Indian Affairs, July 2, 1859, in U.S. Department of Indian Affairs, *Report of the Commissioner . . . for the Year 1859*, 305. Fai-o-tun does not have the sound of a Caddo name, but in this report of Rector's Fai-o-tun is given as the name of the Caddo chief employed as a guide.

19. Rector to Greenwood, Fort Arbuckle, June 15, 1859, in U.S. Department of Indian Affairs, *Report of the Commissioner . . . for the Year 1859*, 285, 286.

20. Rector to Greenwood, July 2, 1859, in U.S. Department of Indian Affairs, *Report of the Commissioner . . . for the Year 1859*, 310.

CHAPTER 24
THE REMOVAL

1. Neighbors to Greenwood, August 18, 1859, in U.S. Department of Indian Affairs, *Report of the Commissioner . . . for the Year 1859*, 329.

2. Burnet, "Letters," 38:377.

3. Lillie (Annie) Whitehorn, conversation with author, Anadarko, Oklahoma, August 1986; Maude M. Simmons, "Statements of Caddo Witnesses," interviews conducted by Jay H. Hoag, attorney, Anadarko, Oklahoma, September 28–29, 1968.

Lillie Whitehorn said her father, Enoch Hoag, who is often identified as the last traditional chief of the Caddo, was José Maria's grandson "in the Caddo way," meaning that his grandmother was José Maria's sister.

4. Neighbors to Wife, August 8, 1859, Neighbors, Letters.

5. Burnet, "Letters," 38:390–391.

6. Census List, Neighbors, Letters, 1859; Leeper to Neighbors, Camp on False Washita, August 31, 1859, Neighbors, Letters.

7. Neighbors to Greenwood, September 3, 1859, in U.S. Department of Indian Affairs, *Report of the Commissioner . . . for the Year 1859*, 333.

8. Neighbours, *Indian Exodus*, 137–138, said any motive for the murder of Neighbors is not clear. Neighbors was shot in the back by Ed Cornett, a man he did not know.

CHAPTER 25
JULIA

1. Dickerson, "History of Anadarko O.T.," 33. This early historical summary was evidently written and privately printed for presentation to Anadarko civic leaders. "A Merry Christmas and a Happy New Year, August 4, 1901–December 25," is on the title page. A copy is deposited in the Anadarko Public Library.

2. This final section is based on visits with Julia Edge at her home and the home of a grandson in Anadarko, at Joe's Cafe in that city, and at her family camp on the Whitebead dance ground at the Hasinai Cultural Center near Hinton, Oklahoma, during the weekend of the annual veterans dance in August 1979. Parts are transcribed from tape-recorded conversation. In 1993 Julia was living at a nursing home in Binger, Oklahoma, but she did attend a Caddo dance, where she sat in a wheelchair watching the Turkey Dance.

3. Miller County, organized in 1820, included all of what is now McCurtain County, Oklahoma, and eastern parts of Pushmataha and Choctaw Counties. It extended a short distance east across the present state line of Arkansas. Foreman, *Indians and Pioneers*, 144–151, covered the outraged reaction of Miller County citizens when the Choctaw treaty included their county within the bounds of an immense tract granted in exchange for Choctaw lands in Mississippi.

BIBLIOGRAPHY

Abel, Annie H. "History of Indian Consolidation West of the Mississippi." In *Annual Report of the American Historical Association for the Year 1906*, 1:233–454. 2 vols. Washington, D.C.: GPO, 1908.

———. "Proposals for an Indian State, 1778–1878." In *Annual Report of the American Historical Association for the Year 1907*, 1:87–102. 2 vols. Washington, D.C.: GPO, 1908.

Almonte, Juan N. "Statistical Report on Texas." Translated by Carlos E. Castaneda. *Southwestern Historical Quarterly* 28 (1925): 177–222.

Barker, Eugene C. "Spanish Texas, 1528–1821." In *Readings in Texas History*, edited by Eugene C. Barker. Dallas: Southwest Press, 1929.

Bean, Covey. "Indians Raid Open Federal Purse—Throwing Money at More Money—One Way to Amass Fortunes." *The Sunday Oklahoman* (Oklahoma City), October 22, 1978.

Berlandier, Jean Louis. *The Indians of Texas in 1830.* Edited by John C. Ewers and translated by Patricia Reading Leclercq. Washington, D.C.: Smithsonian Institution Press, 1969.

Blake, R. B. "Captain Antonio Gil Y'Barbo." Nacogdoches Records, no. 3. Barker Texas History Archives, University of Texas Libraries, Austin, Texas. Typewritten.

———. "Location of Early Spanish Missions and Presidios in Nacogdoches County." *Southwestern Historical Quarterly* 41 (January 1938): 212–224.

Bolton, Herbert Eugene. *The Hasinais: Southern Caddoans as Seen by the Earliest Europeans.* Edited by Russell M. Magnaghi. Norman: University of Oklahoma Press, 1987.

———. "The Location of La Salle's Colony on the Gulf of Mexico." *Southwestern Historical Quarterly* 27 (January 1924): 171–189.

————. "The Native Tribes About the East Texas Missions." *Quarterly of the Texas State Historical Association* 2 (April 1908): 249–276.

————. "The Spanish Occupation of Texas, 1519–1690." *Southwestern Historical Quarterly* 16 (1912): 1–26.

————. *Texas in the Middle Eighteenth Century: Studies in Spanish Colonial History and Administration.* University of California Publications in History, vol. 3. Berkeley, 1915.

————, ed. *Athanase de Mézières and the Louisiana-Texas Frontier, 1768–1780.* 2 vols. 1914. Reprint (2 vols. in 1), New York: Kraus Reprint Co., 1970.

————. *Original Narratives of Early American History: Spanish Exploration in the Southwest, 1542–1706.* New York: Charles Scribner's Sons, 1925.

Brown, James A. *The Artifacts.* Spiro Studies, vol. 4. Second Part of the Third Annual Report of Caddoan Archaeology–Spiro Focus Research. Norman: University of Oklahoma Research Institute: 1976.

Brown, John Henry. *History of Texas from 1685 to 1892.* 2 vols. St. Louis: Becktold and Co., 1894.

————. *The Indian Wars and Pioneers of Texas.* Austin: L. E. Daniel, n.d.

Buckley, Eleanor Claire. "The Aguayo Expedition into Texas and Louisiana, 1719–1722." *Quarterly of the Texas State Historical Association* 15 (1911): 1–65.

Bugbee, Lester G. "The Real St. Denis." *Quarterly of the Texas State Historical Association* 1 (1898): 266–281.

Burnet, William E. "Letters: Removal of the Texas Indians and the Founding of Fort Cobb," parts 1–3. *Chronicles of Oklahoma* 38 (Autumn 1960): 274–309; 38 (Winter 1960): 369–397; 39 (Spring 1961): 15–41.

"Caddo Valley Archeological Project, 1975." Prepared for Arkansas Survey–Society Field School held at Caddo Gap, Montgomery County, Arkansas, June 16–July 4, 1976. Photocopy.

Caddoan Mounds: Temples and Tombs of an Ancient People. Texas Parks and Wildlife Department Booklet 4000-384. Alto, Texas: Interpretive and Exhibits Branch, Caddoan Mounds State Historic Site, May 1984.

Carter, Hodding, and Betty Carter. *Doomed Road of Empire: The Spanish Trail of Conquest.* New York: McGraw-Hill, 1963.

Casañas de Jesús María, Francisco. Fray Francisco Casañas de Jesús to the Viceroy of Mexico, August 15, 1691. Parts 1 and 2 of "Descriptions of the Tejas or Asinai Indians, 1691–1722." Translated by Mattie Austin Hatcher. *Southwestern Historical Quarterly* 30 (January 1927): 206–218, 30 (April 1927): 283–304.

Castaneda, Carlos E., ed. *Our Catholic Heritage in Texas.* Vols. 1–6. 1936–1942. Vol. 1, *The Mission Era: The Finding of Texas, 1519–1693;* vol. 2, *The Mission Era: The Winning of Texas, 1693–1731;* vol. 3, *The Mission Era: The Missions at Work, 1731–1761;* vol. 4, *The Mission Era: The Passing of the Missions, 1762–1782;* vol. 5, *The Mission Era: The End of the Spanish Regime, 1780–1810;* vol. 6, *Transition Period: The Fight for Freedom 1810–1836.* Reprint, New York: Arno Press, 1976.

Cavelier, Jean. "Cavelier's Account of La Salle's Voyage to the Mouth of the Mississippi, His Landing in Texas, and March to the Mississippi." In *The Journeys of René Robert Cavelier, Sieur de La Salle,* edited by Isaac Joslin Cox, vol. 1. New York: A. S. Barnes and Company, 1905.

Chafe, Wallace. "Caddo Names in the De Soto Documents." In *The Expedition of Hernando de Soto West of the Mississippi, 1541–1543: Proceedings of the De Soto Symposia, 1988 and 1990*, edited by Gloria A. Young and Michael P. Hoffman. Fayetteville: University of Arkansas Press, 1993.

Chapman, Berlin B. "Establishment of Wichita Reservation." *Chronicles of Oklahoma* 11 (December 1933): 1044–1055.

Charlevoix, Pierre François Xavier de. *History and General Description of New France*. Translated by John Gilmary Shea. 1870. Vols. 5–6. Chicago: Loyola University Press, 1962.

Clark, Robert Carlton. "La Salle's Settlement and the First Spanish Mission in Texas, 1685–1693." In *Readings in Texas History*, edited by Eugene C. Barker. Dallas: Southwest Press, 1929.

————. "Louis Juchereau de Saint-Denis and the Re-establishment of the Tejas Missions." *Quarterly of the Texas State Historical Association* 6 (1902): 1–26.

————. "The Spanish Occupation of East Texas." In *Readings in Texas History*, pp. 27–33. Edited by Eugene C. Barker. Dallas: Southwest Press, 1929.

Collier, John. *Indians of the Americas*. New York: New American Library, 1947.

Cooper, Douglas H. "A Journal Kept by Douglas Cooper." Introduction by Grant Foreman, *Chronicles of Oklahoma* 5 (December 1927): 385–390.

Corbin, James E. "Retracing the Camino de los Tejas from the Trinity River to Los Adaes: New Insights into East Texas History." In *A Texas Legacy: The Old San Antonio Road and the Caminos Reales*, edited by A. Joachim McGraw, John W. Clark Jr., and Elizabeth A. Robbins. Austin: Texas State Department of Highways and Public Transportation, 1991.

Cox, Isaac Joslin. "Exploration of the Louisiana Frontier, 1803–1806." In *Annual Report of the American Historical Association for the Year 1904*. Washington, D.C.: GPO, 1905.

————. "The Louisiana-Texas Frontier." Parts 1 and 2. *Southwestern Historical Quarterly* 10 (July 1906): 1–75; 17 (July, October 1913): 1–42, 140–187.

Crane, R. C. "Some Aspects of the History of West and Northwest Texas Since 1845." In *Readings in Texas History*, edited by Eugene C. Barker. Dallas: Southwest Press, 1929.

Culberson, James. "Indian Against Indian." *Chronicles of Oklahoma* 7 (June 1929): 164–167.

Davis, Hester A., ed. *Archeological and Historical Resources of the Red River Basin*. Arkansas Archeological Survey Research Series, no. 1. Fayetteville, 1970.

Dickerson, Philip J. "History of Anadarko, O.T.: Its Past and Present and Bright Future, 1901." Anadarko Public Library Archives, Anadarko, Oklahoma. Typewritten.

Dorsey, George A. *Traditions of the Caddo*. Carnegie Institute of Washington Publication 41. Washington, D.C.: Press of Judd and Detweiler, 1905.

Douay, Anastasius. "Narrative of La Salle's Attempt to Ascend the Mississippi in 1687, by Father Anastasius Douay, Recollect." In *The Journeys of René Robert Cavelier, Sieur de La Salle*, edited by Isaac Joslin Cox, vol. 1. New York: A. S. Barnes and Company, 1905.

Early, Ann M. "Progress Report on the Standridge Site." Presentation to members and guests of the Arkansas Archeological Society at Caddo Gap, Arkansas, June 30, 1975.

———. "Turquoise Beads from the Standridge Site, 3mn53." *Arkansas Archeologist* 19 (1978): 25–29.

Early, Ann M., Barbara A. Burnett, and Daniel Wolfman. *Standridge: Caddoan Settlement in a Mountain Environment*. Research Series no. 29. Fayetteville: Arkansas Archeological Survey, 1988.

Elvas, Gentleman of. "The Narrative of the Expedition of Hernando De Soto, by the Gentleman of Elvas." Translated by Buckingham Smith and edited by Theodore H. Lewis. In *Original Narratives of Early American History: Spanish Explorers in the Southern United States, 1528–1543*, edited by J. Franklin Jameson. New York: Barnes and Noble, 1953.

Erath, George E. "Captain Erath's Fight on Elm Creek." In *Indian Depredations in Texas: Reliable Accounts of Battles, Wars, Adventures, Forays, Murders, Massacres, Etc., Etc., Together with Biographical Sketches of Many of the Most Noted Indian Fighters and Frontiersmen of Texas*. Edited by J. W. Wilbarger. 1889. Facsimile reproduction, Austin: Eakin Press, 1985.

Espinosa, Isidro Felís de. Extract from *Crónica de la Provincia Franciscana de los Apóstoles San Pedro de Michoacán*, edited by Nicolas Leon. Part 4 of "Descriptions of the Tejas or Asinai Indians, 1691–1722." Translated by Mattie Austin Hatcher. *Southwestern Historical Quarterly* 31 (October 1927): 150–180.

———. "Ramon's Expedition: Espinosa's Diary of 1716." Translated by Gabriel Tous. *Mid America* 12 (1929): 352–361.

Ewers, John C. *Symbols of Chiefly Authority in Spanish Louisiana: The Spanish in the Mississippi Valley, 1760–1804*. Edited by John Francis McDermott. Urbana: University of Illinois Press, 1974.

Flores, Dan L. "A Final Journey down the Wild Red." *Shreveport (La.) Times Sunday Magazine*, August 14, 1977.

———, ed. *Jefferson and Southwestern Exploration: The Freeman and Custis Accounts of the Red River Expedition of 1806*. Norman: University of Oklahoma Press, 1984.

Foreman, Grant. *Advancing the Frontier, 1830–1860*. Norman: University of Oklahoma Press, 1933.

———. *The Five Civilized Tribes*. Norman: University of Oklahoma Press, 1934.

———. *Indians and Pioneers: The Story of the American Southwest Before 1830*. New Haven, Conn.: Yale University Press, 1930.

———. ed. *A Traveler in Indian Territory: The Journal of Ethan Allen Hitchcock, Late Major-General in the United States Army*. Cedar Rapids, Iowa: Torch Press, 1930.

Fox, Daniel E. *Traces of Texas History: Archeological Evidence of Past 450 Years*. San Antonio: Corona Publishing Company, 1983.

French, B. F. *Historical Memoirs of Louisiana, from the First Settlement of the Colony to the Departure of Governor O'Reilly in 1770*. New York: Lamport, Blakeman, and Law, 1853.

Fulmore, Z. T. *The History and Geography of Texas as Told in County Names*. Austin: Press of E. L. Steck, 1915.

Gaignard, J. "Journal of an Expedition up the Red River, 1773–1774." In *Athanase de Mézières and the Louisiana-Texas Frontier, 1763–1780*, edited by Herbert Eugene Bolton. 1914. Reprint (2 vols. in 1), New York: Kraus

Reprint Co., 1970.

Garrett, Julia Kathryn. "Doctor John Sibley and the Louisiana-Texas Frontier, 1803–1814." *Southwestern Historical Quarterly* 45 (January 1942): 286–301; 45 (April 1942): 380–382; 46 (July 1942): 83–84; 46 (January 1943): 272–277; 47 (July 1943): 48–51; 47 (January 1944): 319–324; 47 (April 1944): 388–391; 48 (July 1944): 67–70; 49 (January 1946): 399–431; 49 (April 1946): 599–613.

Garrison, George P., ed. *Diplomatic Correspondence of the Republic of Texas.* Eighth Report of the Historical Manuscripts Commission, vol. 2. *Annual Report of the American Historical Association for the Year 1907.* Washington, D.C.: GPO, 1908.

Gibson, A. M. "An Indian Territory United Nations: The Creek Council of 1845." *Chronicles of Oklahoma* 39 (Winter 1961–1962): 398–413.

Giraud, Marcel. *A History of French Louisiana.* Translated by Joseph C. Lambert. Vol. 1, *The Reign of Louis XIV, 1698–1715.* Baton Rouge: Louisiana State University Press, 1974.

Gleason, Mildred S. *Caddo: A Survey of Caddo Indians in Northeast Texas and Marion County, 1541–1840.* Jefferson, Tex.: Marion County Historical Commission, 1981.

Glover, William B. "A History of the Caddo Indians." *Louisiana Historical Quarterly* 18 (1935): 872–946.

Griffith, William J. *The Hasinai Indians of East Texas as Seen by Europeans, 1687–1722.* Middle American Research Institute, Philological and Documentary Studies, vol. 2, no. 3. New Orleans: Tulane University, 1954.

Haggard, J. Villasana. "The House of Barr and Davenport." *Southwestern Historical Quarterly* 49 July 1945, 66–88.

Harby, Lee C. "The Tejas: Their Habits, Government, and Superstitions." In *Annual Report of the American Historical Association for the Year 1894,* pp. 63–82. Washington, D.C.: GPO, 1895.

Hardin, J. Fair. "An Outline of Shreveport and Caddo Parish History." *Louisiana Historical Quarterly* 18 (1935): 659–871.

Harrington, M.R. *Certain Caddo Sites in Arkansas.* Indian Notes and Monographs, Miscellaneous 10. New York: Heye Foundation, Museum of the American Indian, 1920.

Hemmings, E. Thomas. "Spirit Lake (3LA83): Test Excavations in a Late Caddo Site on the Red River." In *Contributions to the Archeology of the Great Bend Region,* edited by Frank Schambach and Frank Rackerby. Arkansas Archeological Survey Research Series, no. 22. Fayetteville, 1982.

Henderson, Mary Virginia. "Minor Empresario Contracts for the Colonization of Texas, 1825–1834." In *Readings in Texas History,* edited by Eugene C. Barker. Dallas: Southwest Press, 1929.

Hidalgo, Francisco. Fray Francisco Hidalgo to Fray Isidro Cassos, November 20, 1710. "Descriptions of the Tejas or Asinai Indians, 1691–1722," pt. 3. Translated by Mattie Austin Hatcher. *Southwestern Historical Quarterly* 31 (1927–1928): 50–52.

———. Fray Francisco Hidalgo to Viceroy. "Descriptions of the Tejas or Asinai Indians, 1691–1722," pt. 3. Translated by Mattie Austin Hatcher. *Southwestern Historical Quarterly* 31 (July 1927): 53–62.

Hodge, Frederick Webb, ed. *Handbook of American Indians North of Mexico,* pt. 1. 1907. Reprint, Totowa, N.J.: Rowman and Littlefield, 1975.

Hoffman, Michael P. "Archaeological and Historical Assessment of the Red River Basin in Arkansas." In *Archeological and Historical Resources of the Red River Basin,* edited by Hester A. Davis. Arkansas Archeological Survey Research Series, no. 1. Fayetteville, 1970.

Holden, W. C. "The Development of Agriculture in West Texas." In *Readings in Texas History,* edited by Eugene C. Barker. Dallas: Southwest Press, 1929.

Hollon, W. Eugene. *Beyond the Cross Timbers: The Travels of Randolph B. Marcy, 1812–1887.* Norman: University of Oklahoma Press, 1955.

Hudson, Charles. "Reconstructing the de Soto Expedition Route West of the Mississippi River: Summary and Contents." In *The Expedition of Hernando de Soto West of the Mississippi, 1541–1543,* proceedings of the De Soto Symposia 1988 and 1990, edited by Gloria A. Young and Michael P. Hoffman. Fayetteville: University of Arkansas Press, 1993.

Hughes, Jack Thomas. "Prehistory of the Caddoan Speaking Tribes." In *Caddoan Indians 3,* compiled and edited by David Agee Horr. A Garland Series American Indian Ethnohistory. New York: Garland Publishing, 1974.

Hume, C. Ross. Papers. Hume Collection no. 1, University of Oklahoma Library, Western History Archives, Norman.

Hyde, George E. *The Pawnee Indians.* Norman: University of Oklahoma Press, 1974.

Jackson, Andrew. Letter to Secretary Monroe, October 26, 1814. In *Correspondence of Andrew Jackson,* edited by John Spencer Bassett. Washington, D.C.: Carnegie Institute, 1928.

John, Elizabeth A.H. *Storms Brewed in Other Men's Worlds: The Confrontation of Indians, Spanish, and French in the Southwest, 1540–1795.* College Station: Texas A&M Press, 1975.

Joutel, Henri. "Joutel's Journal of La Salle's Last Voyage." In *Journeys of René Robert Cavalier, Sieur de La Salle,* edited by Isaac Joslin Cox, vol. 2. New York: A. S. Barnes and Company, 1905.

Kinnard, Lawrence, and Lucia B. Kinnard. "Choctaws West of the Mississippi, 1766–1800." *Southwestern Historical Quarterly* 83 (1980): 349–370.

Kinnard, Lawrence, ed., *Spain in the Mississippi Valley, 1765–1794: Translations of Materials from the Spanish Archives in the Bancroft Library.* Vol. 3, *Part II: Post War Decade, 1782–1791.* Annual Report of the American Historical Association for the Year 1945. Washington, D.C.: GPO, 1946.

Kniffen, Fred B., Hiram F. Gregory, and George A. Stokes. *The Historic Indian Tribes of Louisiana: From 1542 to the Present.* Baton Rouge: Louisiana State University Press, 1987.

Koch, Clara Lean. "The Federal Indian Policy in Texas, 1845–1860." *Southwestern Historical Quarterly* 28 (January, April 1925): 223–234, 259–286; 29 (July 1926): 98–104.

La Harpe, Bénard de. "Account of the Journey of Bernard de La Harpe: Discovery Made by Him of Several Nations Situated in the West." Translated by Ralph A. Smith. *Southwestern Historical Quarterly* 62, nos. 1–3 (July 1958–January 1959): 75–86, 246–259; 371–385.

———. "La Harpe's First Expedition in Oklahoma, 1718–1719." Translated by

Anna Lewis. *Chronicles of Oklahoma* 4 (December 1924): 331–349.

Lange, Charles H. "A Report on Data Pertaining to the Caddo Treaty of July 1, 1835: The Historical and Anthropological Aftermath." In *Caddoan Indians 2*, compiled and edited by David Agee Horr. A Garland Series American Indian Ethnohistory. New York: Garland Publishing, 1974.

Lee, Dayna Bowker. "François Grappé and the Caddo Land Cession." *North Louisiana Historical Association Journal* 20 (1989): 53–69.

León, Alonso de. "Itinerary of the De León Expedition of 1690." In *Original Narratives of Early American History: Spanish Exploration in the Southwest, 1542–1706*, edited by Herbert Eugene Bolton. New York: Charles Scribner's Sons, 1925.

———. "Itinerary of the Expedition Made by General Alonso de León for the Discovery of the Bahía del Espíritu Santo and the French Settlement, 1689." Translated by Elizabeth Howard West. In *Original Narratives of Early American History*, edited by Herbert Eugene Bolton. New York: Charles Scribner's Sons, 1925.

Le Page du Pratz, Antoine. *The History of Louisiana Translated from the French of M. Le Page du Pratz, 1774*. Translated and edited by Joseph G. Tregley Jr. Baton Rouge: Louisiana State University Press, 1975.

Lesser, Alexander, and Gene Weltfish. *Composition of the Caddoan Linguistic Stock*. Smithsonian Miscellaneous Collections, vol. 87, no. 6. Washington, D.C.: Smithsonian Institution, 1932.

Marcy, Randolph B. *Thirty Years of Army Life on the Border*. New York: Harper and Brothers, 1866.

Margry, Pierre, ed. *Découvertes et établissements des Français dans l'ouest et dans le sud de l'Amérique Septentrionale (1614–1754). Mémoires et documents originaux recueillis et publiés par Pierre Margry*. 6 vols. Paris. 1875–1886. English-translation in Burton Historical Collection, Detroit Public Library, Detroit, Michigan.

Massanet (Manzenet), Damián. Letter of Fray Damián Massanet to Don Carlos de Sigüenza, 1690. Translated by Lilia M. Casis. In *Original Narratives of Early American History: Spanish Exploration in the Southwest, 1542–1706*, edited by Herbert Eugene Bolton. New York: Charles Scribner's Sons, 1925.

Mathews, John Joseph. *The Osages: Children of the Middle Waters*. Norman: University of Oklahoma Press, 1961.

Mayhall, Mildred P. *Indian Wars of Texas*, Waco, Texas: Texian Press, 1965.

McCrocklin, Claude. "An Intermediate Report on the James Bayou Survey, Marian County, Texas: A Search for Caddo Village." Paper presented at Annual Caddo Conference, Shreveport, Louisiana, March 1992.

McElhannon, Joseph Carl. "Imperial Mexico and Texas, 1821–1823." *Southwestern Historical Quarterly* 53 (October 1949): 122–129.

McGimsey, Charles R. "Indians of Arkansas," In *Indians of Arkansas*, pp. 1–57. Arkansas Archeological Survey Popular Series, no. 1, Fayetteville, 1969.

Miroir, M. P., R. King Harris, et al. *Bérnard de La Harpe and the Nassonite Post*. Bulletin of the Texas Archeological Society, no. 44. Texas Archeological Society, 1973.

Mississippi Messenger (Natchez), September 30, 1806.

Mooney, James. *The Ghost-dance Religion and the Sioux Outbreak of 1890.* Fourteenth Annual Report of the Bureau of Ethnology, 1892–1893, pt. 2. Washington, D.C.: GPO, 1896.

Morfí, Juan Agustín. *History of Texas, 1673–1779.* Translated by Carlos Eduardo Castaneda. Quivira Society Publications, vol. 4, pt. 1. Albuquerque, 1935; reprint, New York: Arno Press, 1967.

Morrison, W. B. "Across Oklahoma Ninety Years Ago." *Chronicles of Oklahoma* 4 (December 1926): 333–337.

Morse, Dan F., and Phyllis A. Morse. "The Spanish Exploration of Arkansas." In *Columbian Consequences,* edited by David Hurst Thomas, vol. 2. Washington, D.C.: Smithsonian Institution Press, 1990.

Muckleroy, Anna. "The Indian Policy of the Republic of Texas." *Southwestern Historical Quarterly* 25 (1922): 248–260, 299–360; 26 (1923): 1–29, 184–206.

Neighbors, Robert S. Letters. Barker Texas History Archives, University of Texas Libraries, Austin, Texas.

Neighbours, Kenneth. *Indian Exodus: Texas Indian Affairs, 1835–1859.* N.p.: Nortex Offset Publications, 1973.

———. "José Maria: Anadarko Chief." *Chronicles of Oklahoma* 44 (1966–1967): 254–274.

Neuman, Robert W. "Archaeological and Historical Assessment of the Red River Basin in Louisiana." In *Archeological and Historical Resources of the Red River Basin.* Edited by Hester A. Davis. Arkansas Archeological Survey Research Series, no. 1. Fayetteville, 1970.

———. "Historical Locations of Certain Caddoan Tribes." In *Caddoan Indians 2,* compiled and edited by David Agee Horr. A Garland Series American Indian Ethnohistory. New York: Garland Publishing, 1974.

Newcomb, William W. *The Indians of Texas from Prehistoric to Modern Times.* Austin: University of Texas Press, 1969.

Newkumet, Vynola Beaver, and Howard L. Meredith. *Hasinai: A Traditional History of the Caddo Confederacy.* Foreword by Arrell Morgan Gibson. College Station: Texas A&M University Press, 1988.

Nye, W. S. *Carbine and Lance: The Story of Old Fort Sill.* Norman: University of Oklahoma Press, 1969.

Padilla, Juan Antonio. "Texas in 1820: Report on the Barbarous Indians of the Province of Texas." Translated by Mattie Austin Hatcher. *Southwestern Historical Quarterly* 23 (1919): 47–68.

Parker, W. B. *Notes Taken During the Expedition Commanded by Capt. R. B. Marcy, U.S.A., Through Unexplored Texas, in the Summer and Fall of 1854.* 1856. Reprint, Austin: Texas State Historical Commission, University of Texas, 1984.

Parkman, Francis. *France and England in North America: La Salle and the Discovery of the Great West.* Boston: Little, Brown and Company, 1886.

———. *La Salle and the Discovery of the Great West.* 12th ed. Boston: Little, Brown and Company, 1886.

Parsons, Elsie Clews. *Notes on the Caddo.* Memoirs of the American Anthropological Association, no. 57. Menasha, Wisc.: American Anthropological Association, 1941.

Paxson, Frederic L. *History of the American Frontier, 1763–1893*. Cambridge, Mass.: Riverside Press, 1924.

Penicaut, André. *Fleur de Lys and Calumet: Being the Penigault Narrative of French Adventure in Louisiana*. Edited and translated by Richebourg Gaillard McWilliams. Baton Rouge: Louisiana State University Press, 1953.

Perttula, Timothy K. *"The Caddo Nation": Archaeological and Ethnohistoric Perspectives*. Austin: University of Texas Press, 1992.

Phares, Ross. *Cavalier in the Wilderness: The Story of the Explorer and Trader Louis Juchereau de St. Denis*. Baton Rouge: Louisiana State University Press, 1952.

Richardson, Rupert Norval. *The Frontier of Northwest Texas, 1846 to 1876: Advance and Defense by the Pioneer Settlers of the Cross Timbers and Prairies*. Glendale, Calif.: Arthur Clark Company, 1963.

———. "Some Details of the Southern Overland Mail." *Southwestern Historical Quarterly* 29 (July 1925): 1–18.

Richner, Jeffrey J., and Joe T. Bagot, comps. *A Reconnaissance Survey of the Trinity River Basin, 1976–1977*. Archeology Research Program Research Report 113. Dallas: Southern Methodist University, Department of Anthropology, 1978.

Sánchez, José María. "A Trip to Texas in 1828." Translated by Carlos E. Castaneda. *Southwestern Historical Quarterly* 29 (April 1926): 249–288.

Santos, Richard G., ed. *Aguayo Expedition into Texas, 1721: An Annotated Translation of the Five Versions of the Diary Kept by Br. Juan Antonio de la Peña*. Austin, Tex.: Jenkins Publishing Company, 1981.

Schambach, Frank F. "The Archeology of the Great Bend Region in Arkansas." In *Contributions to the Archeology of the Great Bend Region*, edited by Frank Schambach and Frank Rackerby. Arkansas Archeological Survey Research Series, no. 22. Fayetteville: 1982.

———. "The End of the Trail: The Route of Hernando De Soto's Army Through Southwest Arkansas and East Texas." *Arkansas Archeologist Bulletin* 27–28 (1989): 9–33.

Schambach, Frank F., et al. "Test Excavations at the Cedar Grove Site (31a97): A Late Caddo Farmstead in the Great Bend Region, Southwest Arkansas." In *Contributions to the Archeology of the Great Bend Region*, edited by Frank Schambach and Frank Rackerby. Research Series, no. 22. Fayetteville: Arkansas Archeological Survey, 1982.

Schmitt, Edmond J. P. "Sieur Louis de Saint Denis." *Quarterly of the Texas State Historical Association* 1 (1898): 204–215.

Scurlock, J. Dan. "The Kadohadacho Indians: A Correlation of Archeological and Documentary Data." Master's thesis, University of Texas, 1965.

Shelby, Charmion Clair. "St. Denis's Declaration Concerning Texas in 1717." *Southwestern Historical Quarterly* 26 (1923): 165–183.

———. "St. Denis's Second Expedition to the Rio Grande, 1716–1719." *Southwestern Historical Quarterly* 27 (1924): 190–216.

Sibley, John. "Historical sketches of several Indian tribes in Louisiana, south of the Arkansas River, and between the Mississippi and River Grande [1805]." In *American State Papers, Class 2, Indian Affairs* 1:721–730. Washington, D.C.: 1832.

Bibliography

404

──────. *A Report from Natchitoches in 1807.* Edited by Anne Heloise Abel. Indian Notes and Monographs, Museum of the American Indian and Heye Foundation. New York: 1922.

Solís, Gaspár José de. "Diary of a Visit of Inspection of the Texas Missions Made by Fray Gaspar Jose de Solis in the Year 1767–1768." Translated by Margaret K. Kress. *Southwestern Historical Quarterly* 35 (1931): 28–76.

"The Standridge Site: A Review and Preview." *Field Notes: Monthly Newsletter of the Arkansas Archeological Society* 135 (March 1976): 2–3.

Swanton, John R. *Indian Tribes of the Lower Mississippi Valley and Adjacent Coast of the Gulf of Mexico.* Bulletin 43. Washington, D.C.: Bureau of American Ethnology, Smithsonian Institution, 1911.

──────. *Final Report of the United States De Soto Expedition Commission.* 76th Cong., 1st sess., H. Doc. 71. 1939. Reprint, Washington, D.C.: Smithsonian Institution Press, 1985.

──────. *Source Material on the History and Ethnology of the Caddo Indians.* Bulletin 132. Washington, D.C.: Bureau of American Ethnology, Smithsonian Institution, 1942.

──────. *Indians of the Southeastern United States.* Bulletin 137. Washington, D.C.: Bureau of American Ethnology, Smithsonian Institution, 1946.

Tanner, Helen Hornbeck. "The Territory of the Caddo Tribe of Oklahoma." In *Caddoan Indians 4,* compiled and edited by David Agee Horr. A Garland Series American Indian Ethnohistory. New York: Garland Publishing, 1974.

Thoburn, Joseph B., and Muriel H. Wright. *Oklahoma: A History of the State and Its People.* Vol. 1. New York: Lewis Historical Publishing Company, 1927.

Tonti (Tonty), Henri de. "Memoir." In *Journeys of René Robert Cavelier, Sieur de La Salle,* edited by Isaac Joslin Cox, vol. 1. New York: A. S. Barnes and Company, 1905.

Torma, Tracy. "Caddo Lake State Park: Where Swamp and Forest Meet." *Texas Highways* (July 1984): 20–29.

"To the People of Texas." *Southern Democrat* (Palo Pinto, Texas), January 27, 1859.

U.S. Department of Indian Affairs. *Report of the Commissioner* for the Years 1840 and 1859. Washington D.C.: GPO, 1840, 1859.

Webb Clarence. "Changing Archeological Methods and Theory in the Transmississippi South." In *Texas Archeology: Essays Honoring R. King Harris.* Edited by Kurt D. House. Dallas: SMU Press, 1978.

Webb, Clarence, and Hiram Gregory. *The Caddo Indians of Louisiana.* Edited by Alan Toth. Louisiana Archeological Survey and Antiquities Commission. Anthropological Studies, no. 2. Baton Rouge, 1978.

Webb, Walter Prescott. "The Last Treaty of the Republic of Texas." *Southwestern Historical Quarterly* 25 (January 1922): 151–173.

──────. *The Texas Rangers: A Century of Frontier Defense.* Cambridge, Mass.: Riverside Press, 1935.

Weddle, Robert S. *Wilderness Manhunt: Spanish Search for La Salle.* Austin: University of Texas Press, 1973.

──────, ed. *La Salle, the Mississippi, and the Gulf: Three Primary Documents.* College Station: Texas A&M University Press, 1987.

──────. "Bonilla's Brief Compendium of the History of Texas, 1772." *Quarterly of the Texas State Historical Association* 8 (July 1904).

Weller, Sadie Bedoka. Interview by Kenneth Beals, July 27, 1967. Tape recording and transcription by Kenneth Beals. University of Oklahoma Library, Western History Archives, Doris Duke Collection.

Wilbarger, J. W., ed. *Indian Depredations in Texas: Reliable Accounts of Battles, Wars, Adventures, Forays, Murders, Massacres, Etc., Etc., Together with Biographical Sketches of Many of the Most Noted Indian Fighters and Frontiersmen of Texas.* 1889. Facsimile reproduction, Austin: Eakin Press, Statehouse Books, 1985.

Williams, J. W. *Old Texas Trails.* Edited and compiled by Kenneth F. Neighbours. Burnett, Tex.: Eakin Press, 1979.

Williams, Stephen. "The Aboriginal Location of the Kadohadacho and Related Tribes." In *Caddoan Indians 1,* compiled and edited by David Agee Horr. A Garland Series American Indian Ethnohistory. New York: Garland Publishing, 1974.

Winfrey, Dorman H. "Chief Bowles of the Texas Cherokee." *Chronicles of Oklahoma* 32 (Spring 1954): 29–41.

Winfrey, Dorman H., and James M. Day, eds. *The Indian Papers of Texas and the Southwest, 1825–1859.* Vols. 1–3. Austin: Pemberton Press, 1966.

Wright, Muriel H. *A Guide to the Indian Tribes of Oklahoma.* Norman: University of Oklahoma Press, 1951.

———. "Some Geographic Names of French Origin." *Chronicles of Oklahoma* 7 (June 1929): 188–193.

Wyckoff, Don W. "The Caddoan Cultural Area: An Archaeological Perspective." In *Caddoan Indians 1,* compiled and edited by David Agee Horr. A Garland Series American Indian Ethnohistory. New York: Garland Publishing, 1974.

Wyckoff, Don W., and Timothy G. Baugh. "Early Historic Hasinai Elites: A Model for the Material Culture of Governing Elites." *Mid-Continental Journal of Archaeology* (1980): 225–288.

Yoakum, Henderson K. *History of Texas from Its First Settlement in 1685 to Its Annexation to the United States in 1846.* 1856. 2 vols. Facsimile reproduction, Austin: Steck Company, 1935.

Young, Gloria A., and Michael P. Hoffmann, eds. *The Expedition of Hernando de Soto West of the Mississippi, 1541–1543: Proceedings of the de Soto Symposia, 1988 and 1990.* Fayetteville; University of Arkansas Press, 1993.

INDEX

410

Index